William Randolph Hearst
Final Edition, 1911–1951

Hearst's inherent eye for beauty appears in this impressive entrance to Casa Grande, San Simeon. Photograph by Victoria Garagliano; Hearst Castle/CA State Parks.

William Randolph Hearst

Final Edition, 1911–1951

Ben Procter

OXFORD
UNIVERSITY PRESS

OXFORD
UNIVERSITY PRESS

Oxford University Press, Inc., publishes works that further
Oxford University's objective of excellence
in research, scholarship, and education.

Oxford New York
Auckland Cape Town Dar es Salaam Hong Kong Karachi
Kuala Lumpur Madrid Melbourne Mexico City Nairobi
New Delhi Shanghai Taipei Toronto

With offices in
Argentina Austria Brazil Chile Czech Republic France Greece
Guatemala Hungary Italy Japan Poland Portugal Singapore
South Korea Switzerland Thailand Turkey Ukraine Vietnam

Published by Oxford University Press, Inc.
198 Madison Avenue, New York, New York 10016

ISBN 978-0-19-532534-8

Oxford is a registered trademark of Oxford University Press

Printed in the United States of America

Book Club Edition

Contents

Preface

Early in the 1980s Robert E. Burke, a longtime friend who was a distinguished professor of history at the University of Washington, proposed that we write the biography of William Randolph Hearst. I would cover his life from 1863 to 1910 and Burke, who was editing the Hiram Johnson Papers for the Bancroft Library at the University of California–Berkeley, would complete the biography (1910 to 1951). Burke's untimely death, however, prevented this ambitious undertaking. Hence in 1998, after Oxford University Press published my book *William Randolph Hearst: The Early Years, 1863–1910,* I decided to complete the biography.

Since Burke often remarked that Hearst was a reflection of his newspapers, I decided to test that premise as part of my investigation—and discovered early on in my research that this proposition was basically correct. As I sat before a microfilm machine for countless hours, outlining one of Hearst's flagship newspapers, I became, in effect, a subscriber. In his daily editions history came alive—huge head lines, well-written stories, exciting political cartoons, trenchant editorials. He was a master salesman and showman, whose newspaper genius had attracted the attention of American readers after his entry into journalism on March 4, 1887. By 1930 he had assembled a media empire of twenty-eight newspapers in nineteen of the largest cities in the United States. One out of four Americans read a Hearst newspaper.

Hearst maintained that his fingers were on the "pulse" of the American people, that his hopes and trepidations, his likes and dislikes, reflected theirs. As a result, the Hearst newspapers were a tremendous source of information in regard to his thinking. After 1900 he seldom corresponded with family and friends concerning his innermost feelings and long-range desires. But as editor in chief, he directed the editorial policies of his weekly and Sunday papers, which in turn reflected his stances concerning the domestic and foreign policies of the United States as well as his personal views on a wide range of subjects. From 1910 to 1939 he averaged between twenty to thirty signed editorials annually (usually on page 1), which clearly enunciated his views. Then from March 1940 to May 1942, he also wrote a daily column, "In The News."

And since no editorial, whether signed or otherwise, appeared without his knowledge and approval, a thorough investigation of the Hearst newspapers was imperative to writing this biography.

Although this method of research was lengthy and often tedious, Hearst was the rewarding factor. He was a fascinating subject. He was no ordinary man, displaying strengths and weaknesses that were, like the man himself, gigantic in magnitude.

Acknowledgments

After six years of researching and writing this second volume of the Hearst biography, I am deeply indebted to a number of professionals. At the Texas Christian University library, interlibrary loan specialist Joyce Martindale was an invaluable resource, obtaining newspapers, magazines, and books from across the nation with utmost speed. Sandy Peoples in circulation kept me up to date on the numerous books checked out in my possession. Reference librarian Pat Austin helped me seek out books and dissertations that were so necessary in researching Hearst. And periodicals librarian Janet Douglass set aside—and kept in working order—a microfilm machine for my daily use.

Other professionals also encouraged and abetted me. Anthony Bliss, Richard Ogar, and Franz Enciso in the Bancroft Library at the University of California–Berkeley imparted their knowledge of the vast Hearst collections housed there. Robert Clark and Robert H. Parks at the FDR Library in Hyde Park, New York, expedited my research by their knowledge of Hearst references. Ned Comstock, the Cinema-Television Archivist at the University of Southern California, was equally informative and helpful, as was Marc Wanamaker, Bison Archives in Los Angeles. And Stacey Behlmer at the Margaret Herrick Academy of Motion Picture Arts and Sciences in Beverly Hills has a comprehensive knowledge of the materials and was of inestimable value to my research. In regard to San Simeon, chief curator Hoyt Fields, library coordinator Judy Anderson, and photographer Victoria Garagliano were extremely helpful. And special thanks go to John Horn, who was the California parks historian at San Simeon; he set aside personal time to help me understand the intricacies of the Hearst castle and its surroundings.

Special thanks also go to the assistant chief of the Manuscript Division of the Library of Congress David Wigdor who, with the help of Mark Sweeney and Georgia Higley of the Newspaper Collection, provided me with Hearst newspapers through interlibrary loan. Wigdor, who is a specialist in twentieth-century U.S. history, was also an invaluable consultant in regard to historical accuracy and content.

Others offering scholarly advice were film historian Louis Pizzitola, whose book *Hearst over Hollywood* is a valuable study of Hearst's contributions to the motion picture industry. Historian Ty Cashion of Sam Houston State University improved the manuscript with helpful suggestions. And Taylor Coffman provided insight through his excellent knowledge of Hearst and San Simeon.

Richard Lowitt, emeritus professor of history at the University of Oklahoma and a walking bibliophile on twentieth-century U.S. history, was a valuable cohort in this undertaking. He continually alerted me in regard to important historical works and carefully read the manuscript. I deeply appreciate his scholarship and friendship.

Most of all, I am inbeted to my wife Phoebe and son Ben, who offered encouragement and then became valuable research assistants. To them I dedicate this book.

William Randolph Hearst

Final Edition, 1911–1951

1 Government by Newspaper

William Randolph Hearst was a formidable force in American life, an awesome power to be reckoned with both in the business and political worlds, a man with a remarkable capacity for reinventing himself no matter how devastating the setbacks. Without question, he was the foremost news media mogul in the United States and throughout the world. During the two decades after 1890 he had enlarged his newspaper empire to include eight publications in five of the largest cities in the United States (New York, Boston, Chicago, Los Angeles, and San Francisco), totaling more than 4 million readers, far outdistancing his competitors in circulation and advertising as well as self-promotion. As early as 1902 he had also ventured into the magazine arena; after purchasing *Cosmopolitan* in 1905, he again proved his marketing wizardry by rapidly attaining a loyal audience of 750,000 readers and a multitude of indulgent advertisers. Hearst was thus girding himself to become even more dominant in the journalistic world through expansion, either by enticing buyouts of poorly run businesses or by engaging in cutthroat competition against rivals.[1]

Upon first encounter Hearst, at age forty-seven, was not a particularly imposing figure. Although somewhat large in stature, particularly for the early 1900s, at six feet, one inch and approximately two hundred pounds, he did not reflect physical strength or noticeable athleticism, mainly because of sloping shoulders and a certain gangliness. Pale blue eyes, which some observers commented were "cold" and "sharp," dominated his face, obscuring a clear complexion that was smooth and unwrinkled; his nose, long and straight, rested beneath a broad brow topped off with brown hair parted slightly off-center. A high-pitched, tenor voice, together with a slight lisp (which San Francisco *Examiner* editorial writer Ambrose Bierce once described as "like the fragrance of crushed violets made audible") deceptively created a first impression of weakness and fragility, of enervation and incapacity. His obvious shyness with strangers, accompanied at times by uncomfortable, if not lengthy, silences, as well as a nervous habit of finger tapping just prior to making a decision, belied his inner strength.[2]

But make no mistake, Hearst was someone whose presence, whether in 1910 or thereafter, had to be dealt with carefully and with utmost concern. And why? He was extremely creative, his proposals concerning the news business bordering on genius or, as biographer John Winkler put it, "so full of ideas that they tumbled over each other." He was also a man of self-reliance and rugged determination, willing to advance any crusade, even though unpopular, in the name of democracy and justice, to confront any individual no matter how prominent and powerful, no matter what the professional or personal consequences. Aggressive and tenacious, he was bent on winning, devoted to providing the means necessary to attaining desired objectives. And when anyone opposed his programs or ideas he was a dangerous adversary who was ready to apply all resources at his command, which were sizable, to incapacitate his foes. He was, indeed, an unrelenting opponent intent upon destroying his enemies. In other words, the Marquess of Queensberry rules went out the window, as did any policy not of his own making. As a result, Hearst was a high-profile public figure who delighted in receiving praise but anticipated criticism. He never forgot a slight and made it his business to repay an affront at least fourfold, if not more.[3]

For almost a quarter century (1887–1910) Hearst had built his huge news media empire on the basis of leadership. Although ably assisted by such gifted editors as Arthur Brisbane and Morrill Goddard in New York, brilliant business manager Solomon S. Carvalho, valued attorney Clarence J. Shearn, and all-around handyman and troubleshooter Max Ihmsen, Hearst alone was responsible. The key to leadership was, he maintained, to instill discipline in his empire from the top down as well as the bottom up. Formality and decorum were therefore essential components in his organizational structure. While Brisbane and a few close friends ventured to call him "W.R.," Carvalho, Imhsen, Goddard, and Shearn referred to him specifically as "Chief." Lesser lights in his expanding news empire addressed him simply as "Mr. Hearst." Only his wife Millicent and mother Phoebe Apperson Hearst called him "Will" or "Bill." Although often confiding in his most trusted employees, Hearst was the decision maker and ultimate authority. Hence he often found himself alone at the top. But that was the way he wanted it; no other system satisfied him.[4]

As a result, Hearst created and maintained his huge news-media empire with entertaining ideas and innovative techniques that revolutionized newspapers, which was, again, a reflection of his personality. He was determined to associate his enterprises with the everyday laboring man and woman, with immigrants and the "huddled masses" in an attempt to gain their interest and support. He believed that his fingers were on the pulse of the American people; therefore, his newspapers reflected his interests—and accordingly theirs. As a consequence, Hearst identified with Americans who loved a winner, with those who appreciated loyalty and close relationships; for example, he concocted slogans that titled the San Francisco *Examiner* as the "Monarch of the Dailies" and the New York *American* as "An American Paper for the American Family." From the very beginning of his career he established a formula for success that demanded an increase in daily circulation, which in turn attracted advertisers and thereby provided him the necessary funds to hire the best editors, reporters, illustrators, and political cartoonists in the country.[5]

The result was "Gee Whiz Journalism." Arthur McEwen, one of Hearst's editors, defined it best: "Any issue the front page of which failed to elicit a 'Gee Whiz!' from its readers was a failure, whereas the second page ought to bring forth a 'Holy Moses!' and the third an astounded 'God Almighty!' "[6]

Sensationalism was the forte of all Hearst papers, with fist-size headlines (succinctly depicting the story) a necessary ingredient. Every edition focused on a myriad of human frailties, such as murder, deception, betrayal, infidelity, as well as major catastrophes and natural disasters.

But his journalism was more than a litany of human suffering and debauchery. Since Americans loved sports competition, he featured college football rivalries and the World Series in baseball on the front page. Anything having to do with women was good copy, whether relating to fashions or cuisines or weddings or beauty contests. Stories about American royalty—the superrich—especially the Rockefellers, Vanderbilts, Carnegies, Morgans, Guggenheims, and Astors, were always prime news.[7]

Hearst demanded that his papers be informative and innovative. Unlike a number of competitors, he was able to provide readers with detailed stories about international incidents. But for those interested in local events, he also initiated mundane but interesting data, such as daily weather forecasts (at the top of page 1), columns registering obituaries and births and weddings (usually on page 4 or 5), repetitive lists that recognized people contributing money to charitable or civic endeavors, letters to the editor, This Day in History, and editorials by syndicated columnists accompanied by trenchant political cartoons, hilariously comical—and brutal—in their depiction.

Hearst insisted that his editors provide a constant stream of entertainment and gamesmanship for readers. Puzzles, contests, at times lotteries, with prizes often totaling thousands of dollars, permeated each edition. Serial stories by renowned authors such as Mark Twain, Jules Verne, Sir Arthur Conan Doyle, Jack London, and Upton Sinclair were equally prevalent, especially in the Sunday editions, which usually ran sixty to ninety pages at a cost of five cents. And Hearst initiated color cartoons, the first being the *Yellow Kid* in 1896, portraying the life of a street urchin in the slums of New York City; hence the sobriquet "yellow journalism."[8]

A major difference between the Hearst papers and competitors was his crusade approach to issues and individuals, or more specifically his technique of orchestrating the news. And herein was the reason for his success, as well as a public danger. He and his editors managed, manipulated, at times falsified news stories, oblivious to charges that such yellow journalism lacked objectivity. Hearst, however, ignored these calumnies by critics, somewhat piously announcing that his system of presenting information was nothing more than "government by newspaper," whereby "the people through popular organs" accurately expressed the "popular will." His daily journals, he expounded, were more closely in touch with the American people than were the politicians. As evidence he cited the Spanish American War to "free Cuba." From 1895 to a United States declaration of war against Spain in April, 1898, his journals had provided the leadership, had "become in fact the people's voice," he asserted, in forcing President William McKinley and Congress to act decisively. Hearst thus reasoned that "we shall see the press fulfill its noble calling, and as the mouthpiece of the people, rule, regulate, and reform the world."[9]

During the first decade of the twentieth century Hearst continued his government by newspaper approach, often with gratifying results. For example, in regard to foreign affairs he campaigned monthly, and often daily in the Hearst papers for what he called the "Journal's National Policy": the annexation of Hawaii, an interoceanic canal either through Nicaragua or Panama, the acquisition of strategic bases in the Caribbean, the maintenance of a mighty navy, and the establishment of "great national universities" at West Point and Annapolis. From 1898 to 1903 the Hearst papers triumphantly expounded on attaining most of these objectives; the power of government by newspaper, by enlisting the help of thousands upon thousands of readers, had forced Congress to do its bidding.[10]

Hearst was an ardent progressive, intent on alleviating (if not eliminating) the economic, political, and social abuses of capitalism in the

United States. He pushed for reforms on the state and national levels, programs that his eight papers called "An American Internal Policy." And again, he trumpeted to his readers, government by newspaper was successful. After 1903 the Roosevelt and Taft administrations busted a number of criminal trusts, especially those engaged in oil, steel, beef, and timber, that had monopolized the natural resources of the United States and that had become more powerful "than the people's government," according to the Hearst papers. He also advocated public ownership of public franchises, especially those that involved water, gas, and rapid transit—in essence, "water and gas socialism." By the early 1900s such states as Wisconsin, Oregon, and California had embraced these reforms partially or in toto. Equally important, the Hearst papers championed the need for postal savings banks, parcel post, a graduated income tax, direct election of senators, currency reform through a federal banking system, and an eight-hour day for labor, all of which were enacted into law by 1913. Only in regard to the improvement of the public school system did the "American Internal Policy" fall short. But here again Hearst remained optimistic; he had devised an effective formula to obtain his objectives for the American people and, of course, for himself.[11]

Hearst fervently yearned to become even more of a contributing factor in American life, to be a significant player in the governing of the United States. Yet at every turn in his career he missed the key opportunity to achieve a position in government "to make a difference." In the 1896 and 1900 presidential elections he backed the losing candidate, Democratic nominee William Jennings Bryan. Consequently Hearst decided that the best way to effect his own policies was to run for public office. In 1902 and 1904 he won election to Congress as a Democrat, representing the Eleventh Manhattan district in New York City, in the belief that such a position would be a solid base of operations for higher office. But at the 1904 national Democratic Convention in St. Louis he placed second to conservative Alton B. Parker of New York—but only after Bryan betrayed him by voting for an insignificant contender. As a result, before entering the presidential fray again, Hearst sought a higher profile job, first as mayor of New York City in 1905 and then as the Democratic nominee for governor of New York in 1906. On both occasions, after hard-fought, rancorous campaigns, he narrowly lost. Disenchanted with Democrats for their lack of support and completely alienated from the Republicans, Hearst almost singlehandedly established the Independence Party, which was dedicated to reforming society and government. And for three years (1906–1909) he became the patron saint of this reform-minded third party movement, applying his considerable wealth and energy and organization into making a viable third party, but again to no avail. Then in the fall of 1909 Hearst once again ran for mayor of New York City, hoping to capture that illusive prestigious rung that would position him as a major contender for the presidency in 1912. In the ensuing campaign he battled Tammany Hall, the most powerful politically run urban organization in the United States, to a standstill, defeating all of its nominees save one, the new mayor of New York City, Judge William J. Gaynor, a former Hearst ally but now, after an acrimonious campaign, an acid-tongued and bitter enemy.[12]

So in January 1910, William Randolph Hearst, as was often his custom after an arduous campaign or an intensive period of strenuous work, sought solace through anonymity, which meant foreign travel and self-indulgence. For the next four months, he became mostly invisible to the news media. He placed his New York papers in the capable hands of Arthur Brisbane, an accomplished editor who was in many respects his alter ego. Hearst then proceeded to California with wife Millicent and their three boys—George, Bill Jr., and John, ages five, two, and four months respectively. Phoebe Apperson Hearst, the proud mother of W.R. and an adoring grandmother who resided at La Hacienda del Pozo de Verona, a luxurious estate at Pleasanton, approximately thirty miles south of San Francisco, had been demanding to see her grandchildren. In anticipation of their arrival she had constructed a two-story, thirteen-room "Boys House," with playrooms filled with toys and outfitted with governesses, tutors, and nurses. As a further inducement she had purchased horses for "her boys" and, even though mere babies, hired instructors to teach them riding skills.[13]

With both grandmother and sons happily settled at Pleasanton, Hearst was free to indulge himself. Speedy transportation had always attracted him. On his European honeymoon in May 1903, he had purchased the fastest motorcar possible to tour France, Italy, and Spain. In the meantime he had cabled business manager Solomon Carvalho to research a British magazine titled *The Car*, and subsequently he produced an American rendition called *Motor* in January 1904. Airplanes equally attracted Hearst. In Los Angeles on January 19, 1910, while checking on the progress of the Hearst *Examiner*, he persuaded the famous French aviator Louis Paulhan to fly him over the city; in October, he promoted a coast-to-coast contest in his newspapers, with a $50,000 prize for the first flier to accomplish such a daring feat.[14]

By March 1910, Hearst and Millicent were touring Mexico. They traveled to Chihuahua to inspect the million-acre Babicora Ranch, where 150 vaqueros tended thousands upon thousands of cattle, sheep, horses, and hogs. Early in the 1880s his father George Hearst, through the cultivated friendship and close business ties with Mexican dictator Porfirio Diaz, had purchased this land for a mere forty cents an acre. After an enjoyable, leisurely stay, they proceeded to Mexico City and obtained an audience with—and rendered their support to—aging President Diaz, who was battling the revolutionary tide that would soon force him into exile. On April 6, they returned to the United States by private car via El Paso, refreshed and rejuvenated.[15]

While on vacation, Hearst constructed a new political agenda. After losing to Gaynor in November 1909, he realized that the Independence Party could not produce a national winner, especially in regard to electing an American president. But if progressives throughout the country joined forces, that was another matter altogether. Assisted by Brisbane in New York, Hearst began corresponding with leading reformers in both parties. To insurgent House members such as Republican George W. Norris of Nebraska and Democratic Minority Leader Champ Clark of Missouri, he offered both aid and newspaper coverage in their fight to undermine the power of House Speaker Joe Cannon of Illinois, who was exploiting nearly every prerogative of his office. A victory of such magnitude, Hearst believed, would signal the beginning of a national resurgence for reformers, regardless of party, to unite under one banner and would pave the way for his return to a possible leadership role within the Democratic Party.

On April 14, three weeks after House insurgents had delivered a stunning defeat to Cannon, Hearst launched a trial balloon while en route to the East Coast. Through his intermediary in Washington, *New York American* correspondent John Temple Graves, he suggested "a union between the Independence League and the Democratic Party for control of the Government." Thus, with the congressional victory over conservatives epitomized by Cannon's loss of power, together with a tremendous enthusiasm by Democratic leaders regarding the Graves overtures, Hearst arrived in Washington elated and triumphant, capping off such favorable endeavors by a thirty-minute audience with President William Howard Taft.[16]

While on vacation Hearst had delegated to Brisbane one piece of unfinished business, that of paying their respects to Mayor Gaynor. The 1909 mayoral campaign had been vitriolic both in tone and substance. Neither Hearst nor Brisbane could forget—or forgive—Gaynor, who had retaliated to vicious slanders. He angrily announced on one occasion during the campaign that Hearst's face "almost makes me want to puke."[17]

Consequently, at the least provocation, the *American* and *Evening Journal* stood ready to exercise government by newspaper, continually reminding

New Yorkers of their mistake in voting for Gaynor. As early as December 15, 1909, the *American* exposed surreptitiously obtained letters from Tammany Hall boss Charles Francis Murphy to his chief lieutenants, stating that the mayor would readily submit to his recommended appointments. After Gaynor assumed office on January 1, the *American* relentlessly linked him to Tammany, despite evidence to the contrary; it then culminated such attacks with a front-page exposé on April 15 that accused the mayor of a political payoff of $48,000 to Daniel F. Cohalan, a prominent Tammany sachem under Boss Murphy. On January 3, 1910, newly appointed City Chamberlain Charles Hyde routinely signed a warrant for work performed during the previous administration. But the *American* implied that Gaynor, after only three days in office, was already using public funds to repay Tammany for its support.[18]

Mayor Gaynor, by temperament irascible and by nature combative, could no longer endure the Hearst–Brisbane assaults, especially after experiencing what he considered to be a gross injustice by the yellow press. He could not—and would not—wait for long. At the Waldorf Astoria on April 28, as the dinner speaker before members of the Associated Press and the American Newspaper Publishers Association, with such distinguished guests at the head table as President Woodrow Wilson of Princeton University, Gaynor rebuked his chief persecutor, verbally excoriating him with every well-chosen word. "You have given me the subject, 'The Press in Its Relation to Public Officials,'" he began, "and to speak plainly and freely." And that, he unsmilingly announced, was what he planned to do. "On the whole," he observed, "the press . . . is just [and fair] to public officials." Yet one among you is not, he asserted. He is a publisher who in no "nook or corner of his head or heart is there the slightest sense of truth or justice." So "in the interests of public morality and decency" Gaynor stated that he could not "remain silent"; for that man was W. R. Hearst, who "as late as the 15th of this month" had "printed in his principal newspaper . . . the facsimile of a draft on the treasury of this city for $48,000, with headlines and an article attributing such draft and expenditure to the present mayor. The headlines and article assert that I fixed the award and amount, and paid it."

While displaying to the audience the page of the *American* that showed the $48,000 draft, Gaynor noted that certain omissions in the facsimile had occurred. He pointed to the obliteration of the pertinent date "December 31, 1909" and an equally important erasure of the city auditor's voucher that had recorded "December 29, 1909." "In plain words," Gaynor proclaimed to the stunned audience, "two state prison felonies, namely, forgery and falsification of a public document, were committed in the eagerness of this publisher and editor to wrong the mayor of the city of New York." For the next several minutes Gaynor continued his assault on Hearst, concluding that "it is high time that these forgers and libelers were in state's prison, and the time is not far distant when some of them will be there."

As the coup de grace for his defense, Gaynor virulently asserted, "And just think of a man who is capable of doing things like this being possessed of the notion that he is fit to hold any public office from mayor to President of the United States! Morally speaking, his mind must be a howling wilderness. Never will the voters anywhere put such a man in office."[19]

What a furor! Complete silence for a moment, then clapping and spontaneous applause. From the audience, however, stormed Tom Williams, the business manager of the *New York Evening Journal* and one of Hearst's "ablest and most trusted lieutenants." Angrily demanding to be heard, he moved menacingly toward Gaynor. As someone yelled, "Three cheers for our honest mayor!" an enraged Williams shook his fist in Gaynor's face and bellowed, "You're a brave man, aren't you! Vilifying a man who is not here! Are you afraid?" After twenty minutes of bedlam and confusion, hotel detectives finally restored order by persuading Williams to leave. The mayor had inflicted his revenge.[20]

But Gaynor would long rue his moment of triumph. He should have remembered the old adage, "You don't engage in an argument with a man who buys ink by the barrel." Hearst and Brisbane immediately proved the wisdom of that statement. With relish they mobilized their forces for a Gaynor crusade, utilizing Hearst's technique of orchestrating the news. They instructed reporters to investigate every aspect of the mayor's administration, to probe for weaknesses and irregularities. They accumulated hundreds of testimonials by prominent citizens throughout the country denouncing Gaynor for scurrilous diatribes, and then printed them weekly and often daily. They assigned gifted editorial writers Alfred Henry Lewis and John Temple Graves, who were masters of invective and purveyors of make-believe, to portray Gaynor "objectively" to New Yorkers. They focused editorials, accompanied by the political cartoons of talented artists Frederick Opper and Robert Carter, that continually denigrated the mayor and his administration.[21]

Hearst himself initiated the onslaught. In a front-page editorial on April 30, he positioned himself as an innocent bystander falsely accused by an abusive and spiteful politician, who had been caught in a scandalous act. "I am not entirely familiar with all the accusations against Mayor Gaynor, or his attempt to divert attention from them by an attack upon the *American*," Hearst began. For "I have just returned from Mexico." But "it is obvious to anyone," he insisted, "that the Mayor's defense is false upon its face. His attack upon *The American* is entirely disingenuous and wholly untruthful." After all, he guilelessly proclaimed, "anybody who knows the high character of the gentlemen who edit *The American* knows that no matter how much they might despise Mayor Gaynor they would never seek to take an unfair advantage of him."

So much for innocence and objectivity! For two printed pages Hearst castigated the mayor and his lackey, City Chamberlain Hyde, who had signed a $48,000 check to Tammany lieutenant Cohalan and had "allowed this padded fee to go through unquestioned." In conclusion, Hearst prophesied, "NOW I KNOW PERFECTLY WELL WHAT IS GOING TO HAPPEN TO YOU, MR. GAYNOR. THE PEOPLE ARE GOING EVENTUALLY TO FIND YOU OUT AND REPUDIATE YOU."[22]

With the Gaynor crusade under way, Hearst saw no reason to interrupt his summer vacation plans. On May 10, 1910, after his attorney Clarence Shearn filed libel suits (eventually approximating $400,000) against the *New York Times* and the Associated Press, Hearst together with Millicent and their two oldest boys George and Bill Jr. sailed for Europe on a five-month tour. They arrived in London soon after the death of the English monarch Edward VII, whereupon for two weeks Hearst witnessed and wrote about the pageantry involving the royal family, the pomp and ceremony of burying the king, and the ascendancy of his successor George V. One *American* headline for Hearst's eyewitness account read, "MOST DRAMATIC AND TOUCHING PAGEANT OF MODERN TIMES."[23]

The foreign press elevated Hearst to celebrity status. The *London Chronicle* acknowledged him as "one of the most remarkable of all living Americans" and asked his opinion concerning American policies and politicians. As the "Napoleon of the American press," he breakfasted with Parliamentary leader Lloyd George and associated with other notables in the English government. When he arrived in Paris late in May, reporters heralded his coming with lengthy interviews that covered a wide range of subjects, especially his estimation of ex-President Theodore Roosevelt, the Taft administration, and the present progressive trend in American politics.[24]

After staying more than a month in Paris, Hearst continued his summer holiday, acting as tour guide (as was his custom) for Millicent and the boys. He investigated—and bought—some Italian treasures, ending his last days in Venice before vacationing in Switzerland. Then the Hearsts traveled back to Paris for an extended visit, before heading to England and a return home early in October.[25]

Yet Hearst could never retreat completely, much less isolate himself from the world at large. His personal interests were so varied, his news media enterprises so enormous and complex that decisions still needed the special attention of the head man. In May, for instance, before sailing to Europe, he sponsored the American Boy Scout movement in New York City and Chicago, with his newspapers providing the necessary publicity as well as application blanks for membership. He was also responsible for establishing a national headquarters in Manhattan. He agreed to accept the American presidency of the organization on June 30 in absentia and several weeks later furthered the movement's solvency by donating $1,000.[26]

At the same time Hearst was maintaining and improving his news media empire. In Chicago, his *Examiner* (the new name for the morning *American*) was involved in a bitter circulation war with Medill McCormick's *Tribune*. The editors of the two papers even hired gunmen to "persuade" newsdealers that one publication was far superior to the other. Beatings and shootings became commonplace. Hearst was aware of the Chicago "problem" and desired a favorable solution, but he remained aloof regarding specifics, especially while in Europe. He was also concerned about financial difficulties at the *Boston American*. Since 1907 he had replaced its editor, business manager, and designated publisher, thereby curtailing yearly expenses by $125,000. Yet "his individual exactions kept the money drawers well-drained," since he constantly upgraded the newspaper.

Equally important, Hearst intended to expand the limits of his empire and assigned one of his brightest young executives, Moses Koenigsberg, to seek out newspaper publishers who would consider a reasonable buyout rather than face, as Koenigsberg noted, "a Goliath [such as Hearst] with club raised to beat them into economic insecurity." As a result, Koenigsberg sought good buys in the United States and, together with Hearst, inquired into the possibility of expanding into the English markets.[27]

The multifaceted Hearst, however, was most concerned about his political involvement both on the state and national levels, and for good reason. Although the patron saint of the national Independence Party, he realized that his reform movement could not defeat the well-entrenched Republicans and Democrats either nationally or statewide. But if neither party nominated standard-bearers dedicated to progressive principles of reform, Hearst announced to a *New York World* reporter late in June 1910, the American people would have to seek relief through "united progressive independents." Hearst even considered aligning with ex-President Roosevelt in September, albeit briefly, asserting that "we independents are whetting our tomahawks for the fray [in 1912]; there is no jealousy in our ranks; we do not care who leads, if only he leads aright." Then, as reports from states in New England and the Midwest proclaimed the nomination of candidates dedicated to political reform "in behalf of the people," Hearst became even more convinced that victory was at hand—but only through the Democratic Party.[28]

Yet Hearst first had to play out his hand with the New York Independence League, at least show meager good faith before bolting. Subsequently late in September 1910, while still in Europe, he agreed to accept the second spot of the Independence League on the New York state ticket, that of lieutenant governor. After arriving home on October 7, he applied himself diligently—but with increasing reluctance—to a month-long campaign.

Hearst, however, never liked the idea of being part of a supportive cast, of playing second fiddle to anyone. Consequently, he received more space in his newspapers than league nominee for governor J. J. Hopper. Even though Hearst was unable to campaign during the last week of October because of illness, the *New York American* printed his speeches in toto, although delivered by a surrogate. On resuming his political commitments early in November, he spoke at rallies in New York City with Hopper, always—as reported by the *American*—as the star attraction.[29]

As a matter of fact, Hearst was the star attraction for the Independence League. As anticipated on Election Day (November 8), he led the ticket in greater New York, outdistancing Hopper by 15,000 votes. And even though the League's statewide results were dismal, the *American* was awash with a tidal wave of praise for Hearst, as political victors throughout the nation, mainly Democratic congressmen and governors, thanked Mr. Hearst, one front-page headline read, "for aid in their election."[30]

Hearst, ever yearning "to make a difference" by becoming a contributing factor in the political leadership of the United States, decided that he must create appropriate avenues for reentry into the Democratic Party. And to that end he arduously applied both time and resources. On November 20, he set the tone for his return by evaluating the outcome of the election in detail. For New Yorkers, and for readers of the Hearst papers nationwide, he optimistically noted that, despite the "personal failure" of some candidates (like himself), "the cause of progressive popular government" had been triumphant. He confidently asserted that "the whole country has rebelled against stand-pat Republicanism" and repudiated its principles.[31]

As was always the case when striving to attain a political goal, Hearst maintained a high profile with the public, orchestrating the news through government by newspaper. As a result, the *American* and *Evening Journal* were awash with his name. In December he was credited with the federal government's victories over huge criminal monopolies that infringed on the rights of Americans, specifically his eight-year fight against the Coal Trust that in turn signified the "end of the beef trust." He was a charitable giver during the Christmas season, with Millicent heading a doll bazaar auction for the poor, while he donated $1,000 to the *American* Christmas fund for 40,000 needy children. He contributed another $1,000 to the wife and family of a recently slain New York City policeman. Hearst attracted further attention by resigning as head of the Boy Scouts of America after discovering financial mismanagement by unscrupulous fund-raisers. Hence he was recognized as a purveyor of honesty and integrity.[32]

But all such activity was mere window dressing for the main event—reentering the Democratic Party and assuming a leadership role. On January 29, 1911, after an extended Christmas vacation in California with Millicent and the boys, an energized and aggressive Hearst returned to New York by way of Washington to implement his political agenda. While lobbying with Democratic congressmen to provide federal funds for a West Coast exposition in San Francisco, he confirmed in an editorial that "I am a Democrat." According to plan he immediately began currying favor with state and national party leaders. At a dinner in Manhattan on January 31 he was one of the principal speakers, paying homage to wealthy philanthropist and political ally Nathan Straus. During the next three months at his huge apartment complex at 137 Riverside Drive, Hearst hosted elaborate receptions and elegant dinner parties. He not only became better acquainted with a number of congressmen and New York state officials but also was on good speaking terms with such political dignitaries as Democratic Speaker of the House Champ Clark of Missouri and progressive Republican Senator Robert LaFollette of Wisconsin.[33]

To experienced politicos Hearst's intentions were obvious. He was attempting to remind Democrats what a valuable asset his return to the party would be. To allay fears regarding his past political stances the *New York American* editorialized that "Mr. Hearst's Radicalism" of yesteryear had become steel magnate "Andrew Carnegie's Conservatism." In several other op-ed pieces the *American* also suggested that the foreign policies of President Taft regarding the U.S. fortification of the Panama Canal were identical with those of Hearst. Rumors concerning the acquisition of more newspapers seemed to crop up periodically, often ending in denials.

Yet the point was obvious; Hearst was an awesome media power who could be a decided advantage to the Democratic Party.[34]

Hearst intended to prove his political value both by word and deed. In Chicago he involved his two newspapers, the *Examiner* and *American*, in a mayoral campaign that promoted Carter H. Harrison. As a first assault team, he sent Brisbane to beef up the journalistic troops of longtime *Examiner* editor Andrew M. "Andy" Lawrence. He intended to win the election for Harrison and control the Illinois delegation to the Democratic National Convention in 1912. After a bitter three-month media crusade, Harrison emerged victorious, grateful although not subservient to the Hearst forces.

Meanwhile in San Francisco the *Examiner* proclaimed that the continual assaults by the boss-run vested interests of the city had failed miserably as evidenced by the trial and conviction of Mayor Eugene E. Schmitz, all of which occurred because of William Randolph Hearst. As a result, his newspapers were already maneuvering to deliver presidential state delegates for the Democrats.

In New York, party leaders welcomed Hearst with all the fanfare of a prodigal son, praising him for his lengthy newspaper crusades to help secure such recent national legislation as the direct election of senators, a graduated income tax, and postal savings banks, as well as a proposed state direct primary. New York Democrats honored Hearst with a series of receptions at Albany, culminating on May 17, 1911, after he delivered a lengthy address to the legislature. Hearst could not have been happier with the results; he was fast becoming a major player in the presidential election of 1912.[35]

With so much accomplished, Hearst decided that rewards were in order. That decision usually meant one thing—a European trip. On May 24 he and Millicent sailed for England on the *Mauritania* and indulged themselves for the next four and a half months. Yet to enjoy this vacation fully he needed to remedy a severe nerve pain that had settled in his teeth, which he called "neuralgia." He thus sought relief in Munich by taking curative hot baths, but to no avail. Then, he exultantly wrote his mother, he received unexpected but total relief from "the funniest little Italian doctor . . . you ever saw." Rejuvenated in body and spirit, Hearst spent time haggling over paintings and collecting rare relics, before experiencing the wonders of the Swiss Alps.

In August the Hearsts enjoyed the sights in and around Paris before channel hopping to England in September, where he really indulged himself. Besides enlarging his journalistic empire in England by buying *Nash's Magazine* and a newspaper titled the *London Budget* (both placed in his wife's name), he became involved in a lifelong passion when he purchased Tattershall Castle near Boston, Lincolnshire, "a fifteenth-century structure built by Lord Cromwell." As reported in the *New York Times*, Hearst intended to "remove it stone by stone and brick by brick for re-erection in the United States." This obsession with collecting and acquiring treasured relics of the past would become even more prevalent during his life time.[36]

Yet Hearst, ever mindful of the 1912 presidential race, devoted considerable time to improving his political image. With Brisbane's assistance he continued to lay the foundation for a blazing reentry into the Democratic Party upon his return in October. Through numerous editorials and interviews while abroad (often appearing on the front pages of his newspapers), Hearst began positioning himself as an accomplished authority on foreign affairs. He especially emphasized the need for reciprocal trade agreements in behalf of the American farmer and businessman, and he became a strong advocate for world peace. The political uncertainties and frictions among European nations disturbed him mightily.[37]

Above all, Hearst understood the importance of self-promotion. Democrats must understand, and appreciate, what an important commodity he was. In rival newspapers such as the *New York Times*, information conveniently appeared concerning the continued growth of the Hearst media empire—that he had bought "the entire block in Columbus Circle" for housing his many publications including the *American* and *Evening Journal*, that he was further expanding into the Midwest market with the "option to purchase" the St. Louis *Star*, and that other journalistic sales were pending. Hearst made these reports all the more credible by acquiring the *World Today*, which he immediately developed into a monthly journal titled *Hearst's Magazine*.[38]

Early in October 1911, Hearst arrived in New York with great anticipation, his plans for a triumphant return well laid. In the span of a week New Yorkers realized that William Randolph Hearst was back in town. Beginning on October 12, he addressed the Italian American Civic Union at a huge Columbus Day banquet in Brooklyn. As expected, the *American* headline noted, he was royally received and "rousingly cheered" each time he mentioned "Italy's career of greatness." Four days later in a signed editorial he won further approval by eulogizing the passing of Justice John M. Harlan as "the last of the constitutionalists" on the Supreme Court who "unalterably opposed . . . the encroachments of the Court" on Congress. Adhering to what he considered the revered ideals of Jeffersonian democracy, Hearst announced that the Supreme Court should never infringe on the rights of the elected representatives of the American people. Then on October 18, Hearst awakened New Yorkers to the clarion call for reform and honest government in the upcoming November city elections. He unleased a venomous attack on Tammany Hall and Boss Charles Francis Murphy, flamboyantly offering $18,000 in reward for the arrest and conviction of illegal registrants, election law tamperers, and a Tammany boss violating voting rights.

And on October 19, as a capstone to an active week of publicity, Hearst spoke at three monster rallies in New York City for fusion candidates (Independents, Republicans, and Democrats). His theme was direct and clear. To a boisterous crowd at Carnegie Hall he repeatedly denounced Tammany chief Murphy, whose actions "drove me out of the Democratic Party five years ago." But no longer! "The commendable course of the National Democracy has brought me back into the fold." And, Hearst proclaimed, "I am registering as a Democrat, I am speaking as a Democrat, and as a Democrat I am going to fight the un-Democratic principles and policies of Murphy and Tammany Hall."[39]

Hearst was delighted with the results. After his reporters garnered scores of interviews from across the nation, Brisbane and fellow editors orchestrated the news, printing only those statements that were glowingly favorable. As a consequence, Speaker of the House Champ Clark proclaimed that "Hearst's return . . . is an asset that will bear full weight. He is a progressive statesman, and his influence and aid will be a blessing to the party." House Democratic leader Oscar W. Underwood of Alabama noted that Hearst "has a world of influence. His fight has always been for the interests of the party." One huge headline read, "Massachusetts Leaders Agree That [the Democratic] Party Should Rejoice at Regaining His Support; California Welcomes Him." Another announced that "Mayor Harrison of Chicago Rejoices in Hearst's Return." Still another proclaimed that "Mr. Hearst's Influence Appreciated at Albany." And while the *Washington Post* editorialized that "Public Life Bettered Through W. R. Hearst," the *Los Angeles Herald* declared that "we welcome him back to the ranks of progressive Democracy."

The response from New Jersey was quite different. Governor Woodrow Wilson sent no letter of commendation, despite a specific request from a Hearst emissary to do so. In fact, Wilson declared: "I am very sorry Mr. Hearst has come back into the Democratic Party. I think it was stronger with him on the outside than on the inside. I do not want him and do not want the support of his paper."

Hearst was not displeased with this response. He had never liked Wilson, and this rebuff provided another reason for future opposition. Not surprisingly, Wilson's comments never reached the printed page in the Hearst newspapers.[40]

Hearst was fast becoming a major player in the Democratic Party as well as in the presidential election of 1912. He still held a lingering hope that Democrats might turn to him should a deadlock for the presidential nomination occur at the national convention. But no matter the choice, he fervently desired to have a positive effect within the federal government, specifically to "make a difference." To accomplish his goals, he must maintain, if not increase, his political momentum. So until Election Day on November 7, 1911, he vigorously campaigned for fusion candidates, speaking to enthusiastic crowds, urging them to free themselves from their bondage to New York City bosses. All the while the *American* and *Evening Journal* denigrated Tammany Hall, upping the tempo for reform with eye-catching headlines, caustic editorials, and devastating political cartoons. To Hearst's delight these crusade tactics were successful. On November 8, 1911, the front-page *American* headline read, "NEW YORK STATE REPUDIATES BOSS MURPHY."[41]

Hearst now energized his growing media organization. His objective was the Democratic presidential nomination, if not for himself, at least for someone who would use his talents in government. Because of his candidacy for the Democratic nomination in 1904, he knew what must be done—bind a two-thirds majority of national convention delegates to him either personally (such as a favorite son) or to his chosen candidate.

In a number of instances, Hearst had political chits to call in. In New England, the governors of Massachusetts, Maine, and Connecticut had sent him public letters of appreciation for the invaluable publicity and financial support rendered by the Hearst newspapers in their November victories. In Ohio, the mayors of Columbus and Cincinnati were equally grateful, while in Illinois, Mayor Harrison of Chicago and Cook County officials, together with several congressmen, were effusive in their praise.

In the West, Hearst was especially strong. He had maintained a close relationship with Democratic politicians in New Mexico, Arizona, and Oklahoma. For instance, in October 1903, he had sponsored a congressional delegation composed of three senators and seventeen representatives on an eleven-day whistle-stop tour, whereupon he had championed immediate statehood for the three territories. He had continued these contacts. In front-page headlines in the *New York American*, the governors-elect of New Mexico and Arizona, together with the two senators-elect from Arizona, credited their victories in November to "the splendid aid" of the *Los Angeles Examiner*—and to Hearst personally. In California, he anticipated favorable reception, especially with the two largest newspapers in the state, the Los Angeles *Examiner* and the San Francisco

Examiner, applying the Hearst crusade for democracy treatment daily to their readers.[42]

Hearst was not ready to anoint a Democratic candidate, to concede the party nomination, to someone other than himself. He therefore appeared quite presidential during the winter of 1911–1912. In editorials and interviews he delivered position papers on foreign affairs, urging the United States to forge reciprocity treaties with Canada, Argentina, and Latin American nations. This action would be economically advantageous to U.S. farmers and businessmen and would help ensure world peace. At the same time in front-page stories, he alerted Hearst readers to his growing prestige and influence within international circles. For instance, the Republic of China was seeking help from him personally for recognition by the community of nations (*New York American*, November 16), and Russia was strenuously objecting to criticisms by the Hearst newspapers, especially by its publisher (December 7). And Hearst continually emphasized his leadership role in the Progressive movement. His newspapers were aggressively fostering such reforms as direct primaries, government protection against "the abuse of power" by huge corporations and trusts, and the dismantling of city and state boss systems, all of which, Hearst asserted, guaranteed greater freedom for the average American.[43]

With the groundwork laid, Hearst embarked on the next phase of his campaign, that of testing his candidacy. For two months his political machine moved forward on cue and without a hitch. On December 10, 1911, with a lavish dinner at his home, he entertained a group of western governors who were meeting in New York City. At the same time in Los Angeles, two hundred Californians honored him at a banquet, praising his business leadership in their community through the efforts of the *Examiner*. The publicity and results in both instances were gratifying. En route to California on December 15 to celebrate Christmas with his mother, he stopped in Chicago to consolidate his Democratic base with the Harrison forces, capping his stay with a huge banquet in his honor. Two weeks later in San Francisco he spoke to an enthusiastic audience of Italian Americans before returning to New York.

But Hearst was still in demand. In Chicago early in January some eight hundred Democrats urged him to be their presidential nominee, while in San Francisco the Hearst machine was busily rounding up endorsements. Then on January 8, before returning home, he attended a prestigious Jackson Day dinner in Washington. Assembled there were House Speaker Champ Clark, Governor Woodrow Wilson of New Jersey, Oscar W. Underwood of Alabama, and three-time presidential nominee William Jennings Bryan. All were considered the front-runners for the Democratic nomination in June; they, together with Hearst, gave victory speeches.

Yet Hearst realized that mere political presence and campaign oratory, no matter how inspiring, were not enough to carry the field; hence, during these months, business information about him continually seeped out in opposition newspapers, providing credence to reports about the magnitude of his financial worth and political power. For instance, during the first five weeks of 1912, the *New York Times* noted that one of his eight newspapers, the *New York Evening Journal*, was worth an estimated $8 million and that the *Atlanta Georgian*, the largest newspaper in the South, would soon be part of the Hearst media chain.[44]

All such preparation and anticipation, however, ended in a resounding crash. On January 27, 1912, a majority of the California Democratic delegation to the national convention, meeting in San Francisco, voted to support Woodrow Wilson. The surprised Hearst forces then decided that the best stratagem was to forgo submitting his name. Thus the Hearst boom for president, which at best had been a long shot was over.[45]

Hearst, ever the optimist, recovered quickly from this defeat. Within three weeks he had devised a new plan of action. Champ Clark of Missouri, who was not only "his friend" but one with whom he would have influence, would be his candidate for the presidency. Hearst thus became Clark's major financial backer and supplied essential manpower when and wherever needed. And, of course, he provided valuable campaign publicity—without cost—through his newspapers and magazines.[46]

In February 1912, Hearst launched his opening campaign propaganda for Clark, both with purpose and focus. In a telegram on February 19, he urged Californians, in "the interests of all Democrats" to support Champ Clark for president. A week later the Hearst–Harrison forces solidified the Chicago delegation for Clark. Hearst was attempting to create a steamroller effect.[47]

But as Hearst had long perceived, Woodrow Wilson was a formidable opponent in Clark's quest for achieving the nomination. That stark realization meant that Hearst must apply a journalistic technique so successful in the past, that of orchestrating the news against an adversary. On March 14, Hearst delivered a blistering broadside in the *Washington Post*, as well as in the nine Hearst newspapers. He announced that Wilson—sarcastically referred to as "The Professor"—was not a Democrat "who believes in the essentials of justice and wisdom of popular government." Nor was he a Republican "who believes in popular government, except where it interferes with his special privileges." Instead, he was an Alexander Hamilton Federalist of the 1790s who "distrusts the people and actually desires to limit and restrict the people's power in government." For that matter The Professor, in his multivolume *History of the American People*, clearly evoked a number of disturbing opinions and un-Democratic judgments such as an avid admiration of the British parliamentary structure over the American congressional system, a disdain for George Washington, and harsh criticisms of the two greatest Democratic Party leaders, Presidents Thomas Jefferson and Andrew Jackson.

But that was not all, Hearst asserted. The Professor, in evaluating "our immigrants from the South of Europe," contemptuously referred to them as "men of the lowest classes and men of the meaner sort . . . of the more sordid and hapless elements of their population." As a result, Hearst concluded, "Professor Wilson . . . is not a Democrat and does not know how to be a Democrat. . . . He is a fish out of water." And "as a candidate for President he would be a pitiful disappointment," and "as an actual President he would be a positive danger to his party and to the country."[48]

These comments set the tone for a deafening crescendo of deprecation and vilification, of ridicule and scorn. *American* political cartoonists Homer Davenport, Frederick Opper, and Tom Powers, satirically humorous and brutally derogatory in their characterizations, depicted Wilson as gaunt and lean, Roman-nosed and bespectacled and tight-lipped, usually attired in a scraggly tail coat and high hat. No matter what the issue, The Professor was at fault. Day after day their cartoons accompanied stories and editorials that ridiculed Wilson so unmercifully that New York City mayor Gaynor urged him not to mind anything having to do with Hearst and his yellow assault.[49]

Yet the tour de force, the ultimate production of this political onslaught and character assassination, was still to come. Hearst assigned Alfred Henry Lewis, a master of invective as well as a purveyor of innuendo and half-truth, if not outright lies, to lay bare to the American public "the facts" about "the real Woodrow Wilson." And early in May 1912, this exposé appeared in *Hearst's Magazine*. Wilson, in Lewis's evaluation, was indeed a Hamiltonian Federalist, a man not "warm" but "cold-blooded" who "felt himself a little above the crowd." In many respects, Lewis asserted, Wilson was a "chameleon," being of one sentiment or "color today and another tomorrow." What other conclusion could an observer reach about a candidate who, in his early years, "practiced love much more effectively than he practiced law," who in his historical writings and college lectures denounced such democratic reforms as initiative, referendum, and recall, yet as a presidential candidate suddenly embraced them? What should the voter think about the honor of a politician like Wilson who condemned steel industrialist Andrew

Carnegie as a "public enemy" for promoting a high protective tariff, yet accepted a $10,000-a-year Carnegie retirement pension for university professors? And, possibly most damning, why should immigrant Americans, especially from Southern Europe, endorse this so-called Democrat who considered the Chinese as "more to be desired as workingmen, if not as citizens, than most of the coarse crew that came crowding in every year at the Eastern ports." Lewis therefore concluded that "were it left up to me . . . Mr. Wilson would not go to the White House."[50]

The effect of such negative campaigning bore immediate and satisfying results for Champ Clark. In the Hearst newspapers headlines built excitement and momentum. For example, on May 1, 1912, the Hearst media jubilantly announced, "Clark Sweeps Massachusetts" and (in an editorial by Hearst) "Why Speaker Clark is Now The Strongest Democratic Candidate for President." On May 2, "Clark [Has] Thrown Wilson From the Race." Again on May 4, "Another Setback for Wilson." Still again on May 7, "Clark Has Easy Victory [in Maryland]." And on May 8, "Clark Wins in Washington." Then came impressive delegate wins in California, Arizona, Iowa, and Arkansas along with an announcement on June 14 that the New York delegation, which was committed to Governor Judson Harmon of Ohio, might switch to Clark after the first ballot. By mid-June, the *American* claimed that Clark was in the lead with an estimated 459 convention votes and the odds-on favorite to be the Democratic nominee.[51]

These astounding political events stunned the Wilson forces. Champ Clark, bereft early on of a substantial war chest and nationwide organization, had not been considered a serious contender prior to Hearst's endorsement in February. But no longer! Wilson managers, in their anger and frustration at coming in second or third best in state delegate counts, suspected some sort of Clark–Hearst deal. For instance, after stunning defeats by the Clark forces in Massachusetts and Illinois early in April, Wilson people pointed out to a *New York Times* reporter that Hearst was "the greatest asset in the Clark boom," then bitterly warned that the Democratic Party was in danger of being "Hearstized."

Yet the Wilson pundits feared that an even greater danger lay ahead for the Democrats and the United States. If Clark were elected president, they intimated, that William Randolph Hearst would have his choice in the cabinet, namely secretary of state. Turmoil and uncertainty roiled the political waters as the Democrats prepared for their national convention at Baltimore on June 25, 1912.[52]

Hearst eagerly anticipated this mighty assemblage of Democrats. Since 1844, national convention delegates had always elected the candidate entering with a majority vote; hence Clark appeared likely to be the anointed one. But Hearst wanted to leave nothing to chance. Besides keeping abreast of the political temperature in many state delegations, he personally attended to the needs of several critical ones. For instance, on June 23, he greeted Chicago mayor Carter Harrison, along with *Chicago American* editor Andy Lawrence and twenty Illinois delegate leaders, at the train station in New York City, then proceeded to his spacious apartment complex on Riverside Drive to discuss convention strategy. At the same time it was rumored, evidently with some truth, that Hearst had reached common ground with an inveterate enemy, Tammany chief Charles Francis Murphy. In return for the qualified Clark support of the 1904 Democratic standard-bearer Alton B. Parker of New York as temporary convention chairman—and with no opposition from Hearst—the two agreed to "bury their political hatchets" if the New York delegation (comprising ninety votes) would switch from Governor Judson Harmon of Ohio to Clark "at an appropriate time" after the first ballot.

Meanwhile, Hearst was mobilizing his media organization to bring the five-month crusade for Clark to a successful conclusion. Although not a delegate, he intended to make his presence felt as an interested observer. In turn, he assigned his most trusted lieutenants and experienced writers to cover the convention—Arthur Brisbane, John Temple Graves, Alfred Henry Lewis, and James J. Montague. They all understood (and in some cases had helped develop) the Hearst crusade technique of orchestrating the news. For the days just prior to and during the week of the convention, they occupied significant space in the *American* and *Evening Journal* with headlines and stories and editorials that extolled the character and leadership qualities of Champ Clark, while denigrating Woodrow Wilson. At the same time in Baltimore, Hearst organizers were preparing to provide a grandiose hoopla of free mementos and rollicking activities for the national delegates—a typical Hearst production perfected in past years. They also inundated the convention hall daily with educational literature, specifically multiple copies of the *American* and *Evening Journal*.[53]

What hectic, exciting days! How great the political stakes! Two weeks earlier in national convention at Chicago the Republican old-guard conservatives had renominated President William Howard Taft as their standard-bearer, with disastrous political consequences. Former president Theodore Roosevelt, angrily proclaiming that "the real and lawful majority of the convention" had been excluded, stormed out of the meeting with 344 loyal delegates, promising to return to Chicago in August to form a new third party and be its nominee. He also vowed to stay the course in the upcoming presidential campaign "even if I do not get a single electoral vote." With the Republicans irrevocably split and in utter disarray, the Democrats for the first time in twenty years seemed primed to win the presidency, provided that the delegates could write a Progressive platform and nominate a Progressive candidate. Both the Clark and Wilson camps readily claimed such credentials.[54]

The Baltimore convention, from the very beginning on June 25, erupted into a bitter affair. In preliminary contests over organization, conservatives—with help from the Clark forces—elected Alton B. Parker as temporary chairman over William Jennings Bryan, who received Wilson's endorsement. But the victory was a Pyrrhic one at best. In the early roll call voting for the nomination Clark assumed a commanding lead, especially after the tenth ballot when the huge New York delegation, controlled by Murphy, fulfilled its pledge by switching ninety votes into the Clark column. Yet his count was still short of the necessary two-thirds majority. Then on the fourteenth roll call Bryan threw the convention into an even greater uproar by switching to Wilson. Although a Clark delegate from Nebraska, Bryan refused to support anyone backed by Tammany Hall. Thus, the deadlock continued hour after hour as the roll calls droned forth, with the weary delegates unable to effect a decision.[55]

Hearst was furious at this turn of events. No matter how detailed the planning, no matter how precise the execution, he was unable to control the final result. Even worse, the man he loathed most, the "judas" who had betrayed him in his quest for the presidency in the 1904 Democratic convention, who had proven to be a politician in the worst sense of the word, William Jennings Bryan of Nebraska, seemed to be controlling the outcome of this convention. In desperation to save the Clark candidacy, Hearst sought to persuade Bryan to return to his former commitment—but to no avail. As a result, he proclaimed in a full-page editorial on July 1 that Bryan, a "man, without conscience or character . . . is bringing wreck and ruin upon the Democracy."[56]

As the Clark nomination was foundering (on the thirtieth roll call Wilson received more votes), Hearst, as well as many Clark supporters, foresaw an even greater danger. Rumors abounded that if a deadlock continued to prevail, delegates in their desperation, might turn to a compromise candidate, namely Bryan. This probability was more than delegates (especially Illinois delegates) could endure. On July 2, 1912, after the forty-sixth ballot, Woodrow Wilson became the Democratic standard-bearer in the race for the presidency.[57]

So once again Hearst had been denied the holy grail of public service. Although Democratic also-rans were expected to play the political game, that of supporting the winner, he did not fit into this role well. How bitterly this loss affected him. At first he initially refused to endorse Wilson when asked his reactions to the outcome of the convention by a *New York Times* reporter. And he was one of a few prominent Democrats who did not send a congratulatory telegram to the nominee. As for the man who, in his opinion, had caused the Clark defeat, Hearst corrected a *New York Tribune* reporter, who alluded that he and Bryan had "shaken hands," such was not the case. "I am rather particular about the people whom I shake hands with," he caustically remarked. "The only time I have noticed Mr. Bryan's hand was when it was extended for campaign contributions." Then in a more practical vein, he added, "We have made a good fight and lost. I will support the ticket nominated, and expect to see it win. I intend to die game in this fight. I am now for Wilson."[58]

But Hearst's support in the 1912 presidential election was lukewarm at best. Within a week he and Millicent, having made plans two months earlier to deposit their three children in California with doting grandmother Phoebe Apperson Hearst, sailed for Europe on the *Mauritania*. For the next five months they gratified their own special needs and whims. They always stayed in the best hotels in London and Paris. This time, they embarked by car upon great adventures, as he reported to his mother, "through Dalmatia, Bosnia, Hertzegovina, Slavonia, Hungaria and places that you see mentioned sometimes but hardly believe that they really exist." The two Americans found themselves "as much of an attraction to the inhabitants as they were to us." As a finale, Hearst frequented the baths and partook of special cures prescribed by a doctor at Bad Nauheim, Germany. In future years he would repeat this same success formula on numerous European excursions.[59]

Even on vacation Hearst did not forsake his business and political interests. *Nash's Magazine* in London, he informed his mother, was gaining over 4,000 subscribers each month and his *London Budget* newspaper was "getting along fine" even though English journalists were "fearfully excited over the advent of the yellow peril as they call it." As for his stance on the upcoming presidential election, despite his distrust of Wilson and a continuing animosity for Bryan, he could ill afford to reject the Democrats. In his opinion, the Republicans, by renominating President Taft, had repudiated progressive ideals, which represented necessary reforms in behalf of the American people. Nor could he support Theodore Roosevelt, whom the newly formed Progressive Party had nominated at Chicago early in August, even though Roosevelt adopted a platform that was reformist in tone and substance. Hearst would never forget, much less forgive the former president for intruding into his race for the New York governorship in 1906. At the behest of Roosevelt, Secretary of State Elihu Root had basely denounced "Hearst with his yellow journals" as the man most responsible for instigating the assassination of President McKinley in September 1901. So Hearst, despite lingering trepidations concerning Wilsonian policies, especially with Bryan as a mentor, decided to endorse the candidate of the democracy. On September 19, 1912, and daily thereafter, the *New York American* (as well as other Hearst publications) announced, "THE *AMERICAN* IS SUPPORTING WILSON."[60]

Yet Hearst, besides this endorsement, may have affected the 1912 presidential election, although negligibly. As early as May, *Hearst's Magazine* began publishing a monthly series of essays titled the "Standard Oil Letters," the contents of which he had first released during the presidential campaign in September 1908. The subject matter was explosively revealing as well as politically damaging. For more than a decade John D. Rockefeller's "hated corporation," as Hearst characterized it, had corrupted American politics both in the Republican and Democratic parties. Specifically, certain congressmen had received sizable campaign contributions or appreciative gifts for fashioning legislation favorable to Standard Oil as well as helping undermine opponents of the corporation. As a result, a number of prominent politicos, including Senators Joseph B. Foraker of Ohio and Joseph Weldon Bailey of Texas, whom Hearst specified as Rockefeller agents, did not seek reelection. Certain letters, through innuendo and association, connected Standard Oil to the Roosevelt White House, and to that extent, these articles in *Hearst's Magazine* damaged the reputation of the Progressive candidate, Roosevelt. And on November 5, 1912, when Wilson won the presidency with a 42 percent plurality but an overwhelming vote in the Electoral College, Hearst reaped a certain grim satisfaction. Through his media empire he had paid his political respects to the defeated Roosevelt.[61]

But Hearst would suffer the consequences of this crusade against political corruption. *Collier's Weekly*, whose editor often referred to him sarcastically as "William Alsorandolph Hearst," assigned a writer, Arthur Gleason, to determine the authenticity of these letters. As expected, the findings in the October 5 issue of *Collier's*, titled "Mr. Hearst's Forgeries," were censorious and condemning. Gleason stated that five of the Standard letters, written from 1898 to 1904, were obvious forgeries, that another eight bore the "traced" signature of Standard Oil executive John D. Archbold, and that Hearst himself had manufactured still others. Since "Mr. Hearst has many genuine facsimiles in his possession," Gleason asked in puzzlement, "why is he using forgeries?"[62]

As a result of these charges, the Privileges and Elections Committee of the U.S. Senate (better known as the Clapp Committee) called the major participants to testify. Since Hearst did not return from Europe until November 22, 1912, his appearance before the committee in Washington did not occur until December 17. Not surprisingly, Hearst easily weathered questioning by the senators. "I am anxious to testify very fully to everything that I am personally concerned in, and to everything that is necessary to the purpose of this inquiry," he candidly addressed the committee.

To some observers, however, his answers were evasive. More than four years had elapsed since his first revelations in 1908, and, he prefaced a number of his answers with "I am quite sure" or "I think" or "I don't think." Besides, Hearst seldom cared about the details of a scheme, especially a sordid one. He needed only to know that any employee assigned an important task was responsible and trustworthy. So as to the charge by *Collier's* that "some of the letters . . . were in fact forgeries," Hearst matter-of-factly replied, "I haven't any explanation to make" because "some explanation was made at the time" of publication. Nor was he too concerned about certain letters being slightly altered or retyped for use in *Hearst's Magazine*, especially since the committee had already authenticated most of his Standard Oil correspondence.

And although one biographer noted that "the Senators were strangely kind to Hearst," not pushing him into an uncomfortable corner, the answer was abundantly clear to all concerned. The Clapp Committee was interrogating one of the most powerful men in the United States, a news media publisher who had ruthlessly destroyed the reputations and careers of several distinguished colleagues and would, without compunction or regret, take on any critic who, to Hearst's way of thinking, was not just his enemy but a defiler of progressive democracy. So the Clapp Committee dismissed him as a witness, seemingly relieved after performing its "public trust."[63]

Hearst discharged another responsibility to the American people and his 5 million readers when he publicly advised (or lectured) Wilson concerning administration policies and cabinet appointments. Since August he had periodically written editorials, often on the front pages of his newspapers, endorsing certain progressive planks in the Democratic Party platform while rejecting those that were, he caustically announced, "a characteristic combination of Bryan's ignorance and egotism." He therefore urged Wilson to enact laws providing for lower tariffs, monetary and banking reforms, protection for the rights of labor through trust regulation, conservation of natural resources, and a presidential primary.

In regard to foreign affairs he ardently advocated a larger navy and stricter enforcement of the Monroe Doctrine. All these planks the Democratic platform touched on but did not adequately define or spell out. And to carry out this progressive program for the "new democracy," Hearst beseeched the new president to be his own man, not to be manipulated or dictated to by Bryan, especially in regard to cabinet posts.[64]

Yet for Hearst the winter of 1912–1913 was one of frustration and disappointment, at least in regard to national politics. As early as December rumors were rife that Bryan would be the new secretary of state, and Hearst was powerless to prevent such a decision. Then on March 4, 1913, Inauguration Day, an informal list of cabinet appointments "evoked restrained approval from all sections and segments of opinion," one prominent historian asserted. Not so, at least as far as Hearst was concerned. Bryan, the man he loathed most in public life, was Wilson's new secretary of state. And what irony! If Champ Clark had won the Democratic nomination, Hearst would have coveted this position in government, this opportunity of being a significant player in the history of the United States. As an outsider, he was cast in the role of a public watchdog—and a highly critical one at that.[65]

2 The Most Hated Man in America

The spring of 1913 dawned auspiciously for Democrats, halcyon days indeed for those advocates of progressivism. For the first time in sixteen years they had a man in the White House, a dynamic leader who advocated policies of economic reform. In 1912 American voters elected Woodrow Wilson, who championed a progressive program titled the New Freedom, one that was intent upon destroying monopoly and privilege, encouraging competition, and thereby unleashing the potential energies of American business in the marketplace. Democrats also gained control of both houses of Congress and were relatively united. But most importantly Woodrow Wilson possessed qualities of leadership that elicited, indeed commanded, their support. Although a stern, somewhat foreboding intellectual in appearance and manner, he was a compelling speaker, an eloquent spellbinder who "lifted men out of themselves" by picturing, through words and ideas, a better world of tomorrow. His concept of effective presidential leadership, influenced by the British parliamentary system of strong executive authority, set him apart as a "national voice," as a moral spokesman for "righteousness and justice" in behalf of the average American.[1]

After Inauguration Day on March 4, 1913, the Wilson administration pushed its exercise of power unrelentingly. The cabinet appointments, headed by Bryan as secretary of state, produced an overall favorable reaction. Five days later, a White House spokesman announced that the president was working on important legislation, specifically a tariff bill. Then, with the calling of a special session of Congress, Wilson shocked many traditionalists on April 8 by addressing both houses of Congress—a custom abandoned by Thomas Jefferson in 1801 on the ground that such an action resembled too much "the King's speech from the throne." And even though Wilson had decided on this course of action because of his unusual ability to persuade from the rostrum, his performance ignited the imagination of the press and the American people. The president was taking the initiative by establishing a good relationship between the executive and legislative branches of government. He then upheld this image by outlining a tariff proposal whose duties would be substantially lower for the purpose of "effective competition."[2]

But not all progressive Democrats shared this national euphoria, especially not William Randolph Hearst. After all, he had gambled on Champ Clark in the 1912 presidential lottery game—and lost. As a result, he was an outsider to the Wilson political family circle, someone who had demonstrated poor judgment in supporting a rival, hence a man with no eminence or influence. As far as New York patronage was concerned, he was not an active player, much less an esteemed adviser.[3]

But no matter! Hearst had always distrusted Wilson, whose actions, especially in addressing Congress, further alarmed him. The president had discarded, Hearst announced in a full-page editorial on April 14, a time-honored precedent initiated by the founder of the Democratic Party, Thomas Jefferson. As a result, Wilson, as Hearst had previously suspected, was not a Democrat but a Federalist—someone who preferred the British parliamentary structure to the American representative system of government. His presentation to Congress "was a mere adaptation of the British usage of a speech to Parliament from the Throne." Even worse, the president proposed a tariff (the Underwood bill) that favored, Hearst asserted, the British merchant to the detriment of the American farmer and businessman. Wilson recommended lowering duties on foreign goods and advocated reciprocal trade agreements, which would be a free trade measure for the British and which any American should condemn. Hearst thus announced his vigorous opposition to this bill in its present form. "I am loath to criticize the policy of the Democratic Party or any man whom I labored to elect," he concluded, "but I am an American first, and a Democrat after, and I cannot consider the interests of my party above the interests of my country."[4]

For the moment Hearst could only alert his readers to the miscues of the Wilson administration. Consequently, over the next few months, although still a national watchdog, he concentrated on a personal project of major importance—his Clarendon mansion at 86th and Riverside Drive. In 1907 he had leased several floors in the nine-story building and then after six years bought it, reputedly for $1 million. By 1913, after considerable renovations to the top five floors, raising ceilings and eliminating walls, the Clarendon took on the appearance of an opulent museum, replete with the treasures of Europe that Hearst had amassed during the past years: a medieval armor collection, recessed wooden cabinets built to house a variety of silver trays, invaluable Renaissance and Gothic artwork, and a superb oversize tapestry. Refurbishing the Clarendon energized his creative juices and kindled a latent architectural flair that developed over the years. For his armor collection he created the Clarendon armory hall, a magnificent domed room, two stories in height, reminiscent of the grandeur in spacious European castles and the forerunner of his California Casa Grande at San Simeon ten years later.[5]

Hearst surely had need of space at the Clarendon; his collecting mania was an incurable passion or, as Millicent later reminisced, "a harmless, if expensive, exercise of vanity" that he and such friends (or collecting rivals) as John D. Rockefeller Jr. and Judge Elbert H. Gary, who headed the United States Steel Corporation, "indulged in to relieve the tension of their workaday lives." One principal culprit in this Hearst obsession was Joseph Duveen, a cunning British art dealer who opened an exclusive shop in New York City known to an even more exclusive clientele of wealthy customers at Duveen's Fifth Avenue gallery. Unavailable, unobtainable, deniable, were words, Duveen realized, that unlocked the Hearst pocketbook. Money was not a consideration; only the need to possess a precious treasure of past ages and thereby attain some measure of immortality was at issue. On numerous occasions Duveen played this game of collecting expertly and with finesse, one in which the customer eventually won, but for a price. For instance, he allowed Hearst to "persuade" him to sell a Van Dyck portrait of Queen Henrietta Maria with Jeffrey Hudson and a monkey, which Duveen claimed his wife cherished and would not part with, that is, until he extracted the then outrageous sum of $375,000.[6]

To house his acquisitions Hearst expanded the top two floors of the Clarendon into a banquet hall and ballroom. Then he and Millicent entertained lavishly and often. On April 28, 1913, they celebrated their tenth wedding anniversary with a party for ninety guests. On Memorial Day, after a cheering crowd of 75,000 watched nine-year-old son George perform an unveiling of the National Maine Monument in New York City, Hearst opened his magnificent home to climax the day's festivities. He and Millicent hosted a lavish reception and dance for such dignitaries as Secretary of the Navy and Mrs. Josephus Daniels, Secretary of War and Mrs. Lindley Garrison, Governor and Mrs. William Sulzer of New York, and Rear Admiral Charles D. Sigsbee (former captain of the battleship *Maine* in 1898), as well as the flag officers of the U.S. Atlantic fleet. And again in June he was entertaining naval officers and sailors from Brazilian, Argentine, and American battleships anchored in New York harbor, treating them to a theater party followed by dinner and dancing at the Clarendon.[7]

But the Hearsts, when not socializing with state and local officials or visiting dignitaries, used the ballroom for their own special pleasure, at times to improve his dancing. While dining one evening at Louis Martin's supper club on 42nd Street, they chanced upon the soon to be famous dance team, Irene and Vernon Castle. Hearst, who made it his business never to take "no" for an answer, soon charmed the couple into teaching Millicent and him the latest steps. For weeks thereafter, a Hearst limousine whisked the Castles to the Clarendon for dinner, where the four danced into the night to popular tunes on a gramophone. Of course Millicent needed no instruction, having performed with her sister in the chorus line of a Broadway musical, *The Girl from Paris*, in 1897. So while Vernon Castle and Millicent glided across the ballroom floor, Hearst concentrated on attaining some semblance of perfection with Irene Castle. Actually, she recalled, he was graceful for so large a man, with "a good sense of rhythm and a nice bounce to the knee." Then she graciously added, "he really didn't need us except to learn the new steps."[8]

Leisure pursuits aside, Hearst focused on his personal ambition to serve his country, even willing, as one biographer observed, to "sell his immortal soul to get into the senate." Late in the spring and summer of 1913 rumors abounded that Hearst might be in line for high office. One obstacle, however, was impossible to overcome—Tammany boss Charles Francis Murphy. What happened was clear enough to all concerned. In the fall election of 1912 Hearst had vigorously supported Democrat William Sulzer of New York for governor, contributing liberally to a successful campaign. Then early in 1913, the two formed an alliance to oust Boss Murphy as a major force among the state Democrats, which would leave them in control. If successful, Hearst would be rewarded with the party nomination for the U.S. Senate. Such endeavors proved fruitless, however. Partly due to the efforts of Boss Murphy, Governor Sulzer came under serious investigation for receiving illegal campaign contributions. And after a lengthy and rancorous probe, a Tammany-led state legislature impeached him in August 1913.[9]

Although thwarted for high office once again, Hearst demonstrated his remarkable ability to bounce back, to reinvigorate himself for meeting new challenges. In the fall elections of 1913 he battled Tammany Hall with a certain degree of success and satisfaction. Hearst, despite a propensity to shift his party allegiance, still had tremendous "political swat" with the Independence League in New York City, the progressive-minded organization that he had been instrumental in founding in 1906; in fact, many of its leaders were urging him to run for mayor. But he had found a candidate worthy of his trust, thirty-three-year-old John Purroy Mitchel, who had fashioned a public record of reform and seemed capable of defeating Tammany Hall. In mid-October Hearst, upon returning from a two-month stay in California, agreed to campaign with Mitchel. To cheering crowds at huge mass meetings, he urged New Yorkers to defeat Tammany candidates and thereby "recognize the right of the people to govern themselves." And on November 5, 1913, the people responded; a *New York American* headline read, "LANDSLIDE; MITCHEL by 100,000." When Murphy conceded defeat, Hearst was cautiously triumphant, announcing that, while "the forces of corruption had been routed . . . the fortresses that they occupied must be razed to the ground."[10]

During this time, however, Hearst did not neglect his national concerns, especially the domestic activities of the Wilson administration. Over the past twenty years he had refined the technique of orchestrating the news, of providing a groundswell of public opinion in support of the Hearst viewpoint, which he continued to define as government by newspaper. No question about it, the *American* editors trumpeted, his media empire had registered one success after another. As a sincere progressive, Hearst loudly echoed such reform triumphs as a graduated income tax (Sixteenth Amendment), the direct election of senators (Seventeenth Amendment), postal savings banks, government supervision and control of the railroads, and the prosecution of criminal trusts. At the same time he kept abreast of the Underwood tariff bill, continuing to editorialize during the summer of 1913 for reciprocal trade agreements, while approving Democratic efforts to lower duties on individual items; Hearst accepted its passage late in September, but with reservations. Concerning the Federal Reserve Act, which was the second essential economic measure of Wilson's New Freedom, he was in complete accord with its passage in December. For years Hearst had endorsed the need for a stabilizing central national bank that would provide elastic currency for the American people while establishing a fine balance between private management and government supervision. But in regard to the third major economic policy of the administration, that of curbing the power of huge corporations, Hearst cynically questioned Wilson's dedication to "bring all trusts and combinations . . . under the supervision and control of the Government."[11]

Hearst was more critical of the Wilson foreign policy. He believed that the president and Secretary of State Bryan, even framed in the best possible light, were visionaries in purpose and unrealistic in approach.

Or, as one prominent historian put it, both were "fundamentally missionaries of Democracy."

But in this age of world imperialism—the building of huge navies, the arms race, the acquisition of territories in undeveloped areas, the competition for foreign markets and goods—Wilson's New Freedom "policy of friendship based on altruism" was to Hearst's way of thinking impracticable, if not astoundingly foolish. He envisioned the United States as a dominant world power. Much like Theodore Roosevelt, he believed that the "civilized" nations (those of "Caucasian" descent) were the purveyors of culture, the protectors of laws and liberty, indeed the practitioners of democracy. Of course, the most practical way to carry out such a civilizing program was through an expanded empire, where American ideals and principles could be implemented immediately. Yet, when such possibilities were either inaccessible or unattainable, Hearst reasoned, the United States must act as a deterrent force against "the threatening and tremendous assault of the Asiatic and the Slav upon the religion, the institutions, and the civilization of us Caucasians."[12]

Hearst therefore crusaded for expanding the American empire. After his active participation in bringing about the Spanish American War, he continued to hail as exemplary the establishment of the military base in Cuba (at Guantanamo Bay) and the territorial acquisition of Puerto Rico.

To secure and safeguard an "American lake" in the Caribbean, Hearst vigorously endorsed the Panama Canal Tolls Act of 1912, which exempted American coastal shipping from paying any fees. When the British protested that this act violated the Hay-Pauncefote Treaty of 1901 (because their ships were paying a toll), Wilson rightly agreed and in March 1914 appeared before Congress, asking for repeal of the U.S. exemption. Hearst was furious, vehemently accusing the president—in full-page editorials—of sacrificing the welfare of American businessmen and farmers to placate his British friends. After all, Hearst argued, the United States violated no treaty, having "acquired by purchase the territory through which the Canal passes." For that matter, "the Canal Zone is now as much the property of the United States as the Capitol in Washington, which the British burned in 1814 as an evidence of their insensitive regard for all international conventionalities and proprieties." The president should therefore realize, Hearst announced, that the American shipping exemption "is as honorable as it is patriotic."

Yet even though Speaker of the House Champ Clark and Majority Leader Oscar W. Underwood concurred with his stance, and despite an all-out crusade by the Hearst media to educate the public in behalf of a toll exemption for American shipping, the Wilson administration carried the day through presidential leadership and the gentle persuasion of patronage. So once again Hearst, as a nationalist foreign policy progressive, was unhappy with Wilson, contemptuously designating him as the "apostle of national concession and contraction" who had become the "advance agent of adversity." At the same time Hearst was equally disgruntled with England—and increasingly Anglophobic—at times referring to Great Britain as the "Perfidious Albion" (the treacherous nation known for its white cliffs).[13]

Hearst became thoroughly frustrated with the New Freedom policies toward Mexico as events continued to complicate and muddle diplomacy between the two nations. In May 1911, after Hearst's longtime friend Porfirio Diaz was forced to abandon the Mexican presidency and seek exile in France, "the revolutionary wheel," one prominent diplomatic historian observed, soon "took an ugly turn" aptly characterized by mayhem and murder. In February 1913, a full-blooded Indian, Victoriano Huerta, seized control of the government after a brutal, bloody coup. Losses in American life and property were alarmingly high.

This international dilemma beset the philosophic conscience of the idealistic Wilson. How could he uphold the tenets of his New Freedom, dedicated to the vindication of moral principles as well as the ideals of liberty and democracy by recognizing, as he once announced, Huerta's "government of butchers"? Even as other nations, such as England, France, and Germany, were recognizing this new regime as the constitutional government of Mexico, what would be his logical reasons for denial—without causing an international affront? And since the large American colony in Mexico City was urging the immediate acceptance of Huerta in order to restore an uneasy peace, what would be the action of the United States, indeed Wilson's own rationale, if nonrecognition affected detrimentally the lives of 40,000 resident Americans with property investments totaling almost $1 billion?[14]

Wilson thus acted in accordance with his principles by refusing to accept the Huerta regime that had come to office, not in a constitutional manner, but as a result of "murder." Putting his policy of "watchful waiting" in perspective, Wilson stated, "My ideal is an orderly and righteous government in Mexico; but my passion is for the submerged eighty-five percent of the people of that Republic who are now struggling toward liberty."

Again Hearst vehemently disagreed. As early as November 1913, he urged immediate intervention in Mexico to protect American citizens, to punish and eliminate "armed bands roam[ing] the country, murdering and marauding," then to restore "peace and order and civilized conditions" in a land where anarchy prevailed. "It has been intimated by a certain leading representative of the administration at Washington that I am moved to the defense of these unprotected American citizens in Mexico by the fact that I have property interests there myself." Not so, Hearst asserted, since "I can take care of myself." And how? He had "one hundred thoroughly armed men" at the Babicora Ranch in Chihuahua as a "safeguarding force." But an average American citizen, Hearst candidly noted, "cannot employ a standing army to give him the protection which his government ought in honor and duty to afford."

The course for the Wilson administration was therefore clear, Hearst concluded. True to his progressive beliefs, he fervently urged the president "to occupy Mexico and restore it to a state of civilization by means of American MEN and American METHODS." In April 1914, when Wilson ordered U.S. forces to seize the eastern port of Vera Cruz for what the *New York American* characterized as continued insults to the American flag, Hearst was only temporarily satisfied. By June, with conditions in Mexico continuing to deteriorate, he argued that annexation was the logical solution. "Our flag should wave over Mexico as a symbol of the rehabilitation of that unhappy country and its redemption in 'humanity' and civilization," because "our right in Mexico is the right of HUMANITY." After all, Hearst reasoned, "if we have no right in Mexico, we have no right in California or in Texas, which we redeemed from Mexico . . . from savagery . . . and for civilization." Indeed, the American people "have always fought for the cause of civilization and the principles of 'humanity.' And what we conquer, let us conserve for the advantage and advancement of all humanity."[15]

During these first Wilson years Hearst also proposed to extend an American "civilizing" influence into the Pacific, especially because of the yellow peril threat, meaning specifically the Japanese, although Hearst opponents termed his "yellow sheets" as the real "yellow peril." He thus exhorted Congress to reject the proposed Jones bill, which was designed to guarantee eventual independence to the Philippines; such legislation might pave the way for Japanese intrusion and eventual conquest of the islands. To protect the growing American empire in the Far East, which included Hawaii and Guam, and to guarantee the safety of all U.S. possessions, Hearst conducted an ongoing crusade to double the naval strength of the nation, especially for the construction of battleships. In frequent editorials in all Hearst papers from 1912 to 1917 he repeatedly pointed to the inadequacies of the U.S. Navy. The British had five times more battleships and cruisers than the United States and the Japanese fleet had at least three times as many. Hearst continually apprised his readers of the ambitious nature of the yellow peril, not just in its attempts to dictate and be the dominant player in the Far East, but its ambition to intrude significantly into Mexican and Panamanian affairs, which could be considered a violation of the Monroe Doctrine. Such pleas and admonitions had little effect on or response from Wilson and Bryan.[16]

Increasingly frustrated by having no voice in the Wilson administration, Hearst became more determined than ever to be a decisive power in American policies, to mobilize and shape public opinion into an awesome force capable of influencing Wilson to his point of view, just as he did with President McKinley in the Spanish American War. With each Wilson misstep, the answer to his dilemma was becoming increasingly clear: molding public opinion through government by newspaper and magazine. And that meant an aggressive program of journalistic growth as well as better organization within the Hearst media empire. As a result, he extended his magazine audience by purchasing *Good Housekeeping* for $300,000 "payable in bonds over a ten-year period" and soon thereafter acquiring *Harper's Bazaar* for an undisclosed sum. Together with *Motor, Motor Boating, Hearst's Magazine, Cosmopolitan,* and two London editions, *Nash's Magazine* and *Vanity Fair,* his publications in 1914 numbered eight and eventually would total seventeen, with five in England. Then he hired Joe Moore, a financial wizard who understood the complex, somewhat muddled fiscal affairs of Hearst's magazine conglomerate and who was his righthand man in that field until 1926. As a result one aspect of this growing empire was stable as well as prosperous.[17]

During this same period Hearst entered a relatively untried and unexplored media area. As early as the spring of 1909 he had organized the International News (wire) Service (INS). Hearst delighted in applying such terms as "cosmopolitan" and "international" to his business ventures because to him they represented hugeness and all-embracing power. And what was his justification for this new enterprise? Syndication! By 1914 he needed to coordinate any number of media projects concerning editorials, photographs, news features, and especially Sunday comics, which by 1908 appeared in more than eighty newspapers in fifty cities. An obvious result soon became apparent. In 1915 Hearst's aggressive troubleshooter Moses Koenigsberg, with the encouragement of Solomon S. Carvalho, who had become the general manager of the Hearst newspapers, organized King Features Syndicate, and voila, another vexing organizational problem of coordinating syndication, was solved.

Hearst, who was unusually inquisitive and at times outrageously impulsive in his business dealings, also decided to delve into, in fact become heavily involved in, the exciting medium of motion pictures. The French company Pathe, which was the largest movie producer in the world, and one of its competitors, Vitagraph, had displayed newsreels in American theaters since 1911, but with little monetary success. Hearst recognized an immediate opportunity for his intrusion into this medium, because he had a number of distinct advantages over these companies. Specifically, his newspapers and magazines provided tremendous advertising outlets; his investigative reporters and foreign correspondents and accomplished photographers were capable of gathering and, whenever imperative, of deftly manufacturing news pictures. And, of course, he had the necessary capital as well as the magic of his name for any new business venture. Hence, in 1913, through persuasion and negotiation, Hearst-Pathe News became a reality. And as soon as Hearst solidified an agreement with newsreel pioneer Colonel William N. Selig, a weekly Hearst-Selig Newsreel appeared in theaters.[18]

Hearst entered into this new market with his customary zest. As usual, cost was no object, but profits surely were. At 127th Street and Second Avenue, he established a New York studio, titled Hearst International Films, where in collaboration with Pathe and Vitagraph he created films and serials, the bases of which were stories often derived from Hearst magazines and Sunday newspapers. Consequently, on March 23, 1914, *The Perils of Pauline*, a serial of twenty episodes, premiered at Loew's Broadway Theatre in New York City, featuring twenty-five-year-old actress Pearl White, whose trademark was a blonde wig that was never mussed no matter (pardon the pun) how hair-raising the action, and whose venue was a "cliff-hanging pattern" of hazardous escapes from villainous cutthroats. Success was immediate, with overflow crowds in attendance. Hearst could not have been more pleased. He had not only conceived the story and written most of the dialogue, but had organized the film's wide distribution.

Hearst-Pathe next produced a thirty-six episodic follow-up with Pearl White, *The Exploits of Elaine*, which proved to be even more profitable. But these serials were not his only successes. By 1915 Hearst was making animated films with Vitagraph; American audiences delighted in viewing their favorite cartoon movie stars: the Katzenjammer Kids, Happy Hooligan, Maggie and Jiggs, Krazy Kat and Ignatz Mouse, Maude the Mule, and Bringing Up Father.[19]

But to consolidate his growing media empire, to institute government by newspaper effectively, Hearst realized that direction by mandate as well as experience and leadership were of utmost importance. In 1914 and 1915 he therefore moved to consolidate his system of operation. He issued directives to his magazine editors, emphasizing his previously proven formula for success. First and foremost, they "must" increase circulation by displaying a better product than their competitors. As a recognition of their progress and success, they "must" publish circulation numbers that compared the present-day totals with those of the past month as well as of the previous year. As a result of such growth, businesses would eagerly clamor to advertise in Hearst magazines, hence greater profits; editors "must" therefore display in each new issue the present number of ads with those of the past month and year. But make no mistake, Hearst announced authoritatively, the order of command and final decision making was his prerogative—and his alone. "I would also like to have it understood," he warned his magazine editors, "that I am to be consulted as much as possible about the purchase of important stories and features, and not merely informed after they are purchased."[20]

As for his growing chain of newspapers, Hearst issued directives to his editors that were specific and challenging, but with an underlying tone of foreboding. To confidants and observers alike, his presence was often intimidating and always dominating. Few could match his seemingly inexhaustible work ethic, his amazing ability to compartmentalize and understand diverse amounts of information even to the point of specificity, his genius in applying new ideas to programs overly traversed and already well discussed. He challenged his newspaper editors to greater heights of efficiency and dedication. In other words, he instructed them to "compete" with others both outside of and within the Hearst organization—or face an ignominious fate. In letters to his editors he emphasized that they must make their "paper more distinctive, more obviously and notably superior" to that of any competitor.

And to the question of how to attain the best results, Hearst laid out explicit criteria to follow. First of all, editors must produce "a compact and complete paper" that would be "appreciated by the public." Accordingly they should apply the Hearst crusade techniques vigorously in support of "good movements." Hearst newspapers always had to strive to be a "leader of the moral and progressive thought of the community." Within each issue editors had to provide "more accurate" stories and "superior" entertainment, with eye-catching, fist-size headlines that succinctly summarized the article's contents. With equal attention they must extend their paper's interest throughout a wide variety of areas—foreign news, financial information, sports reporting, theatrical and society events, and interests of women (etiquette, beauty, fashion, cooking, family)—accompanied by quality photographs that must be devoid of "paint" and "retouching."

In turn, editors must emphasize promotion that has often become, Hearst asserted, "too stereotyped." Advertisements, which were the economic life blood of any newspaper, "should be sufficiently conspicuous to make an impression upon the hasty reader who will not read the whole advertisement." Editors should sustain such promotion through news and editorials that praised their newspaper, especially with testimonials on the front page commending its "various excellences" together with statistics announcing its increasing circulation. But, Hearst advised, to sustain and extend continued growth, editors should hire a staff with "ability," in the main young men of "education, presentableness, and acquaintance, all of which is extremely valuable in our profession." And that meant "recruiting all departments of the paper from the colleges."

Yet the Hearst editors, even those who were most successful, were always held accountable. Within each newspaper structure "a certain division of labor" had to occur; therefore, Hearst concluded, "I would like to know that somebody is going to be directly responsible and be held directly responsible" either for the excellence or mediocrity of every section of each issue.[21]

The *New York American*, the centerpiece of the Hearst media conglomerate with the largest circulation in the United States, epitomized the Hearst formula. On January 1, 1914, the front-page headline announced "1913—Greatest Year of the NEW YORK AMERICAN" with a "GREATER GAIN in Circulation than ALL the other Morning and Sunday [New York] newspapers COMBINED." The *American* then printed its columns of advertising, showing an increase from 27,758 in 1909 to 35,096 in 1913; the average "circulation in December" of the morning edition during those same years swelled from 217,650 to 289,368, and the Sunday edition sales from 606,348 to 786,577. To call attention to these numbers, the *American* offered $10,000 to the charity of anyone who could refute them successfully. In accordance to Hearst directives, the editor updated such statistics monthly and often weekly if not daily.[22]

A new *American* logo heralded its growth and progress. Previously titled "An American Paper for the American family," it now read, "A Twentieth Century Newspaper for the Twentieth Century." And it was. In accordance with the Hearst formula, national and local governmental affairs, foreign news, scandals, human frailties, natural disasters, sports events, individual triumphs, and personal tragedies occupied the front pages, with eye-catching, fist-size headlines summarizing the story. The Hearst crusade technique, which advocated "moral and progressive thought in the community," appeared daily. Editorials and pronouncements, coupled with political cartoons by such talented artists as Frederick Opper, Winsor McCay, and T. E. Powers, crusaded for such important issues as woman's suffrage, child labor laws, public school reforms, municipal subways, and a fair and judicial enforcement of laws by city and state officials. On the national level, the *American* advocated building a modern navy and demanded—in daily editorial pronouncements—"Government ownership and operation of the telegraph and telephones, of the railroads and a merchant marine."[23]

To carry out Hearst's major directive that the *American* be "a compact and complete paper . . . appreciated by the public," the editors assembled an outstanding cast of journalists. Some had been with Hearst for years. Such well-known columnists as Alfred Henry Lewis and John Temple Graves discussed national politics; Winifred Black and Ella Wheeler Wilcox wrote about women's issues; Alan Dale concentrated on entertainment (music, plays, and performers); Cholly Knickerbocker (the pen name for Maury H. Biddle Paul) on New York and Newport societies; Edwin Markham concerning the latest books; T. B. Gregory on "This Day in History"; James J. Montague writing in rhyme about everyday truisms titled "More Truth Than Poetry"; Charles H. Caffin reviewing "New and Important Things in Art"; legendary New York Giants pitcher Christy Mathewson, Ed Curley, Duncan Curry, and Damon Runyon (soon to be a foreign correspondent in Mexico) discussing sports. Augmenting this impressive staff of professionals were such writers as B. C. Forbes (business), Dorothy Dix (society and women), Richard Schayer and Rudyard Kipling (foreign correspondents).

As a complement to many of the news stories, the *American* editors followed one other aspect of the Hearst directives—excellent photographs, devoid of paint and retouching. Such pictures were both frequent and effective. Yet the fabulous depictions produced by the Hearst's International News Service were by far the most striking addition to viewer pleasure.[24]

The *American* was an entertaining, exciting newspaper that provided something for everyone. Cartoons such as Bud Fisher's *Mutt and Jeff* and George McManus's *Bringing Up Father* began appearing daily. Movie serials—and their theater locations—became regular items of interest and information. Within each edition, the editors initiated one and sometimes two contests. In lottery form that required a coupon obtained from a Hearst newspaper, they promoted for months such prizes as five hundred free vacation trips to Europe, Latin America, Canada, and cities in the United States. For sports fans, they sponsored a contest that lasted from June to October, with the ultimate reward being free tickets and travel accommodations to the baseball World Series. And since Hearst had always emphasized education and art in his newspapers, the *American* offered its readers (for six coupons and $1.98) a four-volume work titled *The Great Republic by the Master Historians*.[25]

The pièce de résistance in the Hearst empire was the *Sunday New York American*. Under the direction of Morrill Goddard, an editor justifiably recognized as the "greatest circulation go-getter on earth," it presented all-day entertainment to its readers—and in abundance. For example, in March 1913, the five *Sunday* editions ranged from 88 to 128 pages. They cost five cents and were worth every penny. Goddard, besides applying the winning formula that emphasized stories concerning women, scandal, society, drama, natural disasters, and sports, provided readers with topics about history and mythology, the mysterious and the occult, the grotesque and the bizarre. Included in this mix were novels (in serial form) by famous authors, popular songs of the day, and photos from the International News Service that were impressive by their authenticity. With no competition yet from radio and television, the *Sunday American* was a constant source of knowledge and education and amusement.[26]

Such structural reorganization was, as times and events would prove, both auspicious and propitious. For on June 28, 1914, at Sarajevo, which was the capital of Bosnia and Hercegovina, Serb nationalists assassinated Austrian heir apparent to the throne Archduke Franz Ferdinand and his wife Sofie—and the world seemed to go mad as the major European nations, on the basis of past treaties and friendships, quickly divided into hostile camps. Germany, Austria-Hungary, and eventually Turkey and Bulgaria (the Central Powers) became aligned against the Allied Powers (the Allies), specifically England, France, Russia, Japan, and later Italy. Hundreds of thousands of men were rushed to the so-called Western Front, a battle line between France and Germany, with the opposing armies intent on reaching an advantage and—as erroneously predicted by military experts—a quick victory. Early in August the Germans, regarding a treaty with Belgium as a mere scrap of paper, invaded that country en route to France by way of Brussels. On the Eastern Front, from Prussia to the Balkans, German and Austrian armies met ill-prepared Russian combatants and won resounding victories. By mid-August, with the leaders of European nations either unable or unwilling to stop this madness, World War I had become a stark and bloody reality.[27]

To this cataclysmic world tragedy Hearst reacted immediately. Strict neutrality was the answer, he announced. "The war will help us and we shall help the nations that suffer in it." The Wilson administration should institute posthaste "a constructive American policy" that would "encourage production, extend markets, [and] furnish needed transportation" to U.S. businessmen. Hence "Made in America" should be the patriotic slogan of this country, indeed a crusade that would benefit the United States economically. Hearst also denounced the "useless royalty" that had provoked "this needless war."[28]

During September and into October 1914, the Hearst papers concentrated on orchestrating the news in behalf of world peace. Almost daily, Hearst editorial writers, or Hearst himself—in conjunction with brilliant political cartoons by Frederick Opper and Winsor McCay—preached the gospel of peace to millions of readers. Predictably, hundreds of testimonials soon appeared supporting this effort, without one voice in opposition. On September 5, a *New York American* headline read, "Noted Americans Approve William R. Hearst's Appeal 'Let Us Have Peace.'" On September 6, a follow-up story listed "18 Governors, 24 Senators and 77 Congressmen" who endorsed the Hearst peace plan.

Hearst continued this journalistic barrage on September 7 in a lengthy editorial, but with a different slant. Arguing that American preparedness was the best way to maintain world peace, he declared that building "a navy great enough to protect our east coast and our west coast, great enough to protect our people and our commerce in all parts of the world" would be essential at the end of this great war, especially since the Japanese had demonstrated an alarming aggressiveness and determination to be a dominant world power. They were, he warned, the real threat to the security of the United States. On September 10, in much the same vein, Hearst appealed to Lord Northcliffe and Lord Burnham, publishers respectively of the *London Times* and the *London Daily Telegraph*, to coordinate efforts to stop this senseless conflict "which cripples the nations of Europe," thus "leaving them prostrate before the threat of Asiatic aggression." In fact, Hearst asserted, "the Hun . . . at the gate" was not Germany, as Rudyard Kipling had previously inferred, but was advancing "in successive, almost irresistible tides of invasion from the interior of Asia," notably from Japan.[29]

Even though receiving no reply from his English counterparts, Hearst continued his peace crusade. He concentrated on San Francisco, Chicago, and New York City, where he organized, directed, and paid for marches and rallies in which thousands participated. On September 20, with Vice President Thomas R. Marshall, Governor Martin Glynn of New York, and Speaker of the House Champ Clark as featured orators, 10,000 New Yorkers participated in a peace pilgrimage. On September 22, *American* headlines read, "100,000 Cheer In San Francisco For World Peace." And again on September 26 in New York City participants in a motorcade of 10,000 autos handed out peace pennants and waved American flags en route to a grand finale at Grant's Tomb, then enthusiastically listened to "a chorus of 1,000 girls" sing stirring tunes embracing world harmony and American patriotism.[30]

These efforts helped mold public opinion to support the Wilson administration's stance of strict neutrality but had little effect on the warring nations. During the fall of 1914, for instance, enormous armies on the Western Front, estimated at 1–2 million men, confronted one another. Orders to attack, then retreat, were all too commonplace. Soon trench warfare became the standard operation, with machine guns and huge cannon the keys to repelling enemy assaults, with reports about the resulting physical devastation and human carnage both shocking and sickening. The prospects of a quick war now faded, and a desperate struggle to destroy the enemy became major objectives. In *The Guns of August* Barbara Tuchman vividly described conditions on the Western Front in the fall of 1914: "Running from Switzerland to the [English] Channel like a gangrenous wound across French and Belgian territory, the trenches determined the war of position and attrition, the brutal, mud-filled, murderous insanity known as the Western Front that was to last for four more years."[31]

As the war continued into 1915, as the situation became more desperate for the warring nations, new realities emerged in this world conflagration—the development of the submarine and the floating mine—which in turn affected U.S. neutrality. Hearst, at times considering himself to be "the only powerful sane man on the mad planet" called Earth, fervently believed, as George Washington had once stated, that the United States should remain free of "entangling alliances" and that the welfare of the nation depended on a governmental policy of strict neutrality. And for such convictions he would pay a heavy price over the next two years. No matter that his media empire would endure heavy financial losses, no matter that he would suffer personal opprobrium and vile public criticism, he was determined to weather such unpopularity; history would prove the folly of American intervention in a European conflict—and the correctness of his position.[32]

To follow a policy of strict neutrality, Hearst took on the maritime rules of international law, especially the British interpretation. And in almost every instance he disliked the outcome. When the British navy stopped American ships on the high seas and instituted the right of search, when the Admiralty declared that bales of cotton and foodstuffs were contraband of war, Hearst editorialized to his readers that "people of a neutral nation have a recognized right to sell to a belligerent" and denounced such interference as indefensible. When both England and Germany declared the North Sea a military area and mined it so thoroughly that no American ship dared sail there, Hearst again condemned these actions as a violation of neutral rights. And after German U-boats sank three American vessels without warning, as well as the British liner *Lusitania* (May 7, 1915), Hearst denounced each episode as "cruel and evil," yet pointed out that these acts were an "indictment of the war itself as war is now waged on land and sea." He then adamantly counseled: "LET US STAND FIRMLY IN DEFENSE OF OUR JUST RIGHTS, EVEN THOUGH WE MUST MAINTAIN THEM BY FORCE OF ARMS. BUT LET US NOT PRECIPITATE THE COUNTRY INTO AN UNNECESSARY WAR BY GOING BEYOND OUR OWN RIGHTS AND DEMANDING THE PRIVILEGE OF DICTATING TO FOREIGN COUNTRIES IN MATTERS WHICH HAVE NOT YET RECEIVED THE DEFINITION AND SANCTION OF INTERNATIONAL LAW."[33]

More and more, Hearst became concerned that Americans would enter the war on the Allied side. That moralistic "college professor" from Princeton, he announced, was "OUT OF PLACE as President of the United States" and ill equipped to steer this nation along a safe course of neutrality. Both by actions and statements Wilson was pro-English, as was his cabinet. The exception was Bryan, who resigned on June 8, 1915, in protest of Wilson's stance toward Germany.[34]

Other governmental actions also alarmed Hearst. As early as September 1914, the Wilson administration had allowed American bankers, such as the Wall Street House of Morgan, to send millions of dollars in advance credits to Allied governments. With each passing month these loans had increased substantially. To Hearst, such economic maneuvers were clearly a danger to American security. "It is not for the interest of this country to become too closely identified with either side of this European conflict . . . to begin lending money to what may be the losing side." Indeed, Hearst asked, "Why sacrifice the interest of this country for the benefit of Wall Street?" After all, "Mr. Morgan is practically an Englishman," indeed the recognized "representative of England financially in the United States." Americans therefore should stay clear of this "worst and most wicked of all wars" in which "soldiers of our own Caucasian race" have already been "slain by the thousands—yea, by the millions—upon the field of battle."[35]

Hearst worked ardently to stem the sympathetic fervor for the Allies, to steer the United States away from a dangerous course of military intervention. He had never trusted English benevolence in regard to the United States and even less the foreign policies of the Anglophile Wilson. He therefore instituted a crusade—both persuasive and persistent—that continued in his newspapers for almost a year. To those desirous of ending this "wicked war," he proposed forming "a League of Neutral Nations."

Through solid political unity and extreme economic pressures, the outraged neutrals of the world, led by the United States, could gain the attention of all belligerents and force them to seek peace through an "international board of arbitration." Weekly and sometimes daily Hearst orchestrated this new crusade with all the accoutrements—testimonials by prominent citizens, editorials accompanied by political cartoons, flag-waving parades that convened at a convention hall where orators promoted the sanctity of neutrality and the wisdom of peace.

All such efforts, however, were to no avail. Hearst was preaching his gospel to a limited audience, mainly German and Irish Americans. Nor was the Wilson administration ever appreciative of his sentiments and suggestions. To them, he was an outsider without favor or influence, a critic both unsympathetic and unforgiving, a demagogue proposing unrealistic and impracticable solutions.[36]

Hearst, for what he considered a patriotic stance from 1914 to 1917, deliberately became "the most hated man in the country," one biographer asserted. And no wonder! Although his media empire preached daily such slogans as "America First" and "no entangling alliances," he could not alter the negative image increasingly accepted by the public. Because of his numerous Anglophobic editorials as well as his strong stand in behalf of neutrality, many Americans accused him of being pro-German. He had excused murderous submarine attacks on unarmed ships (such as the *Lusitania*) as "accepted rules of civilized warfare." He had also employed a number of newspaper operatives who were Anglophobes or, in several instances unknown to him, secret agents of the German government. Hence an increasing number of Americans tended to view his statements and actions, along with the New York press, as unpatriotic, indeed bordering just short of treason.[37]

Hearst's enemies seemed to multiply in number while delighting in his growing unpopularity. Whenever possible, they added to such opprobrium and rejection. For example, *Harper's Weekly*, a longtime Hearst basher, assigned H. D. Wheeler to investigate the reporting accuracy of Hearst's International News Service correspondents. On October 9, 1915, Wheeler revealed damaging revelations that especially pleased the New York news media. "Now the Hearst wires lie, just as the Hearst papers lie. Not always—but some," Wheeler announced. After all, Hearst's International News Service claimed to have employed "more than eighty correspondents, many of them of world-wide fame." Then Wheeler sarcastically trumpeted, "Eighty! Count them. You can't. Neither can Hearst." The most famous of these "romantic figures in khaki, braving untold dangers in the field of battle"—staff correspondents Frederick

Werner in Berlin, Franklin P. Merrick in Paris, and Brixton D. Allaire in Rome together with European International News Service manager Herbert Temple in London—did not exist. They were, like their stories, "a common, ordinary, contemptible Hearst fake."[38]

More negatives continued to plague the reliability and integrity of the Hearst empire. In two articles appearing in the *New York American* Sunday magazine, dated September 26 and October 3, 1915, bold headlines proclaimed "JAPAN'S PLANS TO INVADE AND CONQUER THE UNITED STATES, REVEALED BY ITS OWN BERNHARDI." The story blatantly stated that a book, *The War Between Japan and America*, claimed that the Japanese government, with the encouragement and approval of its naval and military leaders, intended to colonize California "shortly" as well as "dynamite" and "destroy the Panama Canal." The Japanese consul-general in New York immediately denied these shocking allegations. He first noted that the Hearst reporter had used as the source for this story a novel, whose correct title was *The Dream Story of the War Between Japan and the United States*; he then denounced the perception that any Japanese public figure had endorsed this "trashy work." In turn, *Harper's Weekly* investigated the Hearst exposé and corroborated the consul-general's statements, concluding that "it was bad enough . . . to lie about our relations" with other countries, but "to make up gross lies to create bad feeling between this country and Japan" was "contemptible."[39]

Such revelations had little effect on Hearst. As in the Bryan campaign for president in 1896 and the journalistic fight to free Cuba from Spain in 1897 and 1898, his crusades for freedom and justice, for the protection of Americans against possible enemies of the United States far outweighed minor errors or misstatements of fact. And with typical Hearst mentality, he was willing to sustain the righteousness of his cause against economic loss and personal unpopularity.[40]

Hearst therefore continued his assault on Japan, and with great media effect. Late in 1915, he decided to educate the American public further by presenting a fifteen-part patriotic serial titled *Patria*, which was produced by his International Film Service. The virulently racist theme concerned a plot by Japan and Mexico to invade and conquer the United States. This thriller, starring Hearst's dancing partner Irene Castle as Patria Channing, "the sole survivor of a patriotic American family of munitions makers," combated the insidious schemes of an evil Japanese baron portrayed by Warner Oland.

And the result! *Patria* played to packed houses until 1917, when the United States entered World War I and Japan became an ally. The Wilson administration then requested that Pathe, which distributed the serial, voluntarily withdraw the films or at least alter and revise the most offensive scenes. Some changes did occur.[41]

During the years from 1915 to 1917, Hearst battled vigorously, often futilely, against the inexorable hand of history. Consequently some of his desires and aspirations proved to be ineptly unresolved or sadly unsatisfactory. For instance, in Mexico, although General Venustiano Carranza, together with his chief lieutenant Francisco "Pancho" Villa, assumed power from the defunct Huerta regime in October 1915, local conditions did not improve. Mexican soldiers killed resident Americans, destroying their property and ravaging the land. They raided border towns, and on March 9, 1916, General Villa looted and sacked Columbus, New Mexico killing seventeen Americans. In retaliation, President Wilson ordered General John J. Pershing, with an army of 12,000 men, to punish the bandit Villa. But in March, 1917, after almost a year of pursuit—and failure—U.S. troops, who were sarcastically dubbed by the Hearst media as the "perishing expedition," withdrew just prior to American entry into World War I.[42]

Hearst continued to be extremely unhappy with Wilsonian efforts in Mexico. In a barrage of editorials he railed against the administration. "American Flag Only One Mexico Does not Respect" (headline, January 16, 1916); "The position of the United States in Mexico is as pitiful as it is painful. . . . Our army should go forward into Mexico, first, to rescue Americans, and, secondly, to redeem Mexicans" (May 3, 1916); "Compel Peace in Mexico. . . . President Wilson has been slow to recognize the fearful conditions prevailing in Mexico" (June 28, 1916); "Intervention in Mexico is not for the purpose of MAKING war. It is for the purpose of ENDING war. . . . Since the policy of neglect of duty has so utterly failed to secure peace and justice, let us try the policy of active performance of duty which has so frequently and so signally succeeded in the glorious history of this Republic" (July 9, 1916).[43]

Hearst, however, had even more reason to be critical of administrative policy. The million-acre Babicora Ranch in Chihuahua once again came under heavy attack. Late in December 1915, a large force of Villa irregulars, reportedly more than 2,000 men, overran the Babicora, forcing Hearst ranch manager John C. Hayes to flee to El Paso. For more than two years Mexican troops used the Babicora as a base of operations, confiscating Hearst cattle, sheep, and swine for supplies and appropriating thousands of horses for cavalry units. Despite protests by Hearst and his mother the Wilson administration was unable to resolve the question. That certain Wilsonians were suggesting that Hearst's stance had to do with personal financial loss rather than concern for national principles was even more aggravating.[44]

As a result, Hearst faced a political quandary during the critical presidential election of 1916. He wanted to help his readers select the right man for president. But, typically, national party nominees limited his enthusiasm. Roosevelt, the logical Progressive candidate, was unavailable because, Hearst sarcastically noted, he was "eagerly searching for a brand new plutocratic suit of Republican clothes." Charles Evans Hughes, the Republican nominee, was even worse. Although "an excellent man in his own way . . . exceedingly honest, extremely moral," he was "not in the least progressive," instead the "diametrical opposite." And Wilson, the Democratic candidate, was by no means a true progressive. His foreign policy was a disaster, and besides, Hearst simply loathed the man.

So what was Hearst's solution? At best, an unsatisfactory standoff. He allowed wife Millicent to become a member of the Democratic National Campaign Committee as a speaker for Wilson while, he maintained a neutral stance. The Hearst newspapers and magazines, while slightly favoring the Democrats, were often highly critical.

On Election Day, American voters reflected Hearst's vacillation and uncertainty. Although the *New York American* headline on November 8 blared forth "NATION SWEPT BY HUGHES," such was not the case. Late returns from California changed defeat into victory. The Democrats and Wilson barely won reelection.[45]

In no way, however, did this election aid and abet Hearst. The Wilson administration considered him unfriendly, if not its most severe critic. Thus the late fall and winter of 1916–1917 was one of bitter discontent, of disturbing turmoil and mounting crises. On October 11, because of his Anglophobic articles and editorials as well as repeated critical exposés by his editors concerning Allied censorship of news, the British government banned the Hearst media from using its cables and mails. On October 29, the French applied like restrictions, and on November 8, the Canadians followed suit.[46]

Hearst was not about to acquiesce quietly to these governmental edicts to submit meekly to foreign pressure. He condemned the Allies for infringing on First Amendment rights, of abridging freedom of the press, of attempting to squelch the truth. His disdain was typically unrelenting to an avowed opponent. "I will not supplicate England for news or for print paper or for permission to issue," he resolutely wrote. "In fact, the more foreign powers endeavor to interfere in America's domestic matters, and the more these foreign powers try to control our American institutions, particularly our free press, the more necessary, it seems to me, that

American papers for the American people shall continue to be published."[47]

Yet Hearst was fighting a losing battle. Events were rapidly pushing the United States toward intervention against the Central Powers. The Wilson administration, the American business community, and the national news media, including an overwhelming majority of the New York press, were becoming even more pro-Allied. Stories of German agents sabotaging American industries, planting bombs in factories and aboard ships fed a growing hysteria against Germany. Hearst, in attempting to present a more balanced view of the belligerents, was increasingly referred to as "pro-German." And with his newspapers' highly vocal and increasingly critical view of British policies, he suffered the bitter harvest of public indignation, the ultimate disdain of his countrymen, the epithet "traitor."[48]

Then early in 1917 a rush of events pushed the United States into hostilities. Whereas Wilson had forced Germany in May 1916 (by the so-called *Sussex* pledge) to agree that its U-boat captains would not sink merchant ships "without proper humanitarian precautions," Berlin proclaimed that unrestricted submarine warfare would commence again on January 31, 1917. Within a week the United States terminated diplomatic relations with Berlin. The German government inflamed Americans even more through an act of indiscretion known as the Zimmermann note. On January 16, German Foreign Secretary Arthur Zimmermann foolishly cabled instructions to his Mexican minister, which the British easily intercepted and deciphered. In the event of war with the United States Zimmermann proposed a German–Mexican alliance. At the conclusion of a victorious war, Mexico would recover Texas, New Mexico, and Arizona. He also intimated that Japan would be favorable to this scheme and revert to the side of the Central Powers. Upon the publication of this document on March 3, after U.S. authorities validated its authenticity, all that was needed to ignite the powder keg of war in the United States was a match, and that occurred in mid-March. Within the space of a few days German U-boats sank four unarmed American merchant ships without warning. With the American people outraged and militant over such ruthless acts of aggression, Wilson appeared before both Houses of Congress on April 2, 1917, to deliver a war message. Four days later the United States declared war on Germany.[49]

Hearst now had to redirect his energies. He had tried to prevent the United States from entering what he deemed to be a disastrous war for all "Caucasians" one that would imperil the safety and security of the United States. He would now face new challenges, those that would concern national unity during the crises of war and, equally important, those affecting a lasting world peace. Always confident in his own ability to educate the American people to his point of view and ever the optimist, he readied himself for these new challenges with unrelenting vigor.

3 The Sword and Shield of the People

On January 2, 1916, eighteen minutes after midnight, William Randolph Hearst assembled at the Clarendon—his sumptuous mansion at 86th Street and Riverside Drive in New York City—a few close friends along with his mother, Phoebe Apperson Hearst. And for what purpose? One of publicity and pronouncement and affirmation. From 3,500 miles away he was congratulated by "wire telephone" Max Ihmsen, the manager of his *Los Angeles Examiner*, who was dedicating a splendid, newly constructed newspaper building, Hearst proudly exclaimed, "located in the center of the world's activities, at the summit of the world's development, at the focus of the world's interest and attention."

Hearst, however, was not about to allow this opportunity to pass without further fanfare and exhilaration. He therefore expounded further his philosophy concerning the mission of the Hearst media empire. His idea of government by newspaper, led by crusading editors who enlisted millions of loyal readers to Hearst's righteous causes, would continue to be the mouthpiece of the people and thereby force local and national politicians to do their—and Hearst's—bidding. But more than that, "a great newspaper is the Sword of the people, to battle for their privileges; the Shield of the people, to protect them from their enemies," Hearst rhetorically announced to those listening in Los Angeles. "It is the banner which leads the march, the lamp which lights the path of popular progress." Indeed, "it is the torch which Liberty lifts aloft for the enlightenment of the world."

In conclusion Hearst provided a true insight into his thinking and intentions for present and future generations of Americans. "The influence of a great newspaper in a great community is almost unlimited," he candidly proclaimed. "It enters into the hearts and homes of the people. It informs the mind of the citizen of today and molds the thought of the citizen of tomorrow."[1]

Hearst surely intended his newspapers to be a "sword" and "shield" for the rights of the average American, but also a protection for him against his enemies, who seemed to be multiplying exponentially in number. For three years he had ardently striven to keep the United States out of entangling alliances with European powers, to safeguard his country from the senseless, murderous catastrophe of World War I. But to no avail. As a result of his neutrality stance, of presenting war news to Americans in what he considered an unbiased fashion instead of a pro-Allied slant, many of his fellow citizens (as well as newspaper competitors) denounced such ideas and actions as pro-German, bordering on treason and sedition, especially after the United States declared war on Germany. During this time of escalating chauvinism and flag-waving patriotism after April 6, 1917, many 100-percent Americans targeted him as someone to hate and revile.

What stance would Hearst take during World War I? To him the answer was obvious: "America First." He directed his media empire to focus on two objectives—winning the war and protecting, with "sword" and "shield," his somewhat exposed flank. Even before the war declaration Hearst directed his newspapers to crusade for universal military service, urging Congress to enact draft legislation immediately. "I believe that it is the only effective system, the only democratic system," Hearst editorialized, because "a citizenry trained in arms makes for democracy and equality," yet "provides for the nation's protection and democracy's defense." Within a month more than 100,000 petitions (from forms printed daily in the Hearst newspapers for reader use) inundated Congress, and Hearst traveled to Washington to persuade his old friend, Speaker of the House Champ Clark, to endorse his point of view. And this campaign, the *American* exulted, was victorious; by the end of April, Congress passed its first wartime measure, the Selective Service Act.

At the same time the Hearst newspapers actively helped recruit men into the army and navy; for example, the *American* established enlistment booths (with government approval) at prominent locations in New York City, often with young Broadway beauties who encouraged young men to do their patriotic duty to God and country. On one such occasion, a budding actress named Marion Davies pledged to be a sister or pen pal to the first four men who volunteered for naval service; the *American* reported that a mad rush to enlist ensued.[2]

Hearst realized that his editors must be in step with national purpose, and that meant the overall support of the Wilson administration. What a turnaround from the past four years! No longer was Wilson ridiculed by Hearst's political cartoonists; no longer did Hearst editorial writers portray the president as a weak, indecisive political novice. They now characterized him as the hope for all democracies, the destined leader against the autocratic aristocrats of Europe, especially Kaiser Wilhelm of Germany. By July 1918, praise for Wilson was so effusive, so laudatory that Senator Hiram Johnson of California, who occasionally represented Hearst as legal counsel and often agreed with his previously disparaging assessments of Wilson, noted that Hearst had "adopted as his defense" against critics "a sycophantic subserviency to the administration," devoting "himself exclusively to the most sickening, slobbering, fulsome flattery of anybody connected with the President."[3]

Hearst, however, did not succumb completely to the Wilson administration. He vigorously opposed wartime issues infringing on freedom of the press, specifically the "autocratic Espionage bill," which would entrust the president with extraordinary powers "to hamper and repress free speech and free publication," he declared. In several editorials Hearst continued to rail against the enactment of such impending censorship, which would be "an invasion of the fundamentals and essentials of a free government." To support this crusade, the Hearst media empire daily orchestrated testimonials of prominent personages condemning the Espionage bill and printed a petition to Congress advocating free speech, which needed only the name and address of the petitioner.[4]

Directing a vast newspaper empire while actively engaging in local and national politics would have overwhelmed most men. But Hearst's appetite for new challenges—or indiscretions—was monumental. Time and advancing age were his major enemies. He mostly scheduled time with his family on vacations. Since World War I had prevented their annual tour of Europe, he took them on holiday to Florida, reserving accommodations during the winter months at The Breakers in Palm Beach. But even then Hearst could not divorce himself from his many interests.[5]

The winter of 1915–1916 was an exception. Early in the morning on December 2, 1915, Millicent was about to give birth for the fourth time. In anticipation of a girl after siring three sons, Hearst had decided to name the newborn after his mother. But Millicent gave birth to twin boys, and Hearst proclaimed in a telegram to his mother: "We cannot call them Phoebe . . . but we could call them Phoebus and Apollo, for just at sunrise two of the loveliest boys you have ever seen were born to Mr. and Mrs. William Randolph Hearst." Over the next few days Hearst referred to his sons as "Romulus and Remus," that is, until "compelled to register them at city hall," Hearst telegraphed Phoebe, as Randolph Apperson Hearst and Elbert Willson (later changed to David Whitmire) Hearst, "taking the names from grandfather and grandmother."[6]

To complicate further his already complicated life, Hearst at times indulged in unconventional activities often frowned on by society. Orthodoxy had never been a part of his behavioral makeup. For more than two decades he had been accused of being a traitor to his own economic class by advocating numerous progressive reforms—direct election of senators, graduated income tax, federal reserve banks, strict antitrust enforcement, child labor laws, and municipal ownership of utilities and transportation. He had even dared to switch parties by forming one of his own. And in no way had these actions hindered his wealth and political prominence. In regard to ethical codes of societal and public conduct, Hearst had wholeheartedly endorsed such mores, but "in the abstract," seemingly unaware, or completely oblivious, that any rules necessarily applied to him.

Hearst was a maverick politically, socially, and in business who personified the cliché, "marching to the beat of his own drum." Since his days at Harvard in the mid-1880s he had persuaded women, without exception young (and often talented), to accept his company and munificence, even at the cost of violating conventional mores. In 1898, during the Spanish American War, he had decided to take the lovely Willson sisters, unescorted, upon "his grand adventure" to Cuba; then in the several years thereafter he introduced them to night life in New York City, at times raising questions of moral impropriety. Yet despite turgid, malicious gossip, he had become the proud husband of a beautiful woman who had borne him five healthy sons.

Hearst was an American success story. To associates and friends his creative genius and imaginary flair, his limitless energy and dominating will to succeed were not just apparent but awesome and overwhelming. An unusual daily schedule, unique in its oddity but workability, also gave rise to the Hearst mystique. He had always been a night person, usually working from midnight to dawn, then sleeping past noon before returning to his office to wind up any loose ends. Despite his unorthodox ways, he was the most powerful media mogul in the world. His continuing success proved that rules for the ordinary man need not apply to him. Nor would he allow such plebeian norms to affect or inhibit him.[7]

Hearst had a passion for the theater—and its participants. In the evening he habitually relaxed by dining at Delmonico's, Sherry's, or Rector's just before or after attending a Broadway play. He especially enjoyed the posttheater parties, reveling in associations with famous producers like

Florenz "Flo" Ziegfeld, acclaimed singer Al Jolson, up-and-coming comedians Eddie Cantor and Will Rogers, as well as such glamorous actresses as Justine Johnstone, who was billed as "America's loveliest woman." He also enjoyed meeting talented young women who might become the future stars of stage and screen. As son Bill Jr. acknowledged, "Pop" customarily took "us backstage at the Ziegfeld *Follies*." He "always was a stage-door Johnny, just always."[8]

Such an assessment far underestimated William Randolph Hearst; those in New York theatrical circles knew his far-reaching importance. He was both rich and famous, the most powerful newspaper publisher in the world, a walking, talking epitome of publicity, indeed, an ultimate link to stardom. With his numerous newspapers and magazines as well as the International Film Service, he had the resources to promote any aspiring new talent into a household name. He was also writing and producing popular, crowd-pleasing serials, such as the *Perils of Pauline*, which had made Pearl White a well-known movie star. Because of his singular attraction to show biz people, he seldom missed a new play. To save valuable time, he leased a bachelor's suite of rooms at the Bryant Park Studios at 49th Street and Sixth Avenue, only a few blocks from the major theaters. Consequently, an invitation to one of Hearst's postshow parties was in itself an acknowledgment of personal acceptance (if not dramatic achievement) and was highly desired.[9]

Hearst soon complicated his passion for the theater with a personal one. Her name was Marion Cecilia Davies, née Douras. Although by no means a classical beauty, she was wonderfully attractive with youthful appeal. Her naturally blond, curly hair framed a pretty face that featured large blue eyes and a flawless complexion. She reminded one of her actress friends of "a beautiful blue butterfly" who enchanted those about her with a flirtatious smile and a fun-loving personality. Approximately 5 feet, 6 inches tall, Marion Davies was lithe and slender, more athletic or tomboyish than voluptuous, making her seem even more girlish and frequently impish.[10]

Born in Brooklyn on January 3, 1897, the daughter of a lesser New York magistrate named Bernard J. Douras, Marion survived some difficult early years. "I stuttered, no school wanted me," she frankly reminisced. "So my mother decided to put me in a convent," first at Sacred Heart on the Hudson, then briefly at a similar school in France. After several depressing months abroad she returned to New York City. Nothing had changed. She continued to achieve special recognition among her classmates by occupying "the dunce seat all the time." By her teenage years, she had escaped to the glamorous make-believe world of the theater.[11]

Although a member (in some capacity) of a traveling road show as early as 1913, Marion Davies did not reach Broadway until the fall of 1915, appearing in the chorus of *Miss Information*. In the next two years she was catapulted to stardom, partly because of her beauty and talent, but also because of a growing crescendo of orchestrated Hearst publicity. By February 1916, she had signed onto the *Stop! Look! Listen* cast at the Globe theater, attracting so much attention that the *New York American* noted that "rumor has it" that she might "soon join the ranks of film beauties." Then on May 21, Flo Ziegfeld announced that she was one of the beauties in the new edition of his *Follies*. In June, three more articles with accompanying photos appeared in the *American*. So by 1917 Marion Davies had the delicious choice between accepting a role in one of several Broadway productions or embarking on a popular new field of theatrics, the motion picture.[12]

But some of these decisions involved Hearst. By the summer of 1915, when he had become somewhat awkwardly aware of Marion's existence, he was a married man with three sons and a pregnant wife. Possibly one reason for his immediate attraction to Marion and his personal vulnerability was that the chemistry in his relationship with Millicent had changed. More and more she complained of physical exhaustion because of continual childbearing as well as having to go on the road with Hearst, whether for business or pleasure. With each passing year, perhaps unknowingly, Millicent placed the needs of family over those of husband. She also was determined to improve the Hearsts' social status. She therefore urged her husband to abandon the crooked game of politics and participate in more rewarding endeavors, specifically civic and charitable events.

Such ideas were repugnant to Hearst. Like his father George, he despised the trappings of high society and avoided lavish parties and formal dinners, unless he was the host or sponsor. And he was never an epicure; plagued with a dyspeptic stomach since childhood, he required that such simple foods as bread, cheese, and pickles be readily available on his dinner table. Hence by the fall of 1915, he and Millicent were drifting apart.[13]

Yet Hearst could not help himself where Marion Davies was concerned; his attraction to her was immediate and irresistible. In his eyes she was simply gorgeous. It was rumored that he reserved two seats every night at the *Follies*, one for himself and the other for his hat. At aftershow parties she was scintillating, lighting up the room with her bubbling vitality while delighting fellow revelers, especially Hearst, with a mischievous disregard for convention and formality. Even her stuttering delighted him; after all, he had overcome an obvious lisp in his own speech.

For a number of months Hearst sent her gifts, unsolicited and without expectations in return, at least not as yet. "He was always a shadow," Marion recollected, ever watchful and protective, ever the silent pursuer, indeed an older, mature paladin. At age fifty-three he was patiently cautious in evaluating this fascinating young actress of nineteen, thirty-four years his junior with whom he would happily share the rest of his life.[14]

While this personal relationship was continuing to unfold, Hearst was still attending to other pursuits. In the summer of 1917, because World War I had disrupted his annual tour to Europe for the past three years, he opted for the next best vacation spot, California. More and more he came to appreciate the old stompin' ground of his youth, the 275,000-acre ranch midway between San Francisco and Los Angeles known as San Simeon. What a wonderful experience! At Camp Hill, where the magnificent Hearst castle would eventually arise overlooking the Pacific, he had the ranch hands erect a tent city for guests and a portable wooden house for Millicent and the boys. For those driving up the mountain from San Simeon Bay at nightfall, the view, often "rising out of the fog," was an exhilarating occasion, the beginning of a memorable vacation.[15]

For several months Hearst rejoiced in the rustic simplicity of his Pacific Coast retreat. He became a combination of director, tour guide, and host, but no matter the title, he was always the leader. A marvelous cook, he enjoyed preparing venison in delicious ways for his guests, together with a specialty from Harvard days, Welsh rarebit. Picnics on the beach or atop a scenic mountain pasture, to which Hearst led his visitors on horseback, were part of the everyday schedule.[16]

As an added pastime, one that soon became a regular event, Hearst produced home movies. Guests were expected to become part of the cast. He, in turn, wrote the silent screen dialogue (often in verse), at times took movies himself, and developed the film. Although a professional cameraman was available, Hearst's expertise equaled, if not surpassed, his specialist's. As a result he produced, wrote, and directed a home movie titled "Romance of the Rancho." In the scenario Millicent played the heroine who was kidnapped by bandits (the ranch hands). Hearst, as the hero of this western epic, formed a posse (composed of the male visitors) and pursued the evil desperados. He crawled stealthily into the enemy camp and rescued Millicent after shooting the bandito leader, who accidently stumbled and fell into the nearby campfire. Hearst ordered the cowhand, whose clothes were burning, to remain dead until the end of the scene. So much for artistic realism![17]

Hearst, however, considered himself a realist in regard to personal political ambition; at least in 1917 he surely did. Late in May, it was rumored that he might run again for mayor of New York City, an idea that he had toyed with during the summer in California. After all, such a prominent political position would automatically establish him as a major Democratic presidential candidate in 1920.

Although more than 3,000 miles away, Hearst readied his forces for an anticipated campaign. To the surprise of many observers, he proffered a peace settlement to former political foe, Charles Francis Murphy, who was disposed to support Hearst because of his popularity with several of Tammany Hall's main constituencies, the Germans and the Irish. The two men had found common ground over the past several years while campaigning in behalf of municipal ownership of utilities and transportation. On any number of critical issues they had also opposed the administration of New York City Mayor John Purroy Mitchel. To create enthusiasm and generate a greater response for his candidacy, Hearst employed in August such time-tested campaign techniques as testimonial endorsements by leaders of Democratic and progressive affiliates—United Workingman's League, Federation of Independent Voters, and Democratic fusion committees. At the same time he launched a petition drive in his behalf, accumulating 8,869 signatures over several weeks, and then capped off these efforts with a ringing affirmation by former Mayor George B. McClellan, who proclaimed that Hearst would "make a stronger fight . . . than any other Democrat."[18]

But not all New York Democrats agreed with this assessment. Tammany leader "Big Tom" Foley, who had defeated Hearst's associate Max Ihmsen for New York County sheriff in the fall of 1907, would never forgive how viciously the Hearst papers had vilified him. At a called news conference on August 25, he vowed that "the editor would not get a vote south of Fourteenth Street." And then he announced, "I prefer Mitchel to Hearst." The next day other Tammany chiefs, including Alfred E. Smith who was campaigning for the presidency of the Board of Aldermen, also voiced their disapproval by threatening to "withdraw from the ticket." And as a final dagger in the heart to the Hearst candidacy, stories appeared in several New York newspapers that no American who had opposed the entry of the United States into World War I could possibly win the mayoral race.[19]

With his candidacy now a major obstacle to a Democratic victory, Hearst made the only logical decision. The defeat of Mayor John Purroy Mitchel was far more important than personal ambition; besides, he realized that the road to the White House in 1920 did not hang upon this election. William Randolph Hearst no longer required an introduction to the American people or the publicity and fanfare so necessary for unknown political candidates. So on August 31 he declined to run, announcing his support for Judge John F. Hylan of Brooklyn, whom Tammany also endorsed, and promised to campaign actively against Mitchel.[20]

Yet Hearst continued his stay in California for more than a month until forced to return in defense of his honor and reputation. Because Hearst's three New York City newspapers had a greater circulation than all other local dailies combined, the Mitchel camp strategized that Hearst must be publicly discredited, his prestige undermined, his influence with voters limited. In the midst of the patriotic ambience enveloping wartime America, the mayor decided to wrap himself in the flag while associating his opponent with the forces of disunity and disloyalty.

Mayor Mitchel, in launching his bid for reelection, clearly enunciated this strategy. And once again he proved that New York politics was not for the faint of heart. On October 1, 1917, accompanied by such prestigious politicos as former President Theodore Roosevelt and the 1916 Republican presidential candidate Charles Evans Hughes, the mayor addressed a spirited crowd of 10,000 followers who had been provided with little American flags. "New York is offered Hylan, the nominee of Murphy and of Hearst," Mitchel solemnly announced. "Their like raise their heads to spit venom at those who have taken a strong and active stand with America and against Germany." Then he fiercely exclaimed, "I will make this fight against Hearst, Hylan, and the Hohenzollerns."[21]

For the next four days the Mitchel camp continued their attacks relentlessly and unabated, with each new charge seeming to revolve around Hearst. On the night of October 3 at several jam-packed meetings, Mitchel again linked him (amid shouts of "Hang Hearst!") with the "Hohenzollerns and Hapsburgs," declaring that "Mr. Hearst puts the Star-Spangled Banner on the front page and tries to stab his country in the back in his editorial columns." On October 4 the mayor garnered support from Judge Samuel Seabury, who had been the state Democratic nominee for governor in 1916. Not only had Hearst not supported him and President Wilson, he charged, but Hearst also "stands as the most pronounced advocate of the pro-German cause." Indeed, "I esteem him false not only to his country, but to every ideal of decency." Again on October 5 still more accusations abounded, this time from State Attorney General Merton E. Lewis, who released documents suggesting alleged activities between Hearst and German representatives. The testimony implied that Paul Bolo Pasha, "a Frenchman now under arrest in Paris as a German spy," had conspired with Hearst to raise $1.7 million to finance subversive activities in France. It also intimated that Hearst had met with Captain Franz von Papen and Captain Karl Boy-Ed, the German military and naval attachés in Washington who were expelled in 1915 for espionage; supposedly they had been Hearst's guests at a Manhattan dinner party as well as at the Clarendon mansion.[22]

Such allegations had to be answered, and Hearst proved equal to the task. Issuing denials of enemy collaboration, he easily dismissed as false his association with Captain von Papen and Captain Boy-Ed; he had never invited them to the Clarendon. Nor had he attended a dinner party with them at Sherry's, especially since this "social repast" had occurred in March 1916, four months after their expulsion from the United States. And as for the Frenchman Paul Bolo Pasha, who presented himself as a representative of the *Paris Journal*, Hearst admitted that Bolo Pasha had gained an audience with him, specifically on how to acquire "the best and cheapest paper" since Hearst used "more print paper than any other man in the United States." Soon thereafter, Hearst explained, Bolo Pasha hosted a dinner at Sherry's that he and Millicent attended, along with other prominent persons, whom he named. Hearst thus concluded, "I defy the Attorney-General to disprove any word in this statement of mine, or to substantiate any one of his own unwarranted implications, except his one truthful statement that my acquaintance with Bolo Pasha was 'purely social.' "[23]

For the month preceding the November election the campaign of innuendo and slander and vilification reached new highs (or lows). After the charges by Attorney General Lewis on October 5, Hearst returned from California to New York and entered the fray with energy and dedication. Within a week he had reactivated his Independence League, dormant since 1911, which wholeheartedly endorsed Hylan. At the same time Hearst mobilized his newspapers for an all-out battle against slanderers and "other scandal mongers." He also bought full-page ads in rival newspapers in an attempt to counter such malicious attacks. By October 12 he had his crusade agenda fully in place and gathering momentum. Until Election Day an increasing number of testimonials denouncing Mitchel peppered the columns of the *American* and *Evening Journal*. Lengthy editorials were equally unsympathetic and, in keeping with the tone of the campaign, abusive and vitriolic. In close accompaniment, Hearst's already famous political cartoonists (Winsor McCay, Frederick Opper, T. E. Powers, and Jimmy Swinnerton) produced vividly humorous creations that brutally denigrated Mitchel and his administration. For instance, on the day before the election (November 5), all four displayed trenchant cartoons in the *American*.[24]

The Hearst assault force tried to conceal its major flaw and inherent weakness, namely, Judge John Hylan. As one prominent historian ungenerously assessed, he was "woefully unfit" so much so that his handlers, mainly Hearst and Tammany chief Murphy, would not allow him to be interviewed by "enemy" reporters. Hence Hylan confined his political comments and personal tidbits and innermost feelings to the journalists of the Hearst newspapers. As a result, Mitchel continually referred to Hylan as the "puppet of Hearst," the "straw man" of Tammany, whose handlers wrote "all of his speeches in words of one syllable."[25]

Hearst, however, was determined to triumph. Hylan, although incapable of deep thought, was not "entirely lacking in intelligence." In one respect, Mitchel was correct; Hylan was a Hearst man. On the other hand, Mitchel and his band of patriots had become, to Hearst's way of thinking, the true foes of democracy. They had besmirched and ridiculed him unjustly, indeed had questioned his patriotism by calling him the "kaiser's friend," the "enemy's hero," the "fosterer of sedition." One aspect about Hearst's psychological makeup was always a given; he never forgot or forgave anyone who attacked him personally. He was intent on maiming, if not destroying, his opponent.[26]

Hearst revealed these characteristics in the mayoral campaign of 1917. For several weeks he purposely avoided answering the question that Mitchel asked at every campaign rally: "Why is Hearst backing Hylan?" With each passing day the drumbeat for a response grew louder, which implied all kinds of negative connotations. Hearst, however, waited until a week before the election to counterattack—and then with a scathing rebuke. In an editorial to Mayor Mitchel, he announced that he had "no personal hostility to Mayor Mitchel. He is an amiable young man, but without character or principles." Hearst then outlined specific reasons for his displeasure: the mayor had "violated the pledges upon which he was elected," had "plunged the city into disastrous debts through his dissipation of the city's wealth to friends and favored corporations," and had grievously undermined the public school system to the detriment of "our children." As a result, Hearst asserted, the Mitchel administration was scandal ridden, and "the re-election of Mayor Mitchel would be an endorsement of utter incompetency and unfaithfulness in public life, a complete surrender of public rights to private interests."

For the next five days Hearst intensified this personal vendetta. In each edition of his newspapers, he wrote editorials, accompanied by a blistering political cartoon, that castigated and condemned Mitchel to the fullest. And on Election Day he savored the full effect of his labors. The headline of the *New York American* on November 7 blared, "JUDGE HYLAN WINS BY 140,000."[27]

With this political victory Hearst enjoyed a euphoric high for the next five months, measured by financial successes and political achievements.

Attending to business matters held in abeyance because of the Hylan campaign, he strengthened the "sword" and "shield" of his media empire. After acquiring the British magazine *Puck* for a nominal sum, he bought the *Boston Advertiser* in November and consolidated it with the *Boston American*, thereby bringing about greater solvency and financial security. Then late in January 1918, the Hearst dailies, along with most competitors, raised their price to two cents a copy, hence even greater earnings. Beginning March 3, he initiated in his three Sunday papers in New York City, Boston, and Chicago the "Gravure Section Supreme," which was, he announced, "the finest picture presentation of world news" ever concocted. He sold an estimated 1.5 million copies, again realizing tremendous profits.

At the same time Hearst strove to improve his national image. Although Hylan's election seemed to be a reaffirmation of public trust regarding his patriotism, he was not satisfied. In article after article beginning in mid-November the *New York American* cited testimony from newspapers across the nation that condemned the "unwarranted tirade of abuse" leveled against him and that praised, as one headline put it, the "Loyalty of Mr. Hearst and His Newspapers." To instill further this idea of public trust, he repeatedly defended the Wilson administration and its conduct of the war, applauding the president for his vision and leadership. And as a final step to confound the opposition, to throw critics off stride, Hearst proposed an ingenious economic project to aid France. On Christmas Day, 1917, his newspapers initiated a huge fund-raising campaign to restore—after the defeat of Germany—six French cities "ruined by the war," a proposal similar to the Marshall Plan of the Truman administration thirty years later. This public relations coup was labeled the "Hearst Plan," which gained widespread approval and for the moment silenced his enemies.[28]

On January 1, 1918, with the inauguration of John Hylan as mayor, Hearst continued to reap the fruits of political victory. While rival newspapers agreed that his influence concerning city patronage was considerable, he claimed all such reports to be false. "I do not in the least care whom Mayor Hylan appoints to office," he announced, "as long as he appoints capable and conscientious men, who will serve the public faithfully and be a credit to the city." But on January 7 neither he nor political observers were surprised that Hylan selected Mrs. William Randolph Hearst to head the prestigious Women's Committee of the Mayor's Committee on National Defense. Then five days later he appointed her to the Mayor's Committee to Rebuild French Cities.[29]

Millicent Hearst thrived in her new assignments. In the spirit of unity and self-sacrifice she was helping make the world safe for democracy.

And as a leader of the city's women she was determined to recruit thousands of volunteers in behalf of the war effort, to demonstrate that this new constituency of soon to be voting women (Nineteenth Amendment enacted in 1920) could make a difference. On January 14, 1918, in anticipation of a bitterly cold winter as well as an impending fuel crisis, she delivered fifty tons of coal to the Mayor's Relief Committee on Coal and contributed $1,000 to its budget. By the end of the month her fifty-five-member Committee on National Defense was in place, with the results soon apparent. For example, over the next four months members transported stars of Broadway shows to entertain soldiers at nearby Camp Upton; others helped stage huge parades in Manhattan to encourage young men to enlist. At the same time members urged New Yorkers to conserve food for export, to enforce voluntary "meatless" and "wheatless" and "porkless" days as well as to grow victory gardens. They also promoted drives to buy Liberty Bonds and to raise funds for the Red Cross. And in May they began establishing social canteens throughout greater New York to show their appreciation to American servicemen.[30]

Hearst had an equally full agenda. Because of the bitterly cold New York winter of 1918, he decided to conduct his affairs in a warmer clime, namely Palm Beach, Florida. Besides keeping in close contact with his editors, he participated in a favorite pastime, the game of politics. For more than two weeks, after persuading John Hylan to vacation in the same location, Hearst conducted a first-class seminar in the art of political propaganda and free publicity. On February 19, along with the mayor, he participated in a charity benefit for the Red Cross, with Hearst typically, the *New York Times* noted, the more dominant figure. Three days later at West Palm Beach he was the featured speaker at the Convention of Education of Florida, where he praised educators as the "torch bearers of democracy." Then that evening he hosted a dinner which included, besides Mayor and Mrs. Hylan, a former enemy-now-turned-friend, William Jennings Bryan. As a result, for the next week such opposition newspapers as the *Times* speculated that the publisher was a prime contender for the Democratic presidential nomination in 1920, especially if Bryan supported him.

Nor did Hylan discourage this feeding frenzy of conjecture by the press. He paid "tribute to that loyal, unselfish, and patriotic citizen, William Randolph Hearst" who, more than anyone else, was responsible for his mayoral victory. Without hesitation he proclaimed his ardent support of Hearst for governor or president or whatever his political aspirations. He was a Hearst man.[31]

For Hearst, however, such halcyon days would soon end; his enemies, malevolent in purpose and toxic in method, would see to that. Even more than *Collier's Magazine* and the *New York Times*, the *New York Tribune* excelled in being pejorative and vicious. On April 28, 1918, the *Tribune* launched a five-part Sunday series, symbolized by a snake spitting venom and titled "Coiled in the Flag—Hears-s-s-s-t." Authored by Kenneth Macgowan, these broadsides, which were extended for five more weeks due to popular demand, employed the Hearst crusade tactics of presenting one side while excluding any rebuttal. In a daily barrage other *Tribune* articles, while branding Hearst as "Germany's Hero," as "The Hearst [enemy] Within Our Gates," also quoted multiple sources—political leaders (especially mayors and town councilmen), executives of women's clubs, veterans, home defense officers, ministers and missionaries, schoolteachers, even bartenders and taxicab drivers—who denounced Hearst for his unpatriotic and pro-German stance. Then with equally critical editorials, accompanied by unflattering political cartoons, the *Tribune* repeatedly bludgeoned Hearst and his newspaper policies before its reading public.[32]

The ultimate goals of this patriotic crusade were to destroy the integrity of Hearst and the credibility of his media empire in the eyes of Americans. And for a time it seemed that his major competitors, particularly the *Tribune* and *Times*, were perilously close to succeeding. The results of their incessant attacks created an ambience of unreasoning hate and blinding fear, a mob hysteria of outraged citizenry in the name of patriotism. Here were but a few reports out of literally hundreds that occurred in the summer of 1918. In Flushing, Long Island, 150 citizens burned every available edition of the *New York American* and *Evening Journal*; in Mount Vernon, New York, the mayor and town council passed a resolution banning the sale of all Hearst publications, and the East Orange Battalion of the New Jersey militia endorsed this action; in Worcester, Massachusetts, members of a local church blacklisted the *Boston American* and *Boston Advertiser*; in Cincinnati, librarians voted to remove all Hearst dailies from their public reading rooms; in California, the South Pasadena Home Guards and in New Mexico, the Albuquerque Rotary Club boycotted the *Los Angeles Examiner* and the *San Francisco Examiner*; in Chicago, bartenders banned the *Chicago American* and the *Chicago Herald and Examiner* from their establishments. And in New York City a woman protested that a sign over the door of a social canteen for uniformed soldiers, prominently displaying the name of Mrs. William Randolph Hearst, should be taken down because of her pro-German sentiments.[33]

To such affronts Hearst reacted quickly. With his dailies and Sunday papers losing circulation in the thousands as well as a resultant number of advertisements, he effected immediate changes. His editors stepped up their support of the American war effort and especially of the Wilson administration. They printed patriotic verse or public-spirited comments by George Washington and Thomas Jefferson on the masthead of the editorial page. They instructed their newsboys on city streets to wear or display little American flags. For a brief time they even changed the name of the famous cartoon *The Katzenjammer Kids* with Hans and Fritz to *The Shenanigan Kids* with Mike and Aleck—while retaining their German dialect. Because of constant criticism for publishing the *New York Deutsches Journal* (the German-language newspaper formerly called *Das Morgen Journal*), Hearst agreed to discontinue it late in April (1918) for the duration of the war. And in an attempt to reach alienated readers, he took out advertisements in the opposition press in an attempt to present his side of the story. On June 1, for instance, the *New York Times* ran a full-page ad titled "What Hearst Papers Have Done To Help Win The War."[34]

Although facing sizable financial losses, Hearst was not discouraged. An habitual optimist, he routinely warded off economic difficulties or personal unpopularity with the self-assurance of a gambler who already knows the outcome of a race, stating that he was "frequently . . . right at the wrong time."[35]

A case in point was his political maneuvering in the summer of 1918. Always keeping an eye on the presidency, Hearst considered running for governor of New York on the Democratic ticket as a first step. As a trial balloon, he tested the political waters—with tremendous fanfare and orchestration, of course. On June 28, four weeks before state Democrats would meet to select their nominees at Saratoga, New York, a rumor floated in the *New York Times*, suggesting that he either would be the gubernatorial candidate or would be instrumental in the party's choice. The next day Hearst attracted more attention by inviting approximately 250 members of Congress, mainly Democrats, to be his personal guests at a July 4 loyalty parade extravaganza in New York City; Mayor Hylan complemented this arrangement by asking the visitors and their wives to be on the reviewing stand with the Hearsts and Hylans. Although the *Times* noted that only twenty-five attended, Hearst provided lodging, transportation, meals, and theater tickets for Secretary of the Navy Josephus Daniels, seven U.S. senators, and forty-nine members of Congress. Then at a spectacular dinner in the Hotel Astor, Speaker of the House Champ Clark and Senator James Reed of Missouri praised the patriotism and loyalty of America's greatest publisher. In the meantime Arthur Brisbane, who was considered Hearst's alter ego, created additional political excitement by announcing in a *Washington Times* editorial: "To William Randolph Hearst: Why don't you run for Governor of New York, beginning your campaign NOW, and give those experts in patriotism something to think about?"

For the next three weeks the political hype continued. Petitions urging him to run and testimonials predicting a Hearst victory in November occupied a considerable amount of space in the New York dailies. In fact, his intentions seemed to be validated after a *Times* reporter learned on July 16 that "Hearst had engaged twenty-seven rooms at the Grand Union Hotel" in Saratoga for the state Democratic convention. After all, he had the backing of Mayor Hylan and, surprisingly, of Tammany boss Murphy, who intimated his willingness to accept a Hearst nomination. Besides, what candidate could generate campaign funds more quickly or had greater name recognition? And over the past decade who among the Democrats had a better record of progressive legislation, especially in campaigning for municipal ownership of utilities, public transportation, and women's right to vote?[36]

Once again Hearst was right but at the wrong time. While Boss Murphy might support him, many in Tammany would not. Over the years he had collected a number of bitter enemies, such as Tammany chief Tom Foley and former ally and close friend Judge Samuel Seabury, who castigated him at every opportunity. He also understood that the pro-German accusation would be a vicious weapon against him, an unnecessary stigma for the Democratic Party to combat. As a candidate, one New York politico aptly observed, "Hearst is a political typhoid carrier, and he does not know it. . . . Political distraction, distemper, and death follow in his trail."

Besides contemplating these important considerations, Hearst also had to assess his competition. Al Smith, President of the Board of Aldermen, was proving to be a formidable opponent, not only as an able New York City bureaucrat but as a gifted consensus builder. As a result, just prior to the election of a Democratic slate on July 24, Hearst withdrew from the gubernatorial race. Two weeks later, he warmly endorsed Smith and pledged the full support of his newspapers, especially if he campaigned "boldly for municipal ownership."[37]

What intuitive timing! Early in August 1918, Hearst again came under a heavy barrage of antipatriotism. Attorney General Lewis, who had charged in the Mitchel–Hylan mayoral contest in 1917 that Hearst had collaborated with the enemy, was now a Republican candidate for governor. Believing that Governor Charles S. Whitman, whom he was challenging in the upcoming party primary, was receiving aid and succor from Hearst, Lewis presented volatile new evidence to discredit Hearst and undermine the integrity of the Whitman campaign by guilt through association.

On August 7 this new assault began. Lewis announced that Bolo Pasha, "the French adventurer who has been executed as a traitor," had met with Hearst, not just once but "at least three times." He also reiterated that Count Johann von Bernsdorff, the former German ambassador to the United States, had been a frequent guest at the Clarendon. To prove that the publisher had lied about these associations, Lewis offered sworn affidavits from six witnesses—the doorman, elevator operator, bellboy, and former superintendent of the Clarendon apartments as well as several taxicab drivers. The *Times* reporter then noted that "Lewis made some comment on the relations between Mr. Hearst and Governor Whitman," implying that the editor was a major supporter.[38]

Hearst retaliated effectively and in kind. In the *American* and the *Evening Journal* he printed his accusers' sworn affidavits, then refuted them in a lengthy editorial. He pointed out that the six men assembled by Attorney General Lewis were either paid informants or ex-convicts. "The whole Pasha Bolo situation is," Hearst asserted, "a good example of the misrepresentation, distortion, and actual fabrication to which I have been subjected by journalistic rivals." He thus challenged Lewis to furnish even "the slightest scintilla of pertinent or competent evidence." Indeed, Hearst defiantly implored, "LET HIM PRODUCE IT."[39]

After this initial salvo, the Hearst sword and shield swung into action. In the *American*, testimonials and editorials rebuked Lewis for his unwarranted attacks. Noted political cartoonist Winsor McCay mocked him continually for associating with ex-convicts and being the tool of the liquor interests—Hearst was advocating the passage of the Eighteenth Amendment (prohibition). In the same editions, nationally known Frederick Opper initiated a cartoon series titled "The Lewis Cabaret," which ridiculed the attorney general for his unwavering defense of "Booze and Boodle." And as a climactic stroke, Arthur Brisbane editorialized in the *Washington Times* (which proved to be good copy in other newspapers as well) that Lewis was the "latest chosen tool" of huge corporate bodies who wished to silence "Hearst's plain newspaper talk."[40]

On September 5, after Governor Whitman defeated Lewis in the Republican primary, this brief furor faded into oblivion. Since midsummer of 1918 Allied forces, especially with American support, had been overwhelming the Germans and Austrians on all battlefronts; consequently, with a conclusive victory—and a favorable armistice pending—anti-German animosity in the United States lost steam. At the same time Hearst curried public favor by using his newspapers as a Democratic mouthpiece for Al Smith, who was steadily gaining popularity in his race for governor.

In turn, Hearst outwitted his business and political opponents with incredible promotional ideas; he continually amazed associates with his marketing genius. For example, at the suggestion of the Hearst papers and with the willing assistance of Mayor Hylan, New York City sponsored its first Heroes Day on Sunday, September 1, honoring "soldiers, sailors, and marines" who had "fallen in this great war for universal liberty." At a parade and in attending activities, New Yorkers by the hundreds of thousands paid solemn homage. During September and October Hearst newspapers helped push to completion the fourth victory loan drive. Then Hearst attained a fantastic public relations coup. On October 19 the front-page headline of the *American* read, "THE HEARST NEWSPAPERS SUBSCRIBE ONE MILLION DOLLARS" with 4,403 of the Hearst staff purchasing $474,750 in bonds while he personally contributed $525,250.[41]

Hearst delivered the coupe de grace to his enemies in yet another brilliant marketing idea. On October 8, the *American* announced that the Hearst newspapers would begin today filming "families for soldiers at the front." At his own expense, Hearst began sending pictures of loved ones to American military men overseas. This project, although at first labeled the "Hearst Plan," soon took on a more euphemistic title, "Smiles Across the Sea."[42]

And, of course, the results of such promotions were easily predictable. The Hearst newspapers, besides helping elect Al Smith as governor of New York in an extremely close race, realized a newfound popularity. Whereas during August the circulation of the *American* Sunday sales averaged 751,883, the figures for November 3 rose to 861,982. Hearst, enjoying this triumph over his competitors, deftly inserted this statement of exultation after publicizing such tremendous growth: "Thus do loyal American men and women answer the eight months' campaign of calumny and misrepresentation against the *New York American*."[43]

Nor did Hearst intend for such fortuitous circumstances to lessen. With Germany agreeing to an armistice on November 11, 1918, American wartime fears and animosities quickly subsided, all of which benefited Hearst. For instance, on December 15, the Sunday *American* reached an incredible circulation of 1,039,242, which was, the editor boasted, "the Highest Figure Ever Attained by a Morning Newspaper in America." At the same time in Washington, a Senate judiciary subcommittee investigating prewar propaganda (better known as the Overman Committee) revealed correspondence from Hearst to his editors just prior to U.S. entry into World War I. After days of study the senators found no evidence of sedition or subversion. They then examined the charges by Attorney General Lewis of New York, which contended that Hearst had lied concerning his relationship with German spy Bolo Pasha. Again, Hearst could not have been more pleased with the outcome. His time for vindication, for an end to months of character assassination, had at last arrived. Accordingly, during December 1918 and January 1919, the *New York American* printed much of the Senate testimony on its front pages. Senator Reed of Missouri, who in many instances saw eye to eye with Hearst, injected himself into the hearings. In a grueling cross-examination of witnesses over several days, he literally tore the Lewis allegations to shreds. As a consequence, Deputy Attorney General Alfred Becker of New York, who had prepared the state's case against Hearst, was forced to admit, lest he face a perjury citation, that his evidence was contrived, that it was a political plot to discredit (if not destroy) Hearst in the eyes of the public.[44]

Hearst was not about to let this favorable momentum subside, much less give peace and respite to his political and business enemies. Early in December he accepted—and with a certain amount of satisfaction—an appointment as chairman of the Mayor's Committee of Welcome to Homecoming Troops. What a furor! For more than a month the political fallout was deafening. Opposition newspapers claimed that Hearst, because of his pro-German stance, was a civic scandal, his appointment an insult to the fighting men of the nation. Former New York governor Charles Evans Hughes unequivocally agreed with this conclusion; Theodore Roosevelt consented to head an independent committee that would more appropriately represent patriotic New Yorkers in greeting returning veterans; and a number of Hylan appointees resigned in disgust, the gist of their feelings summed up in one sentence by an outraged dissenter: "Our boys deserve a red, white and blue welcome, untinged by yellow."[45]

Yet even as Hylan was securing the necessary votes for confirmation, Hearst deftly used his newspapers as a "shield" to protect himself against further enemy onslaughts as well as a "sword" to demolish opponents by fighting for the rights of military veterans. Testimonials in the *American* abounded. On December 6, Secretary of War Newton D. Baker congratulated Hearst for having the foresight to ask for advance information concerning returning troops from Europe in order to afford appropriate recognition upon their disembarking at the port of New York. In another edition cartoonist Winsor McCay wrote a special letter "To the Public" in which he berated the "privileged interests and featherbed patriots" for questioning the patriotism of Hearst. He concluded, "Mr. Hearst is ONE HUNDRED PER CENT AMERICAN! I know! I have never made a pro-German cartoon." Not to be outdone, Mayor Hylan sent a letter to Hearst effusive in praise and somewhat fawning in tone, which the *American* published just before Christmas. He stated that "through your papers you are doing more than any other man in the United States to aid public officials" in protecting the people from "predatory interests." And in timely editorials and praiseworthy articles, Hearst continually countered attacks by critics on his magazines and newspapers as well as on him personally; he appealed to the 15 million readers of the Hearst media empire not to be deceived by the conspiracy that the corporate wealthy had contrived to silence the truth of free papers. On into January 1919, the battle continued to rage. Hearst elicited testimonials from a number of Wilson cabinet members, who praised his contributions to the war effort. Then on January 21, by a vote of 41 to 14, the Board of Aldermen of New York City endorsed Mayor Hylan's appointment of Hearst and the Committee to Welcome Returning Heroes, and the controversy ended as abruptly as it had begun.[46]

New Yorkers, although at times abhorring such journalistic divisiveness, supported it economically. Hearst papers enjoyed widespread popularity, with readers responding to each damning accusation and titillating countercharge. Circulation continued to soar to more than 1 million sales a day. But the flamboyant and entertaining techniques of Hearst journalism were the real keys. His presentation of international and national news, the attractiveness of each edition in comparison to the competition—huge headlines, graphic photographs, tantalizing stories, color comics, brilliant political cartoons—and, most importantly, the Hearst crusades attracted new readers as well as faithful subscribers.[47]

The Hearst approach to the returning boys in uniform was a case in point. During the six months after Armistice Day (November 11, 1918), New York City was the greatest showplace in the world for American servicemen. After all, the head of the welcoming committee was William Randolph Hearst, who really knew how to throw a party. Since all soldiers returning from Europe came through the port of New York, parades were a constant factor in the life of the city. Weekly, and sometimes daily, crowds in the thousands turned out to greet still another boatload of battle-tried veterans, who marched triumphantly down Fifth Avenue to the beat of military bands, with American flags seemingly everywhere and confetti raining down on them. After this initial celebration they often adjourned to one of the numerous canteens established by Millicent Hearst and her Mayor's Committee on National Defense, which provided food and recreation as well as the possibility of companionship. And while stage and screen stars entertained wounded veterans in nearby hospitals, Broadway theaters dispensed free tickets nightly to soldiers.[48]

But Hearst had still more in store for "the boys in uniform." Within a week, he again demonstrated that he "was so full of ideas that they tumbled over each other." On Christmas Day, 1918, he wrote an editorial that urged Secretary of War Baker to "Send the Soldiers Home and Pay Their Wages for Six Months." For their self-sacrifice and tremendous accomplishments, he concluded, "anything less than this would be unjust to the men and unworthy of the nation." He also included a petition for readers to sign and forward to the office of the *American*. During the next six months Hearst newspapers collected over 6 million signatures. Although many prominent politicians, such as New York Governor Al Smith, endorsed this crusade, no legislation, either state or national, would be forthcoming. Hearst also arranged for a local company to sew service chevrons on soldiers' uniforms of "Our Boys," and without charge. New Yorkers were encouraged, upon recognition of such stripes on a uniform sleeve, and at the behest of Hearst, to show special appreciation and a hearty welcome to any soldier in the form of free food or entertainment or gifts. Again the next day (December 26) Hearst instituted still another welcome to the returning soldiers. Because jobs were already at a premium, the *American* announced that for any discharged veteran it was providing space daily—and free of charge—for "Positions Wanted" advertisements. All Hearst papers continued this service well into 1919.[49]

As a master showman and business promoter, Hearst wanted to save the most important part of this welcoming crusade for an extraordinary finale. Once again his ideas proved to be remarkably successful, bordering on brilliance. On January 13, 1919, he proclaimed the establishment of a permanent department within the *American* known as "The Soldiers' Friend." Despite a name change three days later to "The Soldiers' Service Bureau," the aims of this new organization remained consistent. To aid and sustain veterans and their families Hearst installed a national Soldiers' Bureau headquarters in Washington as well as branches in every city where a Hearst newspaper was present to advertise daily. One of the bureau's departments provided legal counsel; its members specifically investigated the severity of certain military courts-martial, afforded representation to soldiers involved in lawsuits, and aided military families threatened with dispossession proceedings. Another department attended to veteran employment needs, listing jobs by employers willing to hire returning servicemen, as well as furnishing information to newly formed World War I veteran associations, which in turn dispensed data regarding activities in the workplace. And while one important department attended to the medical needs of discharged soldiers, another tried to hurry the payment of past-due government allotment checks or promote the Hearst plan for allocating six month's pay to all discharged veterans.[50]

Whether or not Hearst was sincere in promoting the fortunes of veterans may have been questionable—at least by his critics—but the results were not. For almost a year, at the expense of the Hearst media empire, he maintained the Soldiers' Bureau at full capacity, supplying nation-wide information to millions of readers while publicizing its accomplishments and successes. Such exertions both in time and money were well worth it. No longer did Hearst suffer the ignominious epithet of traitor, of a pro-German sympathizer devoid of loyalty and patriotism. He was now the foremost friend of returning veterans, the defender of their individual rights, the protector of the downtrodden and the dispossessed.

For proof Hearst had only to point to the results of his efforts in New York City. "Wounded Heroes Thank Mayor for Appointing Mr. Hearst," one *American* headline blared. "Veterans Glad Publisher Will Welcome Men Home." Eventually more than 7,000 signatures adorned a memorial expressing appreciation of his efforts in their behalf. Of course, such daily publicity about the Veterans' Bureau in all Hearst papers solidified the growing popularity of his media empire. While circulation in the *American* remained above 1 million sales daily, the *San Francisco Examiner* outdistanced its nearest competitor in advertising by more than 30 percent. Hearst had not only weathered the vicious attacks of his business and political adversaries but was thriving at their expense.[51]

Hearst, however, was planning to increase the protective armor of his "shield" and the potent threat of his "sword" with further expansion of his media empire. Within the year he would purchase the *Washington Times* and the *Wisconsin News* (Milwaukee) as well as acquire the services of the widely acclaimed Ray Long, who immediately became one of his most valuable magazine executives. Then on March 12, 1919, Hearst entered a new field of media endeavor, that of motion pictures. In conjunction with Adolph Zukor, president of the Famous Players-Lasky Corporation, Hearst signed an agreement to form Cosmopolitan Productions. The *American*, while stating that this merger involved approximately $5 million, gave no specific details. But no matter what the cost, Hearst was delighted. Given his special passion for the theater and its participants, he now had a personal interest. Besides, he had supreme confidence in his own ability.[52]

Yet Hearst, while riding this new high in business and politics, became painfully aware of the uncertainty of life. His beloved mother, Phoebe, who had devotedly nurtured and schooled him through childhood, who had continually supported his business and political ventures with an open pocketbook, and who had been a constant, stabilizing force in his life, became dangerously ill. While visiting him in New York during the Christmas season of 1918, she contracted a cold and eventually influenza, which soon reached epidemic proportions in Europe and the United States. Upon returning to California in February, Phoebe appeared to have weathered the worse effects of the disease. But late in March she had a relapse, so severe that Hearst and Millicent embarked by train on March 27, arriving at the Hacienda del Pozo de Verona in Pleasanton four days later. During the next week she seemed to rally. But at 4:30 P.M. on April 13, 1919, with family and close friends at her bedside, Phoebe Apperson Hearst drifted into a peaceful sleep and died. She was seventy-six years old.[53]

For almost a week Californians, as well as many Americans, grieved the loss of this remarkable lady who had contributed so much to the American way of life and the many people that she touched personally. She was much admired as a woman who used her money wisely. Over forty years she had contributed more than $20 million to a number of philanthropies, with special emphasis on education. She was one of the first sponsors of free kindergartens in the United States, personally financing seven in the San Francisco area alone. In close conjunction with such activities for children, she helped establish the first Parent Teachers Association, which rapidly attained prominence nationwide. She also endowed free libraries at Anaconda, Montana, and Lead, South Dakota; the National Cathedral School for Girls in Washington, D.C.; and a chair in American History at Mills College in Oakland. In 1897 she became the first woman regent of the University of California–Berkeley. During her twenty-two-year tenure she was its greatest contributor and most prominent backer—in land, equipment for various departments, scholarships for women, and buildings. But as far as she was concerned, her greatest contribution to the United States was her beloved and only son, William Randolph Hearst.[54]

The death of Phoebe was a significant turning point in the life of Hearst. In a handwritten will of twenty-two pages, replete in its specificity, she designated him as the major legatee. While denying him such properties as the Hacienda, the Hearst Building in San Francisco (to her five grandsons), and Wyntoon in northern California (to Ann Flint), she did bequeath the million-acre Babicora Ranch in Chihuahua to him as well as the 275,000-acre ranch along the Southern California coast, known as San Simeon. After consigning approximately $500,000 in gifts to servants and friends and relatives, she left the remainder of her estate to him, well over $11 million. At age fifty-six, Hearst was a man of inherited wealth, owning massive amounts of property. But he had lost a steadying influence in his life. In the years to come he would sorely miss Phoebe's constraining hand and loving support.[55]

4 Notable Successes Except in Politics

By 1919 William Randolph Hearst had not yet realized his lifelong ambition, the illusive dream of achieving high public office, specifically that of being elected President of the United States. Despite considerable wealth, outstanding organizational skills, and exceptional talent bordering on genius, he exhibited character flaws that had thus far denied him that goal. For all of his adult life Hearst had headed one or more businesses in which employees followed his dictates without question. He alone was responsible for all corporate policies and business decisions in the Hearst media empire; he alone was accountable—and that was the way he wanted it. Upon rendering a judgment, he brooked no compromise, unless some unforeseen occurrence or event changed the dynamics of the situation. But whatever the final decision, he expected immediate compliance. As a result, every one of his business enterprises exhibited a definite egotism, a reflection of the owner's utmost command as well as his remarkable achievements, with the Hearst name appearing repeatedly throughout the pages of his newspapers and magazines.

In politics, similar modes of action also prevailed. During a campaign Hearst enjoyed (indeed demanded) center stage; he never liked playing second fiddle to anyone, unless he chose such a role. Even then, most of the election reports in the *New York American* and *Evening Journal* tended to focus more on him than the nominee. When victorious, he predictably became disenchanted with the anointed official. And no wonder! Hearst was a progressive in domestic and foreign affairs, a reformer with high expectations, the most powerful media mogul in the world with definite viewpoints and specific programs. Whether the newly elected official was mayor or governor or president of the United States, Hearst expected promised agendas and party platforms to be implemented—without delay. He also appreciated a certain amount of homage from the anointed candidate as well as demonstrated gratitude, either through public recognition or political patronage that was proportional to his campaign efforts.

For those who disappointed him, the results were again predictable. His editors employed the Hearst crusade technique of personal denigration and character assassination—critical editorials, provocative political cartoons, negative testimonials, and slanted news stories—which lasted over a period of weeks, months, even years. Hearst thus engendered a climate of bitterness, a residue of hatred, long remembered (and seldom forgiven) by the targeted politician and his supporters. As a consequence, Hearst's enemies were numerous, bitter, and aggrieved. Over the past twenty-three years (since 1896) only one candidate had continued to warrant his endorsement and support—New York City Mayor John Hylan, whom opponents sneeringly referred to as a "Hearst flunkie" or "toady" or "stooge."

Hearst, because of an unwillingness (or inability) to play the game of party politics, had incurred further opposition to his dream for public service. Time and again over the years he had endorsed a candidate, regardless of party, who agreed with his ideas and policies, who would give him a chance to make a difference. If a viable choice did not appear, he formed temporary coalitions or, on one occasion, a new party, the members of which appreciated him and, more importantly, did his bidding. After 1910, because national Democrats seemed to embrace progressive planks more readily than Republicans and since third party movements in the United States had proven unsuccessful, Hearst returned to the Democratic fold. But once again he demonstrated inconsistencies. From 1913 to 1917 his media empire had been the most severe critic of the Wilson administration both in domestic and foreign policy, then during the war years of 1917 and 1918 its staunchest supporter.

On the local level, Hearst had fought bitter battles with Tammany Hall for control of New York City, demonstrating the awesome power of the Hearst media "sword" to deliver devastating defeats to the enemies of the people. But again inconsistency prevailed. During several campaigns in New York City he merged forces with Tammany chief Charles Francis Murphy, who had been the express target of many Hearst editorials and political cartoons. Thus Hearst exhibited politics at its sordid worst, his enemies concluded, by compromising principles and ethical conduct for the sake of victory and personal ambition.

Hearst, however, always had the capacity to rationalize such actions, to justify any campaign alliance or political strategy. To his way of thinking the answer was ridiculously simple to grasp. His leadership was essential.

He continually announced that his newspapers and magazines expressed the will of the people, much more so than politicians who placed party over principle and definitely more than businessmen who catered to personal profit over public programs that would benefit the needs of the American people. He therefore decided to undercut those in power by appealing directly to the public. His long-range plans were to enlarge the Hearst media machine of government by newspaper significantly, appeal directly to the people on a daily basis, and thereby achieve his ultimate goal of public service through the popular support of his readers. In May 1919, Hearst still believed that the presidency was an attainable objective.[1]

But for the moment Hearst had to focus on pressing personal problems. Issues arose over the settling of his mother's estate. He willingly accepted most of the codicils in her will, but not all. In an attempt to escape paying a huge estate tax ($949,101), he sought legal clarification that the million-acre Babicora Ranch in Chihuahua was already in his possession; Phoebe had transferred its stock to him a month before her death. He also testified that his mother had showered him with gifts and loans over the past twenty-five years worth "many millions," but required him to repay only $300,000 at 5-percent interest; she believed that such an arrangement would strengthen his business credit. At the same time Hearst strenuously objected to one provision in the will; Phoebe deeded to Ann Flint, her niece and confidante of more than twenty years, Wyntoon Castle, the beautiful summer home on the McCloud River near Mount Shasta in northern California (Siskiyou County). Hearst was determined to keep this property. In 1925, after years of bitter wrangling, he purchased Wyntoon from her for $198,000, achieving his objective but gaining a lifelong enemy. And as one final act of independence (or defiance), he instructed Adele Brooks, whom Phoebe had designated as her official biographer, to "turn over to him" all research and manuscript materials concerning his mother. Then in 1928 he commissioned Winifred Black Bonfils, a trusted employee of thirty years whose pen name was Annie Laurie, to write the official biography. After twelve days and 54,000 words, she completed her assignment. Hearst then published this cosmetic account, a handsomely bound volume replete with errors and misstatements, titled *The Life and Personality of Phoebe Apperson Hearst.* Her life would, and did, merit the attention of future biographers.[2]

Hearst readily approved another condition of his inheritance, with great anticipation. Phoebe deeded him the rugged tract of land known as San Simeon, encompassing approximately 175,000 acres from the Bay of San Simeon to the craggy Santa Lucia Mountains. Some 250 miles north of Los Angeles and an equidistance south of San Francisco, the ranch, as he called it, was a fulfillment of his boyhood dreams. With his father George, he had experienced the joys of roughing it in this beautiful coastal wilderness, sleeping under the stars, hunting and fishing for sport and sustenance, riding spirited and free over wild, tortuous mountain terrain. Early in the 1890s, Hearst had rewarded certain members of his *San Francisco Examiner* staff by inviting them for weekend excursions to San Simeon—a summons that no one dared refuse. And while residing in New York, whenever time and opportunity permitted, he invariably returned to his California roots, seeking solace and respite from the pressures of the world. By the 1910s he had established a temporary tent city on a mountaintop 1,600 feet above sea level, which he called Camp Hill. From this spectacular location overlooking the Pacific Ocean—the eventual site of the Hearst Castle—Hearst entertained family and guests, while dreaming of future plans.[3]

Hearst had a hunger for owning land, for possessing unobtainable treasures of art and invaluable works of literature, for creating a permanent monument that would be a lasting memory to his existence. San Simeon became the embodiment of all such goals and ambitions; it was his lifelong project and a never-ending passion.

Not surprisingly, Hearst wanted to fulfill his dream as soon as possible after his mother's funeral. In May 1919, he sought the expertise of California architect Julia Morgan. He would not be disappointed; she had the credentials that bolstered her ability and talent. In 1902, after having earned a prestigious certificate from the Ecole des Beaux-Arts in Paris, she returned to the United States and within two years set up an office in San Francisco. Although slight of build at five feet and less than one hundred pounds, a "tiny woman" distinctive in appearance in tailored suits and French silk blouses, which went almost unnoticed by her display of large horn-rimmed glasses and an outlandish old-fashioned hat on her petite head, she was nonetheless a consummate professional. Phoebe Hearst had commissioned her for a number of projects at her lavish California estate at Pleasanton as well as for several buildings at the University of California–Berkeley—and always with satisfactory results. In turn, Hearst had contracted Morgan to design his *Los Angeles Examiner* building in 1915.[4]

While the physical contrast between Morgan and Hearst was readily apparent—and in stark contrast—the similarities between the two made for a successful relationship that lasted for more than two decades. From the very beginning, they "just clicked," Morgan associate Walter Steilberg marveled. Both were workaholics, expending unbelievable amounts of energy in their quest for excellence, often exhausting those about them. In their respective businesses both exuded a brilliance, and a formality, that continually awed associates and clients alike. And in these business enterprises they left no doubt who was boss. Yet even more important in this relationship Hearst and Morgan admired each other, an association that turned into a lasting friendship. On more than one occasion she acknowledged that he could have been an outstanding architect; in turn, he truly valued her ability and expertise.[5]

For the San Simeon project, Hearst and Morgan were, Steilberg observed, "long distance dreamers." She was able to identify with his hopes and aspirations, to visualize the end result of a magnificent undertaking. Hearst, even though floating a number of ideas concerning a specific path for his grand venture, needed sympathetic perception and professional direction. During their first year together Morgan gradually began to understand the Hearst mind-set. He was not so much interested in constructing living quarters on what he began to call la Cuesta Encantada (the Enchanted Hill) but "a museum of Renaissance art," a structure unique in design and appearance that would house fabulous treasures of the ages. He wanted to display the things he bought and they had to be used and presented in a creative setting.[6]

After visiting San Simeon for the first time on August 9, 1919, Morgan began developing the Hearst dream. She and Hearst had already agreed on a general plan that included a big master house (Casa Grande) that would dominate three sizable guest houses, which were named House A (Casa del Mar), House B (Casa del Monte), and House C (Casa del Sol).

But procedure and implementation were major problems. They hoped to have the main building completed by the middle of September, which proved to be impossible. Hearst, as well as Millicent, constantly modified and revised the size and content of the individual structures. They also could not decide which building to erect first. In addition, such building materials as wood, brick, and "a remarkable good grade of concrete" were hard to come by and costly. Just to haul these building materials five miles over a winding, narrow trail (euphemistically called a road) to this out of the way mountain retreat was extremely expensive. And to maintain a permanent workforce on location was equally troubling; laborers and their families required adequate housing and satisfactory living conditions. Employment was therefore a chronic concern. As a result, Hearst decided that Morgan should manage (with helpful suggestions from him) these mundane, day-to-day problems, while he focused on financing San Simeon.[7]

Because of his fascination with motion pictures, together with a firm belief that film was "an uplifting and penetrating force" with tremendous "potential for communication with the masses," Hearst devoted both time and energy to his newly formed enterprise, Cosmopolitan Productions. During the spring and summer of 1919 he became involved in the intricacies of the ever expanding movie industry. He surely had specific priorities. Marion Davies, at a beginning salary of $500 a week, would be the star of Cosmopolitan; Hearst publicity as well as a personal interest in her career would see to that. To ensure her continued success, he sought organizational support, no matter what the cost. Ray Long, who was both editor and consultant of his magazines, unofficially began acquiring compelling stories by outstanding authors, whose works would appear in Hearst's *Cosmopolitan, Good Housekeeping,* or *Harper's Bazaar;* in turn, Cosmopolitan Productions would receive first option for a movie script, thereby abetting the Hearst ambition of turning out twenty-four pictures a year. As a further help, Hearst founded the International Story Company in New York City (at 145 West 45th Street) in order to obtain motion picture rights to books, short stories, and plays. In the meantime he sought to hire Joseph Urban, Flo Ziegfeld's fabulous visual illusionist, as his film production designer. In February 1920, after months of Hearst's irresistible persuasion, Urban signed on at the unprecedented salary of $1,200 a week. To complete this grand organizational scheme Hearst bought Sulzer's Harlem River Park Casino, a former New York City amusement center at Second Avenue and 127th Street. By the spring of 1920 he had transformed this project into his own movie studio, typically for Hearst at great expense.

In regard to the overall administration of Cosmopolitan Productions, Hearst again reflected tendencies of egotism, of a disposition to excel. Despite his multifarious and time-consuming business interests, he was determined to maintain control, to oversee and govern his newest media venture. Or as one biographer put it, he intended to be "the top mogul of all cinema impresarios." When his partner Famous Players-Lasky, which became better known as Paramount Pictures, urged him to remove or reassign certain top Cosmopolitan executives, as well as relinquish the presidency, Hearst reacted predictably. At first he stalled any decision making, then perceptibly cooled to such suggestions before concluding, as film historian Louis Pizzitola noted, that "the business methods of Famous Players were unethical and that the hierarchy of the organization was not to be trusted." Within three years Hearst would free himself of such obligations and, true to form, maintain his favorite role, that of leader, alone at the top—and unchallenged.[8]

On September 14, 1919, after five months in California, Hearst ended his West Coast sojourn upon learning that Millicent's mother (Mrs.

George M. "Mama" Willson) had died at the family summer home on Long Island. Upon his return to New York, however, he enjoyed no respite from activities, no lull in demands on his time, because state politics forced him onto center stage. For the onrushing events that developed over the next seven weeks he was mainly responsible—and rather foolishly so.

Hearst was never a patient political follower. After an election he expected his candidate either to fulfill campaign promises or demonstrate proper appreciation for Hearst support through some sort of public acknowledgment. In the case of Democratic Governor Al Smith of New York, who took office on January 1, 1919, neither occurred. As a result, Hearst expounded upon what he considered to be proper excuses for a critical reevaluation of his support. On May 10, after Smith bypassed several Hearst nominees and appointed Robert L. Luce to a vacancy on the state supreme court, the *New York Times* reported that Hearst might have broken with the governor. To suppress this rumor, Hearst cabled from California that he had recommended no one. But he was not convincing. Obviously upset, he concluded that his support of the governor had more to do with Smith's Republican opponent, who was discreditable and therefore a greater evil to the people. Within the next ten days Hearst continued to register his unhappiness in several editorials concerning recent gubernatorial appointments. For instance, Luce had been a lobbyist for the New York Central Railroad, a tool of the Traction Trust, who would undermine progressive legislation for municipal ownership—meaning cheaper subway fares for the people. If such irresponsible patronage continued, Hearst announced in bold headlines, "HEED THIS WARNING, GOVERNOR, or YOU ARE CERTAIN to FAIL."

Whether fearing that Smith might be a Democratic rival for the presidency in 1920 or merely reacting in a fit of pique to his lack of influence in Albany, Hearst continued an all-out media assault. He decided to focus on an emotional issue, one that would arouse immediate consternation and anger, thereby inflicting further criticism on Smith. He accused the governor of allowing two state commissioners, who were responsible for regulating the price of milk (at the outrageously high price of twenty cents a quart) and who were presently under indictment by the New York County grand jury, to continue to prey on the public. And even though the governor correctly replied that he had no jurisdiction to remove these men, the *American* and *Evening Journal* had a field day. Throughout the summer and fall Hearst cartoonist Frederick Opper characterized Smith, almost daily, as a pawn of the Milk Trust who alibied to pleading mothers that "my hands are tied." In turn, Hearst editors charged that "Governor Smith is whimpering and whining" about his lack of power in this crisis, while "babies in New York are dying for lack of milk."[9]

Al Smith, who had successfully worked his way up the leadership ladder of Tammany Hall, was a veteran in the rough-and-tumble game of New York politics. Although vilified in the past by experts, he had never experienced the Hearst treatment. As a consequence, during September and October, as the newspaper assaults on his character and administration increased in vitriolic intensity, he reached his limit of suffering and abuse. Regardless of the political consequences, he decided to meet head-on his chief antagonist, without question the most powerful publisher in the world, who bought ink by the barrel. On October 26, to the surprised delight of many New Yorkers, Smith, breathing fire, challenged Hearst to a joint debate over their differences concerning public issues. At his own expense, he rented Carnegie Hall for the night of October 29 and guaranteed Hearst and his supporters half the tickets.[10]

Whatever the reason, whether realizing that the governor was an accomplished and consummate debater, that he actually had a defensible argument concerning the milk issue, or that he might indulge in personal scandal, Hearst refused the challenge. In such an encounter he would be the one at risk—and he knew it. So his course was clear. Immediately Hearst issued to the press this scathing reply. "I have no intention of meeting Governor Smith publicly or privately, politically or socially. I do not have to meet him, as I am not running for office, and I certainly do not want to meet him for the pleasure of the association, as I find no satisfaction in the company of crooked politicians." For that matter, Hearst announced, "neither have I time nor inclination to debate with every public plunderer or faithless public servant whom my papers have exposed, for the reason that every pilloried rascal in every city where my papers are published always tries to divert attention from the real issue of his political crookedness by making some sort of a blatherskite onslaught upon me."

As a result, Hearst made no apologies for attacking the Milk Trust and the Traction Trust and the politicians who had surrendered to those rich and powerful plundering corporations that foisted on the public twenty-cent milk and ten-cent streetcar fares. He also had "no apologies to make for not supporting the judicial section hands of the New York Central Railroad or any of Mr. Murphy's hand-picked appointments to the bench." In fact, "the only apology I would have," Hearst specified, was "for having supported Governor Smith" who had "repudiated" his pledge to progressive initiatives and proved himself to be "utterly faithless and unreliable." And as for the meeting at Carnegie Hall, Hearst sarcastically commented, "distribute all your tickets to the Milk Trust and the Traction Trust and the politicians they own and the judges they are seeking to control." For that matter, he concluded, "if you . . . are going to hire Carnegie Hall every time my papers expose rascally politicians, you would better take a long-term lease on the property."[11]

Following this blistering rejection, Hearst published a brutal, full-page editorial in the *American* and *Evening Journal* the next day just prior to the proposed confrontation. Over an artist's creation depicting a distraught and forlorn couple with three starving children, together with a photo of Smith, a fist-size headline read, "ANSWER THESE PEOPLE, GOVERNOR SMITH. They Would Like to Know Why You Are Helping the Milk Trust and Traction Trust and Doing Nothing for Them." Then a barrage of debasing questions, one after another, followed.[12]

This media onslaught would have devastated almost any Hearst opponent. But Al Smith, an Irish Catholic from a poor family who was reared within the sounds and smells of the Fulton Fish Market on the East Side of New York City, proved to be the exception. To friends and associates alike he displayed his contempt and anger, emotionally reacting to this challenge. Hearst was like a "cuttlefish" (squid), he proclaimed, whose "foul, dirty pen" continually spewed forth ink both black and slimy. Those "filthy sheets," the *American* and *Evening Journal*, had upset not only his wife and children but especially his ailing, elderly mother who in a delirium reportedly had murmured, "My son did not kill babies." And now, after this latest Hearst editorial, he raged within, more determined than ever to expose the "greatest living enemy of the people."[13]

At Carnegie Hall on the night of October 29, 1919, Smith was at his political best, much like a fine-tuned surgeon intent on saving the New York body politic by deftly removing the cancerous growth within. From the outset he created the tone for the evening with ruthless effect. He appeared on stage together with an empty chair. Then dramatically he began: "Mr. Chairman, fellow citizens: I am going to ask for your absolute silence and attention. (Applause.) I feel that I am here tonight upon a mission as important not only to myself but to this city, to this State, and to this country. (Applause)." And "of course," as he gestured toward the chair, "I am alone. (Laughter and applause.) I don't know whether the chairman of the committee expected that I would be alone, but I knew that I would. (Laughter.) And I felt that I would because I knew the man to whom I issued the challenge. (Applause.) And I know that he has not got a drop of good, clean, pure red blood in his whole body. And I know the color of his liver, and it is whiter, if that could be, than the driven snow."

For the next hour, to the delight of the crowd, Al Smith denounced and denigrated the absent Hearst. On the differences between them, such as judicial appointments, subway fares, milk prices, he established the logic of his arguments, then pointed out where, in each instance, Hearst had lied and deceived and misrepresented. And why, Smith asked the Carnegie Hall audience, had "this man" taken upon himself to assail the governor of New York "in this reckless manner"? Surely "it has got to be jealousy, it has got to be envy, it has got to be hatred or it has to be something that nobody understands." But regardless of the reason, Smith fervently concluded, his own purpose was clear. He intended "to stay the danger that comes from . . . [the Hearst] papers," then rid New Yorkers of that "pestilence that walks in the darkness."[14]

With the absent Hearst successfully rebuked, Al Smith achieved a political stature hitherto unrecognized on the national scene; and emboldened by his apparent victory, he attacked the Hearst media empire at every opportunity. He continually delighted New Yorkers by referring to the *New York American* as the "Mud-Gutter Gazette," which persisted in "spreading lies and misinformation" and "Editorially" it was "in a class by itself." With malicious glee, Smith identified Hearst as that "millionaire ranch owner from California" who on more than one occasion, instead of relieving "distress and suffering among the poor," profited handsomely at their expense.[15]

Hearst, however, had the unusual ability to suffer defeat without affecting his psyche negatively; indeed he continually displayed a remarkable resourcefulness, an all-pervading confidence to overcome any perversity or setback. Within a week he was proclaiming victory over Smith. In the state elections of November 4, voters repudiated the goverener's appointee to the supreme court Robert L. Luce (whose selection Hearst had opposed the previous May) as well as his Democratic running mate Irvin Untermyer. In summing up the election, Hearst exultantly declared in an editorial that "Resentment at Boss Interference with the Judiciary," meaning Tammany Hall and Smith, was the ultimate result. And of course Hearst claimed that much of the credit for this defeat belonged to his newspapers.[16]

Hearst was also able to disassociate himself from any setback for another reason—an incredibly busy schedule that would have undone most men. He had an innate and rare talent to compartmentalize his activities, to keep separate and distinct his multiple business operations and personal interests. In 1919–1920, he displayed this talent repeatedly. In regard to his newspapers, he became anxious when the cost of paper rose exorbitantly. He therefore purchased a paper mill along with twenty acres of timberland near Watertown, New York, as well as increasing the price of all his dailies from two to three cents and the Sunday newspapers from five to ten cents. After lengthy negotiations through intermediary Charles Francis Neylan, he decided to buy the *San Francisco Call* in May 1919, further expanding his influence and power. Within the next nine years he would enlarge his media empire to twenty-eight newspapers in nineteen cities.

At the same time Hearst was corresponding almost daily with Julia Morgan concerning ongoing developments at San Simeon. Despite the high costs of maintenance and building, he agreed to lay out a five-mile, tar-topped road from San Simeon Bay to Camp Hill and to the initial construction of three cottages (identified as A, B, and C) of a Renaissance style, but not strictly Spanish. Typical of his passionate interest in San Simeon as well as a mastery for detail and specificity was a letter to Morgan on February 9, 1920, in which he assessed that plans for House A were "wholly satisfactory," then proceeded to write five pages of detailed suggestions.[17]

But these time-consuming interests were by no means the extent of his involvements. In 1920 Hearst became even more heavily committed to Hollywood. Since he maintained that making pictures was "fundamentally like making publications . . . in each case an endeavor to entertain and interest, enlighten and uplift the public," he stressed the importance of producing pictures with class. Because his goal for Cosmopolitan Productions was twenty-four movies a year, he spent a considerable amount of time enlisting talented directors, actresses, and screen writers to long-term contracts.

Nor was cost ever a deterrent. The word "cheap" was not part of the Hearst vocabulary. He intended to produce quality pictures that, unlike his newspapers, would attract an elite audience. For instance, during the filming of *When Knighthood Was in Flower* (released in September 1922) starring Marion Davies, Hearst insisted on authentic costumes and scenery, regardless of the expense. One story, which became part of Hearst lore, summed up his investment in Hollywood. When recognized at a film industry dinner in New York City in March 1922, he responded with insightful observations about his experiences in moviemaking. He then jokingly concluded, "When anybody asks me if there is any money in motion pictures, I say: 'You bet your life! All mine!' "[18]

Because of personal ambitions as well as an intense interest in politics, Hearst also committed much of his time in 1920 to the complicated national issues of the day. Once again he was at odds with the leadership of the Democratic Party, particularly regarding foreign policy. After the end of World War I on November 11, 1918, Woodrow Wilson had embarked, Hearst believed, upon a disastrous course for the United States. In December, the president had mistakenly opted to lead a huge American delegation to a peace conference in Paris instead of "tending to business" at home. After six months of wrangling over the spoils of victory—and after a number of compromises and concessions—the leaders of England, France, Italy, and the United States, known as the Big Four, finally produced the Treaty of Versailles. Wilson was displeased with many of its provisions, such as requiring Germany to admit "war guilt," being stripped of its colonial possessions, and being saddled with a huge war debt. But he held steadfastly to one unshakable principle—the establishment of a League of Nations, and particularly to Article 10, which pledged all member nations to "respect and preserve . . . against external aggression the territorial integrity and existing political independence of all Members of the League."[19]

Hearst adamantly opposed the Wilson proposition. The policy of the United States should be, he announced, that of enlightened self-interest, a theme of "America First," which George Washington had wisely enunciated in the 1790s as no entangling alliances. Supporting the League of Nations, especially with the inclusion of Article 10, would drag future generations of Americans into the maelstrom of needless European conflicts.[20]

Hearst thus launched a media crusade, lasting for almost two years, to defeat American acceptance of a League of Nations. And although a number of factors came into play to bring about a successful opposition in the U.S. Senate, Hearst surely was responsible for helping crystalize the thoughts of his 10 million readers to oppose the president's plans. Across the country Hearst editors applied the time-tested and proven techniques of past campaigns, which Hearst called "government by newspaper." Specifically they supplied editorials, accompanied by provocative political cartoons, a barrage of testimonials and slanted stories, all with the same theme: condemning the League and putting "America First." Senator Hiram Johnson of California clearly illustrated the Hearst influence on the public and the U.S. Senate. As early as January 19, 1919, in a letter to one of his sons, he wrote, "I dislike to say it, but Hearst is eternally right in saying that our difficulty has been the past two years that we were Pro-Belgian, Pro-English, Pro-French—anything but Pro-American, and that it is time to be Pro-American now."[21]

This crusade against the League, which displayed robust overtones of patriotism accompanied by harsh condemnations of the Wilson administration—and the president personally—greatly affected the Hearst political stance in 1920. Since the president was determined to make acceptance of the League of Nations a major issue in the upcoming election, Hearst set forth his own political agenda. As expected, his first option was to seek the Democratic nomination for the presidency. But after several feelers to test his viability as a candidate, he decided to delay a major push for that office until 1924.

Hearst thus reverted to a second option; he would vigorously support fellow Californian Hiram Johnson, the former running mate of Theodore Roosevelt and the Progressives in 1912, who was an avowed opponent of the League. During the spring of 1920 the Hearst media empire expounded nationwide on Johnson's outstanding political attributes, especially his ability to unite all Progressives under the banner of the Republican Party. As the party nominee and with Hearst's support, he would be an easy victor in November.

If such arguments were not persuasive enough, Hearst raised one more: the specter of a Constitution Party, with Johnson as the nominee, thereby draining off much needed Republican voter support. To emphasize all such appeals or threats, Hearst with an impressive staff of *New York American* writers (including Arthur Brisbane, William Jennings Bryan, Damon Runyon, and Ring Lardner) attended the Republican National Convention in Chicago early in June. But their efforts were to no avail. Despite numerous stories of disaffection and bolting to a third party if Johnson were not the nominee, Republican delegates selected Warren G. Harding of Ohio.

Nor were Democrats any more disposed to heed another option of the Hearst agenda—a plank in the party platform rejecting the League of Nations. Upon meeting in convention at San Francisco late in June, national delegates nominated, after forty-four ballots, James M. Cox of Ohio, who pledged to endorse Wilson's League.[22]

Yet Hearst enjoyed moments of exhilaration and triumph at the San Francisco convention. Much to his delight he had achieved celebrity status. He was, the *New York Times* reported, an object "of curious interest." Any number of "western delegates," upon learning that he was dining at the Palace Hotel in San Francisco, asked that someone point him out, then gawkingly commented within earshot: "Well, that's Hearst, hey? Big fellow, ain't he?" Then on the night of July 2, when the Democratic convention began its initial roll call for president, he received one vote, his first since running for the party nomination in 1904. These incidents, however slight, boosted his confidence that the presidency was attainable in 1924.[23]

The American Constitutional Party, meeting in Chicago, further encouraged Hearst in his illusive quest. National delegates, "representing

35,000 enrolled members" in six eastern states, called on him to be their nominee, *New York American* headlines blared. Although refusing to allow his name to be placed in nomination, Hearst was pleased that many people considered him a viable candidate and agreed with his ideas. In fact the Constitutional Party platform was an extension of the Hearst newspapers' editorial pages. In regard to foreign policy the delegates rejected the League of Nations and adopted the theme "America First." Concerning domestic issues they advocated such progressive legislation as popular election of federal judges, public ownership and operation of railroads and public utilities, and nationwide enactment of initiative, referendum, and recall.[24]

Not surprisingly, Hearst was ready to forgo such reforms, at least temporarily, if given a chance to make a difference through government service. Despite a constant editorial drumbeat in 1919 and 1920 that under Wilson "there is no Democratic Party today" and that even Republicans might be a better alternative, Hearst was willing to dicker with Democratic nominee James Cox for a cabinet position in return for his support. He proposed, according to President Nicholas Murray Butler of Columbia University, that Cox, if elected in November with the all-out promotion of the Hearst media, would appoint him secretary of the navy.[25]

But with no offer forthcoming and his political options exhausted, Hearst faced some difficult choices in the upcoming November elections. For several months he wrestled between party loyalty and what he considered to be best for the American people. On the national level he continually implored Cox—without success—to "get rid of the millstone" that would defeat him, specifically "to throw off the Wilson yoke" of the League of Nations and "lead a truly Democratic party with true Jeffersonian policies . . . to victory." On the Sunday prior to the election, he urged all Hearst readers to "Vote AGAINST Cox, who is pledged to put us into the Wilson foreign policy League" and "Vote FOR Harding, Republican."[26]

On the state level, Hearst faced an equally difficult proposition—supporting his old nemesis, Governor Al Smith, for reelection. Since late in July the *New York American* and *Evening Journal* had been pitiless in their criticisms, belittling Smith in cartoons and editorials as "Governor Booze," the candidate of the whiskey interests, as well as the lackey of the Milk and Transportation Trusts. Actually Hearst favored Farmer-Labor gubernatorial nominee Dudley Field Malone, who promoted progressive principles but had no chance of winning.

Since the Republican candidate, Judge Nathan L. Miller, was totally unacceptable, Hearst endorsed Smith a week before the November elections, but "with reservations," the *New York Times* observed. The governor's "personal attacks upon me are wholly unimportant. I don't consider them at all." But he did. He could not resist inserting a stinging barb into his Democrat rival. No question about it, Hearst announced in a last-minute editorial, Smith "isn't sincere and isn't truthful and probably will not do what he says he will do," but he "will have to do some of it if he commits himself strongly enough" and "to that extent," Hearst grudgingly reasoned, "he is better than Miller who is an open and avowed tool of the Traction Trust."[27]

On Election Day, November 2, 1920, Hearst again proved, at least to his own satisfaction, the power of government by newspaper. By a landslide vote, Harding defeated Cox, while Miller, partly because of Hearst's lengthy vacillation on whom to support, won a narrow victory over Smith. In a front-page editorial in his newspapers Hearst triumphantly proclaimed that "the League of Nations is dead" and implied that, with new leadership in the state and nation, the "Democratic Party can rise again."[28]

Yet for Hearst such attention to political ambitions, to multifarious business concerns, to the construction of a lasting monument to himself at San Simeon, created problems not easily resolved. Although an indefatigable workaholic, he did not have sufficient time to keep pursuing all of his activities; hence, he had to decide what course his personal life should take.

Over the past several years the choice had become increasingly apparent: total commitment to Marion Davies over wife and family. Since 1917, she had become an integral part of his life. He showered her with gifts, talked with her daily, and, like a lovesick schoolboy, wrote amateurish but heartfelt poetry about his feelings of love and endearment. As a further expression of his devotion he tied her family closer to him. At 331 Riverside Drive (near his Clarendon mansion) he refurbished a townhouse for Marion's mother and sisters while persuading Mayor Hylan to appoint "Papa" Douras as a municipal magistrate. He gave Marion a key to a studio apartment at the Beaux Arts Hotel in New York City and, while in California during the summer and fall of 1920, rented a spacious estate for her near Santa Barbara; he was intent on protecting her from the corrupting influences of Hollywood. Hearst was extremely jealous, often directing trusted employees to keep tabs on her afterwork activities—and for good reason. Marion, when angry and hurt that Hearst had "abandoned" her for business or politics or family, tended to retaliate by having brief affairs. Her biographer Fred Guiles explained it this way. "She was not promiscuous, but she frankly enjoyed human contact—in the bedroom and in the parlor." She considered sex "just another form of pleasure" that was "less exhilarating than a fast Charleston or even a particularly gamey joke."[29]

But despite her hedonistic propensities, Hearst loved Marion and wanted to marry her; his days of philandering were over. And despite an age difference of thirty-four years, she earnestly wished to marry him. One person, however, disrupted their plans—Millicent Hearst. Still quite beautiful, the mother of his five sons, who in 1921 would be mentioned seriously as a Democratic candidate for Congress because of acknowledged civic and philanthropic contributions to New Yorkers over the past four years, Millicent thwarted all such designs. No matter that Millicent either suspected or knew about her husband's infidelities with Marion as early as 1918, no matter that he asked for a divorce in 1920, she would not surrender either her position or title.

The two therefore reached an agreement, not wholly acceptable to either, but livable. She would receive all necessary funds for social and charitable events, for extensive travel, and for the education and well-being of their five sons. He, in turn, would perform public duties as her husband, especially in the environs of New York. Nor would he cause her embarrassment with friends by socializing in the city with "that other woman." By this "civilized" compact, both could pursue their interests without too much interference from the other.[30]

Early in the 1920s Hearst thus engaged in a juggling act, trying to give full vantage to his many business and political pursuits while attempting to keep the women in his life happy and contented. It would not be easy, especially since his involvements were so widespread. For instance, during the winter and spring of 1921 while in New York, he engaged—not too wisely for someone aspiring to high office—in political paybacks. Immediately after World War I, the Reverend William Manning of Trinity Church in New York had questioned Hearst's patriotism and vehemently denounced him. Hearst seldom forgot a public slight. As a result, when Manning sought election in convention late in January 1921, as the Episcopal bishop of New York, Hearst wrote a blistering editorial in the *American*, both inflammatory and demeaning, that questioned Manning's qualifications. He then had newsboys distribute his editorial to attending delegates. Although Manning won in a close contest, Hearst was satisfied; he had repaid a long overdue debt.

Again early in February, he incurred further enmity among Democrats by condemning in a scathing editorial lame duck President Woodrow Wilson as lacking "good judgment and common sense" during his eight years in office and thereby discrediting reform and reformers. To emphasize his point he instituted a suit against Wilson's Secretary of the Treasury David F. Houston to restrain loaning "many millions of dollars more of the people's money to foreign governments." He repeatedly voiced the America First idea, which was also the slogan of his newspapers. And in March, to another inveterate enemy, AFL President Samuel Gompers, he paid his respects by initiating slanderous and contemptible attacks in Hearst publications against Gomper's character and work. Such reactions were gratifying to Hearst. Government by newspaper was continuing to protect the people, while inflicting damage on his enemies.[31]

By April 1921, Hearst could not resist his California connection any longer. San Simeon was beckoning and he responded. Work was going slower than anticipated, because costs were excessive. With Hearst's approval, Morgan had reduced the workforce on Enchanted Hill by one-third, from seventy laborers to forty-six; hence, House A (Casa del Mar) had not as yet been completed. San Simeon was a work in progress, ever changing, ever experimental, due to the whims of its creator. His mastery of particulars was amazing, his demand for uniqueness detailed and precise. He wanted mosaic floors with Byzantine or Roman design, fireplaces of a specific pattern, roofs both waterproof and fireproof, and—in deference to Millicent's wishes—cream-colored marble in the bathroom of House A.[32]

Such "suggestions" were but a few of many. For example, Julia Morgan was convinced that the terrain and terrace were of great significance in creating the special charm at San Simeon. Hearst readily agreed. He accepted her ideas about landscaping, of course with some of his own additions. In a letter on December 15, 1920, he indicated the need for a "great rose garden," then specified that she order thirteen plants. A month later (January 19, 1921) he added yellow roses and purple jacaranda to the list. And after another week he proposed color schemes for each season. Hearst left the "mundane" problems of completion to Morgan (although continually proposing a number of solutions) such as transporting topsoil to his craggy mountain crest, piping water for miles from the nearest springs, hiring a head gardener and crew to care for and tend to the magnificent gardens. As a result, visitors would enjoy blooming flowers the year round and thrill to the "miracle" on Easter Sunday of seeing hundreds of Easter lilies covering the hilltop, "the garden crew having set out the plants during the night."[33]

A major concern for Hearst was the construction of the main building, Casa Grande. He and Morgan agreed that it must be a magnificent museum to display his priceless objects of art, a unique showcase for the ages. He therefore accepted her revised plans that the impressive castle-like structure, of neo-Mediterranean and Spanish colonial style, would have two huge stone towers cast in reinforced concrete, its dazzling white facade dominating the countryside that would inscribe forever his signature on the landscape.[34]

Construction of Casa Grande, which would begin in the spring of 1922, could not come soon enough. Hearst had been buying the treasures of Europe for years, especially from Germany, Spain, Italy, and France. His rule of thumb for collecting was not what the dealers and galleries and auction houses of New York City recommended but what attracted and pleased him. His art purchases were so extensive that he established International Studio Arts Corporation "to purchase art for him and, when necessary, to clear customs." Since childhood Hearst had seldom been denied anything (except in the political realm), and he had stored thousands of precious items in warehouses, mainly in the Bronx but also in San Francisco, San Simeon, and Los Angeles. Hearst therefore eagerly awaited Casa Grande.[35]

But the one major obstacle that could delay all such plans and aspirations was Hearst himself. To enlarge on his dream, to attempt exactitude and create perfection, he was continually changing his mind concerning improvements at San Simeon. Hearst was also aware of his propensities for preciseness. In a letter to Morgan dated March 18, 1920, he wrote, "All little houses stunning. Please complete before I can think up any more changes."[36]

During the summer of 1921 Hearst ricochetted back and forth between the East and West Coasts because of business demands. He enjoyed the challenge of new financial ventures, of confronting problems involved in creating a vast fortune. On several occasions he returned to New York to finalize real estate closings: twenty-five city lots in the Columbus Circle area in anticipation of a twenty-five-story skyscraper to house his various enterprises; the purchase of the seven-story Sherwood Studio Apartments at Sixth Avenue and 87th Street (valued at $1 million) as rental property; and a four-story and basement private dwelling at the corner of 52nd Street and Madison Avenue for an estimated $285,000.[37]

Hearst was also trying to juggle his increasingly limited time between the two women in his life. More importantly, however, he needed to satisfy his personal needs by being with Marion. While vacationing with Millicent and the boys at San Simeon during July 1921, he used any number of excuses—real estate ventures, the chance to purchase some rare item at auction, and hands-on decisions concerning the *New York American* and *Evening Journal*—to return to New York, where Marion was starring in a forgettable film, *Enchantment*.[38]

But early in October Hearst became tired of such deception and, casting all caution aside, hit upon a grand scheme for travel and pleasure. He invited Marion, her sister Ethel, and "Mama" Rose, together with film director William LeBaron, scenarist Luther Reed, and talented set designer Joseph Urban and his daughter Gretl, for a private screening of the soon-to-be-released *Enchantment*. After assembling in New York Harbor aboard his 205-foot yacht *Oneida*, they cruised out from the Hudson River into open water en route for a weekend in Baltimore, whereupon Hearst sprang his surprise. If all were willing, they would continue for a much deserved vacation in Mexico, with him shouldering all expenses.[39]

With all in agreement, the grand tour proceeded as planned. Hearst was always at his best in the combined role of travel guide and host extraordinaire. Without interruption the *Oneida* proceeded from Baltimore to New Orleans, where Hearst treated them to a shopping spree. After all, Gretl Urban recalled, "none of us were [sic] equipped for an extended journey" of six weeks. On to Galveston they sailed, then boarded a train to San Antonio en route to El Paso and the Rio Grande.

Upon entering Mexico, Hearst hired a special train whereupon, in the truistic lilt of an old cliché, he mixed business with pleasure. For the first time since his mother's death he inspected inherited properties in Guadalajara and Campeche, but more importantly the million-acre Babicora Ranch in Chihuahua. Under the regime of Alvaro Obregon, the new president of Mexico, Hearst happily reported that the "country was completely and permanently restored to peace and order." Whereas for almost a decade he had been advocating U.S. intervention in Mexico, he now recommended immediate recognition.

Because of the early training and travel indoctrination by his mother, Hearst never forgot the responsibilities of being the thoughtful host. For instance, while on the train, he usually postponed attending to business matters until the early hours of the morning—by habit Hearst was a night person. At the same time he delighted in buying fresh fruit and tamales for his guests when the train stopped at small villages in the interior. Upon arrival at Mexico City, he located them in the best hotels, escorted them to excellent restaurants, and provided them with entertainment of their choice, on one occasion a bullfight. For appearance sake, Gretl Urban noted, Hearst kept Marion "under wraps, albeit rather elaborate ones," but he did ask her to accompany him to the palatial residence of President Obregon for dinner and a lengthy interview. Then by mid-November, either by private train or the *Oneida*, Hearst returned his guests to their homes while he proceeded to Los Angeles and San Simeon. Millicent now had to face the reality of Marion in their lives.[40]

In Mexico, Hearst maintained a constant dialogue with the editors in his media empire, ever aware of pressing political and business concerns. For instance, since the end of World War I he had crusaded in all of his newspapers for bonus pay for returning veterans, an idea that he supported passionately. Much to his satisfaction President Harding and a majority in Congress agreed. Yet no bill was forthcoming because of funding, meaning the lack thereof. In June 1921, Hearst therefore proposed a national sales tax of 1 percent to solve the problem of heavy budget indebtedness. But still no legislative movement. After frustrating months of delay he decided to spur Congress to action. On October 16, while en route to Mexico, he offered members of the House and Senate an expense-paid trip to Canada for the purpose of investigating its national sales tax, tabbed "the painless tax," which had gone into effect in May 1920. After more than a month of preparation, of cajoling and persuasion by the Hearst media, sixty congressmen were off to Montreal as guests of the *New York American* and *Evening Journal*. From November 27 to December 2 the congressmen engaged in an information-gathering sojourn that the *New York American* termed a success. Even though no legislation was forthcoming, Hearst was pleased. His newspapers were continuing to gain popularity (and circulation) as the "sword" and "shield" of the people, and he could count on veteran support in a presidential bid.[41]

Upon returning from Mexico, Hearst directed an even more important crusade, even though at long distance from California, that took on national significance. New York City Mayor John Hylan was running for reelection. His major opponent, Henry H. Curran, received the strong backing of Republican Governor Nathan Miller, who had defeated Al Smith the previous November. Early in October the contest became personal and bitter. Miller and Curran urged voters to reject John "The Faithful" Hylan, so named for his faithful subservience to "Boss Hearst," who was unquestionably, Curran announced, "the meanest man in public life."

To such public slights Hearst reacted with his own brand of calculated retaliation. The *New York American* and *Evening Journal* launched a three-week crusade of malicious denigration and character assassination. Editorials depicted Curran as the tool of big business, the lackey of the Traction Trust, who was bent upon assessing an outrageous ten-cent fare upon the citizens of greater New York. Stories daily characterized Republicans as the party of wealth and greed, of exclusion and privilege, even to the extent that they had opposed a woman's right to vote (Nineteenth Amendment). In contrast, Hylan was portrayed as the protector of the toilers and working people everywhere, who advocated municipal ownership and a five-cent fare. To illustrate the written word, Hearst cartoonists

Winsor McCay, Frederick Opper, and talented newcomer O. P. Williams unleashed their own brand of artistic poison, derisive in tone and demeaning in substance.[42]

Although Curran predicted victory over "John, the faithful, and his "city hall boss," the outcome was never in doubt. The Hearst media machine in New York City, with a circulation that totaled more than all its rivals combined, once again proved the effectiveness of Hearst campaign techniques. On November 8, 1921, Hylan swamped Curran by more than 400,000 votes. In his moment of victory, the mayor acknowledged what all New Yorkers readily understood. In a telegram to Hearst he gratefully asserted, "I wish to thank you personally for the support given me by the *New York American* and *Evening Journal*. These papers have been consistent in championing the cause of the people and not pretending, as some others, to be with the people while secretly espousing the cause of the interests."[43]

During the remaining days of 1921, Hearst gloried in the favorable conditions enriching his life. San Simeon was progressing steadily with House A (Casa del Mar) almost complete, with B and C under construction, and the groundwork for Casa Grande about to commence. Cosmopolitan Productions was anticipating a stellar year with such major films (starring Marion Davies) as *Brides Play, Beauty's Worth, The Young Diana,* and *When Knighthood Was in Flower*. The huge Hearst media empire, consisting of fifteen newspapers and eight magazines, was prospering to such an extent that Hearst was planning to increase its effectiveness with more acquisitions in 1922. And in regard to personal relationships, he was working out arrangements to keep the women in his life placated, if not content. Marion had enjoyed the six-week grand tour of Mexico, while Millicent, although aggrieved by his lengthy absence during the fall, found solace in his return to New York for Christmas with the family and in accompanying him to the White House on December 27 for lunch with President and Mrs. Harding.[44]

But what excited Hearst most of all by the end of 1921 was the apparent favorable turn in his political fortunes. Never had his quest for the presidency seemed brighter. As a self-proclaimed progressive of long standing, he had seen ideas concerning economic and political reform gain popularity with the American people. In Detroit and Boston, mayors had recently won overwhelming victories under the banner of municipal reform. Political leaders in Chicago, Atlanta, Los Angeles, and San Francisco had acknowledged their appreciation for the continued support of the Hearst newspapers in the fight for urban improvement. John Hylan, his close friend and loyal supporter, had won by a two-to-one margin a second four-year term in New York City after only a three-week campaign by the *New York American* and *Evening Journal*, once again proving the tremendous effectiveness of government by newspaper—the journalistic technique that Hearst had honed and perfected over the past two decades. And with the anticipated extension of the Hearst media empire to other major cities, he would have an even greater impact, he editorialized, in influencing popular sentiment against the private mismanagement of public service corporations and in electing faithful public servants who would "understand and remember" the will of the people.[45]

The most deserving of all such "faithful public servants" would be, of course, William Randolph Hearst. For those Americans who were unaware of this truth, he decided to launch a campaign of public enlightenment, a crusade in behalf of this new-style leader of democracy. Early in January 1922, he initiated his candidacy by appointing trusted employee Lawrence J. O'Reilly to the position of private secretary, with a first assignment to establish Hearst political "unions" in upstate New York. He also instructed longtime confidant Max Ihmsen, who was a veteran in organizing campaigns, to solicit members for William Randolph Hearst clubs across the nation. To keep the political pot boiling, Mayor Hylan announced that New Yorkers should "draft Hearst into office," while Democratic leader Jacob Gerling of Rochester strongly supported this idea by urging a state party ticket in 1922 headed by Al Smith for the U.S. Senate and Hearst for governor. In a planned response, Hearst disclaimed any ambition for high public office, asserting that his role as a publisher was his greatest service to the American people. At the same time, however, in order to counter anticipated attacks for supporting Harding over Democratic nominee Cox in the 1920 presidential election, he editorialized in all Hearst Sunday editions that "citizens must abandon partisanship and blind faith in party platforms" and that "the hope for the future, the guaranty of loyalty to the American people and to American institutions, is not in parties or in platforms, but in men."[46]

Increasingly since 1904, after his unsuccessful bid for the Democratic presidential nomination, Hearst had become a lightning rod in state and national politics, engendering strong loyalties and equally bitter animosities. His race for high public office in 1922 exemplified this premise to the fullest. Late in January 1922, Judge Samuel Seabury, a former supporter turned inveterate foe, whom the Hearst newspapers had refused to support for governor of New York in 1916, began organizing against Hearst and wrote an open letter to Al Smith begging him to combat Hearst. Although Tammany chief Charles Francis Murphy was silent for the moment (Hearst publicity and money had "stung" him badly in several embarrassing defeats), Tammany leader "Big Tom" Foley was not. Because of previous campaigns in which the Hearst newspapers had ridiculed and besmirched his character, he prided himself in being the sworn enemy of Hearst, vowing never to support him. These men were representative of literally hundreds of political figures that the Hearst media had maligned over the years, not the least of whom was Al Smith.[47]

As a result, the Hearst boom for high political office began to wane by April, partly because of growing opposition to his candidacy but also because New York campaign coordinator Lawrence O'Reilly had taken ill and died early in February, creating a significant void in the Hearst political organization.

But Hearst rallied his troops and by mid-April the campaign was back on track. He persuaded Buffalo publisher and close friend William J. Connors, a former state Democratic Party chairman, to help revitalize his sagging political operation. Connors' leadership, together with Hearst money, had an immediate effect. By the end of April a *New York Times* headline blared, "HEARST MEN ACTIVE IN UP-STATE FIELD." Hearst betrayed his eagerness for high office by using an acknowledged political ploy, that of "willing to serve only if drafted by the people." On May 2, after briefly returning to San Simeon to oversee construction, he wired the editor of the *Brooklyn Eagle* in response to a calculated question that asked if he was a candidate. His reply was predictable, but insincere in the eyes of Hearst haters. "I am a rancher, enjoying life on the high hills overlooking the broad Pacific. If you want to talk about Herefords, I will talk to you, but not about politics." He then concluded, "I have no ambition to get into politics unless there be some special reason, and I don't see any special reason," the implication being, at least not yet. With momentum building, especially since Al Smith was continuing to reject all pleas to enter the political arena, the Hearst campaign progressed so well that on May 13 Connors confidently predicted that "Mr. Hearst is going to be nominated for Governor by the Democratic Party."[48]

With his political future seemingly in good hands at the moment, Hearst addressed other pressing matters, namely the juggling process with the two women in his life. Millicent was demanding that he spend more time with his family. And what better way than a trip to Europe! Hearst, although fearing a negative reaction from Marion in regard to a two-month tour, reluctantly agreed. On May 23, he and Millicent, with their three oldest boys (George, Bill Jr., and John), an entourage of servants, and several business associates including Guy Barham (and wife)—he was the publisher of Hearst's newest acquisition, the *Los Angeles Herald*—set sail for England on the *Aquitania*.[49]

Hearst, however, correctly recognized the danger signals to his personal life, Marion was furious. "Neglect," her biographer Fred Guiles noted, "was something she could not abide." Nor to her way of thinking was this European trip necessary. After all, Millicent, who was well aware of their affair, had made it clear that divorce was not an option. So just prior to sailing, Hearst met with Marion in an attempt to appease her, but to no avail. Raging out of control, she began throwing things at him, "an ashtray and her slippers," anything she could lay her hands on. And so the matter stood at the time of departure.[50]

But Hearst could not allow this breech between them to fester. His juggling act thus became more complicated. He wired Marion that "life was not worth living without her" and urged her to take the next liner to England. And when she wired back, "What will you do with the Black Widow?" he assured her that "Millicent was busy with the boys" and that he would have the excuse during the day of attending to his British publishing affairs. She sailed for London.

Hearst located Marion in a luxurious hotel suite and assigned a dignified, white-haired Irishman named James Y. McPeake, the Hearst representative of the British version of *Good Housekeeping*, to escort her to dinner and the theater in his absence. Yet his elaborate preparations proved to be inadequate. During Marion's first days in London, Hearst did neglect her. He would not refuse invitations asking him and Millicent to dine at 10 Downing Street with Prime Minister Lloyd George and thereafter with British publisher Lord Beaverbrook at his country estate.

Then the unexpected occurred. On June 10, 1922, Guy Barham, his *Los Angeles Herald* publisher, suffered severe intestinal cramps and was rushed to the hospital. Two days later, after an unsuccessful operation, he died and the European vacation for Hearst was over.[51]

The Hearsts immediately rearranged their schedules. While Millicent decided to tour Europe for another month accompanied by oldest son George, Hearst devised a more elaborate plan. In support of Mrs. Barham, who was taking her husband's body home, he returned to New York on the steamship *Olympic* with sons Bill Jr. and John. At the same time he provided Marion with a ship's suite, which was separate from his, thereby concealing her presence onboard.

Then in an attempt to win Marion's forgiveness for these unforeseen events that had turned into a vacation fiasco, Hearst made amends in his own inimitable way. During the next several months he spent huge sums of money in her behalf, first in the production of *When Knighthood Was in Flower*, which would open in September, and then in hiring Victor Herbert to compose a special song honoring her. At the beginning of each movie showing in which she was starring, the theater was to play *The Marion Davies March*. Hearst also determined that Cosmopolitan Productions handsomely recompense members of her family, especially her sister Reine Douras as head of International Story Company and brother-in-law George Van Cleve as a corporation executive. Contrary to sordid Hollywood scandals that were gaining front-page headlines with increasing frequency, he sought to keep her reputation unsullied and public image wholesome.[52]

Hearst had also decided to return home because of the topsy-turvy contest for dominance of the New York Democratic Party. During his three-week absence abroad, campaign politics had become increasingly bitter. On June 10 his aggressive state manager Bill Connors had terrified the Hearst haters by confidently predicting that Hearst would take New York by storm and, after serving as governor, would be the next president. Mayor Hylan added to their fears by endorsing Hearst as the kind of man needed for governor. In response, a number of Democratic women organized in opposition, with a *New York Times* headline blaring their sentiments: "Hearst Will Not Do." Loyal supporters of President Wilson prepared to contest the Hearst nomination "to the bitter end," sarcastically stating that they would give the publisher anything but a job. And even though Tammany chief Murphy remained neutral for the moment, "Big Tom" Foley and other "wigwam" leaders continued to be almost universal in their loathing and condemnation.[53]

While the controversy over the Hearst candidacy prompted nationwide interest during the summer of 1922, Al Smith remained above the fray. He maintained, as one of his biographers put it, "the virtue of silence." He had let it be known among close friends that he was enjoying his status as a private citizen and that his job as a successful trucking executive was both financially rewarding and personally gratifying. But as the Hearst campaign gained momentum, especially with no prominent Democrat announcing for governor, Smith realized that silence was no longer an acceptable option. He must give the Hearst haters, as well as his own supporters, something to hold on to, someone to rally around.[54]

Al Smith was the obvious candidate to oppose Hearst, and both men knew it. As governor from 1919 to 1921, he had acquired the experience and knowledge necessary for the duties of that office, as well as strong contacts in the Republican areas of upstate New York. He also commanded the loyalty of the Tammany chiefs, except possibly Murphy and a small coterie of friends, who feared Hearst's political power and were playing it coy for the time being. And of course Smith had a large, built-in constituency—those who detested and feared Hearst.

Above all, Smith realized that he must reenter politics if for no other reason than to stop "the greatest living enemy of the people," who spread distortion and filth with his "Mud-Gutter Gazettes." Almost daily during the summer and fall of 1920 he had endured the outrageous charges that as a "tool of the Milk Trust"—by allowing high prices—he had helped "kill babies." And while Hearst often was willing to forget past political confrontations, especially if he was the principal offender, Smith was not. On August 16, in response to a letter from Franklin D. Roosevelt urging him "to take a stand and tell the people what he intended to do," Smith declared his willingness to assume leadership of the state Democrats and run for governor.[55]

Although briefly discouraged by the Smith candidacy, Hearst was not about to abandon his most cherished dream without a fight. Since the state Democratic delegates would convene at Syracuse during the last week of September, he geared his political campaign into a five-week crusade mode. Within a day his state headquarters announced that "Hearst Won't quit." Then a barrage of support appeared in Hearst papers as he began calling in political chits—those who owed him for past support. In an open statement to voters, New York Justice John Ford pleaded that as "a champion of popular rights against the predatory interests, Hearst was duty bound to run for governor." Former state Attorney General William Schuyler Jackson testified that "no man in the state is better qualified for governor." And Mayor Hylan fervently asserted that "the one man who can restore the State Government to the people, regardless of party politics . . . is William Randolph Hearst."[56]

But the key to the Democratic nomination was Tammany chief Murphy; consequently, Hearst focused on his political importance to Tammany Hall in this election as well as in future ones. For financial reasons but mainly for political purposes, he negotiated the purchase of two upstate newspapers—the *Rochester American* in June 1922 and the *Syracuse American* just prior to the state convention in September. Without question, he was emphasizing (with a capital "E") his importance as the foremost media mogul in the state and nation. All political pundits also knew that he was the most influential person in the Hylan administration; and since the mayor controlled city patronage, the threat of damaging the hopes of Tammany office seekers by opposing Hearst was a given.[57]

So on September 28, 1922, as the Democratic delegates to the state convention at Syracuse began to assemble, both Hearst and Murphy were hoping to reach an accommodation—a powerful ticket headed by Smith for governor and Hearst for U.S. Senate. But Al Smith blocked this solution. Under no circumstances would he accept the position of party leadership if part of the bargain was embracing Hearst as the Senate nominee. To repeated pleas by Tammany supporters and personal friends, Smith answered with a resounding no. He literally loathed the man. "Say, do you think I haven't any self-respect? You can tell Murphy I won't run with Hearst on the ticket and that goes!"

For the next two days a parade of emissaries from Boss Murphy filed before Smith at his convention suite in the Onondaga Hotel, with the outcome always the same. To their entreaties, Smith was "unyielding, stubborn, angry, and hurt." And when one Tammany leader asked, "Why hold these feelings against Hearst? He's willing to forget. Why can't you do the same?" Smith angrily replied, "That fellow nearly murdered my mother . . . Hearst said I killed the babies of New York by allowing impure milk to come into New York City—me, the father of five children. And he knows it was a damnable lie. Remember those pictures of the forlorn looking children and the poverty-stricken mothers? God!"[58]

With Smith obdurate and determined, the question concerning state Democratic leadership was no longer an issue. Murphy and Tammany had savored the idea of incorporating Hearst money and his well-oiled publicity machine into the upcoming political campaign—but not without Smith. The choice was therefore easy. On September 29, they ditched Hearst.

In turn, when notified by Conners and Hylan of this decision, Hearst realized that his eight-month crusade for high office faced a shattering defeat. He therefore dictated the following telegram: "Please be sure not to allow my name to go before the convention. I certainly would not go on any ticket which, being reactionary, would stultify my record and declaration of principles, and which would be a betrayal of genuine democracy. My nomination for any public office is not important, but it is important that the party declare for progressive democratic principles, and show the sincerity of that declaration by nominating men who can be trusted to make it effective."[59]

With the Democrats nominating Al Smith for governor, Hearst attempted to mend political fences by playing the role of the loyal party man. He scotched all rumors that he and Hylan might initiate a third party movement in the upcoming campaign. They both pledged their full support to Al Smith—the *New York American* and *Evening Journal* immediately endorsed the Democratic slate. And on November 7, with a Smith victory of more than 400,000 votes, Hearst was seemingly elated with the outcome.[60]

Hearst had personal reasons to rejoice. The *Times* reported that, because of his stance in the campaign, "word had been sent to friends of

Hearst, if not to Mr. Hearst himself, that Tammany would not oppose any fight he might make for the Democratic nomination for President, but would keep an open mind concerning him." As further encouragement, "Big Tom" Foley announced at a Smith political gathering that "he had buried the hatchet in his long-time feud with William Randolph Hearst." Tammany chief Murphy also publicly extended "the gratitude of the democracy . . . to Mr. Hearst for his hearty and loyal support." And Al Smith, because of the monthlong endorsement by the Hearst organization, might possibly have second thoughts about the publisher and relent in his opposition. Hearst, optimistic by nature and at times oblivious to the negative realities of his political image, still nourished hopes for achieving his most cherished dream. The 1924 presidential election was only two years away.[61]

5 End of a Political Dream

On April 29, 1923, William Randolph Hearst turned sixty, a statistic that did not necessarily delight him. Advancing age was becoming a negative factor in his quest for the presidency of the United States. Overall, his political record was an account of continuing disappointment and disheartening failure. For instance, his latest attempt for high public office had ended in a frustrating debacle. During the first nine months of 1922 he had applied the considerable resources of the Hearst media empire to his election either as governor or senator of New York. But late in September, while in convention, Tammany Hall and the state Democrats had rejected his candidacy. In the ensuing months he played the good soldier by supporting Al Smith for governor, the man responsible for his defeat. And while party leaders applauded such acts of loyalty and good sportsmanship with token promises of future backing, lingering questions remained. How could he trust the word of Tammany chiefs Charles Francis Murphy and "Big Tom" Foley, who adopted expediency over principle and who sided in any confrontation with his mortal enemy, Al Smith?

As the foremost figure in American journalism and a major player in the growing motion picture industry, Hearst was unwilling to concede that politics was not his forte. An incurable optimist, he maintained that anything was possible: the word "defeat" was not a part of the Hearst vocabulary. He therefore sought another avenue to achieve his objective, one that had produced excellent results in the past: government by newspaper. True to form, Hearst planned on a grand scale; he continued to build a more formidable political base by expanding his journalistic empire and by educating millions of readers to his point of view, as accomplished in the Spanish-American War and hundreds of times thereafter.

Over the past thirty years Hearst had developed and mastered a new mass media culture in the United States. To his way of thinking, he held the pulse of the American people. In other words, he believed that his hopes and trepidations, his likes and dislikes, reflected theirs. As one of the creators of yellow journalism, he had perfected attention-grabbing, fist-size headlines that revealed succinctly and clearly the gist of a story. He appealed to an American society that reveled in stories that, as R. L. Duffus put it, "reduced everything to the common denominator of two or three instincts and passions." Or as another writer vividly commented, "A Hearst newspaper is like a screaming woman running down the street with her throat cut."[1]

Such descriptions, however, were oversimplifications both of the man and his journalism. Hearst was a master salesman and creative showman who, since childhood, had pursued a personal goal of wanting to accomplish something that no one else had ever done. In a constant quest to achieve greater circulation than any competitors, he directed his editors to employ his crusade techniques for just causes in behalf of the American people. For weeks, if not months, he instructed them to present a litany of testimonials endorsing their position, while unleashing biting editorials accompanied by brutally scathing political cartoons. When necessary to bolster a point of view, they embellished the truth in a story and even fabricated photographs as corroborating evidence.

But always the Hearst newspapers, besides being timely and informative, were entertaining. They focused on the sensational, the lurid, the bloodcurdling, the scandalous. Yet whatever the section—news, advertising, opinion, society, sports, entertainment—the material in every department, Hearst proclaimed, had to be "interesting." To his editors, he stressed, that "people do not read to be bored. They read to be interested, and unless we make our material in every department interesting, it simply is not read; in which case," he philosophized, "we would be like the chap who winked at the girl in the dark—we would know what we are doing, but the public would not." Hearst, for better or worse, personified his newspapers. Although any number of Americans disagreed with him and his policies, they never found him boring. Neither he nor his papers could be ignored.[2]

Hearst was determined not to be ignored. During the first months of 1923, he worked to achieve that end. On January 7, he revived his political creation in New York, the Independence League; members then selected Deputy Commissioner of Markets Edward T. O'Loughlin, a loyal Hearst disciple, to replace Lawrence O'Reilly, who had died the previous year. The specific purpose of this organization, the *New York Times* and

New York American announced, was to support "the civic and political aims of William Randolph Hearst . . . throughout the city, state, and nation." At the same time Hearst was seeking to purchase newspapers in major cities to strengthen his government by newspaper campaign. On March 29, he bought the morning *American* and the evening *News* in Baltimore for an estimated $4 million. He now had twenty-two publications in fifteen of the nation's largest cities—New York, Atlanta, Fort Worth, Washington, D.C., Rochester, Syracuse, Boston, Detroit, Chicago, Milwaukee, Seattle, Oakland, Los Angeles, San Francisco, Baltimore—and the number was growing. On April 2, Hearst further extended his political power base by contributing $100,000 (reportedly) to the Chicago mayoral campaign of Judge William E. Dever, who won an overwhelming victory two days later. With Mayor John Hylan of New York and Dever of Chicago in support, Hearst was gearing up for the Democratic presidential nomination of 1924.[3]

During these halcyon days of political success Hearst could not let well enough alone. While on this victory roll, he decided to repay a debt that had rankled him for almost a year—the betrayal by Tammany chiefs Charles Francis Murphy and "Big Tom" Foley at the state Democratic convention the previous September. For weeks Hearst had suspected that Tammany leaders were involved in a number of illegal activities. He therefore assigned city editor of the *New York American* Victor Watson to uncover the truth. During the second week in April 1923, the *American* registered a bonanza. Murphy had brought suit against Louis N. Hartog, who charged that the Tammany boss had realized tremendous profits by helping fix the price of sugar, specifically glucose. In this high-profile case, the Hearst newspapers raised the level of crusade denigration to new heights. They targeted Murphy (of course, with appropriate cartoon caricatures) as the "GLUCOSE FIXER," a political "Czar for whom thousands would grovel." Then after a week of testimony (and vivid, negative recounting in detail by Hearst reporters), the jury voted to acquit Hartog. As the front-page headline of the *American* put it, "Murphy's 10 to 2 Defeat Shocks [Tammany] Tiger; Jury Verdict Worst Blow Handed 'Boss' In His Career." For the moment Hearst was satisfied.[4]

Yet more was still to come. The payback was not complete. At Hearst's insistence *American* editor Watson assigned Nat Ferber, an ambitious reporter who had previously worked for the *Times* but admitted to having a driving need for "windmills to tilt" and "dragons to slay," to unearth further Tammany corruption. Consequently Ferber investigated bucketshops operating in the city. And again a bonanza! He discovered that the firm of F. M. Fuller and Co., which ostensibly accepted orders to buy stocks for

New Yorkers on margin, was secretly bilking them of their investments (commonly described as a bucketshop operation). Fuller declared bankruptcy and thereby defrauded its clients of an estimated $5 million. On three separate occasions city police had caught the firm's major "bucketeers," Edward M. Fuller and William F. McGee, red-handed and had assisted in bringing them to trial. Yet each time a jury acquitted them.[5]

Hearst demanded to know what—or more particularly who—had kept them out of jail. On May 18, after diligent probing, Ferber came up with a name and an organization—"Big Tom" Foley and Tammany Hall. He discovered a canceled check for $10,000 from Fuller and Co. to Foley.

The "bucketshop crusade," so designated by the *American*, now had roots, and the Hearst newspapers gleefully trumpeted their find. Day after day the *American* announced in front-page headlines, as well as in editorials, that "Big Tom" Foley, the political godfather of Al Smith, was a major participant in the Fuller bucketshop. Because of his involvement with "one of the colossal swindling institutions of the age," Foley was responsible, the *American* proclaimed, for stealing "millions of dollars from the savings of comparatively poor people." How many other Tammany bosses were partners in this plundering scheme, the *American* asked? And how many "serviceable judges," controlled by Murphy and Foley, had kept friends of Tammany "out of jail when they have committed crimes and ought to be there?"

Late in August 1923, the crusade began to lose steam. Hearst, however, was delighted with the coverage and encouraged with the probabilities. The U.S. District Attorney's office was investigating charges of bribery, jury tampering, and massive fraud. Bucketeers Fuller and McGee had "made a clear and truthful statement," which would be "of the greatest benefit to the Government in matters now pending." Murphy and Tammany had suffered withering criticism; "Big Tom" Foley was facing a possible jail sentence; and Al Smith, whom Hearst would never forgive, had been linked to Tammany and corruption. For the moment Hearst's payback was complete; life was good.[6]

For most of 1923 Hearst considered himself blessed. His newspapers were remarkably successful. Both the Sunday *New York American* and the *Chicago Herald-Examiner*, although costing ten cents to their competitor's five cents, reached more than a million in circulation, far outdistancing all rivals. In February, the newly purchased *Washington Herald* sold more than 19,000 copies over the previous four months, although raising its price from one to two pennies. The *San Francisco Examiner*, Hearst's first newspaper, "saw all standing Want Ad records shattered—not only for the month of March . . . but for any month during . . . [its] history." With the economy booming in major American cities during 1923, most of the Hearst newspapers were also prospering by following the Hearst formula of journalistic success—the push for greater circulation, hence increased profits because of more advertisements, resulting in the attraction of top newspaper professionals through high salaries. He reportedly had 38,000 persons on his payroll, and for good reason. As friend and confidant Arthur Brisbane noted in his "Today" column on January 5, 1923, "it is a long time since . . . [Hearst] ceased paying his best men as little as $50,000 a year. Some of them he pays three times that, some more."[7]

No matter the field of business, no matter the nature of the enterprise, Hearst strove to excel, to achieve superior results, if not complete dominance—with cost seldom a factor. His motion picture involvement was a case in point. From 1920 to 1922 Hearst became increasingly tired of the relationship between Cosmopolitan Productions and Famous Players-Lasky (Paramount Pictures). To his chief financial officer Joseph Moore, he complained bitterly about the "raw deal" perpetrated by Famous Players in response to his many good faith efforts. As a result, Hearst sought a new alignment for Cosmopolitan, in which trust and friendship were important factors and profits had reasonable expectations. By February 1923, he signed a contract with Goldwyn Producing Company that created a multimillion dollar corporation titled Goldwyn-Cosmopolitan Distributing Company. Both Goldwyn and Cosmopolitan retained an equal 50 percent in film distribution, while a Hearst foreign affiliation, owned and operated by British publisher and film producer Lord Beaverbrook, received "a controlling interest in 80 percent of the first-run movie theaters in England." At Atlantic City late in May, Hearst, accompanied by Brisbane and Joseph Moore, attended a Goldwyn-Cosmopolitan convention for officers and sales representatives, where the two companies formally announced their merger. In a keynote speech to an exuberant audience, Hearst urged excellence in movie making. "The public has been played down long enough," he declared. "In this business as in the publishing business . . . the best produced pictures are all we should devote our attention to."[8]

And toward that end Hearst set his standards of production; toward that goal he directed the career of Marion Davies, the star of Cosmopolitan. Although a talented comedienne in her own right, she followed Hearst's dictates. In the main, she starred in historical extravaganzas (costume dramas) and sentimental romances. In September 1922, the film *When Knighthood Was in Flower* determined the tone: a screenplay involving legendary characters, detailed stage settings in sixteenth-century France and England, as well as authentic costumes of the period—all at great expense. Since *Knighthood* was both an artistic and financial success, Hearst then produced *Little Old New York*, starring Marion Davies, which turned out to be, in reviews by critics, one of her most celebrated movies. She also appeared in a breezy comedy titled *Adam and Eva* before preparing for two costly major films in 1924, *Yolanda* and *Janice Meredith*.[9]

Besides heralding Marion as a superstar, Hearst focused on making Cosmopolitan an overall success. He spared no expense. Despite a devastating fire in his New York studio at 120th Street and Second Avenue on February 18, 1923, which destroyed scenery and costumes and several valuable art works for the in-progress filming of *Little Old New York*, he forged ahead with dogged determination. While transferring production to the Tilford Studio on 44th Street and the Jackson Studio in the Bronx, he constructed the largest set yet devised by a motion picture studio at the Twenty-third Regiment armory in Brooklyn. He then pushed to completion other successful pictures, such as *Under the Red Robe*, an historical drama starring Alma Ruebens, which was his last film with Paramount; *Enemies of Women* with Ruebens and Lionel Barrymore; *Unseeing Eyes*, also with Barrymore; and *Nth Commandment* with Colleen Moore. Already realizing a banner year, Goldwyn-Cosmopolitan prepared for even greater successes, agreeing late in July to distribute forty-four big films for the 1924 season.[10]

But Hearst was not done; his drive to succeed in this new field gathered momentum. For the premiere of *Little Old New York* on August 1, 1923, he purchased and then lavishly remodeled (under the direction of Joseph Urban at a cost of $700,000) the Cosmopolitan Theatre, which the *New York American* publicized as the "most luxurious New York playhouse." An audience of 1,400 was duly impressed with Hearst's showmanship—and extravagance. Viewers faced the screen ensconced in elegantly upholstered chairs "of silk damask, old gold in hue, in frames of mahogany." Loges on two levels, furnished with huge armchairs, extended around the entire balcony while private boxes were even more lavish and "unique" since the occupants reached them by private, self-operated elevators. While Victor Herbert conducted a fifty-five-piece orchestra, the crowd marveled at the surroundings: an enormous Tiffany chandelier thirty-two feet in diameter and forty feet in height, two magnificent hanging tapestries (presumably owned by Hearst) valued at $25,000, walls covered with live flowers and vines, and four newly commissioned portraits of Marion Davies strategically placed.[11]

The Hearst campaign in behalf of Cosmopolitan continued unabated. Daily advertisements of forthcoming motion pictures, together with photographs of and interviews with Cosmopolitan stars (especially Marion), occupied prominent space in all his newspapers. Hearst realized that a gossip-hungry public wanted to know more about the stars of the silent screen. To feed their appetite, he hired Adela Rogers St. Johns to reveal Hollywood secrets in *Cosmopolitan* magazine. Then he employed Louella Parsons, who was a friend and admirer of Marion, as a syndicated gossip columnist for all his newspapers. Late in October he announced that Cosmopolitan was preparing to acquire the necessary real estate to build three new studios in New York City. By the end of 1923, through production, film distribution, and advertising, "Hearst was finally achieving his long time desire," *Variety* noted, "to be on an equal footing with other Hollywood moguls."[12]

Success in different business ventures pushed Hearst to greater expenditure, indeed to inordinate extravagance. As the only son of a wealthy father and doting mother, he had seldom worried about financial concerns. He had followed the simple adage that anything worth having was worth buying, no matter what the cost. In 1923 Hearst, in action and deed, personified that belief. As one biographer put it, "he was easily the nation's biggest spender." For instance, Hearst had a special affinity for real estate, especially in New York City. He continued to buy plots near his Clarendon mansion at Riverside Drive and 86th Street; its appearance was beginning to resemble a luxurious museum that housed his valuable collections. He also bought the thirteen-story Hotel Essex at the corner of Madison Avenue and 56th Street, where he intended to headquarter his magazines. And his accumulation of about twenty-five city lots and more than 70,000 square feet in the Columbus Circle area as rental property was equally impressive—and costly. Then for Cosmopolitan Productions, besides acquiring and refurbishing the Cosmopolitan theater, he purchased a half interest in the magnificent Capitol theater and took out a twenty-one-year lease on the Park theater at Columbus Circle. His purpose, the *New York Times* reported, was to procure a chain of movie houses throughout the country.[13]

This mania for spending, one contemporary pointed out, continued. At Palm Beach, Florida, where the Hearsts often spent the winter, he contracted with architect Addison Mizner, whose reputation for constructing grandiose mansions was well-known, to build one of his expensive creations. Although this venture fell through, others did not. For instance, in July alone, Hearst announced the construction of a "new $1,000,000 home for the Los Angeles *Evening Herald*" as well as the acquisition of the Rochester *Post-Express* for an undisclosed sum, but estimated at several million dollars. And for some unexplainable reason, he purchased a gas company in Kansas City, possibly because one of his real estate brokers suggested that it was a real deal too good to pass up.[14]

Yet these purchases were not his greatest expenditures. An avid collector with seemingly uncontrollable wants, Hearst alerted auction houses and their representatives concerning his interests in priceless objects of art. He was in constant search for the invaluable treasures of Europe, which were apparently available at rock-bottom prices after a devastating world war. By the mid-1920s, Hearst had one of the finest collections of armor in the world, unsurpassed by any museum; an assortment of precious laces also estimated as "one of the very best"; and an assemblage of silverware worth between $5 million and $6 million. So massive was his collecting that storehouses at San Simeon, Los Angeles, San Francisco, and New York City were brim full, with additional purchases stacked in boxes on wharves. In New York alone, storage space was costing him $80,000 annually.[15]

Construction on the Enchanted Hill at San Simeon therefore became a matter of paramount importance as well as immediate need. Hearst envisioned Casa Grande (the big master house) as his unparalleled gift to the world, a museum of the ages for his fabulous collections, indeed a reflection of his personality and creativity. And it was. So Hearst devoted his energy and his money to its completion. At the first of every month, beginning on April 1, 1923, he deposited $25,000 with Julia Morgan, a sum almost immediately insufficient to meet future work and construction costs. By 1923 the twin towers, which were cast in concrete and faced with stone, were already quite visible, dominating the hillside with their dazzling white facade. On May 20, Morgan learned that a considerable supply of teak from Siam was available at a warehouse in San Francisco—a bargain Hearst could not pass up. The towers would soon have a roof as well as a balcony between them that was beautifully ornamental in design.

Since excavation had begun the previous summer, the ground floor of Casa Grande was also taking shape. Morgan had designed a plan that included three major rooms—the Assembly Room, Refectory, and Trophy or East Room—and two vestibules. Hearst, true to form, revised the original Morgan drafts by enlarging their size. For instance, he lengthened the Assembly Room from seventy-five to eighty-five feet "to provide sufficient wall area for a set of four large Renaissance tapestries." He also expanded the Refectory to seventy feet by twenty-eight feet. And he eventually settled upon the size of the Trophy or East Room at a mere forty-five feet in length.[16]

At San Simeon the accompanying houses (A, B, and C) were finally nearing completion. Morgan had anticipated that all three would be ready for occupancy by 1921. But this forecast was not to be. Hearst was continually changing his mind concerning construction and design. For the eighteen-room House A (Casa del Mar), which "emulated sixteenth-century Spanish Renaissance motifs," he had initially planned for a Library and possibly a Roman pool, that is, until deciding that Casa Grande would be a more suitable location. He also selected a different ceiling design and instructed Morgan to install a bath for each of the several bedrooms. Although not as often, Hearst revised the ten-room House B (Casa del Monte), which was also sixteenth-century Spanish Renaissance style, and the eighteen-room House C (Casa del Sol), which was "Moorish ornament from southern Spain." Although oftentimes in New York, 3,000 miles away, he amazingly became involved in almost every aspect of his magnum opus, whether having to do with door frames, fireplaces, ceilings, grilles, flooring, furniture, or landscaping. Consequently, not until July 1923 were the three houses, which were likened to a hillside Mediterranean village, ready for permanent occupancy.[17]

Hearst had immediate need of San Simeon in 1923. The Duchess de Gramont, who had entertained Millicent extensively in France during the summer of 1922, accepted an invitation to visit San Simeon. On July 31 she and her two sons, Gabriel and Gratien, arrived in Los Angeles en route to the ranch. And for the next week Hearst helped Millicent fulfill a social obligation to European royalty.[18]

For that matter Hearst continued, with relative ease, his "juggling act" performance concerning the two women in his life. Because of his quest for high office, he needed his wife to accompany him on various political events. When a New York ferryboat was named for him, Millicent was at his side—and even more eagerly when Hearst was invited to the White House for a conference with President Coolidge on December 1, 1923. Hearst, in turn, staunchly supported Millicent's New York civic activities, such as the Milk Fund of the Mayor's Committee of Women and the *New York American* Christmas and Relief Fund, both of which she chaired. Although his newspapers usually avoided personal references to Hearst family endeavors, the *American* and at times the *San Francisco Examiner* publicized her various social activities. On April 28, for instance, she gave a fabulous costume ball at the Clarendon mansion for eldest son George and his new bride, with an impressive guest list that included European royalty and the elite of New York society. Yet concerning the Hearsts' twentieth wedding anniversary, which occurred the very next day, the *New York Times* but not the *American* reported their celebration. Overall, Millicent received an inordinate amount of good press from the Hearst newspapers in 1923, which also covered a nine-week tour to Europe beginning in mid-September.[19]

Hearst, however, suffered emotionally by his attention to Millicent; Marion would see to that. After the London trip fiasco during the summer of 1922, she had accepted being the other woman in his life, her biographer noted, not "for the sake of the wealth and power, but out of love, the depths of which surprised even her." But Marion could not abide being ignored. She instinctively retaliated with a brief fling, especially since she knew that Hearst had spies who would report any such incident. To Marion's way of thinking, such an affair was not infidelity but a warning to pay more attention to her.[20]

And Hearst surely did. During the winter and spring of 1923, when Marion was filming *Little Old New York* and *Adam and Eva* in New York, he either talked with or saw her daily, discussing "film deals . . . and related projects *ad nauseam*." But Marion did not mind. Despite the outward Hollywood stereotype of "a dumb blonde," she was an excellent businesswoman, parlaying a personal portfolio in real estate and investments into millions of dollars. She also followed Hearst's advice concerning her career, not only giving lively interviews and frequent photo ops with the press but taking lessons, which Hearst provided, to improve her acting ability.

In the summer, while Hearst was in California for more than a month with Millicent at San Simeon, Marion tested his allegiance and triggered his possessiveness, again with desired results. To prove his love Hearst wrote letters, sent telegrams, and called her at least once or twice a day. In fact, her coolness over the telephone, especially at night, kindled an even greater devotion. So when Millicent sailed for Europe in mid-September, Hearst found reason to attend to Cosmopolitan business affairs in New York instead of California, and not too surprisingly Marion did the same.[21]

For Hearst 1923 was turning out to be a banner year, his endeavors blessed with one success after another. In August, the California state comptroller finalized his mother's estate, appraising its value at $11,012,850. Despite having to pay an inheritance tax of $949,101, despite what appeared to be reckless, even profligate spending, Hearst outwardly seemed to be flush with money. His personal worth in October, the *New York Times* reported, considerably exceeded $25 million "over and above all liabilities."[22]

Hearst therefore decided to crown all his 1923 achievements with one final triumph, that of defeating the corrupt Tammany chiefs, Murphy and Foley, at the polls in November. He surely believed that the present political circumstances would justify this decision. After all, the Hearst newspapers' bucketshop crusade from May to late August had been devastating in its criticism of Tammany Hall, not just for bilking New Yorkers out of personal income but for its corrupt control of the judiciary that allowed the guilty to escape punishment. And late in August when Tammany boss Murphy tried to "placate Hylan and Hearst," the *New York Times* observed, by pledging to support "municipal operation of buses, other transit lines, and public utilities generally" in return for no opposition to ten Tammany nominees to the state supreme court, Hearst delayed before giving his answer. On October 8, however, a *New York American* editorial clearly enunciated his feelings—and intent. The headline blared, "Citizens, the Time to Beat Boss Murphy and Keep Our Courts Clean Is Right Now." Then for the next month a typical Hearst crusade, virulent and vicious, raged unabated.[23]

What a mistake in judgment! As Hiram Johnson noted the previous year in a letter to his sons, "Hearst probably is utterly unable to understand the violence of the antipathy to him." Whereas some Tammany leaders might have tried to explain his bucketshop crusade as simply a demand for good government, Hearst now obliterated that possible excuse. He had rejected their offers for political compromise, their attempts to prolong the uneasy truce from the previous fall. He was launching an all-out war for possession of city and state leadership within the Democratic Party.

Tammany responded in kind, embracing the cliché that its members knew so well, "no holds barred." A week before the November election, an anonymously authored pamphlet appeared, with widespread distribution, titled *Hearst's Life: A Record of Shame,* which scathingly listed "his political activities since he came to New York." Then before record crowds of voters Governor Al Smith, the popular leader of the state Democratic Party who had long considered Hearst a "pestilence that walks in the darkness," denounced him as a surrogate of the Republicans. And his "Mudgutter Gazettes," Smith asserted, typically employed fraudulent, dishonest, and insincere campaign methods."[24]

On November 6, New Yorkers voted their reactions to this all-out political war. While the *American* announced on its front page "TAMMANY LOSSES INDICATED," the *Times* registered the true outcome. Its headline read, "Hearst's Choices Ran Lowest and Tammany Leaders Rejoice." And indeed they did—with smug satisfaction. State party chairman James J. Hoey exultantly observed that "Hearst is dead politically," that "the day of Hearstism, mud slinging and yellow journalism in campaigning is gone beyond recall." Al Smith happily agreed, stating that the election was "a crushing rebuke to the campaign of vilification." Words, however, were not enough for Tammany chieftain Murphy.

To the delight of "Big Tom" Foley, the *Times* reported, he ordered the "filthy, lying newspapers" of the "editor-publisher out of his house," then soon thereafter suggested that the Democrats drop Hearst from their party. Of course, Mayor Hylan, Hearst's faithful friend and ally, also realized the repercussions of this election; Tammany would soon be seeking a mayoral candidate to rid New York of the last vestige of "Hearstism."[25]

Hearst seemed unfazed by this crushing defeat. Although relatively quiet for the remainder of 1923, he still hoped that Democrats would turn to him in 1924 as the only presidential candidate capable of generating huge monetary contributions and favorable newspaper publicity. To support this supposition he purchased the *Albany Times Union* in April of 1924 and the *San Antonio Light* in May. And while failing temporarily to negotiate the sale of the *Salt Lake Tribune,* he instructed his business confidant and West Coast attorney John Francis Neylan to pursue the sale until successful.

At the same time Hearst rallied his political troops to do battle. On January 16, 1924, to test the waters for a presidential bid, he selected former Illinois senator James Hamilton Lewis to address an open letter to the Democratic state chairman, urging the delegation to support Hearst or Wilson's Secretary of the Treasury (and son-in-law), William Gibbs McAdoo, as the party nominee; but, of course, his first choice was Hearst. That same day the Democratic National Committee announced that New York City would host the national convention late in June. Mayor Hylan was ecstatic both for the city and for Hearst who, through his *New York American* and *Evening Journal,* would crusade for progressive platform planks and attempt to influence delegates for a specific party nominee. Then two weeks later the Independence League of New York, with five hundred members from "practically every county," assembled in New York City "to battle for the [progressive] principles constantly enunciated by William Randolph Hearst." And, of course, Hearst could count on potent support from California, where his newspapers in Los Angeles, Oakland, and San Francisco were a dominant political force.[26]

This self-promotion to become a major Democratic contender in 1924 received little outside encouragement. Consequently Hearst wrote Neylan on February 14 that he would not be a candidate "under any circumstances." He then strove to promote a nominee of his own choosing. He first mentioned close political ally, U.S. Senator James A. Reed of Missouri, as a Democrat who "could unite the party." When that suggestion died aborning, he began favoring McAdoo, a transplanted Californian, as the most progressive of the potential candidates. But more importantly no other nominee seemed capable of derailing the presidential aspirations of Al Smith.[27]

Yet late in April, Tammany boss Murphy died suddenly—and for the moment, local politics took precedence over national concerns. With James A. Foley, Murphy's son-in-law, looming as the next Tammany chief, Hearst and Hylan proposed a new method of selection that would allow them a controlling vote. But in this bid for power they were unsuccessful. During the next two weeks Governor Smith assumed a leadership role with Tammany, deftly thwarted attempts by Hylan and Hearst to insert their own man, and rallied the chiefs to choose Foley. After several days of hesitation, however, Foley abdicated in favor of a friend and ally, Judge George W. Olvany. Because of this brief power struggle Smith was more determined than ever to rid New York of "Hearstism."[28]

For the moment, however, Smith had to focus upon a more pressing political problem—his bid for the Democratic presidential nomination. And again an unforgiving, distrustful Hearst paid his respects. During the first weeks in June, prior to the convention, the *New York Times* reported that the Hearst–Hylan and Smith forces had agreed to a political peace pact, whereby Tammany promised to support Hylan for an unopposed third term as mayor in 1925 if the publisher would agree not to fight Smith in convention. But when the governor denied any knowledge of such a deal and his forces refused to accept Hylan as a member of the New York state delegation, Hearst once again felt betrayed. He immediately rejected all compromise, and the visiting national Democrats experienced firsthand the Hearst treatment of Smith.

On June 21, five days before the opening of the convention, Hearst launched the first of many editorials, one of which was repeated over a period of several days. He stated that the Hearst newspapers had "no special enemies and no particular favorites in the coming contest" and therefore would show "the utmost impartiality" in news coverage. He intended, however, to support "any genuine progressive Democrat" as well as "oppose any candidate representing booze and boodle [bribe money]." Of course, no one could mistake this Hearst slap at Smith, who was openly against the Eighteenth Amendment (prohibition) and a significant chief of Tammany Hall.[29]

Since Millicent was an honorary chair of the Mayor's Committee on the Reception of Distinguished Guests, the Hearsts were quite visible at this convention. They attended the opening session together. Yet Hearst, in his typical flamboyant fashion, upstaged everyone. On June 26, the opening night of the convention, he and Millicent hosted an extravaganza, which six hundred delegates and their wives would long remember. They sponsored a magnificent ball which occupied the entire first floor of the Ritz-Carlton. The orchestras of Paul Whiteman and Eddie Elkins provided the music until midnight, when supper was served. Then Clifton Webb, Bonnie Glass, and Will Rogers entertained the delegates.

And what an impressive guest list! The elite of the present and future Democratic Party were in attendance: Mayor and Mrs. John Hylan, William Jennings Bryan, William Gibbs McAdoo, Mr. and Mrs. Franklin Delano Roosevelt, Mr. and Mrs. Nathan Straus, Commissioner and Mrs. James A. Farley, Senator and Mrs. Cordell Hull. But one name was conspicuously absent from the guest list—Governor Al Smith.[30]

For many delegates the Hearst extravaganza had to be the high point of their stay in New York, especially since events went downhill after that evening. Since the Democratic presidential nominee needed a two-thirds vote majority, neither McAdoo nor Smith, the two front-runners, could garner enough support for victory. The convention rolled on day after day with one monotonous roll call after another and still a deadlock, which, as one historian put it, "reduced the value of the nomination." At length, on the 103rd ballot, tired and frustrated delegates turned to John W. Davis of West Virginia as a compromise candidate and ended this disastrous political ordeal on the next roll call. Davis, who had distinguished himself as Wilson's solicitor-general and as U.S. ambassador to Great Britain during World War I, summed up the outcome of his victory after a reporter congratulated him. "Thanks, but you know how much it is worth." And Hearst agreed. He announced that Davis was the Wall Street lawyer of J. P. Morgan & Company and that the "proud old Democratic Party" had "committed political suicide."[31]

To help forget about his latest unhappy political experience and to recuperate from three tiring convention weeks in New York, Hearst left two days later for a vacation at San Simeon, accompanied by Millicent and Mayor and Mrs. Hylan. Consequently he avoided an embarrassing episode, tinged with titillating stories. What happened was partly the fault of *American* editor Victor Watson, but of Hearst as well. In the attempt to excoriate Tammany and "Big Tom" Foley in the bucketshop scandal, the *American* had discovered that slick Broadway attorney William J. Fallon, who exhibited an unusual skill in the courtroom, especially in framing evidence, had bribed a juror to ensure the innocence and acquittal of several bucketshop clients. In the ensuing investigation, *American* reporter Nat Ferber obtained a witness, Fallon's right-hand man, who agreed to a plea bargain and then to testify. Watson, with Hearst's approval, spared no expense in his desire to destroy the Tammany chiefs and anyone connected with them.

But the Hearst media did not anticipate the devious mind and unscrupulous will of "Broadway Bill" Fallon. Faced with a career-ending trial, entailing disbarment and a possible jail sentence upon conviction, he prepared a defense that cast him as the victim of a vindictive newspaper mogul. To Nat Ferber he laid out this blackmail presentation, which would be his trial testimony unless the *American* backed down. Tell Watson, he grimly asserted, "I'll testify that Hearst is having me hounded because I have the birth certificates proving that he's the father of twins born to a certain motion picture actress—you know whom I mean." He concluded that "he's trying to get me because I refused to give them up."

American editor Watson, upon hearing this story repeated almost verbatim from Nat Ferber and perceiving how opposition papers would delight in publicizing it, nervously picked up the phone and called San Simeon. When Hearst answered, the conversation went like this:

"Chief," Watson began, "Nat Ferber has just come from the Fallon trial with a hell of a crack from Fallon."

"What is it, Victor?"

Watson then repeated Fallon's message.

After a brief silence, Watson heard a chuckle and then this reply: "You won't have to worry about your first-page line tomorrow, Victor, will you?"

"You mean we carry it?" Watson queried. To which Hearst replied, "You'll have to, if the other newspapers do, won't you, Victor? You don't want to be scooped on our own story."

Hanging up the phone, Watson turned to Ferber with an obvious look of admiration and announced, "Well, I'll be Goddamned! [He] told me to stick it on Page 1."[32]

The Fallon trial in 1924 proved to be a sensation, the story of the summer. And it surely affected the participants. Fallon, after testifying for several days in August and painting Hearst as the villain and himself as the victim, convinced the jury to acquit him. *American* reporter Nat Ferber and investigative sidekick Gene Fowler would eventually publish books about this episode. Victor Watson, whom Millicent asked Hearst to dismiss because of such embarrassing accusations about their family, received a reprieve and was exiled to the comparatively unimportant Baltimore paper. Millicent, in turn, stayed at San Simeon for the rest of the summer, then evaded questions from scandal-seeking reporters by escaping to Europe early in September for a three-month Continental tour.[33]

Hearst avoided reporters by staying on his secluded mountaintop at San Simeon. Although knowing that the Fallon assertion concerning the fathering of twins with a motion picture actress was blatantly untrue, he realized that such opposition papers as the *Tribune* and *World* were having a field day at his expense, especially after the acquittal of Fallon. In fact, local gossip again gave rise to a growing Hearst legend that he had sired any number of illegitimate children. And surely many New Yorkers began to believe it. Almost overnight, because of the scandal, the *American* lost 60,000 subscribers and thousands of dollars in advertising.[34]

Hearst, however, was much more concerned about Marion; he feared that this scandal would destroy her career, which he had labored so assiduously to fashion over the past five years. He impulsively wrote her that it was time for him to "go out of the motion picture business." After all, she was already at the top of her profession, and his continued public presence might prevent her from becoming one of "the greatest of all movie picture stars past or future."[35]

This gesture of self-sacrifice cemented a relationship that would last for the rest of their lives. Marion, casting aside her fear of encountering Millicent, telephoned Hearst at San Simeon. She "had no intention of remaining in films if he got out," she asserted. "I've done this to please you." Without him, "she would have no more fun making movies." She might delight in punishing him with an inconsequential fling when being ignored, but she loved him—and Hearst knew it.[36]

Nor did the Fallon lies upset Marion. Instead of following Hearst's advice to stay in seclusion, she partied every night in New York, even joking with friends about her alleged offspring. At the same time she did not ignore her professional commitments. On August 5 she attended the world premiere of her latest film, *Janice Meredith,* at the Cosmopolitan Theatre and then appeared frequently for photo ops and interviews. Her only unhappiness was that Hearst stayed in California even after Millicent sailed for Europe in September. He therefore persuaded Marion to relocate in Beverly Hills by purchasing a white stucco mansion at 1700 Lexington Road in her mother's name.[37]

Hearst had other reasons for staying on the West Coast to live at San Simeon, to observe the construction of his most cherished dream, Casa Grande, was in itself a daily reward. But California, as a base of operations, was increasingly beneficial time-wise. He also was becoming more involved in motion pictures. Although deciding early in 1924 that New York was the ideal city for Cosmopolitan Productions, he soon changed his mind. His business associations with Louis B. Mayer and Marcus Loew were personally gratifying. They in turn realized the unique publicity value of the twenty-two Hearst newspapers to their growing industry and therefore involved him in some of their financial affairs. Consequently Hearst, while not mentioned in the official incorporation of Metro-Goldwyn-Mayer (MGM) on May 16, 1924 (or as a member of the board of directors) was, according to Mayer's biographer, a board member "unofficially."[38]

In filmmaking Hearst's propensity for historical accuracy and his desire for perfection occupied a great deal of his time. In July 1924, for example, he purchased the rights to a picture play titled *Zander the Great*, in which Marion would star. For more than a year he fretted over its final result, rewriting the script, taking the film to edit at San Simeon, and suggesting a number of expensive retakes. After months of delay—and at tremendous cost—*Zander* premiered in Los Angeles in April 1925, and in New York City in May.[39]

His change of venue, however, in no way curtailed Hearst's expensive tastes. With the assistance of alter ego Arthur Brisbane, he continued to enlarge his real estate holdings in New York City. In April and May he also completed the acquisition of the *Albany Times-Union* and the *San Antonio Light*. And to add to the astounding costs at San Simeon in construction and labor, he affixed still another. Just prior to Christmas he purchased and shipped to San Simeon forty buffalo "at an average price of $1,000 each."[40]

Without question this mania for spending needed a strong funding base or at least the appearance thereof. Hearst was therefore forced to address this problem by going public. Late in April 1924, he incorporated his twenty-two newspapers and four of his magazines into Hearst Publications, Inc. Their assets were valued at $40 million, with net annual earnings totaling $6,474,133. Under the auspicies of reputable companies in New York and San Francisco, he agreed to offer $12 million in bonds bearing 6.5 percent interest. Within two weeks investors snapped up this enticing issue, and Hearst was temporarily solvent.[41]

Despite his love for California, Hearst could not abandon his political involvement in New York. For thirty years he had been a major player both in the city and state. Even though suffering one setback after another at the hands of Al Smith, he held out unreasoning hope for high office, at least as long as John Hylan was mayor of New York City. His actions during the next several months were therefore predictable. Although highly critical of Smith and Tammany Hall, he toned down his rhetoric after the Democratic National Convention in July 1924, hoping to placate Democrats and soften their opposition to Hylan. He ordered all his editors to be nonpartisan in the forthcoming presidential campaign. At every opportunity, however, the *New York American* and *Evening Journal* praised Hylan as a man of the people, independent-minded and self-sufficient, who had fought for public-owned subways that charged only five cents per ride. Yet as the November 4th election neared, Hearst could not hide his disdain for Democratic contender John W. Davis, who "favored Wilson's League of Nations," and his loathing for Al Smith, who, Hearst editorialized, had "spent more time with corporate attorneys and betraying the people's interests than any other great leader" of New York. To the surprise of no one on Election Day, President Calvin Coolidge overwhelmed Davis, and a popular Al Smith won reelection as governor.

Yet an unrelenting Hearst evaluated the national election results with a front-page editorial. The headline summed up his thoughts precisely. "Coolidge and Smith Elections Personal Triumphs." In a parting shot to his old adversary, he concluded, "Undoubtedly the weakness of the Republican nominee for Governor made Gov. Smith's reelection easy."[42]

As the year 1924 was winding down, an incident occurred that added to Hearst lore and legend. For several months during the fall, Hearst had negotiated with Thomas Ince, a talented independent producer, to form a film partnership for the express purpose of enhancing the career of Marion Davies. To consummate this deal and also to celebrate Ince's forty-second birthday, Hearst hosted a pleasure trip on November 17 off San Diego aboard his floating castle, the 215-foot luxury yacht *Oneida*. Included among the dozen or so guests were Hearst's private secretary Joe Willicombe, production manager of Cosmopolitan Daniel Carson Goodman, Joseph Urban with his wife and daughter, Charlie Chaplin, and, of course, Marion. Early the next morning Ince became seriously ill. Willicombe and Goodman escorted him ashore, put him on a train to Los Angeles (under a doctor's care), where he died after a day of intense suffering. Officially his death was "due to heart disease, superinduced by an attack of indigestion."

Malicious rumors arose quickly, especially among the growing number of Hearst detractors. Since Hearst did not attend the funeral, the most repeated story was that he had caught Ince making love to Marion and, in a jealous rage, had stabbed, shot, or poisoned him—take your choice.

But such a tale has been given little historical credence. None of those aboard the *Oneida* ever corroborated such allegations concerning the most notorious of unsolved Hollywood murders. Nor did Hearst, who understood Marion, ever demonstrate such behavior toward any paramour, no matter how jealous. Film historian Louis Pizzitola has presented the most plausible account of what happened aboard the *Oneida*. Ince, in a celebratory mood that first night, consumed some bad liquor. Neither the participants nor Hearst were willing to admit this fact, especially since the U.S. Justice Department was enforcing Prohibition on the Hollywood scene.[43]

For most of 1925 Hearst remained on his mountaintop at San Simeon, although spending some time in Los Angeles at the Ambassador Hotel. He could not have been happier. Together with Julia Morgan, he supervised the building of his most cherished dream. The pouring of concrete for Casa Grande was now complete, with the second floor taking shape. Above the twenty-four-foot high Assembly Room was the magnificent Library, which extended "the full length of the main facade, fronted by a wide balcony." Then above the twenty-seven-foot-high Refectory they had constructed four guest rooms, called the "Cloisters," which were "divided into eight symmetrical rooms, each with its own bath" and "separated by walls running down the center of their seventeen-foot width," giving a cloistered appearance; hence the name. They also constructed at the east end of the second floor the Doge's Suite (at first called the Royal Suite), composed of two bedrooms with private baths, together with a central sitting room.

Further plans at San Simeon were, in the typical Hearst mind-set of change and improvement, in the works. He and Morgan had already agreed on a third-story suite with two bedrooms and accompanying baths separated by a central living chamber. Hearst continued to emphasize the importance of landscaping, at times buying truckloads of "palms and large shrubs, like camellias and bougainvilleas, arriving fully grown." He also began enlarging his collection of animals for the creation of a Hearst zoo. To existing herds of buffalo and elk and deer he added such wild animals as lions, giraffes, zebras, water buffalo, wildebeests, kangaroos, and rare species of deer. And always on the drawing board was the construction of several pools, which would be recognized for their historic and artistic uniqueness.[44]

At the same time Hearst was securing the future of Marion Davies. In the spring of 1925 he formed a unique alliance with Louis B. Mayer. While both men admired and were appreciative of each other, especially in regard to their capabilities and achievements, "their decision to work together," one film historian observed, "was pragmatic." Marion, however, was central to this alliance. In anticipation of extensive film publicity in twenty-two Hearst newspapers and several magazines such as *Cosmopolitan* and *Good Housekeeping*, Mayer extended to Marion a new contract with a "fat" salary of $10,000 a week. In addition, as a majority shareholder in Cosmopolitan Productions, she was eligible to pocket a considerable amount of its corporate dividends. In turn, MGM agreed to finance Cosmopolitan productions, with Marion in a starring role. Consequently Hearst closed down his New York City film operations and moved to Los Angeles. As a further indication of his movie commitment, he had Marion's fourteen-room, $20,000 "bungalow," famous for its Roman-style sunken bathtub, moved across town from the United lot to Cosmopolitan's new residence in Culver City.

Concerning this alliance between Cosmopolitan and MGM, Hearst was ever protective of Marion and her career. But to do so meant his personal involvement. As *Variety* speculated, he surely had an understanding with Mayer "to have a representative, as well as himself, supervise the casting, adaption of the scenario, and cost of the pictures."[45]

Not too surprisingly, Hearst continued his insatiable passion for spending throughout 1925. With Arthur Brisbane as a partner and at times with Florenz "Flo" Ziegfeld, he invested heavily in real estate, theaters, and rental properties in New York City, amounting to millions of dollars. He also persisted in his quest for political power through his government by newspaper strategy. Although selling the small *Fort Worth Record* to Amon G. Carter, he acquired the society magazine *Town and Country* in June for an estimated $1 million and the evening *Syracuse Telegram* in November for $600,000 to $1 million.[46]

In his passion to acquire and possess, Hearst at times seemed fiscally out of control. Alice Head, who headed up his two English magazines, *Nash's* and the English version of *Good Housekeeping*, witnessed his compulsion firsthand. Late in the spring of 1925 Hearst returned to New York and met with Head intermittently over a six-week period. One evening in a casual dinner conversation he expressed an interest in buying "a country home in England," she later recalled, "and that if ever Leeds Castle in Kent or St. Donat's Castle in Wales were for sale," she "was to let him know." Having seen "pictures of both of them in *Country Life*," he professed an "interest in purchasing one or the other." Soon after returning to England in June, she alerted Hearst that the eleventh-century, 125-room St. Donat's, which rested on 13,000 acres near Cardiff, was for sale. Without asking the cost, he telegraphed her to buy it. And Head, while admitting to having a "kind of sinking" feeling about purchasing a castle that neither she nor Hearst had ever seen, consummated the deal in August for $120,000.[47]

Despite so many business interests, any one of which would have exhausted the energies of most men, Hearst did not neglect his political ambition, his desire to make a difference through public service. He therefore focused on the reelection of John Hylan as mayor of New York City. But therein lay the problem. Tammany Hall, under the leadership of George Olvany and with the invaluable support of Governor Al Smith, was determined to rid itself, as well as New York City, of a final Hearst stigma—namely John Hylan.

To combat their political maneuvers Hearst returned to New York late in April specifically to bolster the campaign of his faithful friend. But instead of securing Hylan's candidacy, Hearst roiled the political waters of the city even more. He announced that the mayor's "honesty and uprightness" had helped erase the public shame attached to "the very name of Tammany Hall" and that the chiefs ought to be grateful. He then suggested that if the Democrats did not renominate Hylan he would support the mayor as an independent.

To this threat of a third party candidate, state Democrats reacted immediately. A front-page headline in the *New York Times* announced that "Smith Won't Back Hylan, But Will Aid Any Other Nominee." Tammany, under the leadership of George Olvany, continued to strengthen its resolve. And the Women's Democratic Union responded by endorsing a number of disparaging resolutions, the gist of which denounced Hylan as an understudy. They then asked, "Is William R. Hearst to be continued as the virtual ruler of the biggest city in the Western Hemisphere, or is the government of the city to be restored to native New Yorkers?"[48]

Hearst, however, was determined to win this fight for Hylan through his time-tested technique of "government by newspaper." He would gain the support of New Yorkers with a well-crafted crusade that would overwhelm Tammany and Al Smith. Emerging victorious over such prestigious enemies, he would elevate his own stature with Democrats nationwide as well as save Hylan's job.

Before leaving for California late in June, he laid out plans with his editors for the forthcoming contest. The Hylan campaign rested on two themes: a popular leader who had restored honesty and integrity to the mayor's office over the past eight years and a man of the people who, unafraid of the political consequences, had ardently fought against the powerful railroad interests for a five-cent fare on municipal-owned subways. Consequently, a daily barrage of headlines inundated *New York American* and *Evening Journal* readers over the next six weeks: "Leaders Assure Hylan of Big Majority in Primary" (June 20); "GOVERNOR'S AIDES TELL HIM HYLAN WAVE GROWS" (June 30); "Thousands of Women are Joining the HYLAN 5-CENT FARE CLUB. SAVE THE CITY FOR ITS PEOPLE" (July 20); "Public's Duty Is to Re-Elect Hylan Mayor, Says Hearst" (front-page editorial, July 26); "Mayor Hylan Foes in Air Over Candidate" (July 30); "105,000 MEMBERS HAVE JOINED THE 5-CENT FARE CLUB" (August 1); "The Five-Cent Fare Is Safe Only So Long as a Mayor Elected by the People Is Safe" (full-page editorial, August 3); "Hylan Sure of Victory" (August 5).[49]

Equally effective were the nationally known political cartoonists that Hearst loosed on the Hylan opposition. Frederick Opper and O. P. Williams daily portrayed Al Smith and Tammany as representatives of Big Business, as cohorts of Wall Street, who were greedily lining their own pockets to the detriment of the public good. To emphasize one of Hylan's major issues, that of a five-cent fare on all municipally owned subways, Opper created a daily cartoon series titled "The Ten-Cent Troubadours." Two overstuffed men, depicted as the Transit Trust, playing banjos, merrily serenading an emaciated, overtaxed, and harried "plain citizen" with this lilting refrain:

> Will you love us in December as you did in May?
> When a ten cent fare is what we'll make you pay!
> Though your hair turns gray with grief
> It will cause us great relief
> If you'll love us in December as you did in May![50]

Against this well-orchestrated Hearst crusade the anti-Hylan forces retaliated vigorously and with equal effectiveness. On August 6, with the Democratic primary set for mid-September, Tammany chiefs selected James J. "Jimmy" Walker of Greenwich Village, a Democratic leader in the state senate who was, as the *New York Times* headline blared, "A HEARST FOE AND HARD HITTER." They then released a list of Walker supporters, including two of the borough chiefs in Hylan's home base of Brooklyn as well as several ex-Hylan aides. But their most important political weapon was Al Smith, who was mainly responsible for the Walker nomination. During the last week in August he began campaigning in New York City, speaking to huge crowds of enthusiastic voters.[51]

Political pundits soon cast this campaign correctly as a personal confrontation between Hearst and Smith for control of the state Democratic Party, one that placed Hearst at a considerable disadvantage. As a stump speaker, Smith had few equals, and his prestige with New Yorkers as possibly the next president of the United States was never greater. While Hearst wrote front-page editorials in the *New York American* and *Evening Journal*, Smith replied in person and in a public letter to the voters. He was personal and denigrating, once again revealing his animosity and contempt for the "greatest living enemy of the people." Referring to Hearst "as the Overlord of the Pacific" to whom "Mayor Hylan was subservient," he urged New Yorkers to pay no heed to a man whose example in life was morally undesirable to "our youth." For that matter, why should Democrats adhere to any political advice that Hearst offered? "He has not got a vote." On Election Day he would be on his landed estate in California; therefore, Smith announced, they should "read the editor-politician out of the Democratic Party."[52]

To this personal diatribe, Hearst replied in kind. "The distinguished Governor of the great State of New York has taken three days laboriously to prepare a vulgar tirade," Hearst began in a front-page editorial, "that any resident of Billingsgate or any occupant of the alcoholic ward in Bellevue could have written in fifteen minutes in quite the same style, but with more evidence of education and style." But "the Governor," he acidly continued, "has added new force to his sobriquet of 'Alibi Al' by dodging all the real issues of the campaign and sheltering himself behind a free flow of characteristic blackguardism." Hearst then discussed several points of difference in this campaign before arriving at one on which they did agreed. Governor Smith "inadvertently tells the truth once," Hearst announced, "when he says that I am not a Democrat and did not vote for . . . [him] at the last election. He is right. I am an independent in politics and always have been, and I did not vote for Governor Smith at the last election or for a party which seemed to have surrendered disgracefully to the Wall Street interests. I cannot be a Democrat in the State of New York," he bitterly asserted, "while a brazen instrument of the traction companies sits in the Governor's chair and claims to be the Democratic leader of the State."[53]

What a mistake! With his admission that he was "not a Democrat," Hearst destroyed Hylan's candidacy as well as his own credibility within the party. For the next ten days Democrats throughout the city, at the instigation of Tammany, cited Hearst's confession; many party loyalists who had endorsed Hylan quickly disavowed their support or were silent. At the same time Al Smith gleefully upped his rhetoric. In campaign speeches he repeatedly referred to Hylan "as a Hearst-trained demagogue" who was dragging the dignity of mayor's office "into the gutter." And with Tammany organizing its troops to get out the vote, the outcome of the primary election became a mere formality. On September 16, Jimmy Walker overwhelmingly defeated John Hylan. The *New York Times* reported, "WALKER'S LEAD IS 95,543."[54]

Over the next six weeks Hearst suffered the bitter seeds of defeat. On September 18, two days after the primary, he offered Hylan enthusiastic support if the mayor would run as an independent. The next day state progressives, obviously with Hearst's encouragement, asked Hylan to be their nominee. But Hylan refused both entreaties. Besides having his fill with politics, he was a Democrat. A week later (September 25) Hearst renewed his pledge to aid a Hylan candidacy, but again to no avail. Then for more than a month the *New York American* and *Evening Journal* were surprisingly noncommittal, paying little more than lip service to the mayor's race, their owner seeming to have lost heart in the political process. Not until October 30, four days before the election, did New Yorkers again hear from Hearst concerning local politics. In an eleventh-hour decision he and Hylan decided to endorse Walker.[55]

Hearst, however, did not find any solace in Walker's landslide victory of almost 400,000 votes on November 2. In an interview with the *New York Post* published the next day he revealed his intense disappointment and deep-seated bitterness. When asked, "Will you take any part in the Democratic state convention or the shaping of next year's campaign issues?" Hearst replied, "I shall take no part in party politics of any kind, but shall continue to advocate in my papers the principles and policies which I consider essentially Democratic." To a second question, "Do you think Mayor Hylan has a chance to come back?" Hearst candidly stated, "I certainly think that Mayor Hylan will have many chances to go back into politics, but I earnestly hope he will not do so." To a third question, "Whom would you suggest as possibilities for Democratic Senatorial nominations next year?" he retorted, "I wouldn't." To still another question, "Do you think George W. Olvany is as strong in Tammany now, after his primary victory, as C. F. Murphy ever was?" he retorted, "I think a leader to be as strong as Murphy must be as wise as Murphy. I do not think Mr. Olvany is wise. I think his attitude toward Mayor Hylan was an evidence of unwisdom if nothing else." And to the pertinent question, "Will you support Smith as a fourth term Governor candidate?" Hearst adamantly responded with a resounding no. He then elaborated. "I supported Smith three times and that was three times too many. . . . I made the same mistake three times. That is enough."[56]

This interview revealed one inescapable truth: Hearst's quest for the presidency of the United States was over—and he knew it.

Montage of Hearst at work and play. San Francisco History Center, San Francisco Public Library.

Young Millicent Hearst. San Francisco History Center, San Francisco Public Library.

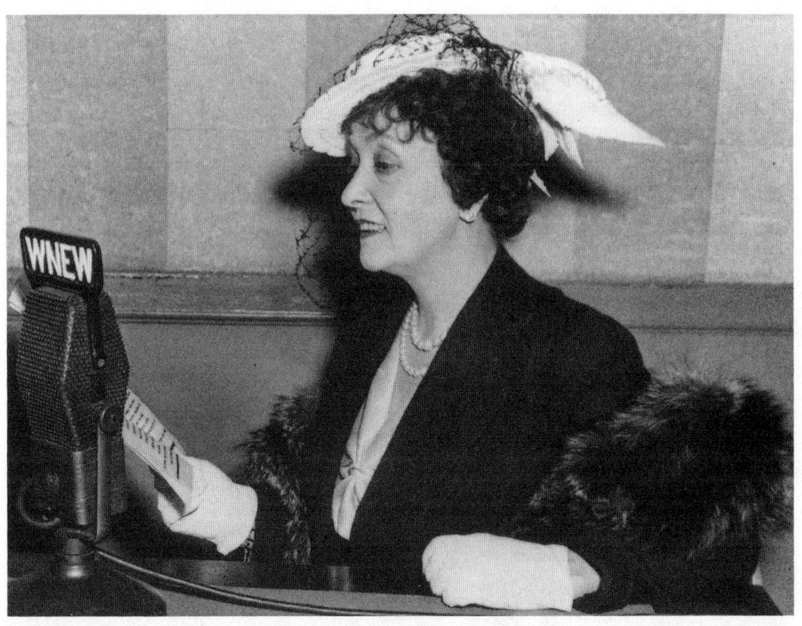

Millicent Hearst in 1940 speaking in behalf of one of her charities. San Francisco History Center, San Francisco Public Library.

William Randolph Hearst and his five sons at San Simeon in 1938. Hearst Castle /CA State Parks.

One of the houses at Wyntoon that make up Hearst's Bavarian Village in northern California. Courtesy Academy of Motion Picture Arts & Sciences.

Aerial view of La Cuesta Encantada, "The Enchanted Hill." Photograph by Victoria Garagliano; Hearst Castle /CA State Parks.

The breathtakingly exquisite Gothic Study on the third floor of Casa Grande. Photograph by Victoria Garagliano; Hearst Castle /CA State Parks.

Kindred Spirits, Hearst and architect Julia Morgan. Photograph by Irvin Willat; Marc Wanamaker, Bison Archives.

The Refectory, so named by Hearst and Morgan, shows Hearst's magnificent collection of silver pieces. Photograph by Victoria Garagliano; Hearst Castle /CA State Parks.

The grandeur of the sitting room in Casa del Mar (House A) competes with the spectacular view of San Simeon Bay. Photograph by Victoria Garagliano; Hearst Castle /CA State Parks.

Hearst and Marion Davies, seated across from each other, entertain in the 70-foot-long Refectory. Hearst Castle /CA State Parks.

Marion Davies Beach House (also called Ocean House) in Santa Monica. Courtesy Academy of Motion Picture Arts and Sciences.

Elegant dining room at Marion's Beach House for dinner parties for as many as fifty guests. Courtesy Marc Wanamaker, Bison Archives.

Costume party at the Beach House for Hearst's 74th birthday in 1937. L to R: Hearst, unidentified man, Marion Davies, Robert Montgomery, Mrs. Montgomery, Chester Morris. Courtesy Academy of Motion Picture Arts and Sciences.

1938 costume party—a favorite entertainment by Hearst and Davies. Courtesy Academy of Motion Picture Arts and Sciences.

Hearst photographs a favorite subject: Marion Davies. Hearst Castle /CA State Parks.

An avid collector, Hearst looks over Italian glass. Courtesy Academy of Motion Picture Arts and Sciences.

Hearst displaying his life-long interest in photography. Courtesy Academy of Motion Picture Arts and Sciences.

Hearst with movie producer Robert Vignola and Arthur Brisbane, often called Hearst's alter ego. Courtesy Academy of Motion Picture Arts and Sciences.

Impressive head table: Hearst, Winston Churchill, L. B. Mayer, Fred Niblo, John Churchill. Courtesy Academy of Motion Picture Arts and Sciences.

Marion Davies holding her beloved dachshund, Gandhi. Courtesy Motion Picture Academy of Arts and Sciences.

6 Hollywood, San Simeon, and Expansion

Early in the 1900s, nestled in the valleys and foothills of the Santa Monica Mountains in northwest Los Angeles, lay the peaceful community of Hollywood. Because of the warm southern California climate, with a terrain caressed by Pacific Coast breezes and "aglow with orange groves, fruit trees, palms, and poinsettias," Hollywood was considered an ideal place to live. But by 1926 the business and economic complexion of the area had changed significantly "from a paradise for retired Iowan farmers into a seventh heaven for youth." More than eighty percent of the motion picture trade, which was the fourth largest industry in the world, now resided in Hollywood and the surrounding area. As this golden age of the 1920s continued, population doubled, trebled, then quadrupled, with Hearst's *Los Angeles Examiner* publicizing California growth in a daily headline, "2nd Million Population Is Coming to Los Angeles." As a consequence real estate exploded in value; accompanying businesses arose to meet urban demands, and local leaders struggled to solve the problems of municipal expansion.[1]

Hollywood was a special place. While Los Angeles was known as the Emerald City, Hollywood became the City of the Stars, a modern-day Babylon of the rich and famous, of the young and beautiful, that attracted tourists from all over the world to its haunts. Through the daily accounts of such movie columnists as Louella Parsons, Americans eagerly read about their favorite film idols. They reveled in the most intimate tidbits concerning such silent screen luminaries as Charlie Chaplin, Mary Pickford, Douglas Fairbanks, Gloria Swanson, Rudolph Valentino, Greta Garbo, and (for those who identified with the Hearst newspapers) Marion Davies. Although sympathizing with the sad plight of beautiful young girls who were flocking to Hollywood by the thousands only to find their chances of success at "less than one in a hundred," Americans were fascinated by the private lives of their favorite stars, their likes and dislikes, their illicit love affairs and scandalous divorces, their continuous striving to achieve or hold on to that "golden rung" of stardom. No news about them seemed insignificant; an adoring public had to be served. For instance, the magnificent homes of screen celebrities served as backdrops for a succession of fabulous parties. The name "Pickfair," where Mary Pickford and Douglas Fairbanks royally entertained the in crowd of the motion picture industry, became a familiar word in the American lexicon of the 1920s.[2]

But in 1926 Hearst and Marion Davies supplanted Fairbanks and Pickford as the leading host and hostess of the Hollywood scene. It was not by accident. In May, Hearst surprised Marion while on an outing at Santa Monica beach. As the two waded in the ocean surf, he nonchalantly asked her if she liked this location. When she replied, "it's fine," he announced that he was going to build a beach house there for her immediately.

In less than a year Hearst constructed an ocean house on the Santa Monica beach that met not only his standards of grandeur and magnificence but Marion's as well. Typical of his mind-set, he constructed a mansion that dwarfed all others on the Hollywood scene. The white, three-storied Georgian building exemplified his creative, architectural impulses: a lavish dining room large enough to seat comfortably twenty-five to fifty guests; a luxurious gold room resplendent in gold leaf with crystal chandeliers from Tiffany's; a huge library equipped with a movie screen rising out of the floor; and an expansive gallery large enough to display Marion's growing collection of art treasures.

Four other structures of the same architectural style circled the main building, giving it the appearance of an immensely luxurious compound. And it was. To the rear of the mansion were tennis courts as well as a 110-foot heated swimming pool lined with Italian marble and traversed by a Venetian marble bridge. In all, the Davies compound housed fifty-five spacious suites, each with two bedrooms, a private bath, and a sitting room. Hearst provided separate suites for Marion and himself, which were connected by a hidden door. And the cost? When Hearst finally finished his inevitable tinkering and constant changes, the estimated price was $7 million—$3 million for construction and $4 million for the furnishings and artwork.[3]

While becoming a major social player in Hollywood, Hearst also ingratiated himself with the film industry in other ways. Over the past two years, through his newspapers and magazines, he had promoted Cosmopolitan and MGM studios, and rival concerns in general, not just weekly but daily. Hearst always had a special touch for creating publicity.

In April 1925, the *New York American* sponsored a coast-to-coast party for its readers, which provided—for $600 per person—a round-trip train ticket from New York City to Hollywood; the high point of this tour was the shooting of actual scenes that starred Marion Davies at the MGM studios in Culver City. Early in September the innovative Hearst came up with another publicity gimmick, a souvenir movie star spoon. For three clipped coupons from the *New York American* and nineteen cents, fans could purchase a silver-plated spoon, embossed with the facsimile and signature of their favorite actor or actress. An adoring public bought these collectors items by the thousands. Late in September Hearst continued his screen promotions by sponsoring a nationwide contest that would select the next baby movie star between the ages of two and seven. After months of excitement, a *New York American* panel of judges chose a young boy named Edwin Hubbell. They failed to mention that his father was Joe Hubbell, who was Hearst's senior newsreel executive.[4]

Hearst identified himself even more solidly with the motion picture industry by the grandest of all his promotions—a weekend excursion to San Simeon, which film historian Lewis Pizzitola dubbed "Hollywood on the hill." What a unique experience it was, one unlike any other. While Marion customarily selected the guest list from the Hollywood crowd, usually twenty to sixty in number, Hearst issued formal letter invitations—with enclosed train tickets—through his secretary, Joe Willicombe. Such "invites" were like a summons from on high that the selected participant, while greatly honored, seldom if ever refused. Hearst was considered that powerful. Guests were to arrive at the Southern Pacific station in Los Angeles, usually between 7:00 and 8:00 P.M. on Friday, where a special train awaited them. After being served a cocktail with dinner, they eventually settled into private compartments for the night. Upon arriving at the sleepy California town of San Luis Obispo early in the morning, the train was sidetracked, allowing the guests to sleep until 7:00 A.M. Some ate a quick breakfast before disembarking into assembled taxis (actually limousines), which Hearst provided for the forty-five-mile ride north to San Simeon. Upon arrival, they presented their credentials to armed sentries at a huge iron gate, which was the entrance route to the Enchanted Hill. Then they made their way slowly up a winding mountain road for five miles, halting intermittently to avoid roaming herds of cattle or exotic animals and birds from the Hearst zoo: zebras, camels, buffaloes, ibexes, and emus. Upon reaching the top of the hill, they stopped at still another gate, where Hearst's designated housekeeper walked them to luxurious private suites and, with the help of servants, settled them in.[5]

For his guests Hearst set an agenda that was organized but flexible, orderly yet relaxed. Despite a staff of at least three butlers and, as Marion put it, "God knows how many maids," Hearst did not allow room service. The honored guests ate breakfast buffet style in the Refectory between 9:00 A.M. and noon, then lunch at about 2:30 P.M. For dinner, which usually occurred at about half past eight, they began gathering in the Assembly Room an hour earlier for one cocktail, the maximum amount that Hearst allowed at San Simeon. As a topic of conversation, the Assembly Room itself was enough, especially with the dazzling grandeur of Hearst's creation on display: his priceless objects of art and exquisite furniture and huge fire mantel, primarily from the Renaissance, encompassed by four magnificent tapestries. Marion was an effervescent hostess, mingling easily with her friends while challenging them to partake in her pet passion—a giant jigsaw puzzle located prominently on a convenient table. All the while the guests awaited the entrance of their host who customarily entered from a well-concealed elevator (constructed in 1928), which was linked to his living quarters, the Gothic Suite, on the third floor of Casa Grande.

Hearst's appearance signaled the time for dinner in the Refectory, an experience which by itself was memorable. Like royalty, Hearst sat at the center of a huge elongated table, with Marion across from him. Printed cards designated the place for each guest, with those nearest Hearst deemed the most honored. Except on special occasions the dress code was casual and informal, although the waiters were outfitted in white jackets and bow ties. As in the Assembly Room, the guests luxuriated in the opulence of the Refectory's impressive setting, that of fourteenth-century Spanish choir stalls and gilt iron church grille, with colorful Tuscan silk flags hanging twenty feet overhead.

Amidst such astounding opulence the guests marveled at the contrast, the incongruity of the setting. While impressed with a table adorned with plates of fine China, delicate crystal, sterling silverware, and resplendent with three-foot silver candlesticks, they were amazed that bottles of ketchup, mustard, and other condiments, as well as paper napkins, were on hand—a reminder that Hearst called San Simeon "the ranch." But "the dinners were elaborate," Charlie Chaplin recalled, the main course often featuring "pheasant, wild duck, partridge, and venison," because Hearst selected the menu.[6]

With the completion of dinner by 11:00 P.M., Hearst invited his guests to see a first-run movie or, at times, one of Marion's classics. Until the completion of the theater on the ground floor of the North Wing (early in the 1930s), he held such showings outdoors, following the tradition of the early days at Camp Hill.

The guests, however, had many things to occupy their time. For some, the grandeur of San Simeon, the awe-inspiring view westward to the Pacific, the magnificent gardens and trees, the zoo with exotic animals and birds, and the presence of Hollywood's beautiful people were entertainment enough. For the more energetic and athletic, the choices could be tennis with a young tennis pro such as Alice Marble, a swim in the breathtakingly beautiful Neptune Pool or Roman Pool, or a Hearst-led horseback ride to a scenic picnic spot. He also provided his guests with "you-name-it-and-Hearst-had-it" clothes—swimsuits, riding habits, evening attire, with appropriate shoes or boots.[7]

The only negatives of the San Simeon experience had to do with certain Hearst rules. Somewhat surprisingly, amidst such generosity, any guest making a long-distance phone call had to pay for it before departure. But the cardinal sin involved liquor. Hearst would not allow anyone sneaking a bottle onto the premises. For those few who foolishly ignored this edict, Hearst's majordomo packed their bags and summarily escorted them to a waiting taxi for the long ride to San Luis Obispo and the even longer trip to Los Angeles.[8]

At departure time on Sunday evening, the honored guests agreed that the weekend at San Simeon was an unforgettable experience. Or putting it another way upon viewing Casa Grande and Enchanted Hill, George Bernard Shaw quipped to Hearst, "No doubt, this was the way God would have built the place if he had your money."[9]

During 1926 Hearst appreciated more and more his California environment and lifestyle. A return to his native state signaled a new beginning for him, a revival of mind and spirit. No longer did he have to endure the bitter political fights with Tammany Hall, the acerbic barbs of such politicians as Al Smith that rival New York City newspapers delighted recounting in their publications. In California he controlled the major news outlets—*Los Angeles Examiner, Los Angeles Herald, San Francisco Examiner, San Francisco Call,* and *Oakland Cal Post Enquirer*—which, like all Hearst newspapers, presented him in a favorable and, with few exceptions, a laudatory light. As in past years he instituted a proven crusade formula for success with his readers by advocating progressive legislation that would enhance the lives of fellow Californians and, at the same time, promote his own popularity. For instance, the *Los Angeles Examiner* advocated daily on its editorial pages the building of the Boulder Canyon high dam and a Colorado River aqueduct, which would help alleviate the pressing need for water in the state. To address the growing transportation demands of southern California, the *Examiner* also demanded a rapid transit system and the construction of major traffic highways, which would attract industries.[10]

On the national level, Hearst championed causes that attained further approbation and favor with Americans. In editorial after editorial his newspapers praised seventy-one-year-old Secretary of the Treasury Andrew Mellon for his policies of fiscal responsibility—of balancing the federal budget and paying off the national debt. But more importantly Hearst editorials approved of Mellon's insistence on tax reductions, especially high surtaxes, which inflicted an intolerable burden on "producing" (meaning the wealthiest) Americans. At the same time Hearst suggested a possible reevaluation of the Volstead Act (Nineteenth Amendment). He argued that Prohibition had "aroused a great deal of dissatisfaction among perfectly honest, decent, 'God-fearing' people" because they questioned "whether or not prohibition makes for increased temperance."[11]

Hearst also continued to espouse another popular theme, one that he had advocated for years—"America First." To substantiate this viewpoint he repeatedly quoted on the Hearst editorial pages George Washington's revered foreign policy slogan of the 1790s, "No Entangling Alliances," which to American isolationists meant U.S. rejection of the League of Nations as well as a denunciation of the World Court.[12]

To demonstrate his firm belief in this "America First" foreign policy, Hearst applied his government by newspaper technique against politicians who disagreed with him. Specifically, he directed the editors of his media empire to seek and destroy them whenever possible. In 1926 he had cause to rejoice. In Illinois, Iowa, and Wisconsin, U.S. senatorial candidates (whether Republican or Democrat) who backed American participation in the World Court suffered defeat in primary elections mainly because of, Hearst exultantly trumpeted, opposition by his newspapers. At the same time he vigorously supported Senator Hiram Johnson, who held similar foreign policy sentiments and who was campaigning, the *New York Times* noted, to reestablish himself as the political leader in California. With the Johnson slate of candidates favored to win in November, Hearst reveled in his seemingly revived political power and in having such a potent ally as Hiram Johnson.[13]

As a result of such political successes nation-wide, Hearst decided to invade the dank recesses of New York politics once again. Unwilling to admit that he could no longer sway New York voters to his way of thinking, he chose to support Representative Ogden L. Mills, "a gentleman of wealth and social position" who was the Republican candidate for governor. Hearst could think of no better way to exact sweet revenge on Al Smith—and Tammany as well—than to defeat them at the polls in November with a relatively obscure Republican congressman. A Mills victory would also undermine the presidential aspirations of Smith.[14]

On October 5, 1926, Hearst endorsed Mills for governor, praising him as "a man of brains and courage, more democratic than many Democrats and independent in thought and action." He then threw the full weight of his newspaper organization into a whirlwind, monthlong campaign for Mills. In some ways this gubernatorial race was reminiscent of the first Hylan mayoral contest of 1917. Hearst controlled the major aspects of the campaign, intending to leave nothing to chance. To head up the Mills election committee, he assigned one of his New York editors, T. E. Watson, as the congressman's political caretaker. In other words, Mills delivered no speeches except those written by Hearst operatives, allowed no interviews with the hostile press, and accepted only approved campaign appearances. He even adopted as the central issue in this election a Hearst slander first conceived in 1919 that accused Smith of being in league with the Milk Trust and, due to prohibitively high milk prices, of being responsible for killing babies.[15]

With Congressman Mills well in hand and the political program set, the Hearst media empire assailed Smith and Tammany viciously—and with relish. For Hearst it was payback time. The *New York American* and *Evening Journal* were at their yellowest. Front-page stories daily attacked Smith as "one of the milk crooks" and Tammany chief Olvany as a major profiteer of the Milk Trust graft, charging that both were unconcerned that children in New York were continuing to suffer. The Hearst editorial writers and political cartoonists were equally savage in their written and pictorial displays, at times supplying Mills with acerbic punch lines for his speeches. To entertain and enliven his audience while making his point, Mills repeatedly proclaimed at every campaign stop that Governor Smith "is afraid to look a cow in the eye." And for that matter, "if the . . . [governor's campaign] train met a milk train, Smith's car would jump the track."[16]

Al Smith was a skillful politician with few equals. Since 1919 he had experienced the Hearst treatment from the "Mud-Gutter Gazettes" innumerable times and had emerged victorious each time—although not completely unscathed. He would do so again. Smith recognized the problem facing him and addressed it. "Hearst is the real opponent," he candidly announced in the *New York Times* on October 15. "It seems," he asserted, that "the fates have decreed that in every political contest in which I take part I am called upon to wage the real fight against the sinister figure of

Hearst and all that he stands for in the eyes of American public opinion." New Yorkers should recognize, he pointed out, that "this campaign is the same which Hearst employed to vilify and slander William McKinley, Grover Cleveland, Theodore Roosevelt, Elihu Root, Charles E. Hughes, and practically every decent leader of both the great parties." And to carry out this campaign of calumny and mudslinging, Smith announced, "Hearst's man Watson in the Mills headquarters, at a salary greater than that paid to the Governor for a whole year's work" was in charge.

Over the next two weeks, while the Hearst newspapers waged their journalistic war against Smith and state Democrats, the governor intensified his personal attacks on Hearst. "I have seen some men in my time who are hungry for office," he declared in a public debate with Mills on October 16, "but I know of no one [hungrier], unless it be his partner Hearst." Again, he bluntly stated, "the support given to Mr. Mills by the editor-politician . . . [has] tended to 'degrade' the Republican campaign." And still again, Congressman Mills has come to realize during this campaign "the undisputed fact that William Randolph Hearst . . . [has given] him the kiss of death."[17]

The "kiss of death" for Mills arrived one week before the election. In a detailed report submitted to Mayor Walker, New York City Commissioner of Health Dr. Louis I. Harris announced that the milk in the state was, as the *New York Times* headline blared forth, "SAFE AND GOOD."

As a result, Smith issued this statement that summarized his month-long onslaught. From the beginning of this brief canvass, Mills "took advice from the past grand master of mudslinging campaigning, William Randolph Hearst." And now, Smith concluded, "the milk prop has fallen to the ground. The Congressman may be able to shake the milkcan off his neck, but he'll never get rid of Hearst. That black scar will always be across the end of his neck, and he will carry it to his grave." His assessment was correct. On November 2, 1926, Smith crushed Mills by more than 320,000 votes in a Democratic sweep.[18]

Hearst was not downcast for long over this political defeat. A consummate optimist who sought to displace a setback with some victory or success, he characteristically addressed other problems as soon as possible. San Simeon was always a therapeutic retreat for him, a healing balm for any disappointment. In 1926 he delighted that workmen had already laid the Esplanade on Enchanted Hill, which he enhanced with palms and large shrubs, like camellias and bougainvilleas. At the same time he eagerly anticipated the expansion of the largest private zoo in the world, with pens for more animals under construction. Time and again Hearst demonstrated his love for animals. And as for Casa Grande, he continued to enhance its magnificence, to house a museum that was unlike any other the world had ever seen. On December 14, the *New York Times* reported that Spanish art experts Arthur Byrne and his wife had purchased for Hearst "one of the most valuable romanesque cloisters" from the province of Segovia, dating from the tenth century, and had carefully packed it stone by stone for transport to San Simeon.[19]

Since the quest for political office was no longer a dominant influence in his life, Hearst became heavily involved in business affairs. Both acquisition and ownership continued to be compelling factors. For instance, on August 1, 1927, he and a longtime friend, publisher Paul Block, purchased four Pittsburgh newspapers and merged them into two, with Hearst acquiring the *Pittsburgh Sun-Telegram*. He was now publishing twenty-seven newspapers in sixteen of the largest cities in the United States—and was still in search of other "good buys." The fact that approximately one out of every four American families daily read his news copy was personally gratifying. These estimates, however, did not include the nine Hearst magazines that were printed monthly in the United States and England, the largest being *Cosmopolitan*, whose sales in September and October topped 1.5 million copies. Nor did such statistics involve his planned extension of Hearst Corporation radio broadcasting privileges for eleven cities: New York, Baltimore, Washington, San Francisco, Seattle, Detroit, Boston, Albany, Rochester, Syracuse, and Chicago. As a result, the Hearst media empire, despite prolific business expenditures by Hearst, netted more than $15 million in 1927 alone.[20]

During this high time of business prosperity, of flush economic growth in the United States, Hearst was a willing participant, especially in regard to real estate development in New York City. With the encouragement and support of business partner Arthur Brisbane, he actively indulged his mania for spending. In February 1927, they bought land at the corner of Sixth Avenue and 55th Street, "diagonally opposite the new Ziegfeld Theatre," thereby adding to other choice parcels between 54th and 56th Streets, such as the thirty-six-story Warwick Hotel. Again in May, Hearst snapped up a five-story building near the Brooklyn Bridge for a mere $53,000. And in August he improved his block front property on Eighth Avenue with the purchase of an old YMCA building on 57th and 58th Streets.[21]

Hearst also attended to the financial needs of Millicent who, in the main, shouldered the responsibility for rearing their five children. During the winter of 1926–1927, in a brief moment of melancholia and self-recrimination, he confessed his relationship with Marion—and guilt—to John Francis Neylan, a trusted friend upon whom he relied heavily for advice. "Jack, always remember that Millicent is my wife and the mother of my children. I know I'm the villain of the piece."

After 1926, except on rare occasions such as a costume ball at New York's Ritz-Carleton Hotel late in April celebrating their twenty-third wedding anniversary, Millicent lived a life completely apart from Hearst. In accordance with their "civilized" arrangement, she received all funds necessary to maintain a lifestyle befitting the wife of the world's most prominent publisher as well as substantial support for her several charities.

Millicent had established a year-round routine much to her liking. From January to mid-March she participated in the Florida social whirl at Palm Beach. With the approach of spring she returned to New York for several months, spending much of her time in organizing and promoting benefits for the Free Milk Fund for Babies. By May, she customarily set sail on a European tour, engaging in the lively social season in Paris for several weeks (with headquarters at the Hotel Crillon), often in the company of her close friend, the Duchess de Gramont. Then she traveled to Spain in search of rare artifacts that would interest Hearst; U.S. Ambassador to Spain Alexander P. Moore proved to be an accommodating host. By late July, she returned to New York before boarding a train with her sons for a summer vacation at San Simeon. (After 1927, Hearst, along with Marion, vacated Enchanted Hill whenever Millicent chose to visit.) By October, Millicent reappeared in New York in ample time to head, as she had for the previous fourteen years, the *New York American* Christmas charity in behalf of the city's poor and crippled children.[22]

As a further gesture in his "civilized" arrangement with Millicent, Hearst attempted to equalize living arrangements with the two women in his life. Typically for Hearst, cost was not a factor. After completing Marion's Santa Monica Beach House in the summer of 1927, at an estimated cost of $3 million, he wisely protected his backside. In October he purchased for Millicent a between-season residence—Beacon Towers—for an undisclosed but substantial sum; it was part of the lavish, seven-acre estate of Mrs. Oliver H. P. Belmont (formerly Mrs. William K. Vanderbilt) at Sands Point, Long Island. This prestigious acquisition attempted to balance his largesse between Millicent and Marion, which apparently was satisfactory to both.[23]

Marion accepted the lifestyle that Hearst had scripted for her. As the major star of Cosmopolitan Productions, she continued in much the same vein with MGM. Although an accomplished comedienne, she abided by his wishes to accept roles in historical period pieces. In 1926, she starred in *Beverly of Graustark*, in which she demonstrated "no mean ability," the *New York Times* commented, "in the handling of her [dramatic] role." In 1927 she expanded the range of her talent by playing diversified characters as the lead actress in four films—*The Red Mill, Tillie The Toiler, The Fair Coed,* and *Quality Street*—two of which were lighthearted comedies. Overall, however, she followed Hearst's direction and wishes.

Hearst was determined to make Marion one of Hollywood's top stars and himself a premiere mogul in the film industry. Late in November 1926, he sold his New York Cosmopolitan studio at Second Avenue and 127th Street to the Shuberts for an estimated $1 million. Although still a legal resident of New York, he preferred to devote more time to West Coast projects. Consequently he rented a full floor of the Ambassador Hotel in Los Angeles both as a home and business office. He also provided more space in his twenty-seven newspapers for Hollywood gossip, a journalistic decision that MGM colleague Louis B. Mayer and other motion picture producers appreciated. For the next two decades he promoted Louella Parsons as the foremost tattler of movie personalities. And because of her close friendship with Marion, some Davies tidbit appeared weekly and sometimes daily in the Louella column.

Increasingly Hearst dominanted Marion's life. "He had moved into all of her dependencies," biographer Guiles noted. "He was lover-father-mother as well as her conscience. 'W. R. wouldn't like that' became a frequent comment, said mostly to herself." At San Simeon over the next decade Hearst elevated her "to the position," her biographer observed, "of being one of the world's most favored and interesting hostesses." She welcomed not only the rich and famous of Hollywood but also such world dignitaries—whom Hearst invited to San Simeon—as George Bernard Shaw, Winston Churchill, Calvin Coolidge, Herbert Hoover, Andrew Mellon, Albert Einstein, Charles Lindbergh, and the king of Siam.[24]

During 1927, Hearst was determined to remain a participant in the public forum, although no longer as an aspirant for political office. Early in January he decided to launch a crusade for world peace, a proposal that provoked widespread discussion and placed him at the center of a controversial debate. In a front-page editorial in all his newspapers, he argued that the "English Speaking Nations of the World Should Join to Maintain the Peace." After all, the League of Nations was "a phantom with form but no substance" and "was unable to present a united front on any question." Nor was the World Court any better. Both institutions would involve the United States in "entangling alliances" with Europe. Hearst therefore reverted to the argument held by him and other progressives regarding American foreign policy prior to World War I that the "civilized nations" (meaning those of "Caucasian" origin) were the purveyors of culture, the practitioners of democracy, indeed the protectors of law and liberty.

Because of a common language as well as similar cultural and historical traditions, English-speaking nations such as the "United States, Great Britain, Ireland, Canada, Australia, New Zealand, and South Africa" should be responsible, Hearst announced, for maintaining world peace.[25]

Although this crusade for peace received little support, except in the Hearst newspapers, it served a necessary purpose. Hearst received academic acceptance from a little-known quarter. On May 22, Oglethorpe University in Atlanta, to which Hearst had donated four hundred acres of land and $100,000 and where third oldest son John Randolph was attending, conferred on him an honorary doctor of laws degree with this simple accolade: "William Randolph Hearst, counsellor of millions, lover of America, exponent of a perpetual peace entente among the . . . [English] speaking peoples of the world." In turn, he delivered the baccalaureate address on this subject and then let the subject drop.[26]

Hearst quickly focused on another event. On the day that he received his honorary doctorate, newspapers across the world announced that a twenty-five-year-old American aviator, Charles A. Lindbergh Jr., had landed at Le Bourget airport in Paris; he was the first man to cross the Atlantic Ocean in a solo flight. Boyishly handsome, with a seemingly impeccable character, he became a true American hero overnight. During the Roaring Twenties, with its emphasis on moneymaking coupled with excessive living, Lindbergh represented something that Americans were not. As historian Arthur Schlesinger Jr. put it, Lindbergh "was a symbol of redemption. He personified all that the twenties passionately wanted to admire—adventure in a time of calculation, faith in a time of expediency, youth in a time of gross middle age. He carried people away from the furies that consumed them back to motives deeper and higher than the pursuit of private gain."[27]

Hearst recognized the Lindbergh phenomenon that was mesmerizing an adoring public and planned to use it to his advantage. When President Coolidge sent the cruiser *Memphis* to escort Lindbergh home from England early in June, Hearst engineered his own scenario. Patience and timing were of the utmost importance. On the morning of June 13 Lindbergh, after being cheered in Washington by crowds numbering in the hundreds of thousands and after being offered every hospitality by the president, proceeded on his triumphal tour to New York City. More than 4 million people roared their approval in an hour-long parade up Broadway from the Battery. At makeshift grandstands before city hall, Chairman of the Mayor's Committee on Reception, Grover A. Whalen introduced him to Mayor Jimmy Walker, who officially welcomed him for a holiday celebration of Lindbergh Day and pinned a specially made medal of New York City on his lapel, in effect offering him the keys to the city. For the next two days New Yorkers celebrated their hero as he attended every function on a crowded schedule and met the state's most important personages, including elderly Cardinal Hayes of New York and Governor Al Smith.[28]

After dinner on June 15, at a little past 9:00 P.M., Lindbergh motored to a reception at 86th Street and Riverside Drive, which was "the home," the *New York Times* succinctly reported, "of Mr. Hearst." Whether purposefully or not, Hearst did not arrive until thirty minutes later—and then the Hearst treatment, that of pressured persuasion, began. From several sources, including the recordings of Lindbergh biographer Scott Berg, the meeting proceeded in this fashion. Hearst, after dealing with the usual preliminary amenities, such as showing Lindbergh his fabulous collections of armor and art objects, set forth an offer of such "extravagance" that was so typically Hearst. Lindbergh would star in a motion picture about aviation opposite Marion Davies of Cosmopolitan Pictures. As compensation he would receive $500,000 plus 10 percent of the gross receipts, a bonus that should eventually total in the millions of dollars.

Hearst then handed Lindbergh a contract that needed only his signature. As a further point of assurance—and persuasion—Hearst stated that this production would not be a motion picture in the ordinary sense. Rather, it would be the actual story of Lindbergh's life, in reality, Hearst confidently predicted, "an historical record of a fine life and a great achievement to be preserved in pictures for others to see in years to come." In fact, Lindbergh should not consider this proposed motion picture as a testimonial to his own glorification, Hearst concluded, "but as an inspiration to others."

Lindbergh, however, withstood the Hearst treatment, at least temporarily. He later revealed in his memoirs a wholesome disdain for Hearst personally and his newspapers in particular. "They seemed to be overly sensational, inexcusably inaccurate, and excessively occupied with the troubles and vices of mankind." For that matter, he continued, "I disliked most of the men I had met who represented him, and I did not want to be associated with the organization he had built."

Lindbergh thus evaded Hearst's entreaties. "I wish I could do it if it would please you," he diplomatically replied, "but I cannot, because I said I would not go into pictures."

After moments of awkward hesitation, Hearst replied, "All Right—but you tear up the contract; I have not the heart to do it."

Lindbergh was now "more embarrassed than ever" and "attempted to hand it back." But Hearst applied more pressure. "No," he sadly stated, "if you don't want to make a picture, tear it up and throw it away." Lindbergh thus reacted, ripping the contract in half and depositing it in the nearby fireplace as Hearst watched, Lindbergh would long remember, with "amused astonishment."

But Hearst, unaccustomed to suffering a rebuff or a defeat except in politics, was subtly persistent. Lindbergh, upon leaving, "stopped at a table to admire a pair of silver globes, fourteen inches high," one "terrestrial," the other "celestial." He was informed that they were crafted in Hanover in 1700 and were the only pair in existence, with their value estimated at $50,000. The next day Lindbergh received a package at his Fifth Avenue apartment "bearing these two silver spheres." Within six months Lindbergh's life story—from birth to Le Bourget, titled "We"—ran in chapter form daily in the Hearst newspapers.[29]

Hearst realized how the thrill and romance of flying captured the public imagination. To boost newspaper circulation, he instructed his editors to publicize the exploits of aviators the world over, particularly their fantastic feats of derring-do. To Clarence Chamberlin and Charles Levine, who flew to Berlin within weeks after Lindbergh touched down at Le Bourget on May 21, 1927, Hearst offered a contract of $100,000 for a return trip to New York City, with them giving the Hearst newspapers exclusive rights to the accounts of their experiences. Soon thereafter he sponsored the so-called Dole flight to Hawaii that ended with the death of two pilots. And early in September, he promoted the Old Glory flying expedition, a nonstop trans-Atlantic flight from New York to Rome. Yet, because of the increasing number of aerial disasters late in the summer of 1927, Hearst tried to persuade the pilots to forgo this trip, "accept the prize" of $25,000 that he had offered, and "give up [this] dangerous expedition." But his efforts were to no avail. On September 13, the *New York American* headline blared, "OLD GLORY WRECK FOUND! NO TRACE OF THREE FLIERS." This disaster ended his aviation promotions, at least temporarily.[30]

Toward the end of 1927, another disaster awaited Hearst, one of his own making that damaged him professionally as a newspaper man, one that caused a Hearst biographer to proclaim his actions as "something approaching lunacy." It had to do with official documents, obtained through stealth from Mexican archival files, which supposedly authenticated the existence of anti-American plots by Mexico. Beginning on November 14 and then running daily through December 9, the Hearst newspapers broke the story that accused the Mexican government under President Plutarco Elias Calles of conspiring against the United States. These documents charged that Calles had financed an anti-American rebellion in

Nicaragua with "a million dollars in one lump sum to the rebel cause" and had fostered communism among Guatemalan Indians who were being trained to fight U.S. marines stationed in Nicaragua. Then to protect Mexican interests and gain favorable consideration in Washington, President Calles agreed to spread money to important personages among the press as well as politicians, the most prominent being "four United States senators," the *New York American* announced on December 9, who were "to be paid $1,215,000" for their services to Mexico.[31]

Such allegations required immediate validation. Although no senators were mentioned by name in the Hearst exposé denoting bribery, that information quickly came to light. On December 10, Hearst editors turned over the Mexican documents to a Senate committee headed by David Reed of Pennsylvania. Within days the committee issued subpoenas to major participants in this scandal—the Mexican consul general in New York, Arturo M. Elias, who purportedly paid for the documents; Victor Watson, who was presently Hearst's managing editor of the *New York Daily Mirror* and a key participant in the exposé; John Page, whose name appeared over the articles; and the man responsible for the promotion of this scandal, William Randolph Hearst.[32]

After three weeks of testimony, the Senate committee members agreed that the Mexican documents were a canard, a malicious fabrication having absolutely nothing to do with the truth other than the fact that Hearst had fully endorsed the project. For instance, Hearst admitted in testimony before the committee that his newsmen had not considered the Mexican documents to be forgeries, even though such "official" papers, untypically, were replete with grammatical mistakes. Nor at any time did they hire a handwriting expert to verify the signature of President Calles or, for that matter, question the validity of such startling revelations.[33]

In regard to the four U.S. senators, the documents not only revealed their names but also the amount of tainted money each one allegedly received; and again the question of authenticity arose. All four senators—William Borah of Idaho ($500,000), George Norris of Nebraska ($350,000), Thomas Heflin of Alabama ($350,000), and the younger Robert La Follette of Wisconsin (a mere $15,000)—were prominent members of Congress; they had never suffered the taint of scandal.

Testifying before the committee, Hearst was soon in full retreat. He admitted that his staff could not produce any evidence that the senators in question had ever received any payment. He then replied concerning the question of their guilt, "I do not believe the charge."[34]

Although the Senate committee hearings continued into the second week of January 1928, Hearst's testimony on December 15 actually settled the issue. But the reverberations of disdain and contempt for this type of journalism gathered momentum, reflecting a growing disrespect for Hearst and his journalistic creation. The investigation proved that the Mexican documents were forgeries, slipshod in research, spurious in content, and malicious in purpose. On December 19, Senator Norris summed up this sordid affair by reading into the *Congressional Record* these scathing comments. "A fair analysis of the recent articles published in the Hearst papers," he asserted, "leads to the inevitable conclusion that you are not only unfair and dishonest, but that you are entirely without honor." He then delineated numerous misstatements of fact produced in the four-week-old Mexican documents story (occupying four full columns of fine print in the *Congressional Record*) before summarizing the feelings about Hearst by a growing number of Americans: "The record which you have made in this matter is sufficient to place your publications in disrepute in the minds of all honest men, and it demonstrates that the Hearst system of newspapers, spreading like a venomous web to all parts of the country, constitutes the sewer system of American journalism." The members of the special Senate committee agreed. They immediately declared the four senators innocent. But the reasons why Hearst promoted this ugly incident, while open to speculation, still remain a mystery.[35]

Yet Hearst was unperturbed by these public reprimands. "He welcomed attack," Moses Koenigsberg marveled. "It was a pretext for the expression of his greatest talent. No publicist of his generation surpassed him in polemic writing." Besides, with so many interests, life was too full, too gratifying to be distracted by temporary setbacks. In politics, for instance, despite bitter defeats by Al Smith and Tammany Hall, he found solace in the Republican Party. After his strong support in the 1924 elections, Republican leaders sought his favor and understandably so. On November 22, 1927, President Coolidge invited him for lunch at the White House. Secretary of the Treasury Andrew Mellon, a fellow art collector, considered him a personal friend who had similar political views, especially in regard to federal tax cuts. And Senator Hiram Johnson deemed him to be a staunch ally; they were battling the potent Power Trust, urging the federal government, not private industry, to build Boulder Dam on the Colorado River, which would be a tremendous economic boon to Californians.[36]

In 1928 Hearst again applied his energies to the accumulation of more property. His competitiveness, his all-encompassing need to excel in any endeavor, and his utter disregard for money pushed him to be a top landowner in New York City. On February 6, despite warnings to the contrary by trusted realtor Martin Huberth, he bought the forty-one-story Ritz Tower on Park Avenue and 57th Street from business associate and close friend Arthur Brisbane, who had overextended his financial reaches; Hearst assumed a mortgage loan of $4.5 million. Yet he was seemingly unconcerned, because eleven days later he purchased a six-story building on 56th Street and Madison Avenue that adjoined some of his other properties, including the twelve-story Hotel Essex. Then in August, October, and November he added three more sizable holdings as part of his development projects, the *New York Times* stated, for rental and publishing enterprises.[37]

Yet Hearst continued to expend both time and money on his grand passion, his monument to posterity on Enchanted Hill. In January 1928, although persuaded by Julia Morgan and John Neylan to reduce costs at San Simeon from $50,000 to $30,000 per month, Hearst had difficulty staying within such budget constraints. San Simeon demanded his attention and energy, indeed his creative genius. With the luxurious Gothic Suite and the fabulous Gothic Study now completed on the third floor of Casa Grande, where Marion and he would reside, an elevator became an immediate priority.

Other San Simeon projects also demanded attention. As a consequence, workmen expanded and laid tile for the Central Plaza, which encompassed a quatrefoil marble pool. They also enlarged a terrace west of Casa del Sol (House C) in proper proportion to the nearby Neptune swimming pool, with its Neptune Pavilion containing seventeen dressing rooms. With great care they replanted large oak trees and full-size date palms, following Hearst's preservation and scenic dictates. Prompted by numerous helpful suggestions from the master of San Simeon, they remodeled and lengthened the pantry and kitchen on the South Wing near the Refectory, while constructing twelve bedroom suites in the three floors above.

At the same time other workmen attended to the Hearst zoo. With the acquisition of three hundred animals by 1928, including "three cougars, five lions, two bobcats, a leopard, a cheetah, three kinds of bears, a chimpanzee, three java monkeys, a tapir," as well as two kangaroos, a wallaby, and (in 1929) an elephant, Hearst directed Morgan to erect shelters and feeding troughs in safe locations but in sight of San Simeon guests. He therefore suggested the construction of "exceedingly picturesque log houses" that would be "in certain picturesque locations not far from the main road," the cost of which San Simeon historian Victoria Kastner estimated at $75,000.[38]

Hearst had still other creative and expensive ideas. With San Simeon halfway between Los Angeles and San Francisco, the need for swift transportation was essential. Hence, besides providing for his guests a special train from Los Angeles to San Luis Obispo and then a fleet of limousines to transport guests to San Simeon, he decided that air travel would be necessary at times. Late in June 1927, he placed an order for an eight-passenger, single-engine plane with Fokker Aircraft Corporation, with an initial down payment of $20,000. He then directed Morgan to construct a landing field near the highway at Sam Simeon. At first it was little more than a graded strip in a pasture.[39]

Hearst was thus preparing San Simeon for its ultimate purpose and his most cherished dream. In a letter to Morgan as early as February 1927, he announced that "many fine things" from the storage warehouses would soon "be arriving for the ranch." Somewhat amazed, he pointed out, "I had no idea when we began to build the ranch that I would be here so much or that the construction itself would be so important." But "under the present circumstances," he happily concluded, "I see no reason why the ranch should not be a museum of the best things that I can secure."[40]

During 1928 Hearst was pleased with the patterns of his hectic existence; overall, life was good. For instance, when second son Bill Jr. married Alma Walker of San Francisco on March 24, Hearst arranged to celebrate this happy occasion with Millicent. In May, Simon & Schuster published *W. R. Hearst: An American Phenomenon* by John K. Winkler, who was a former reporter for the *New York American*. In two full pages a reviewer of the rival *New York Times* hailed Hearst as "A MODERN MONTE CRISTO" and proclaimed the biography to be "the best . . . I have read in some time." With the book enjoying brisk sales, Hearst had to be pleased, although indicating to a friend that he would not buy a copy because, he explained: "If it doesn't tell the truth it will make me mad, and if it tells the truth it will make me sad."[41]

By habit an active participant in politics, Hearst watched the national parties select their leaders for the 1928 presidential election. For the first time in years he neither dealt with nor affected the nominations. At the Republican convention meeting in Kansas City early in June, Hearst favored Secretary of the Treasury Andrew Mellon for president. Despite vigorous efforts by Hollywood associate Louis B. Mayer to swing him into the Herbert Hoover camp, he remained committed to Mellon, whom he had previously endorsed in several editorials.

With the nomination of Hoover, however, Hearst soon committed himself to the Republican agenda. Two weeks later the Democrats, meeting in Houston, selected Al Smith as their standard bearer. Once again Hearst intended to "pay his respects" to an inveterate enemy. Over the next several months in the Hearst newspapers (now numbering twenty-eight with the purchase of the *Omaha Bee* in July), he systematically did just that.[42]

With his business enterprises in good order, Hearst planned to indulge himself by resurrecting an old custom that his mother had designed for him: a trip to Europe. Of course, it had to be on a grand scale, one of epic proportions, which would be under his meticulous direction. On July 20, 1928, Hearst and Marion sailed from New York, but on separate ships—he on the *Olympic* and she on the *Ile de France*. With precise instructions he ordered his man Friday, personal secretary Joe Willicombe, to direct their twenty-six trunks of luggage to the proper ships. He also provided an extensive guest list that included not only Marion's sisters Rose and Ethel, niece and nephew Pepi and Charlie Lederer, but a number of her closest Hollywood girlfriends. Hearst also included third son John and bride Gretchen, who had married the previous December; this trip was Hearst's honeymoon present to them. And to round out this increasingly large cast of travelers, he included several of Millicent's relatives, his society columnist Maury Paul (whose pen name was Cholly Knickerbocker), and Harry Crocker, who had been designated as his traveling secretary. Upon reaching Paris, he invited Alice Head, editor of his London magazines (who had purchased St. Donat's for him in 1925), to join the grand tour. Well in advance of departure, Hearst had let it be known that he would shoulder all expenses; his sole compensation, he repeatedly told the group, was that "they would take something home with them in the way of a new cultural experience."[43]

What a cultural experience it was—not just for the Hearst expedition but for those villagers who witnessed this American invasion. As tour director extraordinaire, Hearst orchestrated every step of the trip. He planned all meals and when to partake of them. For transportation, he rented four large touring cars. Then into the French countryside they proceeded, to Versailles, Rambouillet, Chartres, and Tours. At each step of the way, they drew large crowds and photo ops. The villagers were fascinated with the unannounced arrival of "extremely beautiful and attractive girls from Hollywood dressed in the smartest of summer frocks from Magnin's." Somewhat amused, Hearst remarked to Alice Head on one occasion, "We're much the most important people, but nobody wants to photograph us."

Onward the Hearst entourage leisurely continued, to Vichy, Grenoble, and south through the French Riviera en route to Lyon and Monte Carlo. Determined that his guests appreciate this rare privilege afforded them, he led them on tours of palaces, cathedrals, and galleries, all historically inspired and wonderfully endowed with cultural gifts of the ages.

Then at the end of the day, during dinner, Hearst examined his charges on their day's discoveries and pointed out the importance of each.

On to Italy they proceeded, as the days turned into weeks. By the end of August they had visited "palaces and galleries and churches in Florence" before journeying to the Lido, where they "spent a thrilling fortnight at the Hotel Excelsior." Then on to Venice they continued, where Hearst sponsored a shopping spree for his guests. With shopkeepers seemingly aware of his reputation for extravagance, he became, Alice Head marveled, "a kind of perpetual Santa Claus."[44]

After two months the tour began to wind down. Hearst decided to invade Germany for several days, to take "the cure" (hot baths) at Bad Nauheim, then sail down the Rhine for a scenic view of the historic castles before returning to Paris. Then on to London he proceeded for the last leg of the tour.[45]

Once here Hearst continued to build upon his growing legend, to astound onlookers by his actions, to create an image unexpected of mortal men. Since he had bought, sight unseen, the twelfth-century Welsh castle St. Donat's three years earlier, he announced to Alice Head as well as Richard E. Berlin, one of his magazine executives who happened to be in London, that his curiosity had to be quelled. "Let's go down to St. Donat's and look it over."

This request was a summons from on high, which Head and Berlin immediately complied with. Anticipating Hearst's propensity for architectural revisions, especially of this medieval fortress, they prevailed on Sir Charles Allom, a distinguished architect who had won knighthood for redecorating Buckingham Palace, to accompany them. Their reading of Hearst's disposition was surely correct. They drove 160 miles to St. Donat's, arriving late in the evening. Hearst was so excited that, true to form, he "suggested" an immediate tour of the grounds as well as the entire infrastructure. So by the light of kerosene lamps, they investigated this dimly lit, ancient castle, all 135 rooms, before retiring for the night. Upon arising the next morning, they drove to Southhampton, where Hearst boarded the *Berengaria* and sailed for New York. Several weeks later Allom received a twenty-five-page letter, listing in detail alterations for every aspect of St. Donat's.

Thus the Hearst legend, that of a man oblivious to financial costs, who was a creative genius in journalism as well as castle building, who flaunted social customs by his pursuit of a Hollywood actress, who attacked his own economic class by advocating progressive legislation, and who was a dominant figure in any field of endeavor in which he participated (except as a candidate for political office) continued to grow. Added to this expanding list of remarkable abilities was a hitherto unknown talent, that of a photographic memory.[46]

Returning to New York on October 5, 1928, Hearst made his presence known. To a *New York Times* reporter he announced, "I am inclined to favor Mr. Hoover on the basis of continuing the administration that seems to have been a success and a benefit to the country." He then disingenuously stated, "I am not opposed to Mr. Smith. I merely think that Mr. Hoover is better for the country," especially since no "deep democratic principles are at issue."

Without question, Hearst sided with the Republicans. For the next three months the twenty-eight Hearst newspapers conducted a nationwide straw poll that publicized a Hoover victory daily. And on Election Day, November 5, all predictions became a happy reality. The *New York American* headlines on November 8 stated Hearst's elation best: "ONLY 8 STATES FOR SMITH." And then, "SMITH THROUGH WITH ALL POLITICS."[47]

Yet for Hearst not everything was picture perfect. Toward the end of 1928 he became increasingly concerned about the economic condition of his newspaper chain, especially with the crown jewels of his empire, the *New York American* and *New York Journal*, suffering circulation attrition due to fierce competition from the *New York Times* and the *New York Daily Mirror*. He therefore applied his showmanship techniques, which encompassed fresh as well as proven ideas, to attract new readers. On Christmas Eve the Hearst newspapers, in cooperation with the National Broadcasting Company, sponsored an hourlong concert, beginning at 11:00 P.M. It was, the *New York American* trumpeted, "a spiritual service of unprecedented magnitude" in which carolers spread holiday joy into millions of American homes over the radio.[48]

As a follow-up to this successful venture, Hearst initiated several crusades in 1929 that stirred up considerable controversy. On January 3, he conducted a contest in his newspapers, offering a $25,000 first prize for the "best plan to repeal the Eighteenth Amendment and," he announced, "substitute in place of prohibition a more liberal and more American measure which will secure for the public a more genuine temperance." On June 1, after more than 70,000 temperance proposals by readers nationwide denounced prohibition, the plan submitted by Judge Franklin Chase Hoyt of the Children's Court of New York City won the $25,000 first prize. He proposed that "Congress repeal the Volstead Act and substitute a law defining the words 'intoxicating liquors'" as "'all alcoholic products of distillation.'" Congress should then "ban the manufacture, sale, and transportation of such products throughout the country, except for commercial and medicinal purposes, but at the same time let . . . each State . . . regulate and control the manufacture and sale of all malt, brewed and fermented beverages within its own borders." Hearst immediately endorsed the Hoyt plan, although realizing that the repeal of the Eighteenth Amendment was the ultimate solution.[49]

A second crusade targeting Hearst readers related to an appeal for income tax revision, indeed a demand for Congress and the incoming Hoover administration to give the people a tax break on earned income. Although previously praising Andrew Mellon for such a stance, Hearst began this crusade anew with an editorial in the *New York American* on March 2, 1929. Two days later he published a petition to Congress that appeared daily in all Hearst papers "in behalf of the earned income class." This crusade was wildly popular; within two weeks it had collected 150,000 signatures, representing what the *American* called the income tax army. By the end of May, membership had surpassed several million, a fact that pleased Hearst.[50]

But Hearst was determined to breathe new life into his newspapers, to involve as well as educate his millions of readers. In the past he had always found one journalistic technique to be highly successful that of appealing to the patriotic impulses of Americans. Early in February 1929, the Hearst chain of newspapers thus established a nationwide flag contest revolving around seventy-five questions concerning the history of the flag, which would appear in the Hearst newspapers daily, usually four at a time. The purpose of the contest was to spread understanding of and appreciation for American ideals and institutions represented by the flag. Those eligible would be boys and girls between the ages of fourteen and eighteen enrolled in "public high schools or their equivalent in private or parochial schools." The winners—two boys and two girls—to be announced on June 14, 1929 (Flag Day), would receive from the Hearst newspapers an expense-paid trip around the world, escorted by a chaperon of their choosing. They would also be provided with appropriate clothes and luggage for this grand adventure. Again Hearst was jubilant. He intuitively understood how much Americans enjoyed entering contests, especially patriotic ones, and having their children receive the financial benefits from a competitive victory.[51]

To attract subscribers Hearst decided to provide reading entertainment unparalleled by his competitors. He persuaded outgoing President Calvin Coolidge to write about his life experiences both in and out of office. At considerable expense Hearst signed contracts with leading authors of the day to allow their works to be serialized in the Hearst newspaper chain. For example, such classics as *All Quiet on the Western Front* by Erich Maria Remarque and *Little Caesar* by W. R. Burnett entertained *New York American* and *Evening Journal* readers with single-chapter presentations from July 14 to September 21. Then from September 29 to October 16, they enjoyed a journalistic biography of *The Life of Jimmy Walker* (the popular mayor of New York City) by O. O. McInty.[52]

But for further rejuvenation of his journalistic empire, Hearst needed a major dramatic production that would capture the imagination of the people. Since Lindbergh's Atlantic flight to Le Bourget in May 1927, Americans had become enamored with anything having to do with airplanes and aerial endeavors, with the romantic adventures of aviators attempting to conquer the heavens. Hearst was no different. As a result, he concocted a pièce de résistance, bold in conception and dramatic in purpose. On August 1 he announced that the Hearst newspaper chain was sponsoring an "around the world flight of the great Graf Zeppelin," the giant dirigible captained by the "famous skipper, Dr. Hugo Eckener." Passengers included renowned polar explorer Sir Hubert Wilkins, "brilliant British woman" Lady Drummond-Hay, and noted newspaper correspondent Carl H. von Wiegand, who would record their experiences each day exclusively for Hearst readers.

Hearst projected this flight into a media extravaganza. While radio commentators interviewed the travelers at each stop along the way, RKO Cameo produced a talking film, the *New York American* announced, of the "flight that thrilled all nations."[53]

For Hearst, the year 1929 was proving to be a huge success. Besides stimulating circulation in the Hearst newspapers and magazines, he continued to expand his multiple business operations. In Hollywood late in June, he concluded an "important and far-reaching deal" with Louis B. Mayer, the *New York American* announced, whereby MGM would "continue to produce and release the pictures starring Marion Davies," and in turn Hearst would merge his sound newsreel service (Hearst Metrotone News) into a new company known as the MGM International Newsreel. During the summer of 1929, within the space of six weeks, he increased his already impressive New York City real estate holdings with three major properties, costing approximately $6.5 million. And on September 1, he purchased the *San Francisco Bulletin* for an estimated $1 million, merging it with the *San Francisco Call* while leaving renowned editor Fremont Older in charge.[54]

In his personal life Hearst seemed to have few complications. Millicent continued to follow an expensive, high-society schedule—winter at Palm Beach, usually summer in Europe followed by a brief stay at San

Simeon, then charity functions and parties during the holiday season in New York City. Hearst also placated her in other ways, such as including her in a special invitation for lunch at the White House with President Hoover in May and helping arrange a party for Winston Churchill at her Riverside Drive home in October.[55]

At the same time Marion continued to accept the role that Hearst had created for her. With a lucrative new contract from MGM she was assured of job security and continued stardom as well as unlimited publicity from the Hearst media. During the summer of 1929 she was taking singing and dancing lessons for her first talkie, *Marianne*, which appeared late in the fall. And except on rare occasions when Hearst became too obsessive in structuring her life and career or ignored her needs—whereupon she lashed out at him—Marion seemed quite content. On weeknights she often entertained members of the Hollywood crowd and Hearst's special friends with lavish parties at her Beach House; on weekends she was mistress of San Simeon. Late in September, for example, Marion and Charlie Chaplin delighted in performing a burlesque on Shakespeare for Hearst's honored guest Winston Churchill at her Santa Monica mansion, then proceeded with him to Hearst's ranch for several days. Like Louis B. Mayer, who marveled at Hearst's unusual lifestyle, Churchill must have been amazed after Millicent's party for him in New York the next month.[56]

During the last week of October 1929, however, a devastating turn of events occurred that no American would ever forget—and surely not Hearst. The great bull market of the New York Stock Exchange collapsed. On October 29 alone, 23.5 billion shares changed hands and by the end of the day stocks had declined by approximately $18 billion from September 1 values. The Great Depression had begun, gravely affecting the economy of the United States and, equally so, the business empire of William Randolph Hearst.[57]

7 Solutions to Depression and President Maker

By the spring of 1930 severe economic depression inundated the United States, creating a contagion of anxiety and fear in its wake. After the Wall Street crash on October 29, President Herbert Hoover repeatedly downplayed the seriousness of the calamity, announcing in conference after conference with the nation's business leaders that the economic downturn was only temporary, that prosperity was "just around the corner." It was inconceivable to him that the business and financial structure of this nation was in danger of total collapse. But the president was wrong. Bread lines began to appear in many of the larger cities, and by the fall of 1930 soup kitchens to feed lines of hungry masses became commonplace. Banks closed, with millions of investors losing their life savings. Wages declined and unemployment rose; hence, debts mounted and purchases dwindled as the downward spiral of depression signaled an even greater economic catastrophe.

In rural America conditions were equally as bad, if not worse. Farmers and cattlemen found little or no market for their produce; and when they did, prices were cut-rate. To make matters worse, a crippling drought, beginning in 1930 and lasting seven years, spread like a pestilence over the Great Plains states, withering and searing all in its path. As a result, bitterness and distress became all too familiar, indebtedness and foreclosure a way of life, paving the way for the Okies and Arkies—as John Steinbeck graphically described in *The Grapes of Wrath*—to travel belatedly on Route 66 to California. In summing up the economic malaise in which Americans found themselves, economic historian John Kenneth Galbraith put it this way: "The singular feature of the great crash of 1929 was that the worst continued to worsen."[1]

At first Hearst was unwilling to accept such judgments, to concede that the depression was catastrophic. On November 15, 1929, some two weeks after the Wall Street crash, he published on the front page of all his newspapers "An Open Letter to President Hoover." His purpose, he announced, was to propose solutions which would restore people's confidence in "the present situation," which would end a "contagious" distrust of the American economic system. He thus urged the president to stay the panic with an immediate "reassuring utterance," then provide a "great psychological uplift" through "vigorous action" by the federal government. He suggested that the Federal Reserve "would do much to restore the confidence of the public" by affording "an opportunity for legitimate investment under the most favorable circumstances," specifically, the lowering of interest rates. Equally important, the president should assemble "the banking and financial leaders of the nation" to take an active role in "reviving confidence and restoring normal prices." Such immediate responses, Hearst concluded, would "compel respect for the sincerity and the determination of the administration" to offset further misfortune.[2]

Through the winter of 1929–1930 the response by the Hoover administration was gratifying to Hearst; the president seemed to be following his advice. Along with the Federal Reserve lowering interest rates, Hoover announced a huge cut in taxes. He also promoted a series of meetings at the White House with the nation's business leaders, with one immediate result; on November 22, the *New York American* headline proclaimed, "Ford Increases Workers' Pay to Boom Prosperity." And with the Hoover administration promising a $6 billion business expansion through construction as well as loans at low-interest rates to farmers, the Sunday *American* editorial confidently proclaimed on December 1, 1929: "Hoover Leads Nation Back to Normalcy."[3]

Although sickening drops in the stock market did occur intermittently during the first three months of 1930, signs of a "substantial recovery," John Galbraith noted, were evident. And as the president continued to prophesy that "Prosperity Is Returning" (March 17 and 19), the Hearst newspapers joined lock step in such predictions. For instance, *New York American* editorials repeatedly bolstered administrative propaganda with optimistic reports and statements about the economy. As a further means of promoting confidence and support with the public, all Hearst newspapers, from late in March to June—in a daily front-page article, titled "Good News of Good Times"—alerted readers to encouraging stories within the paper that justified the subtitle, "Prosperity Is Returning!"[4]

Hearst became a true believer of the administration propaganda, indeed a willing participant in the Hoover recovery plan. While amateurs were selling their stocks at disastrously low prices and thereby cutting their losses, he decided to take advantage of the panic—and buy. To his way of thinking, real estate was always a worthwhile investment. In December 1929, he therefore purchased a large plot in Brooklyn. Early in the spring of 1930, he added two more substantial buildings to his growing property consortium in New York City on West 57th and 58th Streets.

Hearst's spending during this first year of depression seemed to magnify in proportion to his voracious need to possess the previously unobtainable. In March 1930, he rejoiced, along with Welsh antiquarians, in buying priceless English furniture as well as many Gothic and Tudor antiques in order to grace St. Donat's Castle. At the same time he instructed renowned English architect Sir Charles Allom to restore immediately—and regardless of cost—this treasured historical landmark to its former glory, even to the point of replacing stones and paneling as well as improving the lighting of the living rooms.[5]

Nor did Hearst control his appetite for spending. In April he enlarged the circulation of his magazine empire by purchasing *Smart Set-McClure's*. In May he pledged $100,000 to Oglethorpe University, whose board of regents had bestowed upon him an LL.D. degree in 1927. All the while he was intent upon improving Marion's Beach House at Santa Monica—again, no matter the expense. Hearst had a special talent, a rare imagination for embodying precious relics of the ages into unusual architectural settings. For instance, he hired seventy-five woodcarvers to construct balustrades throughout the Davies mansion; he selected an exquisite mural wallpaper specifically for Marion's suite (costing $7,500); and he inserted thirty-seven fireplace mantels, mainly acquired from stately English homes into rooms throughout the Davies compound.

Although all such acquisitions or improvements amply demonstrated Hearst's need to possess—and his willingness to spend—one business venture with Will Rogers, however, became a part of Hearst lore and legend. Hearst discovered that the humorist, whom he had known since the Ziegfeld *Follies* days in New York, owned a small piece of adjacent land on which Hearst contemplated building a tennis court. Rogers refused to sell. But when Hearst persisted through his realtor, Rogers proposed an outrageous price of $25,000. Hearst countered by offering $20,000. This cat-and-mouse game continued, with both men seeming to enjoy the haggling as the price proceeded to rise, even though at Hearst's expense. At length, Rogers agreed to sell for $105,000. And Hearst was pleased. To his realtor, he philosophically justified the final transaction by commenting, "Pleasure is worth what you can afford to pay for it."[6]

Hearst thus conducted his business affairs during 1930 as if no depression was occurring, as if economic hard times did not exist. At San Simeon construction was never ending, with monthly costs at a minimum of $30,000. For example, in December 1929, workmen began pouring concrete for the Recreation Wing at Casa Grande. By February, Hearst was urging Julia Morgan to focus on finishing the theater. By June workmen were plastering the walls; by July, they had cast big caryatids and on August 22 those majestic columns went up. And with the ordering of chairs and carpets, Hearst wrote to Morgan on December 15 that "we will have ground floor perfect if we proceed with music room theater and projection booth." Hence, another piece of Hearst's building odyssey at Casa Grande, which was a constant reminder of his creativity and personality, came to completion by the end of 1931.[7]

At the same time Hearst vigorously promoted Cosmopolitan Productions and Marion Davies as the major star. But he decided to change the thematic direction of his motion pictures. Partly because Americans were suffering difficult economic times but also because of the popular advent of talkies (beginning with Al Jolson in the *Jazz Singer* late in 1927), he wisely emphasized entertainment over serious theater, lighthearted comedy over historical drama.

To this change Marion responded well. After all, she excelled at comedy as well as song and dance. Even so, she spent hours in rehearsal, taking singing and dancing lessons in preparation for the talkies. As a result, she performed like the trouper she had always been. In the *Hollywood Revue of 1929*, emceed by actor Conrad Nagel and rising young comedian Jack Benny, she was one of many MGM stars who entertained the American public in a series of vaudeville-type acts. In the summer of 1929 she also starred in *Marianne* (her first leading role in a talkie) and had the lead role in *Five O'Clock Girl*, which never reached the screen presumably because Hearst was unhappy with the songs slated for her. Early in 1930, however, she rebounded by starring in a light comedy titled *Not So Dumb* and then received wide acclaim for her next performance, *The Floradora Girl*.

As always, the Hearst newspapers were glowing in their praise of Marion's talents. One California comedian aptly characterized the situation. "If an earthquake should suddenly send Los Angeles sliding into the sea," he joked, "the Hearst headline would read: HOLLYWOOD VANISHES: MARION NEVER LOOKED LOVELIER."

Louis B. Mayer, besides being a good friend and fervent admirer of Hearst, was in total agreement with her treatment. As the head of MGM, he recognized the tremendous importance of the Hearst newspapers to the motion picture industry in general and to MGM in particular. For instance, after addressing a company conference in Los Angeles, Mayer opened the floor to questions. When a salesman somewhat indelicately asked, "Why do we handle the pictures of Marion Davies" since only one of her first four "had been a money-maker?" Mayer replied in no uncertain terms. Besides "the personal charm of Miss Davies" the fact remained, he emphatically pointed out, "that she was the friend of Mr. Hearst, whose newspapers were in a position to be a great help to the company." He was surely correct in his assessment. The cinema coverage in the *New York American* alone was usually two to three pages daily and sometimes as many as four pages on Sunday. In return, MGM paid Marion $10,000 a week, financed all Cosmopolitan films, and gave Hearst a share in the profits of her pictures.[8]

Hearst, however, focused on more than one business enterprise. He was a miraculous juggler, *Cosmopolitan* author and screenwriter Irvin S. Cobb marveled, who "could keep a dozen spheres in the air at once—newspapers, radio stations, magazines, syndicates, press bureaus, mines, ranches, real estate, moving pictures, book publishing . . . yet find time for building fabulous palaces and gorgeous playhouses; for collecting the finest . . . antiques and art treasures ever assembled by any individual since Lorenzo the Magnificent."[9]

Yet because of his penchant for leadership, of preferring to be alone at the top, Hearst was unable to tolerate any organization for long, unless he headed it. Consequently his honeymoon with the Hoover administration was short-lived. In foreign affairs he was deeply suspicious of the president, who, he believed, had always been a Wilsonian, hence an internationalist. Hearst therefore preached his own patriotic brand of isolationism: "America First" and "No Entangling Alliances." Hearst and his editorial writers leveled a constant barrage against U.S. involvement in the League of Nations and the World Court, while his political cartoonists scathingly mocked those who advocated world involvement.[10]

U.S. participation in the London Naval Conference was a case in point. On January 17, 1930, Hoover sent a distinguished American delegation to London, headed by Secretary of State Henry L. Stimson, its purpose that of further limiting naval tonnage regarding warships of the five major Allied powers. But Hearst vehemently opposed participation. Alliances or treaties meant involvement, which in turn could lead to war. Surely, the diplomacy of World War I amply exemplified that premise. As a consequence, Hearst initiated a fervent crusade in front-page editorials that addressed a special plea to each individual member of the American delegation. In headlines titled "COME HOME" he announced to them that "minding OUR own business" was "MORE THAN ENOUGH." In fact, noninvolvement would be their greatest show of patriotism. Then in a lengthy editorial Hearst implored President Hoover to avoid a "consultative pact" and "BRING THE AMERICAN DELEGATION HOME" not only "for your own sake" but "for the sake of the nation." And even though the Senate would finally approve the subsequent terms of the London Treaty (58 to 9) on July 21, 1930, Hearst adamantly reaffirmed his position—the president was lacking both in leadership and judgment.[11]

During the spring of 1930 Hearst became increasingly critical of the Hoover administration. In fact, he found little to his liking. Republican support of the Smoot-Hawley Tariff was "NOT ONLY A DISGRACE TO THE PARTY IN POWER BUT A BRAKE UPON THE WHEELS OF RETURNING PROSPERITY." The failure of the administration to support a bonus bill for deserving World War I veterans was shameful; the government owed those heroes a debt of honor, which was long overdue. But most importantly for Hearst, the president seemed more intent on attending to international matters than in solving the economic problems at home. And to Hearst such inaction was not only disheartening but unforgivable; unemployment was increasing, distress heightening, and a contagion of fear and want among the people a stark reality. On June 2, 1930, an editorial headline in the Hearst newspapers summed up his growing disillusionment: "We Need an American administration. Bring Back Coolidge and Americanism, Coolidge and Patriotism, Coolidge and Confidence."[12]

Yet Hearst's concern for the woes of the republic in no way affected his personal routine. From January to May, in keeping with his "civilized" arrangement with Millicent, he financed a luxurious trip to Europe and Egypt for her. When she returned in May, they hosted a dinner for Dr. Julio Prestes, the president-elect of Brazil, at their Riverside Drive mansion in New York City. In turn, he was preparing his own European tour with Marion, one that he greatly anticipated.[13]

Late in June 1930, Hearst sailed to England, arriving at Southampton on June 27. As always, he was the ultimate tour guide and coordinator, planning every detail in advance—travel, housing, meals, entertainment, and sightseeing excursions. With Marion's help, he had selected a favored entourage of friends and employees who would enjoy an expense-paid educational tour of Europe. Other than a number of Marion's friends (Hollywood starlets), the party included editor of the *New York American* Edmund D. Coblentz, Hearst's personal secretary Joe Willicombe, and Harry Crocker, his favorite staffer on the *Los Angeles Examiner.*

After a weekend in London, Hearst directed his charges to St. Donat's Castle for an experience they would long remember. For the next four weeks Hearst radiated true contentment in his regal possession. Architect Sir Charles Allom had refurbished this historic Welsh treasure tastefully. The sixty bathrooms were new and in good working order; the 135 rooms, fitted with appropriate lighting, were artfully redone; and Hearst's bedroom, containing the bed of Charles I and "a collection of priceless Charles II lacquer cabinets," was truly impressive. And the great hall, where Hearst presided at mealtime like a medieval king over obedient vassals, was a satisfying reminder that he was lord and master over this expansive 1,300-acre domain.[14]

At the end of July this part of their European sojourn came to a close. Off to London and Paris en route to Germany, they leisurely made their way, the therapeutic hot baths prescribed by resident doctors at Bad Nauheim beckoning them. Hearst could not have been happier. In between treatments that required a three-day rest period, he escorted his minions on boat rides up the Rhine, so reminiscent of the trip to Germany with his mother when he was a boy. Alice Head, who joined the Hearst party at Bad Nauheim, fondly remembered such occasions. "On these trips Mr. Hearst is just like a boy out of school. He makes me feel at least old enough to be his mother. He jokes with the boatmen and the itinerant musicians, does a little yodelling on his own account, and buys wooden animals and carved inkstands, and gaily coloured scarves and sweaters, and sweets and wines and cheeses—whatever there is to buy." In fact, she marveled, he "all the time tells us in the most interesting way the history of the places that we visit."[15]

Toward the end of August, after a month at Bad Nauheim, the German doctors dismissed Hearst, with advice to seek continued rest and comfort during the next four weeks. He therefore toured southward for several days at a leisurely pace, showing his guests the pleasures of the Italian lake district. He then decided that the exclusive Hotel Crillon in Paris would be more relaxing and curative.[16]

But shortly after Hearst arrived at the Crillon on September 1, circumstances altered his plans for the prescribed aftercure. He discovered—and not too surprisingly—that the French did not welcome his presence. Over the past two years a confrontation had been building. Late in September 1928, Hearst correspondent in Paris Harold J. T. Horan had secured an official document that outlined terms of a proposed secret naval pact between France and Great Britain. The subsequent newspaper exposé embarrassed both governments, especially the French, who were caught "red-handed" violating one of the principles of the Treaty of

Versailles: "Open Covenants Openly Arrived At." As a consequence, the French arrested Horan and soon thereafter expelled him. The treaty died aborning, but continued follow-ups by the Hearst press did not. Hearst editors branded the French as hypocrites who hid their deceit by attempting to silence "freedom of the press." Then in August 1930, near the end of his stay at Bad Nauheim, Hearst exacerbated the situation even more. In a widely publicized interview in the *Frankfurter Zeitung*, he proclaimed "very friendly" feelings toward Germany as well as his disdain for French foreign policy in regard to the treatment of Germany.[17]

As a result, a "polite French official," Hearst reported, announced that the French government considered him to be persona non grata and a danger to the Republic. He was given four days to wind up his affairs before being expelled. Hearst could not have scripted a better scenario for himself. He was at the center of an international incident in which "freedom of the press" appeared to be the major issue—and his defense.

Hearst's responses and reactions were classic. "They made me feel quite important," he candidly stated to reporters. "They said I was an enemy of France and a danger in their midst," but that "I could stay in France a little while longer, if I desired, that they would take a chance on nothing disastrous happening to the Republic."

In a voice etched in sarcasm, Hearst retorted that he "did not want to take the responsibility of endangering the great French nation, that America had saved it once during the war," and that he "would save it again by leaving."

Nor did Hearst mind this eviction. "He was like the man who was told that he was going blind, and who said he did not mind, as he had seen everything anyhow. Similarly," he philosophized, "I had seen everything in France, including some very interesting governmental performances," which were "a little bit foolish but extremely French."

Hearst then surmised the reasons for his expulsion. Surely the exposé of the secret Anglo–French naval pact was the main cause, but the Hearst press opposition to the League of Nations and his criticism of the French attitude toward Germany were also contributing factors. Consequently, "if being a competent journalist and a loyal American makes a man persona non grata in France," he concluded, "I can endure the situation without the loss of sleep."[18]

Whereas a dozen years earlier Hearst had been targeted as the most hated man in America, he now experienced new-found popularity. He was upholding the "tradition and pride of American journalism," and he was never one to waste such an opportunity. After taking several days in London to negotiate the purchase of the famous Elizabethan "Great

Chamber" of Gilling Castle in Yorkshire for "a sum running into six figures" and arranging for its removal to St. Donat's, he sailed for New York on the *Europa*. With his personal business completed, he now assumed the mantle of a patriot who was willing to suffer public humiliation in defense of the United States against French intrigue.[19]

Any important Hearst venture inevitably had the makings of an extravaganza and, when possible, of epic proportions. The expulsion decree was no exception; the French proved to be the perfect foil for him. Even before he arrived home on September 15, the Hearst media empire was working at optimum speed. Hearst newspapers peppered the front pages with testimonials by prominent U.S. statesmen. Actions by the French government were "a disgrace," Senator C. C. Hill of Washington asserted, "and should arouse the resentment of the lovers of freedom of the press the world round." The French expulsion of Hearst was "an ungracious act," Senator Royal S. Copeland of New York opined, "a petty reprisal . . . a poor response to adverse newspaper opinion." Senator George H. Moses of New Hampshire, however, was the most penetrating in his analysis, at least as far as the Hearst press was concerned. The Hearst "publication [of the secret Anglo-French naval pact] seriously interfered with negotiations which might have been of inestimable damage to the United States," he pointed out, and therefore furnished the "reason for the futile resentment now displayed by the French Government."[20]

Upon Hearst's arrival in New York, a celebration glorifying his Americanism began. Although Hearst sent telegrams to his editors insisting that no demonstrations be held in his behalf, a delegation of congressional leaders headed by Senator Robert F. Wagner of New York, together with veterans of the Spanish American War and World War I greeted him, lauding his performance as an act of courage in defense of the United States. Hearst was obviously pleased. At the same time Mayor James M. Curley of Boston invited him to be the city's chief guest of honor on September 17 at a parade and banquet commemorating the three-hundredth anniversary of the Bay State, which signified the beginning of free government.[21]

From New England and New York, the celebration moved westward, with the results predictably the same. On September 22, the Chicago city council passed a resolution praising Hearst for his patriotism and inviting him to be the guest of the city. For the next two days he reveled in Chicago hospitality. He was the honored participant in a monster parade of 5,000 cars and 50 bands, attracting an estimated 150,000 people, that culminated with a reception at Soldier Field. Although 15,000 Polish Americans accused him of being an international troublemaker,

Mayor William Hale Thompson voiced the prevailing sentiments of Chicagoans by introducing him as a citizen who had demonstrated by his actions against the French not only "the fine qualities of Americanism" but also "the citizenship and patriotism of any great country."

As a fitting climax to this day of triumph, the National Broadcasting Company persuaded Hearst to present his version of the French expulsion edict over a nationwide hookup. After several days of preparation Hearst delivered the first of many such radio talks to the American people. The president of NBC set the tone for the speech. The *New York American* aptly observed in introducing Hearst, he "paid a glowing tribute to his patriotism," calling him "a citizen of the entire U.S."[22]

Well into October the Hearst celebration tour continued triumphantly to a final stop in California. In Los Angeles on October 14, a distinguished group of citizens, headed by chamber of commerce president John C. Austin and MGM chief executive and colleague Louis B. Mayer, honored Hearst with a homecoming banquet at the Hotel Biltmore, where he once again recounted his oft told experience to an admiring audience. And miraculously thousands of "Hearst for President" buttons appeared. Although Hearst stated to reporters that "I know nothing about it, and do not approve of it [and] I am not a candidate for any public office," Hearst opponents were in skeptical disbelief and wary of his future political intentions.[23]

Such skepticism did not diminish during the next week. On October 16, Hearst received a thunderous ovation in San Francisco. Before a huge gathering at the train station, Mayor James Rolph Jr. welcomed him as a native son whose exposé of French diplomacy was an act of heroism. At a luncheon, after recounting his French experience to a receptive audience, Hearst received a citation for meritorious service from the Veterans of Foreign Wars, the first ever bestowed on a civilian. In much the same vein this celebration extended into the next day. Across the bay at Oakland Hearst attended a reception at city hall followed by a public dinner in his honor at the Hotel Oakland. "Hearst for President" buttons again surfaced not only in California but in St. Louis and even in the offices of the *New York Times*. Again to the consternation of his enemies Hearst claimed no knowledge of their source and disavowed any thought of seeking political office.[24]

To a certain extent Hearst was being truthful. His age was a factor. At sixty-seven he admitted publicly in December that "I have had my day in politics," yet he hoped not completely. He still wanted to serve his country, to implement policies that would be of benefit to the American people, to say that during his lifetime he had made a difference in behalf of the United States.

Others had already publicly recognized his ability. Late in August 1930, James W. Gerard had listed him as one of fifty-nine men who rule America. During the next three months, following Hearst's return from Europe, Americans from all walks of life acknowledged his contributions through countless proclamations and celebratory functions. And as the owner of twenty-eight newspapers and thirteen magazines, he was the foremost publisher in the world with an estimated 20 million readers.[25]

Hearst surely believed that many of his ideas were vital to the welfare of the American people and needed to be implemented as soon as possible, especially with the depression so debilitating. In his opinion the Hoover administration was not only a disappointment but a miserable failure. Already the nation was approaching the second winter of depression and conditions were worsening. "The shadow" of fear, of a growing economic downturn, one prominent historian put it, "fell over the city and towns," introducing millions of Americans to a humiliating way of life. With joblessness approaching six million, soup kitchens and bread lines signified a dismal daily existence, while Hoovervilles—makeshift shanties of boxcars and tarpaper shacks at the edge of communities—sprang up, the name identifying the cynicism and bitterness of the American people toward their government.[26]

Both the president and Congress seemed to be in a constant state of paralysis concerning what to do—but not Hearst. He was never without ideas and seldom in doubt as to their viability. As he hypothesized to his readers, the causes of the depression were "not merely overspeculation, but overcapitalization." In other words, "there was no money left to build up the purchasing power of the masses, and MAINTAIN THE CONDITIONS WHICH MADE FOR PROSPERITY. Excess capitalization took money away from the masses WHEN MONEY OUGHT TO HAVE BEEN GIVEN TO THEM IN THE WAY OF INCREASED WAGES AND SHORTER HOURS." During the dismal winter of 1931 he therefore pleaded in vain to Congress, as well as to the Hoover administration, that "employment, not the dole, should be America's program for the needy." In fact, he repeatedly stated, "MILLIONS FOR EMPLOYMENT BUT NOT ONE CENT FOR THE DOLE should be the American motto of an American government."[27]

With President Hoover and Secretary of the Treasury Mellon urging tight fiscal policy in order to balance the national budget, Hearst decided to outline to the American people his own plan for recovery and back it with his proven crusade tactics. Through government by newspaper—and also over the airwaves—he intended to convince the American people as to the soundness of his proposal, then regiment them into a powerful force that would compel the Hoover administration to initiate his plan.

On the night of June 2, 1931, in a nationwide radio broadcast, he introduced his blueprint to restore prosperity to the United States. It would be a $5 billion bond issue, financed totally by the federal government. The Hoover administration should immediately focus on a comprehensive program of internal improvements in every part of the country that included "highways, waterways, flood control, and water and power conservation." This plan of national development through public works would create jobs for thousands of unemployed Americans, who in turn through their newfound "wealth in government wages," would help restore prosperity.

Nor was this the time "to reduce the national debt through burdensome taxation and thereby REDUCE prosperity," Hearst declared. Rather, just the opposite was true. "It is a time to INCREASE the national debt and INCREASE the expenditure of the Government in public works in the employment of labor and thereby INCREASE prosperity." Then "out of prosperity," Hearst concluded, the United States could "PAY OFF THE [$5 billion] DEBT."[28]

After this opening salvo delivered on nationwide radio, Hearst launched his campaign to win the approval of the American people. Over the next two weeks, all Hearst newspapers, through editorials and political cartoons, as well as endorsements by prominent citizens from all walks of life, crusaded daily for the Hearst $5 billion loan, inundating readers with the soundness of his plan. Even though the Hoover administration did not react favorably to his proposal, Hearst was determined to prevail. Over the next twelve months his newspapers continued to remind readers (and voters) that the Hearst $5 billion plan was the legitimate solution to the problems of depression. Then with the approach of a presidential election in 1932 he sought another solution, one that would eliminate Hoover from the equation.[29]

At the same time Hearst planned to take time off for personal indulgences. With the approach of summer, that meant one thing, another trip to Europe. Already the steam baths at Bad Nauheim were beckoning to him, but so were the ancient castles along the Rhine and the marvelous treasures of Europe. Consequently he followed his prescribed method of travel. As always, he had to be the leader of this expedition, selecting the participants and planning every detail of the tour well in advance, while verifying to his guests that this expense-paid educational trip was a Hearst benevolence. By mid-June 1931, the Hearst entourage, consisting of Marion and several of her friends as well as a few of his high-level business associates, sailed for Europe. After stopping over in London to check on his business enterprises, such as *Nash's Magazine* and the British version of *Good Housekeeping*, Hearst proceeded to Bad Nauheim by way of Holland, careful to avoid French authority and "beneficence." After taking the cure for several weeks, he and his entourage proceeded to Rome, where he met Italian dictator Benito Mussolini, who had written a number of articles for the Hearst Sunday newspapers. On first encounter Hearst was highly impressed. Mussolini "is a marvelous man," he later wrote. "It is astonishing how he takes care of every detail of his job."

By August, Hearst and his merry band of American tourists were on a leisurely return trip home. Hearst carefully skirted France again via Germany and Holland en route to England. He then proceeded to St. Donat's, where he treated his guests regally. As a special bonus for them he invited longtime friend and former British Prime Minister Lloyd George to visit, all the while providing every luxury of this historic twelfth-century Welsh landmark to all. Then early in September he somewhat reluctantly ended this three-month vacation, sailing to New York City on the *Europa*.[30]

Back on American soil, Hearst immediately addressed several important problems afflicting the United States. He became an ardent crusader for better government, a conscientious citizen who wished to help extricate his fellow Americans from the failed policies of the Hoover administration. On September 12, through the auspices of NBC radio, he addressed the American people in a nationwide speech on the continued perils confronting the United States. The problems were many and becoming more acute. Although disappointed, but not surprised, Hearst pointed out that the Hoover administration had failed to act in time of national crisis. Specifically, "the Hearst $5 billion loan plan," dedicated to ending joblessness through public works and thereby restoring prosperity, had received no consideration since first proposed in June. Hearst was equally concerned that the United States was continuing to become more embroiled in European affairs; therefore, he again preached Washington's philosophy of "No Entangling Alliances." While touring Europe, he asserted, "I found . . . conditions so bad that our own depression in comparison seems like only a small dent in the smooth surface of prosperity." Hearst thus predicted that the debt-ridden European nations were heading toward another world war. As a consequence, the Hoover administration should shun European politics and as a "part of patriotism," Hearst concluded, "keep our money and our men and our minds at home."[31]

In spite of editorial after editorial in his twenty-eight newspapers vigorously supporting the logic of his assertions, Hearst failed to persuade the president to accept his point of view. Nor did he foresee any hope for the future under the Hoover administration. In foreign affairs, for instance, one issue alarmed him greatly—a moratorium concerning war debts. Late in October 1931, it was reported that Hoover had agreed with French Premiere Pierre Laval "to link war debts to reparations, and to consider plans for the permanent disposal of both." The story, although later proved to be inaccurate as to purpose and content, outraged Hearst. Besides his suspicion of and dislike for the French, he suspected an administration betrayal of the American taxpayer. War debts owed the United States by foreign powers such as France would be delayed, if not eventually forgotten. This so-called moratorium policy, Hearst asserted, was un-American. And "if the American Congress does its American duty," he announced, "it will quash at the outset Mr. Hoover's un-American moratorium policy."[32]

By December, Hearst concluded that a change in national leadership was an utmost necessity. But selecting the right candidate was the problem. As early as June he had petitioned former President Calvin Coolidge to run again for the presidency, but to no avail. Political wisdom indicated that Hoover would be the Republican choice. Hearst, in turn, questioned the leadership of the Democratic Party. "It has no leaders and apparently no principles," he editorialized on December 24. Governor Franklin Delano Roosevelt of New York and Newton D. Baker, former Secretary of War (in Wilson's cabinet), were "Wall Street internationalists," hence unacceptable. And Al Smith—for whom Hearst could have given a litany of negatives—was the same. Hearst then dropped a name to his readers. "The hope of the Democratic Party," he suggested, "is John N. Garner."[33]

On New Year's Day 1932, in a nationwide broadcast on NBC radio, Hearst exploded his candidate onto the American political scene. He informed the public as to the qualifications of John Nance Garner of Texas. As Speaker of the House of Representatives since 1931, the sixty-three-year-old Garner was an experienced legislator, having served in Congress since 1903. He "is a loyal American citizen," Hearst proclaimed, "a plain man of the plain people, a sound and sincere Democrat; in fact, another Champ Clark. His heart," Hearst emphasized, "is with his OWN PEOPLE. His interest is in his OWN COUNTRY." And "unless we American citizens are willing to go on laboring indefinitely merely to provide loot for Europe, we should personally see to it that a man [such as Garner] is elected to the Presidency this year, whose guiding motto is 'America first.'" In a fervent appeal to his audience, Hearst then concluded, "Seldom in the whole history of the nation has the selection of a good AMERICAN for President been so important to the people as it is today."[34]

The selection of Garner was not by accident. Hearst had researched his nominee. Because the two men had not spent any length of time together since Hearst's last days in Congress (1906), he directed George Rothwell Brown, one of his most gifted syndicated political writers, to discover where Garner stood on major issues.

The Brown report was immensely gratifying. Garner had voted against the Smoot-Hawley Tariff Act, was unalterably opposed to Hoover's moratorium on (or cancellation of) American war debts by European nations, and "believed in thrift, prudence, and economy in government." But the clincher for Hearst had to do with the League of Nations. Even though the House of Representatives had no part in that "great battle over the League"—and therefore "no public stand"—Garner was, Brown confidently reported, "opposed to all foreign entanglements." In fact, "Garner was," Brown concluded, "an old-fashioned, patriotic American and a rugged Democrat of the Andrew Jackson school."[35]

Since Garner seemed to resemble in many ways another Champ Clark, Hearst decided to create a Garner boom (as he had with Clark twenty years earlier), even without the consent or agreement by the candidate. On January 3, in all his Sunday newspapers, Hearst launched his crusade, writing a front-page editorial titled, "Who Will Be the Next President?" He essentially summarized his radio talk of the previous night. Then during January, while presenting editorials and political cartoons continually in praise of his newly discovered American hero, Hearst expanded his publicity machine by transferring the highlights of his radio speech onto newsreel hookups in theaters across the United States.[36]

Yet Garner in many ways was an enigma to associates and close friends as well as to Hearst. "I do not know whether Mr. Garner takes very seriously the movement to make him a candidate or not," congressional confidant Sam Rayburn remarked after the Hearst radio endorsement. "I do not think it is offensive to him now, but what it will be later on I do not know."

Nor did Garner's appearance signal the arrival of a new political star. Although recently elected Speaker of the House, he was not, on first encounter, impressive physically. Short of stature but somewhat fierce of mien, Garner was a challenge to Hearst's ability to sell a political product. With a ruddy complexion, short-cropped white hair, and prickly eyebrows that focused attention on steel-blue eyes and a small, tight-lipped mouth, Garner "presented at once an appearance," historian Arthur Schlesinger Jr. observed, "of an infinitely experienced sage and of a newborn baby." Besides all such hindrances, Garner proposed one other; he did not consider himself a viable candidate because he was from Texas.[37]

Despite such misgivings and reservations about his candidacy, Garner agreed to cooperate with the Hearst political juggernaut. While doing nothing to promote his own nomination ("his only interest was to fulfill the duties" of the Speakership), Garner assigned Congressman John McDuffie of Alabama to be his contact man and keep him fully informed on the progress of the campaign.[38]

McDuffie would have a great deal to report; the Hearst media editors would see to that. They closely associated their readers with Garner, familiarizing them with every aspect of his life. On February 21, all twenty-eight newspapers produced in serial form (one chapter each day) a Garner biography, which columnist George Brown had hurriedly written. Americans soon began referring to Garner by his nickname "Cactus Jack"; he had once proposed a bill changing the Texas state flower from the bluebonnet to the cactus. In April *Cosmopolitan* produced for its 1.6 million readers a laudatory piece titled "Fighting Jack Garner." And in May *Good Housekeeping* presented a sympathetic article to the American public about Mariette Garner, the Speaker's "old-fashioned wife" of thirty years who, besides being a devoted homemaker, was her husband's secretary.[39]

Yet while the Garner boom gained momentum during the spring of 1932, while Texas Democrats organized to support him as their favorite son at the upcoming Chicago Democratic Convention late in June, a Roosevelt landslide loomed as a real possibility. By the end of April, FDR was winning most of the Southern delegates in primary battles against his major opponents, Al Smith and Garner. Although the Roosevelt forces suffered a disappointing defeat by Smith in Massachusetts and temporary setbacks in Pennsylvania and New York, more than half the convention delegates favored FDR—and the necessary two-thirds majority for the party nomination was indeed plausible, if not a certainty.[40]

Hearst, however, was not yet ready to concede defeat. The California primary for delegates was early in May. Although most political pundits predicted that the Roosevelt and Smith forces would do battle for control of the state delegation, he was not convinced. He therefore applied all the resources at his command in favor of Garner. After all, he would never be able to exact enough political hurt on Al Smith, and he was not completely convinced that Roosevelt was not an internationalist, even though FDR had repudiated the League publicly in February. In his five California newspapers, which were by far the state's largest and most influential, Hearst kept his readers apprised of Garner's activities and statements, so much so that one Roosevelt backer exasperatingly remarked, "Hearst gives almost as much space daily to Garner as he gives to the Lindbergh baby [kidnapping] or the Japan-China War."[41]

On May 3, the Hearst campaign reached its zenith. With former presidential hopeful William G. McAdoo heading the list of Garner delegates, California Democrats endorsed Garner for president in their primary, casting 222,385 votes for him, 175,008 votes for Roosevelt, and 141,517 votes for Smith. With forty-four state delegates registered for Garner and forty-six more from Texas, Cactus Jack was no longer in the favorite son category. Nor could he be looked upon as a serious contender.[42]

As for the national party conventions, both of which were in Chicago, Hearst decided not to attend, bypassing those important political events for the first time in almost three decades. Yet he was not a disinterested spectator; the American people were in their third year of dire depression and national leadership was at stake. Although he remained ensconced on his lofty perch at San Simeon, his most trusted lieutenants—personal secretary Joe Willicombe and such *New York American* all-star writers as Damon Runyon, Louis Seibold, and Arthur Brisbane—kept him fully informed.

As for the Republicans, no surprises occurred. On June 14 their convention "began in apathy," one historian noted, its proceedings both "desultory and dreary." With little fanfare and enthusiasm they proceeded to adopt a party platform, then nominate Hoover as their standard-bearer. As a result, delegates "acted as though defeat in November was inevitable."[43]

On the other hand, the Democrats, meeting two weeks later, were confident of victory, that is, if they could select a candidate without party bloodletting. That, of course, was their greatest fear—and an ever-present danger. The Roosevelt forces, whose delegate count was approximately one hundred votes short of the necessary two-thirds majority for nomination (770 votes), hoped to acquire favorite son delegates at the end of the first ballot, or soon thereafter. Otherwise, looming ominously before them was the history of the 1924 Democratic Convention at Madison Square Garden, in which Smith and McAdoo deadlocked for more than one hundred ballots.

With the Roosevelt strategy for victory in place, the first roll call for the presidential nomination began on July 1 at an un-Godly hour, 4:28 in the morning. But the stampede to FDR did not materialize. The count after the first ballot was Roosevelt 661¼, Smith 201¾, Garner 90¼, with seven other candidates having a smattering of votes—but no switches in state delegations. The second roll call thus began immediately, and again no significant break in ranks for the three major participants. Hence, the Roosevelt floor leaders moved for adjournment. But the opposition forces, "hoping that they could crack Roosevelt on the third ballot," defeated this ploy, and the third roll call commenced, again ending with no major delegate switches. The tally was Roosevelt 682⅘ (an additional sixteen votes), Smith 190¼ (a loss of ten votes), and Garner 101¼ (a gain of eleven votes). The Roosevelt floor leaders were now reaching the panic stage. Word on the convention floor was that the Mississippi delegation, weary of the impasse, was about to abandon Roosevelt and that Arkansas was soon to follow. Thus the matter stood as the exhausted delegates agreed to adjourn after this fatiguing early morning session. They would reassemble at 8:30 that evening.[44]

The next few hours were critical to the political life of the Roosevelt candidacy. The convention was in danger of deadlocking. Already rumors were spreading in regard to a compromise candidate; the 1924 Smith–McAdoo scenario seemed to be playing out all over again. During the next harried hours, party leaders worked to reach some accommodation. With Roosevelt needing less than one hundred votes, his nomination rested with Garner, who had 101 loyal delegates. Consequently Roosevelt manager and field commander James A. Farley worked unflaggingly to achieve Garner support on the fourth ballot. To Congressman Sam Rayburn, a Garner confidant who had been in close touch with the Roosevelt forces, he entrusted the responsibility of persuading the Texas delegation to switch to FDR. The vote would be close.[45]

The California delegation was another matter altogether. Farley had to deal directly with Hearst, who had no great liking for Roosevelt but much less for Al Smith. He therefore telephoned Hearst at San Simeon to solicit needed help. In a lengthy conversation Farley and several other Roosevelt floor leaders explained the gravity of the situation facing them on the fourth ballot. A deadlock was imminent if support for FDR deteriorated and the delegates turned to a compromise candidate such as Al Smith or Newton Baker. Farley therefore asked Hearst to persuade Garner to release his votes to Roosevelt.

With the threat of a brokered convention seemingly at hand, Hearst agreed to do so. He instructed his Washington correspondent George Brown to relay a message personally to Garner, who was at the Speaker's office in Washington. The conversation went like this: "Mr. Speaker, I have a message for you from Mr. Hearst," Brown began. "Mr. Hearst is fearful that the nomination will go either to Baker or Smith, unless you throw your strength to Roosevelt. He regards Baker as an internationalist and a reactionary. If Smith should be nominated, we will have the fight of 1928 all over again, with the party torn asunder, and all hope of electing a Democrat gone."[46]

To his credit, according to historian Norman Brown, "Garner showed statesmanship." The Speaker was in full accord with Hearst's assessment concerning the convention and agreed to release his delegates to Roosevelt. On the fourth ballot that evening, after the convention clerk called for the vote from California, delegation chairman William McAdoo, upon approaching the microphone, announced that "California asks the opportunity of explaining its vote to the convention." With the packed arena hall in an uproar over his anticipated statements, he explained that California had complete faith in the "leadership, character, and ability of John Nance Garner" but realized that the Texan could never be nominated. "Therefore," with the consent of Garner, McAdoo dramatically proclaimed, "California, believing the majority should rule, casts its entire forty-four votes for the unmistakable choice of the majority—Franklin D. Roosevelt."

This switch was the key to a Roosevelt landslide. At the end of the fourth ballot, Franklin Delano Roosevelt was the Democratic standard-bearer. In turn, the convention, at FDR's request, selected Garner as his vice presidential running mate.[47]

Hearst was especially pleased with the outcome of the convention. To his way of thinking, he had acted with patriotic fervor and sound judgment; he was responsible for helping nominate the next president and vice president of the United States, men who had the capacity of leading this nation out of difficult depression times. After all the years of disappointment in politics, he now hoped to claim as one of his lasting accomplishments the title of "President-Maker."[48]

For the next four months Hearst geared his news media empire to elect Roosevelt and Garner. In articles and editorials he extolled the vitality and wisdom of their leadership, of their plans to extricate the American people from stark, dire depression. On the other hand he attacked Hoover unmercifully, laying bare his failed presidency. A master at formulating attention-grabbing headlines, at coining a memorable phrase that readers would appreciate and oft repeat, Hearst took it upon himself to present the case for a Democratic victory. In personal editorials (always prominently displayed on page 1) to his 20 million readers in twenty-eight newspapers, he accused the Hoover administration of being "Neither Republican nor American." In fact, the president was a "man without a country," more concerned "with foreign interests," than with "effective plans for relieving the depression." Hearst characterized Governor Roosevelt as having a record of success, a man who, although despised by "Wall Street," would "lead us out of depression." To all within the sound of his voice Hearst also took great pleasure in reiterating this catchy phrase: "Vote for Hoover and lose your job."[49]

In the meantime Hearst had to attend to a personal health matter. He fully realized that he had reached celebrity status, that he was good copy, no matter how minor the incident or trivial the event. For instance, the *New York Times* noted that he checked in as a patient to the Cleveland Clinic Hospital on October 2. Eminent Ohio surgeon Dr. George Crile then announced that he had operated on Hearst, performing minor throat surgery "without the aid of a general anaesthetic," and the patient's condition was good. The next day his medical progress report was evaluated as excellent.

Yet the story still had legs. Two and a half weeks later, when Crile finally discharged him, commenting to the *Times* that the "operation was not important," Hearst endeared himself to many Americans with this reaction. "The surgeons say the operation was 'not important,' but whenever folks begin plowing around in my interior, the situation becomes important as far as I am concerned." Then he added, enjoying the moment, "Dr. Crile says he has been doing operations like mine for years and has never had a fatality. Of course, I do not want to spoil such a good record and am particularly pleased to say I did not."[50]

Despite his penchant for creating controversy as well as attracting powerful political enemies such as Al Smith, the time-period from September 1931 (his expulsion from France) through the end of 1932 seemed to be a period of redemption, a time of reidentification with the American people, no matter how contentious his political stances had been over the years. On October 11, a French deputy, in an attempt to end his country's well publicized dispute over Hearst's ouster, stated to the *New York Times* that "France will lift its ban on Hearst." In reply to the *Times* reporter, Hearst was in fine form. He "invited the French Government to visit him at his ranch at San Simeon" in order "to enlarge their experience and broaden their minds." He then delighted his fellow Americans with this stinging barb: "They will not be ordered off the premises for being loyal to their own country."[51]

Hearst also gained in popularity because of his political stances and proposals during the past year. Over nationwide radio broadcasts, he identified with the average American in trying to solve the growing crises of depression. The Hearst $5 billion loan plan would not only put money in the pockets of the millions of jobless but would rebuild the infrastructure of the United States through public works projects—dams on the largest rivers and interstate highways linking sections of the United States closer together. In regard to foreign affairs Hearst was equally in tune with many Americans. His promotion of Washington's policy regarding no entangling alliances was a ringing endorsement for the patriotic slogan "America First."

Yet more than anything else, Hearst's resurgent popularity rested on his return to the Democratic Party. His all-out support of Roosevelt who "will fulfill his promises," who will "give consideration to the FORGOTTEN MAN," who will bring "prosperity for us all" through dynamic leadership, was a recurring theme in all Hearst newspapers prior to the fall elections of 1932. And with Roosevelt winning an overwhelming victory over Hoover on November 8, Hearst rejoiced in the Democratic presidential theme song "Happy Days Are Here Again" as he eagerly anticipated "A New Deal for the Forgotten Man." At long last, he might have an opportunity to play a role in national affairs.[52]

8 A Jeffersonian Democrat Versus the New Deal

With the inauguration of Franklin Delano Roosevelt as the thirty-second president of the United States on March 4, 1933, William Randolph Hearst faced an uncertain future, filled both with hope and anxiety. Like other Americans, he anticipated a change of direction in the policies of the United States as well as a rejuvenation of political leadership sensitive to the needs of the American people. At the same time Hearst believed that he could help the Roosevelt administration solve some of the horrendous problems of the Great Depression. Yet even though blessed, or cursed, with a colossal ego and an intellect bordering on genius, Hearst grudgingly had to admit that he did not have all the answers for the economic debacle of October 1929.

Over the past thirty years the world had changed dramatically, and so had Hearst. Late in the 1890s he had believed that his journalistic efforts had helped shape American foreign policy. The symbolic American eagle had unleashed its fierce talons, forcing Spain into granting independence to Cuba, then instituting a new American empire, and fashioning a way of life for people in Puerto Rico, Hawaii, Guam, and the Philippines. Yet, with the onset of World War I, that period of buoyant optimism, of supreme confidence in Americans' ability to recast the world into their own image began to deteriorate. The slaughter of thousands of soldiers on European battlefields from 1914 to 1918 had seen to that. As a result, Hearst had turned isolationist, preaching "America First" and "no entangling alliances" with European powers. Such Wilsonian creations as the League of Nations and the World Court were anathema to him; inevitably, those "loathsome" institutions, he continued to editorialize, would involve the United States in foreign wars and thereby threaten the very existence of this nation.

Soon after the turn of the twentieth century, a youthful Hearst had also been a militant progressive, vigorously advocating in his newspapers economic and political changes that would free the average American from the evils generated by the capitalist system. He had campaigned for such industrial reforms as factory inspection laws, an end to child labor, minimum wages and maximum hours for workers, and a laborer's right to strike and join a union. On the political front Hearst had advocated such reforms as direct election of senators, a graduated income tax, a federal reserve banking system, direct primaries, and initiative, referendum, and recall. Yet early in the 1930s, with a catastrophic depression ever present in an uncertain world, with economic collapse spreading hopelessness and despair, even to the point of revolution, American progressives such as Hearst became fearful of unchecked federal power. Although continuing to follow the Jeffersonian tradition, which maintained that freedom was threatened by collective power, economic or political, he was, for the moment, willing to support an incoming Democratic administration headed by a charismatic president who was pressing for additional powers to meet a national emergency. Although ever cognizant that a Jeffersonian prerequisite to preserving liberty was a certain distrust of federal authority, Hearst decided that Roosevelt and his New Deal were worth the gamble.

Approaching age seventy in 1933, Hearst was surely cognizant of these changes during his life span as well as his shifts in focus and points of view. As he candidly reminisced about his career, "Those were the wonderful days and happy achievements of youth. No grandiose performance of later years ever equaled them in satisfaction. Life was not 'one damn thing after another' then. It was one wonderful adventure after another."[1]

In 1933, however, "one damn thing after another" seemed to be affecting Hearst's life. The Great Depression was taking its toll on him financially. John Francis Neylan, his legal adviser and unofficial second in command, counseled him to retrench immediately or face bankruptcy. Hearst, although balking at first to this advice, reluctantly concurred. He slashed salaries across the board by 39 percent, with only a forty-eight hour advance notice. But even after cutting $7 million from the payroll, he was still facing financial ruin. By 1933 advertising income from his newspapers and magazines had dropped from $113 million to $40 million and was still falling. More than half of his twenty-eight newspapers were losing money; the *New York American*, the bellwether of his media empire, was sneeringly referred to by rivals as "the vanishing American." And, at times, when some banks had refused to loan Hearst money to cover an increasing number of debts, he had resorted to raising new capital by going public and selling Hearst Consolidated stock at $25 a share. At other times, however, he enjoyed playing the game of keeping one step ahead of his creditors. Yet Hearst continued to spend without compunction. He continually acquired treasures from abroad, then lodged them in warehouses in New York, San Francisco, and Los Angeles until the monument to his posterity at San Simeon could appropriately house them. Ever so gradually the day of financial reckoning was at hand.[2]

The specters of old age and declining health were also matters of concern to Hearst. Since his boyhood days he had suffered the lingering discomfort of a dyspeptic stomach, which trips to the curative baths at Bad Nauheim had attempted to relieve. In October 1932, after a three-week stay at a Cleveland hospital following a throat operation, the concern regarding his physical well-being was even more pronounced.

Overall, however, Hearst had enjoyed relatively good health. Casual observers, as well as those close to him, marveled at his seemingly boundless energy. At San Simeon he enjoyed exercising with guests thirty to forty years his junior, playing tennis, riding horseback, and swimming. Then after dinner and a late-night theater presentation, he often worked until dawn. Through the use of night telegrams he advised his newspaper editors and reporters concerning the strengths and weaknesses of their previous day's edition, with specific recommendations for immediate improvement.

But the aging process was gradually taking its toll on his body. With each passing year life was becoming more precious and the presence of death an unwelcome visitor. To Walter Howey, one of Hearst's favorite editors and a designated troubleshooter, he assigned a certain delicate mission for investigation. Hearst was interested in the scientific research of a Dr. Serge Voronoff, who claimed to rejuvenate the elderly by transplanting monkey glands into the human body. After a story appeared that a Chicago millionaire had undergone such an operation, Hearst dispatched Howey to inquire as to the results. When the outcome proved inconclusive, Hearst's interest flagged. Yet delaying the inevitable became a growing Hearst obsession. As one Hollywood friend put it, "an unwritten law never to mention death in his presence" was a constant.[3]

Hearst could not escape the realization that he was not immortal. Reminders appeared regularly. For example, on April 29, 1933, some fifty of his closest friends and associates celebrated his seventieth birthday at San Simeon. *Time* magazine editors, while marveling at his career as "a master journalist-showman" who "is still unreconciled to age," raised the question, "*After Hearst?*" They then speculated, somewhat doubtfully, if any of his three oldest sons—George, Bill Jr., or John—could, so to speak, "fill the shoes of the mighty man."[4]

Hearst, for the time being, had no intention of retiring. Besides attending to his many business interests, he focused on the problems facing the Roosevelt administration. Prior to Inauguration Day on March 4, he had communicated with FDR and several members of the president-elect's transition team regarding cabinet posts or lesser positions in government. The *New York Times* reported incorrectly that his eldest son, George Hearst, "will be Assistant Secretary of the Navy." Even though Roosevelt did not accede to any of his recommendations, Hearst was satisfied for the moment. He had an open communication with the White House.[5]

Hearst reacted positively to such presidential recognition. In signed editorials during January and February 1933, he applauded FDR for the vigor and intensity of his actions in preparation for taking office. On several occasions he sent an emissary, editor Edmond Coblentz of the *New York American*, to Roosevelt with suggested priorities for fixing the economic crisis and thereby helping restore prosperity. He also instructed his editors to initiate a "Buy American and Spend American" crusade in hopes of improving the economy and, in turn, aiding the incoming administration. And as further support for the New Deal, he directed Hearst Metrotone News to record "a complete sound motion picture of the INAUGURATION of PRESIDENT ROOSEVELT" for immediate release to theaters across the nation.[6]

At the same time Hearst planned an even greater propaganda coup for the president. He and Walter Wanger, the newly hired producer at MGM, agreed to work together for the filming of *Gabriel Over the White House*, which was a fictional account about an American president assuming office late in the 1930s. Portrayed by actor Walter Huston as a Tammany-style politician who addresses the serious problems of the day with "blatant cynicism," the new president suffers a severe blow to the head in a near-fatal car wreck but is saved from death—and spiritually enlightened—by the archangel Gabriel. As a result, the restored-to-life and now truly dynamic president, with heavenly help—and intentionally crafted to resemble FDR—restores prosperity to the depression-ridden United States and brings peace to a war-torn world. With the advice and help of Roosevelt, this propaganda piece hit the screens in April and was an immediate success.[7]

This movie rendition by Hearst seemed to typify the first days of the New Deal—speed and innovation. Beginning on March 9, 1933, Roosevelt called a special session of the Seventy-third Congress, and for the next one hundred days lawmakers, with the forceful direction of the administration, worked to meet the most pressing needs of the national emergency. They rushed through legislation with such unbelievable speed that no Congress has ever come close to equaling their record of production. Following FDR's relentless prodding, they enacted fifteen major laws affecting the immediate needs of the nation: the stabilization of banking and currency, the restoration of agriculture, the refinancing of homes and businesses, the building of roads and dams through immense programs of public works, and the employment of millions of Americans. In characterizing the efforts of these first one hundred days, Arthur Schlesinger Jr. wrote, "For a deceptive moment in 1933, clouds of inertia and selfishness seemed to lift. A despairing land had a vision of America as it might some day be."[8]

To say that Hearst was pleased with such legislative progress was an understatement; however, he did have some reservations. The New Deal incorporated many of his ideas concerning relief, recovery, and reform; and for that he was appreciative. Yet even though such laws appeared to be progressive in nature and followed the dictates of the Democratic platform, Hearst was uneasy concerning the method of enactment and, seemingly, the overextension of powers to the executive branch. The progressive tradition that feared unchecked federal authority by one arm of the government was of paramount concern to him. In its haste to solve the economic crisis, Congress, he feared, was relinquishing its prerogatives to the executive branch. While "Mr. Roosevelt is a good President," Hearst editorialized, and might not abuse his powers, "the wisdom of the founders" of the republic "contemplated the possibility of a bad President who would misuse powers which were too largely entrusted to him." Hearst therefore urged Congress not to abdicate its constitutional responsibilities, not to be supine and hesitant in performing its duties, but to exercise its authority as a branch of government equal to that of the executive.[9]

During the spring of 1933 Hearst continued to vacillate in his opinions about FDR. He had never encountered anyone with such finesse in dealing with people, with the ability to amass information and formulate arguments quickly in a sound, convincing way. For that matter, Hearst had not known many men whom he considered to be his equal in brain power and experience. Hence his first meeting at the White House was baffling and perplexing. When asked by Ed Coblentz his reactions, Hearst replied, "I was greatly disappointed. The President didn't give me a chance to make suggestions. He did all the talking."[10]

Hearst did not remain silent for long. In his areas of expertise and interest—newspapers, magazines, newsreels, national radio, and motion pictures—he was a media giant, unparalleled in power and unconstrained in expression. The National Industrial Recovery Act, which Congress passed on June 16, 1933, proved to be a case in point, exemplifying the growing differences in philosophy and action between Hearst and the president.

With the creation of the National Recovery Administration (NRA), the New Deal focused on industrial recovery and reform through government leadership. Under the direction of General Hugh Johnson every industry would establish a blanket code, drafted exclusively by representatives of the industries concerned, each of which contained these specific provisions: the prohibition of child labor, maximum hours of labor per week at thirty-six for industrial and forty for clerical workers, a minimum wage of forty cents an hour, and mandatory protection of labor to strike and bargain collectively (Section 7a). In turn, the act prohibited monopolistic practices; hence, the government suspended the antitrust laws.[11]

Although realizing the need for industrial recovery and reform, Hearst believed that the NRA was a gigantic mistake. In its eagerness to bring about recovery and reform, Congress had erred in its rush to restore industrial prosperity. By setting standards for minimum wages and maximum hours as well as the right of unions to strike and bargain collectively, it had benefitted organized labor, he argued, to the detriment of business. And even though "I always have been and always will be in favor of organized labor," he asserted, "the abuses" of "unionism," which would "compel," manufacturers to employ or retain "larger forces" than needed and which were "less competent," would "limit productivity." As a result, manufacturers would price themselves out of competitive markets, when forced to meet enlarged payrolls. The NRA codes were therefore killing "the Goose that Lays the Golden Egg."[12]

But for Hearst a much more serious problem—having to do philosophically with the role of government—had arisen in the formative stages of the NRA. During the spring of 1933, prior to congressional enactment on June 16, it was rumored that the president intended to control newspapers with a provision to license the press. Hearst reacted emotionally to this news. He instructed Ed Coblentz to convey the following message to the White House:

> Please tell the President that I consider his proposal to license the press under [the] NRA is in direct violation of the Bill of Rights; that it is an abridgment of the freedom of the press guaranteed by the Constitution; and that I will fight his proposal with every means at my command, even

if it means taking it to the Supreme Court of the United States, and even if it costs me every nickel I possess.

As instructed, Coblentz phoned in Hearst's declaration. The response was immediate. Louis Howe, who was secretary to the president, upon hearing the opening words of Hearst's dictated ultimatum, stopped Coblentz in midsentence by saying, "Just a minute, I'll put Frank on the phone." And, shortly thereafter, Roosevelt was on the line, listening to Hearst's dictated words.

Upon hearing the message, Roosevelt paused briefly and then replied in a manner that would continue to befit his reputation for thorough knowledge of impending legislation as well as his ability to enunciate the administration's position with clarity. "My proposal is a regulatory measure and in no sense will it abridge the freedom of the press," FDR announced to Coblentz. "It is similar, in a sense, to the fire department rules. When you violate the fire department regulations, the Chief steps in and compels you to conform, does he not?"

"Yes, Mr. President," Coblentz replied, "but he does not stop the presses." The president laughed good-naturedly and then in all sincerity said to Coblentz, "Tell Mr. Hearst there . . . [is] nothing to worry about."[13]

For several months Hearst seemed to accept such assurances, but with increasing reservations. The progressive tradition that federal powers might infringe upon individual liberties continued to gnaw at him as the NRA grew in size and power. In August 1933, Hearst announced his satisfaction with the American Newspaper Publishers Association code, especially since he and his big business allies formulated the rules to benefit themselves. But he still questioned whether or not, in the long run, the codes would prove to be advantageous. After all, "the government is entering in a new field . . . is initiating measures which are more Socialistic than Democratic." Nor do "we want a dictator," Hearst declared in a lengthy editorial, "who will go so far away from the Constitution" and who might persuade the American people, in their "alarm and distress," that a powerful government "is preferable to the Do-Nothing [Hoover] administration that preceded it." He then concluded, "Surely, there is a happy medium."[14]

During September and October, Hearst tried to find that happy medium. The NRA codes, even though geared to benefit labor unions, he asserted, should be "modified to make due allowance for business profit." Corporations should be able to raise prices without fear of violating antitrust laws and should receive "relief from onerous income and corporate taxes through the substitution of a Federal General Manufacturers'

Sales Tax." But if prices continued to remain low, he suggested that the government pursue a policy of inflation.

At the same time Hearst attempted to boost NRA programs with his readers by promoting daily a "Buy in September" crusade, and in October a similar one titled "Buy Now and Buy American—Spend a Dollar and Make a Job." But by the end of October, Hearst was thoroughly disenchanted with the NRA. The administration had not adhered to his corrective suggestions. Nor, in his opinion, had the codes enhanced prosperity. On October 31, he cynically announced in a front-page editorial that "the letters NRA" appropriately stood for "No Recovery Allowed."[15]

Although demonstrating a growing disenchantment with the New Deal, Hearst still devoted time to his California concerns. San Simeon was a never-ending project. Because money was tight, building came to a standstill in the spring of 1933, but soon resumed at a modest pace. For instance, construction superintendent George Loorz completed the Billiard Room (on the first floor of Casa Grande) by November. When late in April of 1934 Hearst decided to celebrate his seventy-first birthday, Loorz received a rush order to complete "for occupancy" thirteen rooms on the upper floors of the North Wing. After six days of frantic work—and without regard for cost—he reported eleven rooms fully furnished "with closets, bathrooms, including showers, ready for use." Two other rooms in the tower were "quite comfortable for use but [with] no bathrooms." To be expected, Hearst would relish the opportunity to provide a number of suggestions for further improvement.[16]

Hearst was short of cash because of another architectural challenge: the constructural configuration of a property in northern California—Wyntoon. Early in 1930, this secluded estate on the McCloud River in the shadow of Mount Shasta, which he had inherited from his mother, received renewed attention. Fire had destroyed the seven-story stone Gothic structure known as Maybeck's Castle, where Hearst had vacationed during the 1920s while seeking relief from the summer heat. But with its destruction, Hearst's compulsion to create, to design and build immediately came to the fore. He instructed Julia Morgan to draw plans for a new construction based on a model in her San Francisco office that showed a medieval castle with two main towers, large enough to encompass sixty-one bedrooms with private bathrooms.

But Morgan soon devised another model for Wyntoon that intrigued Hearst even more. It was a Bavarian village composed of three half-timber three-story guest houses, each with four to eight bedrooms together with accompanying baths, and two sitting rooms. Half mile down the river would be a second siting, which would include a swimming pool, tennis courts, a croquet court, and the Gables for dining and movies. And then a quarter mile farther down the McCloud would be a third siting where an elaborate central structure called the Bend, so named because the river turned at that point, would provide formal entertainment and dining for guests in a magnificent frontier setting.

While the concept of a Bavarian village was in itself unique, it proved to be utilitarian in result. Hearst would have a place to house his vast collection of Germanic art and furniture that was piling up in his warehouses. He could also use Wyntoon, especially in the summertime, as the headquarters for his many business enterprises. And whereas San Simeon would accommodate thirty to fifty guests luxuriously, Wyntoon would serve as a weekend retreat for as many as one hundred.[17]

Because of his "civilized" arrangement with Millicent, Hearst was free to lead a life that satisfied his own needs and desires—however, with discretion. He therefore devoted an increasing amount of time to Marion Davies. In the Hollywood community Marion and he were a recognized item, the focus of a celebrity social swirl second to none. Gradually a pattern to their lives began to evolve. On location during the week Marion hosted parties nightly at her Santa Monica Beach House, inviting friends from the MGM and Cosmopolitan studios as well as favored Hearst corporation employees and executives, or such distinguished celebrities as George Bernard Shaw and Winston Churchill, who happened to be visiting Hearst. On weekends or between pictures, the ongoing social moved two hundred and fifty miles northward to San Simeon, to the grandeur of Casa Grande on Enchanted Hill. And again life was unique and far from ordinary.

Since Hearst would not—or could not—obtain a divorce from Millicent, the decision for Marion became evident. If she was willing to be the other woman in this relationship, she would have to endure the vicious gossip, the humiliating tales accompanying their affair. She would also have to forgo the conventionality of marriage, the security of home and family, the acknowledged acceptance of society.

A vivacious and effervescent actress, indeed a striking beauty with the potential to be an outstanding comedienne, Marion could easily have chosen another lifestyle, but she did not. At age thirty-six in 1933, she was the star of Hearst's Cosmopolitan Productions and a main attraction at MGM. In the fall of 1932 she was the lead actress with Robert Montgomery in *Blondie of the Follies;* the following May she headlined the cast of an appealing love story titled *Peg O' My Heart;* and in December she starred with Bing Crosby in a "warm, modest and good-humored" musical (so said the *New York Times* reviewer) titled *Going Hollywood.* Then early in 1934 she signed on to do a Civil War melodrama with Gary Cooper, which Cosmopolitan and MGM called *Operator 13*.

Marion was, by no stretch of the imagination, a dumb blonde; indeed, she was bright and multitalented. A shrewd, independent-minded businesswoman, she had reached the economic status of a millionaire through sound investments and hard work—and Hearst's beneficence. And like Hearst, she was not miserly. In 1933 she was reelected president (for a fourth term) of the Motion Picture Relief Fund, which was an industry wide charitable organization. She also earned a reputation at Cosmopolitan and MGM for being extravagantly generous, helping understudies and staffers financially without any repayment. And for her closest girlfriends she became a matchmaker, who inevitably participated in weddings as a bridesmaid but never a bride.

Marion's decision to stay with Hearst, a septuagenarian twice her age, could have played out like a Greek tragedy. But it would not. The major reason was that she had an unfailing love for the man, despite his faults. One other personality trait affected this relationship; she and Hearst both had a strong sense of loyalty to each other. What made the situation even more pronounced was that Hearst simply adored her. He seemingly overlooked, or ignored, her reputed "friendship" with leading men, especially Charlie Chaplin. After all, Marion was, and continued to remain, his staunchest ally and supporter, his most steadfast friend. And other than the loss of some personal desires, the positives in their existence far outweighed the negatives. They were leading lives that most people would have envied. Both were recognized celebrities—of the rich-and-famous status; they lived in magnificent surroundings; and they had achieved recognized distinction in their chosen fields of endeavor.[18]

By the end of spring 1934, Marion and Hearst needed a break from their overcrowded agendas. Tired and overworked, she was pushing to finish *Operator 13*, which was behind schedule. He, in turn, needed a reinvigoration of spirit, a rejuvenation of mind and body. And that signified one thing to him—a vacation and another tour of Europe.

Hearst, according to habit, left little to chance. On any lengthy, expense-paid excursion he was the ultimate educational director as well as tour guide extraordinaire. With the help of Marion, he selected such movie friends as Mary Carlisle, Buster Collier, Arthur Lake, Dorothy Mackaill, and Eileen Percy, together with such Hearst personnel as *Cosmopolitan* movie executive Edgar Hatrick, Marion's secretary Ella Williams, and youthful *Los Angeles Examiner* reporter Harry Crocker, who acted as Hearst's personal secretary and general flunkie on the trip. Hearst also included his three eldest sons—George, Bill Jr., and John—and their wives. And he finalized the guest list with the inclusion of two essential companions, his German dachshund Helena and Marion's dachshund Gandhi.[19]

By May 22, Hearst had made all necessary preparations. His entourage left Los Angeles by private car en route to New York City. In Chicago the next day he spoke at a luncheon in his honor, while commemorating the Century of Progress Exposition (Chicago World's Fair). Then, on reaching New York, he delayed the tour one more day while taking a side trip to Washington at the invitation of the president.[20]

Once again Hearst encountered the Roosevelt charm and the aura of the White House—and, for the moment, again succumbed to both. Whereas during the winter and spring of 1934 he had been highly critical of certain New Deal legislation, especially the NRA and a proposed income tax increase, he showed no signs of discontent with the administration. In an interview on May 26, just prior to sailing to Spain on the Italian liner *Rex,* he proclaimed that the "U.S. Is Definitely on the Road to Recovery," or so the *New York American* headline blared forth. In fact, after visiting with President Roosevelt in Washington, Hearst asserted that the NRA "is much better than it was" and "I am entirely in sympathy with the President." He revealed only one negative concern, that of the Newspaper Guild which, he asserted, dictated union policies unfavorable to "the public" and, of course, to his business enterprises. Overall, however, Hearst seemed satisfied. Such was the compelling influence of the Roosevelt presence; such was the desire of the world's most powerful publisher to make a difference in behalf of his country.[21]

But for now the Hearst traveling troupe was bound for Europe, having no apparent difficulties as long as Hearst was in charge. Within a week they were touring the Spanish countryside en route from Granada and Cordova to Madrid, where Hearst was to be welcomed as an official guest of the city in an elaborate reception. On June 21 they took leave of Spain for London, with most of the party traveling by car through France. Hearst, however, decided to charter a plane to England, thereby reminding Americans of his disdain for the French after being expelled from that nation four years earlier. His memory for insults was lengthy and often unforgiving.

In London, Hearst directed his charges to the lavish castle at St. Donat's, where they luxuriated for several weeks in the Welsh countryside. But they did not tarry for long. By mid-July they were off again, this time across the English Channel by steamer, then into Holland and Belgium by train, and through Germany and Switzerland to Italy by car. At

Rome, they were truly American tourists, visiting numerous historic sites in the ancient city, and delighting in taking pictures of Italian dictator Benito Mussolini haranguing a crowd. Then north to Venice en route to Germany they proceeded, returning late in August through Austria to Munich and the curative baths at Bad Nauheim.[22]

Hearst was in prime form. "He was a wonderful guide," Harry Crocker admiringly recalled. Because of his extensive travels to Europe, "he knew the proper hour of day to arrive in any city to enhance its natural beauty; he knew the best hotel, the best restaurants, the characteristic dishes of all countries and all cities, and the entertainments." For instance, Hearst chose to arrive in Venice at dusk, which he considered to be the most picturesque and impressionable time to visit. He then, as deftly prearranged, had assembled "a flock of gondolas," designating for comfort only two of his entourage in each one. The gondoliers poled their boats, "like black swans," Crocker reminisced, in and out past dimly lit historic palaces and luxurious hotels, while the sounds of the city at eventide greeted them. Hearst had a penchant for the dramatic.[23]

Hearst loved Germany, especially Munich. "What do I like best about it?" he proclaimed to a reporter. "Everything—the city, the surroundings, the climate, the bright and kindly happy Bavarian people, the shops, the theaters, the museums—and the beer. Let us not forget the beer. . . . In fact, it is such a delightful place that one has to be careful not to want to live here instead of going home and attending to business."[24]

Hearst also had another objective in mind. On departing from New York late in May, he had told a *New York Times* reporter that he hoped to meet Adolf Hitler. But he soon began to have some misgivings. Ernst "Putzie" Hanfstaengl, a Harvard graduate from New York City who was now the press officer for the German Reich and an intimate adviser to Hitler, was determined to arrange a meeting between Hearst and the Fuhrer at a major Nazi Party rally in Nuremberg. But Hearst reviewed the situation and decided not to get mixed up in Nazi politics. He therefore declined, stating that medical treatments at Bad Nauheim were essential to his health. When Hanfstaengl then proposed a conference at a certain castle in Germany, the same excuse was forthcoming.[25]

With Hanfstaengl as a persistent go-between, Hitler asked Hearst to name a place and date where a discussion could occur. Cherished friend and confidant Arthur Brisbane correctly counseled Hearst in a long-distance telephone call against such a meeting, stating that "no matter what you say or do, persons in America will not understand . . . they will hold it against you that you even talked to Hitler." But Hearst listened to other advice. MGM mogul Louis B. Mayer, for instance, troubled by the reported Nazi persecution of German Jews, wired Hearst to intercede in their behalf: "You may be able to accomplish some good."

Hanfstaengl argued even more persuasively. He pleaded with Hearst to see Hitler, who was "surrounded by provincial men" who would not point out to the Führer that "his anti-Catholic, anti-Semitic programs" would produce "world disapproval" and eventually "lead Germany to a debacle." Hitler was "fully aware," Hanfstaengl contended, "that Hearst knows what he is talking about," and "I am sure" that such a "conference would have far-reaching results."[26]

No further discussion was necessary. Hearst, an old news hound tantalized by the idea of having the scoop interview of the year, found this opportunity irresistible. On September 16, he flew to Berlin in a private plane to meet Adolf Hitler.

And in so far as this event being memorable, Hearst was not disappointed. At every turn, precision and military order were much in evidence. A high-ranking German officer met Hearst, who was accompanied by Crocker as secretary and Hanfstaengl as interpreter, and deposited them into a waiting black Benz limousine. After a brief ride they arrived at the "Reichs-Konslerei [sic]," Crocker recollected, which was "a gray stone building crouched behind an impressive black, grille fence." Everywhere, it seemed, Hitler's elite guard, the ominous Brown Shirts and Black Shirts, were hovering. When the Hearst party of three entered a reception room, which was evidently the intended destination, "a series of booted heel-clicks, sharp like castanets," and Nazi arm salutes with an automatic "Heil Hitler" rent the air. Then, within a few minutes, as if on cue, Hitler entered through the same door—and again "a barrage of heel-clicks exploded" and obedient military salutes saturated the room.

As the lead participant in this brief drama, Hitler reached a psychological high in role-playing at least as Crocker so noted. With "a quick forward jerk" he shook hands with each of his guests, almost toppling each one with the suddenness and strength of such a maneuver. He then waved them to be seated, sinking Hearst into a deep sofa while he selected a high straight-backed chair, which gave him a definite downward-look advantage over Hearst in one-on-one conversation.

After exchanging a few formal amenities, Hitler directed the conversation toward the point of the meeting. "Why am I so misrepresented, so misunderstood in America?" he accusingly asked. "Why are the people of America so antagonistic to my regime?" When Hearst replied that "the people of the United States believe in democracy and are averse to dictatorship," Hitler abruptly interrupted and held forth for several minutes. He vigorously argued that the German people had elected him to office by an overwhelming vote and that they had endorsed his policies by more than a two-thirds majority. And under Germany's Weimar constitution he was legally following their dictates. After several more minutes of similar contentions expressing the righteousness of his position, Hitler asked somewhat rhetorically, "That is democracy, is it not?" Seemingly unaffected by Hitler's avalanche of words, Hearst succinctly replied, "That might be democracy, but it is also dictatorship in view of what those policies are."

And so the conversation continued, which provided Hearst the opportunity to justify his grounds for this meeting. He suggested a second reason for Hitler's unpopularity in the United States. "A very large and influential and respected element" of Americans, he pointed out, were concerned about "the drastic treatment by the German government of . . . [many] subject people" either because of race or religion. In response, Hitler assured Hearst, in no uncertain terms, "that all discrimination is disappearing and," he concluded, "that is the policy of my government, and you will see ample evidence of it."[27]

At the end of this interview, which lasted almost an hour, Hearst went away from it highly impressed. To Colonel Joseph Willicombe, his secretary and trusted friend, he wrote, "Hitler certainly is an extraordinary man. We estimate him too lightly in America. He has enormous energy, intense enthusiasm, a marvelous faculty for dramatic oratory, and great organizing ability." He then added quite prophetically, "Of course, all these qualities can be misdirected."[28]

Hearst soon realized that Arthur Brisbane had been prophetic in his earlier counsel that "no matter what you say or do, persons in America will not understand, they will not want to understand . . . that you even talked with Hitler." Hearst's editor and biographer John Winkler readily agreed. As he put it, "this encounter set in motion a chain reaction of tempestuous, percussive events, engulfing governments and peoples and arraying against Hearst powerful, organized forces which all but accomplished his ruin." Hearst's inquisitiveness to meet Hitler also gave further voice and meaning to the nursery rhyme, "Curiosity killed the cat."[29]

In the fall of 1934 Hearst was not completely aware that powerful negative reactions were materializing. Nor was he obliged to heed any dire warnings. For instance, upon emerging from his meeting with Hitler, he allowed a photographer to snap pictures of him with a group of waiting Nazis, including a high Reich official, Dr. Alfred Rosenberg, who was vehemently anti-Semitic. He also disregarded a plea from one of his New York executives, who asked him please to sail for home on a "Cunarder, or anything but a German boat" because his "hobnobbing with Hitler" was already creating "a bad impression in America." In reaction to such advice, lest he appear intimidated, Hearst arrived in New York on September 27 aboard the north German Lloyd liner *Bremen*, with his full entourage of guests in tow.[30]

After four months in Europe, Hearst immediately addressed a number of important concerns. Even while on vacation he had continued to oversee and juggle his various business and political activities. One situation in his native California was especially worrisome. Upton Sinclair, a renowned writer who had first achieved a national reputation in 1906 for *The Jungle*, a gruesomely detailed best-seller describing the unsanitary conditions in the Chicago meatpacking industry, had decided in the spring of 1934 to switch from the Socialist Party to the Democrats and run for governor. Late in August, after a vigorous campaign, Sinclair won the party nomination in an upset victory.

At first Hearst had been amused by Sinclair, whom he considered a well-meaning man and visionary. But the possibility of Sinclair's election posed an economic threat to those engaged in the motion picture industry and to Hearst personally. With thousands of unemployed down-and-outers flocking to California in 1934, reminiscent of the Okies and Arkies on Route 66, Sinclair had gained considerable notoriety and support for his campaign platform, which he called EPIC—End Poverty in California. To sustain such a program meant higher taxation on those citizens and businesses who could best afford such fiscal burdens. As Shakespeare's Hamlet would have appropriately remarked, "Ay, there's the rub."

As a result, with Sinclair's nomination, Republicans and well-to-do Democrats such as Hearst launched an all-out political campaign to defeat this threat to their economic security. It was not pretty—or fair. Motion picture moguls, led by Louis B. Mayer, were particularly vicious and unprincipled. They manufactured newsreels of well-dressed, nice-looking people backing their candidate, Republican incumbent governor Frank Merriam, while showing criminal-looking types with long, unkempt beards, who spoke with distinct Russian accents, endorsing Sinclair. They then distributed their handiwork to theaters throughout the state free of charge. They also suggested that if Sinclair won, the major studios would relocate to Florida.

To complement this fiction Hearst added his own brand of campaign vilification. His newspapers, besides containing two to four pages daily of Sinclair negatives, pictured trainloads of hobos arriving in Los Angeles. These "communists," attracted by Sinclair's promise to "End Poverty in California," were going to take over the state. Such a charge had little foundation since the pictured communists were later identified as screen actors in Warner Brothers' *Wild Boys of the Road*.

Hearst then upped this campaign of vilification. He turned his five California newspapers into screaming testimonials to save the state from "the control of an unbalanced and unscrupulous political speculator." In the "performance of his unsound and sinister program [EPIC]," Hearst editorialized, Sinclair would "wreck the very foundations of all prosperity for years to come." On November 6, 1934, Mayer and Hearst proved the power of the media. The final vote was Sinclair, 879,537; Merriam, 1,138,620.[31]

While agreeing with Mayer on the gubernatorial race, Hearst was at odds with MGM over Marion's career, which was, motion picture historian Louis Pizzitola noted, "very much on Hearst's mind." Prior to sailing to Europe late in May, he had attempted to secure a starring role for Marion in the projected production of *The Barretts of Wimpole Street,* but MGM selected Norma Shearer instead. After returning to California, Hearst and Marion focused on another prized screen part, that of playing the French queen in *Marie Antoinette.* But again Mayer intervened in favor of Norma Shearer; he could not envision a song-and-dance comedienne shouldering such a dramatic role.[32]

Yet other dynamics were also at work, straining the decade-long relationship between Cosmopolitan Productions and MGM. Mayer, a staunch Republican, was the state party chairman; he greatly admired Herbert Hoover and intended to promote his renomination for the presidency in 1936. Upon seeking support from Hearst in August 1934, he received this blunt reply: "Dear Louis: I am sorry but I cannot conscientiously support that man. He is selfish and stupid. . . . He will harm his own party, handicap the whole conservative movement, and strengthen the hands of the radicals." For that matter, Hearst asserted, "the present incumbent [Roosevelt] would be immeasurably better than this discredited failure, and if you don't suppress this hoodoo, your party will lose its chance, too, of electing a Congress as well as a President. His name is an anathema to the American public. W.R."

This slashing rebuke deeply hurt Mayer. Early in October, when the *Los Angeles Examiner* headlined on page 1 that Hearst had spent the night at the White House as FDR's guest and in conjunction with the president had forecast genuine recovery, the strain on the Hearst–Mayer relationship increased. And even though "they were not to abandon their friendship," Mayer's biographer noted, "the old glamour of the 1920s was gone."[33]

When Mayer rejected the *Marie Antoinette* proposal in October 1934, the commercial association between MGM and Cosmopolitan Productions ended. Hearst quickly set in motion an arrangement with Jack Warner which established a five-year association with Warner Brothers.

And within a few days, Hearst disassembled the fabulous Marion Davies bungalow on the MGM lot and moved it in three large sections from Culver City to Warner studios in Burbank.[34]

During this same time period Hearst was also focusing on national politics. After visiting the White House on October 9, Hearst again succumbed to the Roosevelt charm. Despite his concern about the NRA favoring labor unions to the detriment of business and the threat of higher taxes "to soak the thrifty," he concluded that the president "is willing to learn by experience" and that "the United States has a great mission" not only for economic recovery but for world peace. Proclaiming himself a Democrat, Hearst thus directed his media empire to support the New Deal.

As in California against Upton Sinclair, so it was across the nation that Hearst enjoyed sweeping political success. On November 6, Americans overwhelmingly endorsed the New Deal. To the president he wired this telegram: "I congratulate you, sir, on your historic victory. There has been no such popular endorsement since the days of Thomas Jefferson and Andrew Jackson. . . . I believe your just and judicious measures will soon restore a national prosperity in which all will share with contentment and gratitude." He then concluded in typical Hearst rhetoric: "The forgotten man does not forget."[35]

Two days later Hearst, in the mood of a jubilant Democrat but concerned over losing the momentum of victory, was already advising Roosevelt—and Hearst readers. In an editorial on page 1 of his newspapers he urged the president to understand that "the lesson of the election should be" that "the public" was not just demanding "continued" progressive reform but, more importantly, "SOUND progressivism." He warned against "excessive and unreasonable expenditures" that would accelerate the evils of "an unbalanced budget," which in turn would deter "a speedy return to normalcy" in "business and employment and government costs." Otherwise, he feared, "an extremism" might evolve throughout the nation, arising from protests and demonstrations by the Communist Party in the United States, and thereby "threaten our American institutions."[36]

Although a crusade against communism would increasingly occupy his energies during the first six months of 1935, Hearst still labored to be an effective supporter and friend of the Roosevelt administration. But he found this task increasingly difficult. The president had surrounded himself with a number of intellectuals who affected legislative policy detrimentally, at least to Hearst's way of thinking. The so-called Brain Trust, composed of scholars Raymond Moley of Barnard College, corporation and private property expert Adolf Berle Jr., and agricultural authority Rexford Guy Tugwell (both professors at Columbia University)was especially irritating to Hearst. Having "no actual experience in business and no practical experience in economics," they were the Democratic Party's cross to bear, its "white elephant," Hearst publicly announced. In regard to their political advocacies of the past two years they had proven to be "chuckle-headed reformers and asinine theorists" who were hell bent on "wrecking . . . American business" and bringing the nation "to the brink of despair."[37]

Many New Deal programs and policies were examples of their handiwork. Although Hearst had previously advocated a $5 billion public works project as one panacea for coping with the depression, such massive New Deal programs as the Agricultural Adjustment Administration (AAA), Civilian Conservation Corps (CCC), Public Works Administration (PWA), and Tennessee Valley Authority (TVA) had created enormous deficits, thus causing Hearst considerable worry and concern regarding their implementation and cost. Yet the president was willing to veto a bonus for veterans (the Patman Bill), one of Hearst's long-term pet projects. With "billions . . . being distributed freely, liberally, almost recklessly, in every direction, why should not some of this money GO TO THE VETERANS?" Hearst challenged Roosevelt in an editorial. "Why economize only in the case of the veterans?"[38]

Even more galling to Hearst, the New Deal seemed to be unfair to business, at times likening profits in the marketplace to ill-gotten gain of "crooks" and "criminals." In a scathing editorial Hearst stated that "the government seems to think that business, instead of being the great benefactor of the nation, is 'Public Enemy No. 1,' and that it is the duty of Democracy to destroy it." As for the National Recovery Administration (NRA), which increasingly appeared to favor labor unions to the detriment of business, Hearst could become almost apoplectic at the mere mention of its name. Consequently, "Government should let business alone," he announced in still another editorial, and not hobble it with the "back-breaking burden" of multiple taxation—city, state, and national—which would impede prosperity. Thus in May 1935, when the NRA was declared unconstitutional, Hearst predictably rejoiced in a front-page editorial titled "Thank God for the Supreme Court!"[39]

Although during the spring of 1935 Hearst and the Roosevelt administration tried on several occasions to settle their differences, to orchestrate a truce concerning editorial criticism that appeared daily in the Hearst newspapers, such an arrangement could not—and would not—prevail. For instance, while praising the New Deal for its build up of American naval strength, Hearst sensed that Roosevelt, and especially Secretary of State Cordell Hull, were internationalists. To his alarm and chagrin, Hearst suspected that the United States intended to join the

World Court, thereby giving sanction to the League of Nations. Once again in editorials he raised the rallying cry of "America First" and "No Entangling Alliances." Once again he demanded that Roosevelt keep the promises of the Democratic Party platform and not make a mockery of the term "Splendid Isolation."[40]

The administration's stance on taxation was equally disturbing. On June 19, 1935, Roosevelt proposed increasing taxes on personal incomes and inheritances, a levy on gifts, a graduated assessment on "very great individual net incomes," and provisions for a corporation income tax. To Hearst this proposition was pure madness, a robbery of the wealthy by government; it was foolishly raising taxes on the producers of the nation—on the "seed corn" of society—in time of depression.

Hearst responded immediately to this administrative proposition, which seemed to be targeting him specifically. Whereas his editors had been using the phrases "Soak the Thrifty" and "Soak the Rich" in reference to administration tax proposals, he now instructed them to substitute "Soak the Successful." And henceforth they should allude to Roosevelt's New Deal as the "Raw Deal."

Because of his anger—and disillusionment—with the president, Hearst went a step further. To his editors he wired this harsh observation: "President's taxation program is essentially Communism. It is, to be sure, a bastard product of Communism and demagogic democracy, a mongrel creation which might accurately be called demo-communism, evolved by a composite personality which might be labeled Stalin Delano Roosevelt."[41]

By August, attempts at reconciliation were no longer possible. Vicious attacks by the Hearst press on "Raw Deal" programs continued unabated. "WHICH? American Democracy or Personal Dictatorship?" Hearst asked his readers in one Sunday editorial, pointing out that Thomas Jefferson had warned that a prerequisite to preserving liberty was a certain distrust of federal authority. "The Roosevelt regime has so thoroughly invaded and dominated the states and counties and cities of this country," Hearst asserted, that "the President has assumed, unconstitutionally in most cases, more power than European constitutional monarchs, and, in fact, practically the same powers as the European dictators [Hitler and Mussolini]." By the end of August, Hearst was so fearful of Roosevelt that he was contemplating the formation of a Constitutional Democratic Party. Indeed, the old progressive of yesteryear was even willing to accept as the leader of this third party movement an inveterate enemy, Al Smith.[42]

At age seventy-two, Hearst was once again adrift in the uncertain waters of national politics. His past judgment in this arena had often been sorely lacking. But with the nation teetering toward "Socialism or Fascism" through the policies of the "Raw Deal," he was determined to fight for the benefits of liberty under a constitutional government. With FDR as a formidable adversary and with the future of the nation at stake, Hearst resolutely girded himself for the presidential campaign of 1936. In this time of crisis he must not fail his fellow Americans.[43]

9 Promoting the Red Scare

On November 26, 1934, approximately three weeks after the congressional elections in the United States, William Randolph Hearst alerted the editors of his various publications to a growing threat to American democracy. Without question, the Communist Party was the real menace facing the nation. "Today," he asserted, it "is largely composed of agitators with the greed for power, position, and property, but without the competence to acquire them except by criminal violence, and certainly without the ability or the will to exercise them for the general benefit." During his summer tour of Europe Hearst had noted that fascist movements in Italy and Germany, headed by Benito Mussolini and Adolf Hitler, had acquired power because of their opposition to communism. "We do not want to have to resort to a Fascist movement in order to prevent such misgovernment," he announced. Hence, "let us realize that there is no danger of Fascism as long as there is NO DANGER OF COMMUNISM."[1]

Hearst, however, was not entirely convinced of this statement. Radical forces were being unleashed in American politics, having little understanding of democracy and even less appreciation of constitutional government. During the summer of 1934 a series of labor strikes had erupted throughout the United States and had continued with unabated violence.

The one in San Francisco was especially bitter, spurring Hearst into demonstrative action. While in Europe he had directed John Neylan, who was the West Coast director of Hearst enterprises as well as a close confidant, to settle this labor dispute against striking dock workers in behalf of the business community. With Hearst's knowledge and approval, Neylan used the Hearst media empire, including the five California newspapers, to denounce the strikers as communists and use whatever means necessary to defeat them. During the summer of 1934 Neylan collaborated with the San Francisco business community and those in power to do just that, applying both force and violence to achieve a "satisfactory" peace.[2]

But Hearst believed that the main source of communist infiltration into American society was much more sinister. Communists were indoctrinating students with Marxist philosophy through the public school system and higher education. Hearst therefore worked assiduously to blunt such un-American activities. Late in November 1934, he initiated plans for an "Anti-Red Crusade." He instructed a number of his editors to send reporters, posing as prospective college students, to obtain study outlines of university courses, especially those having to do with the comparative investigation of socialism, communism, and democracy. After a so-called interview with one unsuspecting professor at Syracuse University about the content of his course, Hearst reporters of the *Syracuse Journal* ran a front-page story on November 22. The headline read, "DRIVE ALL RADICAL PROFESSORS AND STUDENTS FROM THE UNIVERSITIES." Not above manufacturing evidence, the reporters labeled the professor in question as a communist. He was quite outspoken "even to strangers" about the "coming revolution."[3]

From this beginning the "Red-Scare Crusade" spread rapidly. A number of Hearst reporters, using the same tactics as their colleagues at Syracuse, invaded other institutions of higher education. At New York University and Columbia University they were able to procure course outlines but were unable to interview professors, who were no longer unsuspecting. In the meantime Hearst editors attempted to investigate such eastern colleges and universities as Harvard, Yale, Dartmouth, Princeton, and Amherst, as well as prominent midwestern institutions—the University of Illinois, the University of Chicago, Northwestern University, and the University of Wisconsin. In published exposés reporters linked as communists those professors who had written scholarly works on Russian history, who taught courses on comparative economic theories, and who were members of, or associated with so-called pink organizations. And since these institutions were funded partially or completely by public money, the Hearst editors demanded that professors and students alike should take an oath pledging their loyalty to the United States.[4]

The academic community, because of these ploys to besmirch the reputation of its constituency, reacted with justified outrage and alarm. On December 23, twenty prominent New York educators, including Charles A. Beard of Columbia, who was a past president of the American Historical Association, noted pastor Harry Emerson Fosdick of the Riverside Church, honorary president of the National Education Association

John Dewey, and Willard Beatty, who was president of the Progressive Education Association, denounced the Hearst newspapers for conducting a red scare and called on the McCormack-Dickstein Congressional Committee (on un-American Activities) to investigate the "un-American activities of William Randolph Hearst." The group concurred that Hearst, if successful in his red scare campaign, would destroy institutions of higher education that were preparing students "for intelligent democratic citizenship" or "reduce American universities and schools to the ignominious condition of the German schools and universities under Hitler."

In Boston a week later, members of the National Student Federation were equally vehement in their criticism, condemning the Hearst newspapers for "promoting the suppression of minority political beliefs on American campuses." Again on January 14, fifteen college editors from the East and Midwest accused Hearst of attempting to "stifle freedom of inquiry and expression" and vowed to use their editorial influence in opposing "this crusade aimed at Hitlerizing American education." Late in February, a thousand educators, meeting in convention at Atlantic City for the National Education Association (of superintendents), applauded Columbia Professor Beard repeatedly for denouncing the "insidious influences of William Randolph Hearst."[5]

The results of this academic denunciation were immediate and far-reaching. In planned demonstrations students censured Hearst, urging Americans to boycott his newspapers, magazines, and newsreels. Other citizen groups burned him in effigy after listening to rousing harangues of denunciation. For instance, at a mass meeting in New York City early in February 1935 called by the Provisional Committee for Nonpartisan Labor Defense, some 2,000 members unanimously voted for a resolution that condemned Hearst for paving the way in his newspapers for a fascist reaction to the working classes and therefore dubbed him "Labor Enemy No. 1." Three weeks later 15,000 New Yorkers gathered at Madison Square Garden to censure him not only for advocating fascist views in abridging academic freedom but for criticizing the recognition of communist Russia by the United States. Once again Charles Beard summed up the growing disdain and hatred for Hearst by writing that "I have never found one single person who for talents and character commands the respect of the American people, who has not agreed with me that William Randolph Hearst has pandered to depraved tastes and has been an enemy of everything that is best in the American tradition. . . . There is not a cesspool of vice and crime which Hearst has not raked and exploited for money-making purposes. No person with intellectual honesty or moral integrity will touch him with a ten foot pole."[6]

Such criticism did not deter Hearst in the least. When convinced of the righteousness of a cause, no matter how unpopular, he was unwavering in his commitment. He continued to instruct his editors to hunt out and reveal to the public those "communists" who were intent on undermining American democracy. In 1935 the Hearst newspapers publicized a growing list of subversives, those individuals and organizations who opposed the furtherance of constitutional government.

In some cases the accusations bordered on the ridiculous. President Nicholas Murray Butler of Columbia University, who was also president of the Carnegie Endowment for International Peace, was singled out as an "arch-propagandist for un-American principles." President Robert Maynard Hutchins of the University of Chicago, who refused to allow a public investigation of communism on his campus, was equally unpatriotic and a Moscow adviser. And the American Civil Liberties Union, for its opposition to sedition and teacher's oath bills by state legislators, was a communistic organization that supported subversive unions.[7]

Hearst editors soon extended the parameters of the red scare crusade. Reporters announced that communists were infiltrating all walks of American life, sinisterly invading churches and labor unions as well as positions of importance in local and state governments. They even suggested that leadership in the YMCA and YWCA were in danger of being taken over.[8]

As a growing number of detractors identified his name with fascism, Hearst defended his red scare crusade with unwavering determination and without apology. In signed editorials he declared that "the Hearst papers stand for Americanism and genuine democracy," that "they are opposed to Communism, Fascism or any form of despotism," and that "they believe that America should be for Americans and that Americans should be for America." And for "those who do not approve of these policies," Hearst declared defiantly, they would be better off "not . . . [subscribing to] these papers, because these are the policies which will be adhered to as long as these papers are published."[9]

Hearst was not alone in his convictions; he took comfort in a number of successes which alerted fellow Americans to the dangers of communism. For instance, forty-four state legislatures considered sedition and loyalty oath bills. And at such leading universities as Harvard and Yale, the presidents required their faculties to denounce communism and swear allegiance to the United States.[10]

While conducting this crusade, Hearst did not neglect the Roosevelt administration. During the summer and fall of 1935 he continued a brutal assault on the "Raw Deal." In one editorial after another (with accompanying political cartoons) the Hearst newspapers condemned the administration's excessive spending, its antibusiness–prolabor stance, its unreasonable taxation policy of "soak the successful." But equally alarming to Hearst was Roosevelt's international stance toward recognition of the World Court that in turn would sanction the League of Nations. And what was equally frustrating to him was the realization that he was powerless to affect such wrongheaded policies. The president had surrounded himself with "chuckle-headed reformers and asinine theorists," many of whom, he asserted, were socialists, if not avowed communists.[11]

As a consequence, Hearst decided on another course of action, one that would remedy his growing anxieties and fearful concerns for the future of the American people and his country. The answer, of course, was new leadership. He must discover—and anoint—a formidable political candidate who had the wherewithal to defeat the charismatic Roosevelt, someone who would restore the United States to the true principles of Jeffersonian democracy and constitutional government.

Seemingly uncertain as to the correct political course of action to pursue, Hearst considered his options—and those for his readers. In a front-page editorial on August 30, 1935, he proposed several possibilities. One would be the formation of a third party—the Constitutional Democratic Party—whose platform would be the very one that the Roosevelt administration had discarded after the 1932 presidential election and had replaced, Hearst asserted, with the policies of "the imported, autocratic, Asiatic Socialist Party of Karl Marx and Franklin Delano Roosevelt." Hearst even suggested that Al Smith, his archenemy of yesteryear, "would make a powerful candidate . . . of the genuine Democratic Party." Hearst also raised the prospect of supporting a southern Democrat, such as Senator Harry Byrd of Virginia, Governor Eugene Talmadge of Alabama, or Governor Albert Ritchie of Maryland, as the nominee of the "true" Democratic Party. But he did not consider this proposal as having much feasibility. Another alternative would be for Democrats to support a Republican not closely identified with Herbert Hoover but who was imbued with the philosophy of Jeffersonian Democrats. Hearst "innocently" suggested for consideration Governor Alf Landon of Kansas and publisher-businessman Frank Knox of Illinois.[12]

His "innocent" proposal was a typical Hearst ploy. He was already preparing the American public for the proper candidate to defeat Roosevelt. It was Governor Alf Landon of Kansas. As early as July 1935, the Hearst media empire had been gearing up to explode this relatively unknown face onto the American political scene. Richard E. Berlin, who headed the Hearst magazine chain, had already assigned such talented writers as Adela Rogers St. Johns of *Good Housekeeping* and Damon Runyon of *Cosmopolitan* to introduce Landon to the Hearst audience while others checked the governor's credentials. After Ed Coblentz and other Hearst insiders acknowledged that Landon met the Hearst standards for ultimate approbation, Hearst marshaled his forces for a lengthy campaign against Roosevelt and the "Raw Deal."[13]

On September 30, Hearst launched his support for Landon. The *New York Times* headline read, "HEARST SAYS HOPE FOR '36 IS LANDON." He then explained his endorsement by resolving the political dilemma that he had presented to his readers in the August 30th editorial. He first ruled out the possibility of a Constitutional Democratic Party; third party movements had never been successful in American politics. As for a candidate to oppose Roosevelt, Hearst asserted that a Jeffersonian Democrat such as Al Smith or Eugene Talmadge would be an acceptable choice—they "could do the trick." But, he lamented, they had not stepped forward or shown any real inclination to do so. Yet Roosevelt "can be defeated," Hearst asserted, "if he continues to repudiate the declaration of the Democratic platform . . . if he continues to dishonor his own personal pledges, and if he persists in trying radically to modify our American form of free government." Hence, through the process of elimination Hearst brought his readers to one ultimate conclusion. Vote Republican! Since the often maligned Herbert Hoover would be a disastrous choice as the Republican nominee, "I figure," Hearst concluded, that "the Republican party will have to depend on Governor Alfred M. Landon of Kansas," who "believes in action rather than conversation" and whose "record is one of deeds instead of promises."[14]

The Hearst pronouncement produced mixed reactions from those closely involved. William Allen White, the dean of American editors and a Landon adviser, was disturbed by the endorsement but then rationalized philosophically, "Doubtless any statesman many times has to ally himself with worse men than Hearst. Probably in my own career I have worked with deeper-dyed villains. But a man should be allowed his fancies in villains, this being the glorious free country that it is." Landon, having never met Hearst or even having spoken with him, was also taken aback by the endorsement. But he soon agreed with his consultants that "it was better that Hearst be for him than against—as long as he exacted no promises and did not interfere." And as for Hearst, with his disdain for Roosevelt increasing at a fever pitch, the commitment to Landon was total and without reservation. He had joined that clique of "Roosevelt haters," biographer John Winkler noted, "who lived only to get That Man out of the White House."[15]

To justify this all-out commitment, Hearst arranged a meeting with Landon. On December 10, he traveled by special train to Topeka, accompanied by columnist and alter ego Arthur Brisbane, close friend and newspaper publisher Paul Block, and Eleanor "Cissy" Patterson, publisher of the *Washington Herald*. After lunch at the governor's mansion and a lengthy exchange of views, they all went away impressed. To assembled reporters Paul Block predicted the defeat of the New Deal and was all smiles when asked if he and Hearst had pledged their support to the governor. With equal exuberance, Cissy Patterson concurred, announcing that Landon "was simply grand. He's just the solid, common type of man we need in the White House." And Hearst, although unable to find agreement with Landon on several campaign issues, summarized their meeting by stating, "I think he is marvelous. To say I am favorably impressed is putting it mildly."[16]

In January 1936, the Landon campaign for the Republican presidential sweepstakes began with little fanfare. As a relatively unknown candidate from a Great Plains state, underfinanced and bereft of political experience on a national scale, Landon appeared to be a long-shot aspirant for the presidency. But he soon changed all such prognostications. His political organization was unique and surprisingly effective. By the end of February Landon-for-President clubs, although not always authorized officially, sprang up across the nation. Photographers took pictures of him with his family, which were subsequently labeled "America's Best-loved Family." By March, a pro-Landon biography by Richard B. Fowler, *Deeds Not Deficits: The Story of Alfred M. Landon*, with an introduction by William Allen White, appeared; by May 10 it had gone through a fifth printing. At the same time hundreds of enthusiastic volunteers, facts in hand, hit the campaign trail, spreading the good news about this progressive "financial wizard" from Kansas, who had balanced the budget in a depression-ridden state and was now preparing to lead the United States out of depression into a new prosperity.[17]

The Landon inner circle also handled the Hearst problem deftly and with aplomb. William Allen White, while noting that "professionally, Hearst is a form of poison" and that "politically he has degenerated into a form of suicide," advised the campaign to accept his backing without direction or conformation. Hearst should be considered "a hitch-hiker on the Landon bandwagon," White philosophized. "Sooner or later Landon will have to throw him off." But for the moment Hearst's support was of utmost importance. His disdain for Roosevelt and the Raw Deal, as well as his approval of Landon, would keep the Hearst presses going at full tilt, providing ample amounts of favorable—and free—publicity. Such backing might also bring in needed campaign contributions.[18]

White was correct in his assessments. The *New York American*, for example, typified the political coverage of the twenty-eight Hearst newspapers. On January 11, 1936, the *American* announced that its Sunday edition would have full-page color pictures of Governor Alf Landon. Two days later an article noted gains for Landon in California, and again on January 16 another favorable reference about him appeared. By the end of the month Hearst reporters recorded his activities on at least six occasions, while Hearst editors denounced New Deal measures and cast harsh judgments about the president.[19]

By the end of March, as the Landon campaign gained momentum, so did activity in the Hearst media. Articles in the *American* appeared daily, creating the aura of a sure-fire winner. On March 17, page 1, the *American* announced that "Landon Gets 21 Oklahoma Votes," then on March 19, page 1, that "New Jersey Delegates Favor Landon." Again on March 20 and 21, similar stories touted even more Landon gains, which seemingly portended to Hearst readers a preconvention landslide victory. As the Republican nomination sweepstakes intensified for national delegates during April and May, the *American* took on a crusade mentality in anticipation of a Landon coronation at the Republican National Convention at Cleveland late in June.

Even Hearst was beginning to believe his own propaganda about Landon. As early as May 4 he wrote to trusted lieutenant Ed Coblentz that Landon was "a man of destiny," indeed "a man who understands public sentiment, public psychology and political situations, and who is consequently capable of succeeding in an astonishing manner." Thoroughly convinced that Landon would win the Republican nomination, Hearst marveled: "Observe Landon's conduct . . . He has had no money, no organization, no previous nation-wide support of any kind, no recognition until six months ago." Hearst therefore predicted that Landon, "a man of destiny," would defeat Roosevelt in November.[20]

Events of the next six weeks seemed to justify Hearst's confidence. At Cleveland on June 11, Republicans in national convention nominated Landon without rancor or divisiveness, then selected Chicago publisher Colonel Frank Knox—a former Hearst executive—for vice president. Nor did it bother Hearst that Secretary of the Interior Harold Ickes, whom he considered a New Deal hatchet man, asserted that Hearst, while not attending the convention, was in actuality Landon's "absentee boss." Presumably disturbed by this "rather absurd" accusation, Hearst was not displeased. Such recognition, although intended to be derogatory, acknowledged his standing in the political scene. Besides, both he and Landon knew that younger delegates at Cleveland, militant and energetic, were responsible for nominating Landon and Knox. They had replaced the Republican old guard and were determined to carry the man from Kansas to victory in November.[21]

For Hearst, Landon's nomination alleviated a number of disappointments both on a personal and business level—but not completely. In 1936 his continued media attacks on the Communist Party in the United States earned him the title in some quarters as "America's No. 1 Red-baiter." His meeting with Hitler in September 1934, his constant assault on the academic community with the demand for loyalty oaths, and his denunciation of New Deal programs (especially concerning labor) reinforced the view of Hearst as one of the most hated men in the United States. As Norman Thomas phrased it, "nearly Public Enemy No. 1." For instance, during January and February 1936, stickers stating "I Don't Read Hearst" were much in evidence in San Francisco and New York City, signaling the demand for a nationwide boycott of the Hearst media. Late in March, at a national meeting of Farmer-Laborites who were planning a third party movement, delegates adopted a resolution condemning "the Fascist laborbaiting tactics of William Randolph Hearst" and promised financial and moral support to striking editorial workers of the *Wisconsin News,* which was a Hearst publication in Milwaukee. And in New York City on April 13, a group calling itself the League Against War And Fascism denounced "Hitler, Mussolini, and William Randolph Hearst" as "traitors to their own people, bent on gaining power and glory for themselves at the cost of sacrificing the lives and welfare of others."[22]

Nor did the Hearst image improve. In March, two biographies, unsolicited and unsanctioned, appeared. One was by Ferdinand Lundberg, *Imperial Hearst: A Social Biography,* with a scathing preface by Charles A. Beard, and the second was by Oliver Carlson and Ernest Sutherland Bates titled *Hearst: Lord of San Simeon.* The *New York Times* book review section summed up the authors' conclusions in its headline: "Two Unflattering Views of William Randolph Hearst," which are "condemnatory" of "the publisher's life and work."

To combat these assaults on his reputation, Hearst asked friend and editor Fremont Older to write an authorized biography. Because of advanced age, Older assigned wife Cora, who adored Hearst, to this welcome task; and together they published the life and achievements of "the most misunderstood man in America." Somewhere between Older's glowing assessment of Hearst and the two negative tomes (especially by Lundberg), readers could attempt to decipher the personality and contributions of the real Hearst. Yet these offsetting works did not resolve the Hearst legacy or satisfy its chief recipient.[23]

In 1935–1936, Hearst had also begun to realize a severe financial pinch. The Raw Deal policy of "soak the successful" was galling and upsetting, but so were other revenue laws. In 1935 the California legislature enacted a state income tax, which Hearst vehemently opposed. As a result, he would announce in October that circumstances compelled him "to close my places" in California "and live almost entirely in New York." The new law, he explained, contained a "peculiar provision," stating that anyone, even a citizen of another state, who resided in California for six months would be subject to its income tax that "goes to 15 percent." If you "add this to the Federal income taxes and the New York taxes, plus many other taxes," he complained, "I find that over 80 percent of my income will go to taxes—in fact, it may be 90 percent."[24]

Yet excessive taxation was only a part of his financial worries. Hearst specifically was the problem. He had demonstrated a disregard for money all his life; it was "something to spend," and that he did well. Although *Fortune* magazine estimated his worth at $220 million in October 1935 (even at deflated depression prices), Hearst had acquired liabilities at a disastrous rate. He was widely recognized as the "nation's No. 1 spender" and, without question, *Fortune* magazine affirmed, "the world's No. 1 collector of *objects of art*." As early as 1925 he tried to address these tendencies by appointing John Francis Neylan as his financial watchdog. As the second in command of the Hearst empire, Neylan stayed the course of debt for a time by going public, selling Hearst Publications, Inc. stock at $25 a share.

A builder of mansions, a creator of businesses, a collector of rare objects, and an accumulator of real estate, Hearst could not be constrained. For instance, San Simeon was a work always in progress, a monument to his life. Without effort or concern he spent $50,000 a month on the Enchanted Hill. Even when he put limits on construction and cut the workforce, the costs were staggering—but not to Hearst. On weekends during depression times who else would hire a special train from Los Angeles to San Luis Obispo for fifty to sixty guests, maintain a taxi service of thirty-five cars for the forty-five miles to San Simeon, and then supply all necessities—food, clothing, entertainment—for a weekend of fun and relaxation? Who else would sustain the upkeep on the largest private zoo in the world? And who, other than Hearst, would continue to buy priceless treasures of Europe, often sight unseen and without regard to cost, only to store them in warehouses in New York City, San Francisco, Los Angeles, and San Simeon?[25]

Nor did seven years of depression, of lost profits and severe economic trends diminish these whims and indulgences. On May 31, 1935, his representatives at Sotheby's Today auction in London outbid all competitors for four pieces of rare English silver—the famous great mace and sword of the old city of Galway, Irish Free State for £5,000 ($24,675), the famous Pusey Horn for £1,900 ($9,376.50), a rare William and Mary toilet set for £1,700 ($8,389.50), and a set of four early Charles II beakers for £1,141 ($5,630.84), all of which amounted to £9,741 ($48,071.84).

The next spring was equally expensive. On April 28, 1936, Hearst purchased *Architecture to the American Architect* from Charles Scribner's Sons and immediately merged it with his *American Architect*, thereby cornering that restricted reading market. A week later he maneuvered the takeover of radio stations in Texas at Austin and San Antonio, while attempting to acquire three more in Fort Worth, Waco, and Oklahoma City.[26]

Other than his obsession to construct or possess castles and mansions (St. Donat's, Marion's Beach House, Wyntoon, and San Simeon), Hearst's most expensive preoccupation was his grandiose trips to Europe. To be the host, in essence to pick up the tab for fifteen to thirty guests over a three-month period was the ultimate in extravagance. On August 8, 1936, with a party of sixteen, including Marion, son George and his wife, Arthur Lake (the film star in the *Dagwood and Blondie* series) and his wife Pat (Marion's niece), and several of Marion's starlet friends, Hearst sailed for Italy on the *Rex* of the Italian line. Somewhat bemused, Hearst's personal secretary Harry Crocker noted that at the last minute at least half a dozen art dealers also booked passage, ever ready to make a sale to the nation's No. 1 spender.

Not so amusing to the Roosevelt administration, however, was a parting shot by Hearst. To reporters covering his departure, he announced that the presidential race in November "will not be close at all. Landon will be overwhelmingly elected and I'll stake my reputation as a prophet on it."

Upon arrival in Italy, Hearst was, as always, the ultimate tour guide, following the family tradition established by his mother Phoebe. For several weeks he directed his charges to the wonders of ancient Rome and the surrounding countryside. He accepted an invitation to meet with fascist dictator Benito Mussolini, who for a number of years had written a column in the Sunday *New York American*. As a result of this meeting Count Galeazzo Ciano, Il Duce's son-in-law, royally entertained Hearst and his entourage at a magnificent villa overlooking Rome.[27]

After recovering from a brief bout with dysentery, Hearst led his merry band northward across the Alps into Bavaria, carefully avoiding any "invasion" of France; he still had not forgiven the French for evicting him in 1930. For several weeks in September he again enjoyed the hot baths at Bad Nauheim, while carefully avoiding any contact with Hitler and the German government.

By the end of September the Hearst travelers were on the move, proceeding eastward into Belgium and Holland. Then at Amsterdam the collecting bug attacked Hearst in full. Upon visiting the famous Rijksmuseum, he viewed several priceless paintings, one by Joost van Cleve and another by George Morland, that he had to possess. Before escaping to the financial safety of England, he had purchased both canvases for "more than $70,000," as well as "three cupboards costing several thousand dollars."

Although unable to complete negotiations on two other paintings valued at $30,000, Hearst provided little relief for his dwindling bank account. He proved once again that "money is meant to be spent." Two weeks later, on October 24, the *New York Times* reported that he had contributed three campaign gifts to the Republican National Committee totaling $30,000.[28]

Hearst and his troupe, now on the last leg of their trip, rested for several weeks at St. Donat's, luxuriating in the grandeur of the historic Welsh castle and the picturesque countryside. Visitors such as actress Sally Eilers, together with Marion's Hollywood producer Jack Warner and wife Ann, enlivened their stay, while the prospect of returning to the United States on the brand-new *Queen Mary* heightened their anticipation. On October 26, they sailed for home in ample time to vote for Landon.[29]

While in Europe for three months Hearst, as usual, kept abreast of his various enterprises and directed policy in regard to them. His surrogates at home knew that they were just that. Except for John Neylan, who dealt with the Hearst finances, Hearst was "the Chief" both in name and reality, whom they must keep informed down to the merest detail, that is, if they wished to keep their jobs. Even at age seventy-three, he had the memory, the work ethic, the mental capacity to command their respect and devotion, as well as their fear.

The presidential campaign of 1936 exemplified this case. Prior to sailing to Europe early in August on his Roman holiday, Hearst ordered his lieutenants to support Landon in every possible way. To propagate the truth about the Republican nominee, Hearst editors and writers first had to familiarize themselves with their subject. As a result, the governor's mansion at Topeka became a Mecca for Hearst employees, often resembling one of their home newspaper offices.[30]

During July and August, the Hearst men did their work well, following the Chief's instructions without a hitch. The *New York American* typified all twenty-eight Hearst papers. The crusade technique was readily apparent. At a daily minimum of three to four pages, editors prominently displayed campaign accounts, editorials, and political cartoons that either praised Landon and the Republicans or debunked Roosevelt and the Raw Deal.[31]

But the Landon quest for the presidency differed perceptibly from his earlier race for the Republican nomination. An internal struggle for control of the campaign soon became apparent. Indecision abounded concerning what issues to stress, what schedules to approve, what speakers to enlist. Yet equally distressing was the candidate himself. Landon seemed to reflect a disturbing political malaise. His speeches lacked force and conviction, the fervor and intensity of firm belief. By the end of August, because of the mounting pressures of the campaign he "had now reached the point," his biographer noted, "where he was doing less listening and more speaking, occasionally with a sharp tongue." William Allen White aptly described the rudderless Republican attempt to defeat Roosevelt in 1936 by saying that it turned out to be "a nightmare."[32]

From the reports of his surrogates, Hearst realized the difficulties facing his candidate and, without anyone's consent, decided to intensify the level of the campaign. He surely had good reason to do so. He announced in a signed editorial that Democratic national chairman James A. Farley was "a national disgrace," who was using the powers of his cabinet position as postmaster general to extend "Tammany politics" (implying corruption) onto the national scene.[33]

Secretary of the Treasury Henry Morgenthau Jr. was also a proven enemy. He was responsible for the administration's 1935 tax measure, which the Hearst newspapers termed "soak the successful" and which was, Hearst asserted, a robbery of the wealthy "through confiscatory taxation." As part of his job Morgenthau was laying the groundwork to incapacitate Hearst's impending onslaught. As "I told the President on Tuesday," Morgenthau recorded in his diary on September 11, "it would be much better to proceed at once on Hearst's and Marion Davies' income tax [returns] before he attacked." He then assured Roosevelt that after a brief investigation "there was plenty there."[34]

Secretary of the Interior Harold Ickes was far more provocative. For months prior to the Republican National Convention, he had made it his business to connect Landon with Hearst, to place upon the Republican nominee the publisher's political kiss of death. During the latter part of August Ickes, as the administration's major hatchet man, escalated this assault over national radio and through timely press releases. Hearst was Landon's "Republican Boss," Ickes announced, who had placed his media empire at the disposal of the Republican Party and who, in turn, expected to receive tax relief, both corporate and personal, after the defeat of Roosevelt. Because of these allegations the *New York Times* speculated that Hearst might be "an important issue" in the campaign.[35]

Hearst soon confirmed that supposition. On September 6, Hearst newspapers across the country began a prolonged assault on the administration. The *New York American* published a front-page editorial titled "The Radical Brand on the New Deal." It charged that radical and communist leaders had already given their approval to support Roosevelt against Landon. During the next two weeks Hearst editors trumpeted these recurring themes: that communists had infiltrated the New Deal; that communism was un-American and undemocratic; that "America can only judge Mr. Roosevelt and his administration by the strange silence that has prevailed in official quarters."[36]

Because of this journalistic barrage, Roosevelt realized that a "defense" against such accusations was imperative. Leveling a charge against Hearst of possible income tax evasion was too late in coming. Thus on September 19, Presidential Secretary Stephen T. Early issued this brief but sharply worded statement: "The White House today . . . [has] learned of a planned attempt, led by a certain notorious newspaper owner, to make it appear that the President passively accepts the support of alien organizations hostile to the American form of Government. Such articles," Early declared "are conceived in malice and born of political spite. They are deliberately framed to give a false impression—in other words to 'frame' the American people." Consequently "the President does not want and does not welcome the vote or support of any individual or group taking orders from alien sources." Early then concluded with this political zinger aimed directly at Hearst. The "simple fact is, of course, obvious. The American people will not permit their attention to be diverted from real issues to fake issues which no patriotic, honorable, decent citizen would purposely inject into American affairs."[37]

To this stinging rebuke Hearst (who was in Amsterdam) replied immediately with a front-page editorial in all his newspapers, titled "A Reply to the President by W. R. Hearst." As far as he was concerned, the campaign had now become personal—and his editorial revealed as much. He castigated Roosevelt for not having the "frankness" and "sincerity" to address him personally instead of directing his criticism to "a certain notorious newspaper owner." Assuming that the White House statement was directed at him, "I may courteously endeavor to correct Mr. Roosevelt's misstatements and to set him right."

So much for "I may courteously endeavor." For two full columns Hearst demeaned the president and his administration. "I have not stated at any time whether the President willingly or unwillingly received the support of the Karl Marx Socialists, the [Felix] Frankfurter radicals, Communists, and anarchists, the [Rexford B.] Tugwell Bolsheviks, and the [Donald] Richberg revolutionists, which constitute the bulk of his following. I have simply said and shown," Hearst pointed out, "that he DOES receive the support of these enemies of the American system of government, and that he has done his best to DESERVE the support of all such disturbing and destructive elements." As a consequence, Hearst declared, the "Bolshevist tyranny in Russia has ordered all its Bolshevists, Socialists, Communists, and revolutionists in the United States to support Mr. Roosevelt . . . and urges his election."

After several paragraphs in support of his accusations, Hearst set the stage for an acrimonious conclusion. "However, I want to be perfectly fair to Mr. Roosevelt—and I HAVE BEEN." Specifically "I have never said by direct or indirect personal statement that he willingly or unwillingly, passively or impassively, receives the support of the bloody Bolshevist tyranny at Moscow. I have simply said, and proved by actual and accurate quotation, that he DOES RECEIVE such support from the enemies of our system of government, and that he has done his utmost in act and utterance while in office to secure and justify such support."

To many Americans Hearst then went beyond the pale in political rhetoric, revealing how deeply the Steve Early memorandum had wounded him. "I do not find any pleasure as an American in saying this of an American President, but it is the truth." And since "I am not a shifty, prevaricating politician, but for over fifty years have endeavored to serve my country as an honorable and patriotic journalist, I am compelled in fairness to my readers to tell the truth."[38]

The Hearst editorial produced the desired reactions. The administration could not have been more pleased. Hearst had demonstrated once again that in politics his support was "a kiss of death." Typical was the experience of U.S. Senator Robert Wagner of New York. On the evening of September 21, while delivering a campaign speech to a boisterous Democratic crowd of 14,000, he departed briefly from his prepared text. He aroused the crowd by mentioning the Hearst editorial. After a "prolonged and sustained booing at the name of William Randolph Hearst," Senator Wagner delighted his audience by stating, "I have been accustomed to reading so many things that were not true in the Hearst papers that I was not surprised to find myself listed as a revolutionist." As a consequence, "I have come to the conclusion that Mr. Hearst is an unconscious comedian; he doesn't know when he is being funny, or how funny he is."[39]

For the next six weeks the campaign for the presidency continued with unabated vigor and venom. Hearst newspaper editors dutifully continued their daily assault on the administration, apparently unaware that the Democrats, with a dynamic president leading the way, were in command.

Hearst seemed oblivious to the momentum swing toward the Democrats. Predictably, just prior to Election Day on November 3, he wrote signed editorials, one proclaiming that Landon "will positively be elected President" and the second one urging his readers to retain "A CONSTITUTIONAL DEMOCRACY" rather than "become a SOCIALISTIC nation." On election eve, while approaching New York City on the *Queen Mary*, Hearst broadcast on national radio a final appeal for a Landon victory, the gist of which was the title of one editorial: "Tomorrow: The American Way or Socialism?"

Upon embarking in New York, Hearst again confidently predicted a Landon victory. And as trusted friend and editor Ed Coblentz observed, "As a political prophet, Mr. Hearst registered zero." Roosevelt carried all but two states, Maine and Vermont. The Electoral College vote was 523 to 8.[40]

Yet Hearst's reaction to the Roosevelt victory was unexpected, if not bizarre. On election night, as the returns proclaimed a Democratic landslide, FDR's son-in-law John Boettiger was answering congratulatory telephone calls at the Roosevelt family home at Hyde Park. To his surprise one was from Marion Davies, followed immediately by Hearst. "Hello, is that you Boettiger?" a high-pitched voice inquired. "Well, I just wanted to repeat what Marion said, that we have been run over by a steamroller, but that there are no hard feelings at this end." Then two days later Hearst wrote a front-page editorial congratulating the president for achieving an "overwhelming majority of the popular vote." What a strange turn of events! For the better part of six months the Hearst media empire had unmercifully condemned the Roosevelt administration daily. "The cardinal principle of our American democracy is government by majority," Hearst announced to his readers. So "let us hope and pray that the President's policies will be wise and just, and that they will prove beneficial in the highest degree to the great country of which we are all loyal citizens." In other words, Hearst was once again emphasizing "no hard feelings at this end." To make sure that his message was received and understood, Hearst hired Boettiger as the new publisher of his *Seattle Post-Intelligencer* on November 26.[41]

Yet Roosevelt's reelection was a bitter setback for Hearst, a disappointment that temporarily affected his philosophy in publishing as well as doing business with the American people. Since first becoming the owner and editor of the *San Francisco Examiner* in March 1887, Hearst had established a three-part formula for success. He focused on increasing circulation (and bragging about it in print), which in turn attracted advertisers. Then with added revenue, he hired the most competent newsmen and editors. Equally important, however, he believed that he had his fingers on the pulse of the American people. He was convinced that his likes and dislikes, his desires and interests, his eccentricities and unconventionalities were much the same as theirs. He maintained that since his newspapers were a reflection of his thinking and creativity, of his genius in sales techniques, of his emphasis on publishing only interesting and exciting stories, the American people would respond appreciatively with their support.

For almost half a century Hearst had pursued this successful philosophy. As the dominating, all-powerful figure in this business arrangement, he was the catalyst that inspired his editors and reporters to scoop the opposition, the glue that held together this mighty media empire of twenty-eight newspapers, thirteen magazines, and ten radio stations. But during the six months after the November election of 1936, a change in Hearst became apparent. Since he had always maintained that his newspapers were a reflection of him, an examination of the *New York American*, the flagship of his media empire, was quite revealing. In almost every edition prior to the presidential election the Hearst name appeared numerous times; readers knew who owned the publication, especially since Hearst wrote as many as four signed editorials a month. But from December 1936 to June 1937, only ONE appeared (February 4). In the past, the *American* editors involved readers in a crusade for a righteous cause—most recently the fight against communism and/or the campaign to defeat Roosevelt for a second term. Hence stories supporting the *American*'s point of view appeared daily. Blistering editorials accompanied by devastatingly comical political cartoons supported the written word. Readers could only anticipate more of the same in the weeks and months to follow. The *American* regularly reported interesting and entertaining stories having to do with natural disasters or the frailties of society and mankind, headed by bold, fist-size headlines that summarized the major points of the article.

But in 1937 the *American* noticeably changed. It seemed to lose its personality, its *raison d'etre*. A new reader would have been hard put to know that the *American* was a Hearst paper. During January and February, his name rarely appeared, and not once in March. Many stories were routine, often lacking flair and flamboyancy. The editorials were brief, usually pertaining to local issues or personal gripes. And the accompanying political cartoons were equally unimaginative, bordering on the commonplace. To compound this journalistic malaise, the *American* editors abandoned their crusade technique of exciting and involving readers. Only in passing commentaries did they rail at the communists, and their attitude toward the New Deal was at times praiseworthy to the point of ingratiation. Except for displaying two to three pages about Hollywood (including

Louella Parson's columns), opinions and observations by Damon Runyon, a special business commentary by B. C. Forbes, and several pages of comic strips, the *American* had lost its heart, its will to surpass the competition. No wonder that the editors announced that they were combining the *American* with the *New York Evening Journal* after June 24, 1937.[42]

Adding to this winter and spring of discontent, personal tragedy also affected the Hearst psyche. In December, Arthur Brisbane suffered several heart attacks. Concerned about his long-time friend, Hearst persuaded his German doctor in Bad Nauheim to come post-haste to New York to attend Brisbane. But such efforts were to no avail. On Christmas Day, 1936, Brisbane died. And with his demise ended a relationship of forty years duration. Brisbane was not just a business partner and Hearst columnist, he was, one observer noted, Hearst's alter ego, one of the few close friends on whom Hearst relied.

In Brisbane's column, "TODAY," which always appeared on page 1, Hearst wrote this poignant essay titled "A Tribute by W. R. Hearst." In almost every word the reader could feel the pain, the anguish and sorrow. While Americans and the nation have lost the "enlightenment" of a remarkable professional newsman, Hearst lamented, "all I can think of at the moment is that I have lost my friend—my close and dear and long time friend." And "I grieve inconsolably," Hearst declared, "that the long, long friendship, uninterrupted by a single quarrel or definite difference of any kind, is ended—that I will no longer know his enjoyable and helpful companionship, and that the world in which I must spend my few remaining years will hold for me a blank space, which had been so unforgettably filled by my more than friend and more than brother, Arthur Brisbane."[43]

But for Hearst another grievous situation was looming ominously on the horizon—financial insolvency and bankruptcy. Late in December 1935, with the resignation of his financial expert, John Neylan, Hearst realized that his vast empire was in grave danger, that creditors were no longer willing to forestall payment of his mounting debts no matter how powerful his image, no matter how great his reputation. William Randolph Hearst, who had always maintained that money was something to spend, was facing the perils of deficit expenditure, the confusing intricacies of bankruptcy, the humiliation of financial failure. He would not appreciate the experience.[44]

10 Nightmare of Insolvency in a World at War

On August 10, 1937, John Francis Neylan, who had agreed several months earlier to return as the chief financial officer and attorney of the Hearst media empire, wrote to William Randolph Hearst concerning the desperate condition of the corporation's finances—and his struggles to right them. Somewhat bewildered and definitely perturbed, he reviewed in this letter their hectic relationship. Over "the last nineteen months I have endeavored with whatever ability and ingenuity and earnestness I had to aid you . . . and I was frequently rebuffed for my pains." Consequently, he had resigned, in frustration, late in December 1935, only to be persuaded by a submissive Hearst, almost to the point of childlike compliance, not to abandon him. Early in June 1937, Neylan agreed to come on board again and "lay the foundation to restore . . . [Hearst's] current credit which had been terribly shattered." After skillfully obtaining assurances of cooperation from the major banking creditors, he had directed his headstrong client, who was unaccustomed to accepting supervision of any kind, to follow an effective and advantageous course of action. And for almost two months all went smoothly, that is, until Hearst had second thoughts and sought other counsel. Neylan again submitted his resignation, lamenting that the rejection of his strategy would result in financial disaster.[1]

Neylan was right in his prediction. On September 1 Hearst Magazines, Inc., and Hearst Publications, Inc., which had previously filed with the Securities and Exchange Commission for permission to float $35.5 million in debentures, were allowed to withdraw the registration statements because of their possible inability to meet fiscal obligations. With the government unwilling to help support such proposed refinancing, the Hearst empire evolved into a state of sheer panic; the public was now alerted to its financial difficulties.[2]

Yet more disquieting monetary news was forthcoming. A U.S. Treasury report stated that Hearst was the highest paid business executive in 1935 with an annual salary of $500,000, topping screen actress Mae West, who earned $480,000. Hearst, who carefully avoided mentioning any details concerning his private life, especially abhorred this disclosure. But the report by Secretary of the Treasury Morgenthau revealing wealthy tax dodgers whom the government intended to prosecute—and naming Hearst as one—was much more upsetting. Through the manipulation and use of holding companies, the report asserted, Hearst had avoided paying $2,371,133 in corporate taxes in 1934 and $2,740,575 in 1935. But Morgenthau promised that the government would soon put a stop to such financial skullduggery.[3]

These reports were the least of Hearst's fiscal worries. In order to have better control over his vast empire, he decided to dump Neylan and place his financial future in the hands of Judge Clarence Shearn, who had been his legal counsel in New York early in the 1900s when the Hearst newspapers were combating Tammany Hall and such powerful corporations as the railroads and Standard Oil. Now an attorney for the Chase National Bank of New York, Shearn seemed to be the logical successor to Neylan. And Hearst, believing that he would have the last word in all major decision making, agreed that Shearn would have an irrevocable ten-year term as trustee as well as sole voting rights over all stock in Hearst's principal holding company. Shearn also received authorization to appoint a Conservation Committee to wrestle with all fiscal difficulties. It comprised seven organization executives, including Thomas J. White, general manager; Richard E. Berlin, head of magazines; William Randolph Hearst Jr., publisher of the newly formed *New York Journal-American* and Hearst family representative; and Martin Huberth, a real estate expert. Hearst understood that he would retain control over his publications, with the proviso that Shearn would have full authority to oversee spending.[4]

Shearn needed such authorization. Hearst had run up a staggering debt totaling $126 million while demonstrating no evidence, much less a pretense, of changing his spendthrift habits. Despite marvelous technical skills and exceptional media expertise, he had proven to be an irresponsible chief executive. As the ultimate authority in his empire and accountable to no one, he was, as one biographer observed, "a chump when it came to the ledger." His philosophy was that money was something to spend, that no matter the amount of indebtedness creditors would overlook his shortcomings because of his business standing as the world's most powerful media king, and that in actuality "the master of San

Simeon," who ruled in a magnificent castle atop a California mountain overlooking the Pacific, would be held in regal awe and therefore never be held accountable—surely not William Randolph Hearst. After all, he was, besides a builder of castles, a collector of rare objects of art, and a prominent New York City real estate magnate. Indeed, he was the world's foremost media mogul whose empire encompassed twenty-eight newspapers, thirteen magazines, ten radio stations, and a motion picture studio. Of course, such reasoning of unaccountability bordered on sheer folly, if not irrationality. But Hearst was not just any man, at least no one outside of the political world had ever treated him as such.[5]

Judge Shearn, however, forced Hearst to face reality, to assume the position of a mortal man—even though unwillingly and surely not with graceful acceptance. All his life Hearst had coveted possessions and thirsted for power. But now the long winter nights of bankruptcy darkened his outlook and shriveled his spirit. Neylan and then Shearn agreed that he must dump some of his treasured newspapers. On June 25, 1937, the debt-ridden morning *New York American* was the first to go, combining with the *New York Journal* to become the evening *Journal-American*. Then a week later the *Rochester Journal* and the *Sunday American* folded. And rather than sell the *Washington Herald*, Hearst leased it to Cissy Patterson, while agreeing to consolidate Universal Service with International News Service. Yet he stubbornly refused to consolidate the *Chicago Herald-American* with the *Examiner*, postponing that union for several years.

Each sale inflicted great anguish on Hearst, much like a sinister ritual of bloodletting that plunged a dagger into the heart of a victim. The dismantling of the Hearst media empire would continue, however, until by 1940 only nineteen newspapers remained.[6]

The long nightmare of financial insolvency, of business failure and personal embarrassment, seemed to gain momentum with each passing day. At San Simeon, where expenses were enormous, the household staff was reduced. But more importantly Shearn informed Hearst that "if he wished to live at San Simeon he would have to pay rent for it" as well as "cover the costs of maintenance, future construction, and noncorporate expenses." Over vigorous and lengthy protests by Hearst that San Simeon was a "business headquarters," not a "private residence"—that if need be, he would close down "the ranch" rather than reside there only "three months a year as a renter"—Shearn held firm; and Hearst, no longer "the Chief" and in charge, acquiesced.

Humiliation continued to build. Hearst now had to deed Wyntoon to the Committee, together with most of its fabulous German art collection. St. Donat's, which Hearst had spent millions to modernize and truly loved to own, was also put up for sale. And even though the listing price was prohibitive, the rental was even more so, costing $342,500 a month or approximately $11,400 a day. The castle's immensely valuable art objects were soon put up for auction.[7]

In turn, Hearst was forced, at age seventy-four, to revise the spendthrift habits of a lifetime. He had to live within the limits of a budget. Shearn cut his annual salary from $500,000 to $100,000 and terminated payment on $700,000 in preferred stock dividends that were due him. Equally distressing, if not humbling, Hearst could not buy objects of art without permission from the Committee. Even worse, he realized that treasures he had spent a lifetime collecting were about to be sold at a reduced price under an auctioneer's gavel. This realization was almost impossible for him to bear.[8]

Personal embarrassment had no limits. Millicent learned of Hearst's financial crisis through John Neylan. She therefore cut her allowance in half, informed her five sons that they must do the same, and prepared to leave the magnificent five-floor Clarendon apartment, where she had lived since 1908. The Committee remodeled this elegant real estate into business suites and then sold them to ready buyers.[9]

Other Hearst property in New York City, estimated by inflated pre-depression prices as much as $50 million, was also subject to immediate liquidation. Martin Huberth, the Committee's real estate expert, proved invaluable in this regard. The Ritz Towers, appraised at $6 million, attracted no buyers in the depressed New York market. Hence the Committee, at Huberth's suggestion, decided to consign this property to the Continental Bank and Trust Company of New York, thereby saving $500,000 in annual mortgage indebtedness. In turn, Huberth continued to sell other Hearst real estate properties that were not registering a profit.[10]

Shearn approached the problem of corporation bankruptcy in a coldly efficient manner, seemingly oblivious to Hearst's personal feelings about the loss of treasured collections or the public shame accompanying economic failure. On October 10, 1937, the heartbreak of losing "cherished friends" began again. Sotheby's in London announced that the fabulous collection of old English silver that Hearst had purchased over the past eight years and housed at St. Donat's would be auctioned off. As a result, on November 17, silver experts had a bargain-hunter's field day, acquiring eighty-three items for £22,000 ($108,570)—a fraction of the original cost. As the *New York Times* noted, thirty-two of the purchased items had originally cost the publisher £25,000 ($123,375). For example, one of Hearst's prized possessions, an Elizabethan silver gilt cup and cover, designed by

Simon Brooke in 1565, brought only £500 ($2,467.50), although Hearst purchased it in 1930 for £3,275 ($16,162.13).[11]

In the meantime Shearn and the Conservation Committee were in complete control of the bankruptcy proceedings. To simplify as well as hasten the process for solvency, they generously earmarked $11.5 million worth of art and antiques to Hearst personally and an equal sum to International Studio Arts Corporation, a subsidiary holding company that had often paid for Hearst's art. Then they assigned teams of experts to inventory every item that was negotiable. What a tedious task it was. At warehouses in the Bronx, San Francisco, San Simeon, and Los Angeles as well as at the magnificent Hearst residences—San Simeon, Wyntoon, St. Donat's, the Clarendon, and Millicent's Sands Point estate—they catalogued and priced for sale thousands of Hearst treasures and memorabilia, a lifetime of priceless collecting, indeed his special genius in regard to art and literature and history.[12]

On March 21, 1938, with the formal public announcement in the *Times* that Shearn was the Hearst trustee, whose task was to reorganize his vast properties for a gradual liquidation, buyers eagerly anticipated the Hearst sell-off. They did not have long to wait. On April 10 Shearn announced that a fifteenth-century French Gothic tapestry (valued at $85,000) and two carved oak stalls from the Hearst collection would be on display at the Hotel Commmodore. Then eleven days later, through the firm of Parish-Watson & Co., he advertised that a large part of the William Randolph Hearst collection, valued at $15 million, would be on display and sale in a five-story building at 46 East 57th Street.

The dismantling of these marvelous collections continued from 1938 to 1940, with Hearst's grief and sorrow mounting with every sale. As a further heartache, he often had to verify the authenticity as well as ratify the sale of his treasures. Nor was Shearn's explanation for liquidation consoling, much less believable. Connoisseurs of the arts, who knew Hearst's passion for collecting, gave little credence to the idea that Hearst, approaching seventy-five, had suddenly become "conscious of the uncertainties of life" and wished to have a "more comprehensive plan of management" in order to avoid the complications of "death taxes."

But no matter the explanation, much to the delight of other collectors, Hearst was selling. For instance, at a special showing in New York City on April 20, John D. Rockefeller Jr. bought $100,000 of rare English silverware for installation at the Governor's Palace in historic Williamsburg, Virginia. On another occasion, Van Dyck's portrait of Queen Henrietta Maria, which Hearst had purchased from the Duveen Gallery for $375,000, was a buyer's delight. In fact, many of Hearst's treasured beauties—armor, tapestries, antique furniture, rare paintings, china and glassware, jewelry and precious stones, flags and banners, Indian art, autographs of the famous, as well as rare books and manuscripts in history and literature—sometimes sold at auction for as little as twenty cents on the dollar.[13]

Still needing cash to meet the empire's financial obligations, the Conservation Committee received some welcome help. In desperation—and somewhat embarrassed—Hearst asked Cissy Patterson to loan him $1 million. When she readily agreed, he insisted on paying her 5-percent interest. On the other hand, he said nothing to Marion. But in a crisis of this magnitude no secrets could remain hidden for long. As a result, she immediately negotiated a cashier's check for $1 million; and when more money was needed, she began hocking her fabulous jewelry collection, much of which he had given her. Although Hearst, understandably humiliated, obstinately refused to accept her assistance, the Committee had no such inhibitions. Consequently Hearst insisted on giving her the two Boston papers (*Record* and *American*) as collateral.[14]

During these difficult times Hearst found life equally trying in motion pictures. Still intent on micromanaging Marion's career, he sensed, as did Marion, that the stories and screen scripts provided by Warner Brothers were not of star quality, that—unlike at MGM—they were not about and for her. Surely her first picture with Warners, *Page Miss Glory* in 1935, costarring Dick Powell, and her next one, *Hearts Divided* in 1936, also with Powell, did not display her acting talent at its best. Nor did her third film with Clark Gable, *Cain and Mable*, late in 1936, and a fourth one with Robert Montgomery, *Ever Since Eve*, released in June 1937, fare any better at the box office. In each case the screen revealed a mature actress miscast in the role of a young woman. Her biographer correctly noted that at age forty she had "begun to lose some of the ingratiating, kittenish appeal" exhibited earlier in her career.

Marion also had to deal with a number of personal problems that deeply affected her. In April 1935, her father—"Papa" Douras—died at age eighty-two. Eighteen months later her favorite niece, Pepi Lederer, committed suicide. As a result, Marion lost control in dealing with the magnitude of death and began drinking heavily. Whereas she had always looked forward to advancing her career as "fun," she lost her enthusiasm for making movies, at times not appearing on the Warner set until noon and on some days not at all. And when all four of her Warner films turned out to be financial flops and reviewers were less than kind in appraising her performances, (except in the Hearst newspapers), Marion manufactured an excuse to retire. "I've been working so long," she announced, "and I felt that I would rather be a companion to him [Hearst]" at this critical time in their lives. "So I got out—made up my mind just like that."[15]

In much the same tone and manner Hearst sadly agreed. In 1919 he had arrived in Hollywood, intent on becoming the top mogul in the movie industry as well as displaying Marion as its most brilliant star. But the Warner scripts were not to his liking; regrettably, they did not show a proper appreciation for Marion's talent. To negotiate a deal on the outside, he therefore asked for her release. And when Warners agreed, his dream of almost twenty years ended.[16]

The lessening of motion picture responsibilities, however, did not alleviate Hearst's financial problems. By March 1939, in order to meet the demands of creditors, Shearn had been forced to sell seven of the ten radio stations in the Hearst media empire. At the same time Hearst, although withstanding an offer of longtime friend Joseph P. Kennedy to buy his thirteen magazines because the price was too low, had decreased instead the number of his prized newspapers from twenty-eight to twenty—and still was facing insolvency. So bad had the financial situation become that, much to his surprise and utter horror, he learned in February that rival publisher Harry Chandler of the *Los Angeles Times* held a $600,000 mortgage on San Simeon but decided to extend the note "rather than embarrass his strapped debtor."

Another grave economic crisis was at hand in March 1939. Besides owing millions of dollars to Canadian paper mills and New York banks, the Conservation Committee under Judge Shearn was about to encounter an angry group of stockholders. In 1925 and 1927, under John Neylan's direction, Hearst had gone public with successful multimillion-dollar bond issues. Then in May 1930, always in need of money, he had offered another stock option under the name of Hearst Consolidated Publications, Inc. It was a rousing success because stockholders were to receive a quarterly 7 percent dividend or, as advertised, "a depression safety-net check." But on June 1, 1938, Hearst Consolidated was forced to defer its quarterly payment, stating that over the previous four months advertising revenues had decreased from $15 million to $12 million and that income had dropped by almost $2 million. Subsequently, with two more defaults occurring in 1938 (and a fourth looming in March), Hearst attempted to wrest control of his business interests from Shearn as the sole trustee and place himself in charge again. For nearly two years he had been unable to manage his own destiny; and now, much to his distress, he had almost lost his most treasured possession, San Simeon. Using as an excuse a Hearst Consolidated contract proviso, stating that reorganization would occur after four consecutive dividend deferments, he readied for the moment when he would regain power. But at the last moment Shearn and the Conservation Committee secured a loan from Chase Manhattan in order to pay the March dividend, thus thwarting the Hearst coup. *Time* magazine recorded his reaction to this defeat. Its cover page displayed the picture of a disconsolate-looking Hearst, belatedly saying, "At my time of life, you just sit here."[17]

Yet Hearst would not just sit for long. Optimistic by nature and confident in his own capabilities, he had previously survived crushing setbacks with remarkable resilience. In fact, his life had been a constant example of a strong-willed individual destined for success. Because of a strenuous work ethic and uncommon energy that would have humbled most men, together with a talent to compartmentalize multiple enterprises, he realized his advantage over almost any competitor. And his ability to ward off defeat with relative ease was in itself a strength, if not a blessing.

Hearst, at age seventy-five, was a constant reflection of extraordinary will and determination. For example, who would have dared, at age twenty-two in 1887, to have assumed control over a dying newspaper, the *San Francisco Examiner*, and within four years have transformed it on the West Coast into the proposed logo, "Monarch of the Dailies"? Who else would have dared in the mid-1890s to have challenged the foremost publisher in the world, Joseph Pulitzer, to a contest for supremacy of New York City newspaper circulation? For that matter, how many men could have overcome the disadvantages of a noticeable lisp and high voice, as well as incredible shyness among crowds to become an effective political campaigner and stump speaker? And how many men could have withstood unreasoning public disdain and criticism for denouncing British naval activities against neutral nations prior to U.S. entry into World War I? Indeed, how many men could have suffered the devastation of bankruptcy accompanied by public humiliation in the national press from 1937 to 1940—and still have had the will to persevere?

Late in the 1930s, however, foreboding world events would shock Hearst into concentrating on the suffering of fellow Americans and the dangers facing his country rather than focusing on personal problems. Since the end of World War I he had demonstrated a consistency of thought, a steadfastness of conviction concerning the role of the U.S. government both at home and abroad. In philosophy and action, Hearst was still a Jeffersonian democrat, ever fearful that "big government," with a popular chief executive in control, would infringe on the personal liberties of individual citizens. Hence, in editorials he continually referred to Roosevelt as a dictator and to the New Deal as an instrument of government that was gradually subverting the Constitution. After the November presidential election of 1936 Hearst tried to make amends to Roosevelt for his support of Alf Landon, to smooth over his bitter campaign against the New Deal, but a rapprochement would not occur. The president would never trust Hearst either as a supporter or a friend. On one occasion, he "brooded darkly" concerning the publishers of "fat cat" newspapers, having Hearst specifically in mind. As FDR put it, "I sometimes think that Hearst has done more harm to the cause of Democracy and civilization in America than any three other contemporaries put together."[18]

Nor should the president have entertained a different judgment. Hearst could follow only his own leadership. He was highly critical of the New Deal, especially regarding its approach to industry and agriculture. And after the Supreme Court struck down the major legislation in those areas (the National Industrial Recovery Act in 1935 and the Agricultural Adjustment Act early in 1936), Hearst was even more perturbed by Roosevelt's response. The president proposed a "Court-packing" plan, a reorganization of the judiciary, whereby he could appoint as many as (but no more than) six judges to the Supreme Court provided they had served at least ten years and were six months past their seventieth birthday.

On April 24, 1938, in a Sunday editorial titled "An 'Especial' Revolutionist," Hearst lectured the president who, in an address to the Daughters of the American Revolution a few days earlier, had announced in an opening statement: "Remember you and I especially are descendants from immigrants and REVOLUTIONISTS." Hearst then, in thoughtfully worded sentences, demonstrated his disdain for FDR'S New Deal. The Revolutionists of 1776 had intended "to OBTAIN freedom, not to despise and discard it." They had "created a Supreme Court to interpret the Constitution, and maintain exact justice and equality before the law," not like the New Dealers "try to PACK THE SUPREME COURT and personally DICTATE the laws of the land." And they had established "a Congress to represent the WHOLE PEOPLE," not "a venal body subservient to the will of a dictator, receiving their reward in patronage for betrayal of the people's rights." Hearst then announced to his 10 million-strong Sunday readership that "if Mr. Roosevelt is 'ESPECIALLY' descended from immigrants, he should remember that most of those immigrants came to this country to escape despotism, oppression, and extortion, and to find liberty, opportunity, and prosperity in those basic American institutions which misguided modern revolutionists" of the New Deal "are mistakenly endeavoring to disparage, demolish, and destroy."[19]

As evidenced by this biting editorial, Hearst was once again alive and well, demonstrating a fighting spirit for constitutional government rather than wallowing in the abject self-pity and embarrassment of bankruptcy. But for his millions of readers he displayed even greater zeal in helping formulate and shape their thinking concerning American foreign policy.[20]

In the period of American history from the Treaty of Versailles (1919) to Pearl Harbor (December, 1941) Hearst was the very picture of a model isolationist. His newspapers trumpeted the slogan "America First" while at the top of the editorial pages he deified George Washington's foreign policy statement of "No Entangling Alliances." Although in the decade after 1895 he had been a militant progressive, like Theodore Roosevelt advocating American expansion into the Caribbean and the Pacific, he mollified his position after World War I. He endorsed the idea of the United States as a safe haven from any foreign threat as long as 3,000 miles of ocean served as a protection. During the 1920s, however, he continually harped on the necessity for American security, advocating the buildup of the U.S. military, especially the navy and air force. In keeping with the "no entangling alliance" theme, Hearst strenuously denounced any administration, whether Republican or Democrat, that favored American participation in the League of Nations and the World Court. He was therefore highly critical of England and France, who tried to embroil the United States in European affairs, yet who were unable, or unwilling, to honor their World War I commitments, specifically the payment of American loans.

In regard to the Far East, Hearst warned his readers of the "yellow peril" as early as the first decade of the twentieth century. At first he displayed a xenophobic reaction to Japanese and Chinese immigration in California. But after World War I he became more assertive in his editorials, more aggressive in his charges. He stated that Japan intended to be the dominant power in the Pacific and eventually would find reason to attack the United States. On more than one occasion during the 1920s and 1930s, he proclaimed that the real enemy was not Russia or Germany but the "barbarians" of the Orient. He repeatedly cited an editorial theme (March 9, 1918) that "all the world is threatened by the advancing empire of Japan."[21]

Hearst surely considered himself justified in harboring these beliefs. During the 1930s, as it was in the summer of 1914, the nations of the world—specifically Italy, Germany, Russia, and Japan—seemed to have gone mad. Italy under Benito Mussolini in 1922, Germany in electing Adolph Hitler as chancellor in 1933, Russia in selecting Joseph Stalin as general secretary of the Communist Party in the 1920s, and Japan under Emperor Hirohito in 1926 promised economic security to their countrymen in a depression-filled world and advocated the expansion of empire to their growing populations. When necessary, they preached war as a positive good and united "in an unholy alliance against the democracies," initiating what diplomatic historian Thomas A. Bailey termed "international gangsterism." In September 1931, the Japanese manufactured an excuse to invade Chinese-held Manchuria, crushing all resistance by January 1932. Japanese troops also clashed with Chinese forces in Shanghai, slaughtering thousands of civilians in savage aerial and land assaults. In March, the Japanese gave notice that they were withdrawing from the League of Nations.[22]

With the League proving ineffective and collective security rapidly diminishing, the European dictators successfully challenged the world democracies. Early in 1935 Hitler began openly to rearm Germany and the next year to occupy the Rhineland. Meanwhile, Benito Mussolini championed Italian nationalism by invading the hapless North African kingdom of Ethiopia, promising to return Italy to the glories of ancient Rome. In turn, the United States tried to avert the prospect of war, historian Bailey graphically noted, "by retreating to the storm cellar of neutrality."[23]

The outbreak of the Spanish Civil War in 1936 intensified the threat of international conflict. After three years of fighting, General Francisco Franco emerged victorious and pledged his support to fellow dictators. As a consequence, Germany and Italy formed an anticommunist alliance against Russia in 1936 (Rome–Berlin axis) and the next year extended the pact to include Japan (Rome–Berlin–Tokyo axis).[24]

With the dictator nations uncontested by the world democracies, appeasement and conciliation became the new diplomacy, a strategy that served only to encourage future aggression. Japan invaded China in 1937, intent on further conquest and seemingly unconcerned with British, French, and American reactions. In March 1938, German troops overran Austria without firing a shot. Then during the spring and summer Hitler threatened Czechoslovakia, seeking to reunite 3 million Germans in the Czech Sudetenland with the Fatherland. Yet the Czechs held firm against Hitler's bullying, secure in the fact that they had a negotiated defensive alliance with France and Russia. But with Hitler seemingly ready to launch a full-scale invasion, the major powers agreed to meet at Munich on September 29–30, 1938. In a last-ditch attempt to avoid open conflict, British Prime Minister Neville Chamberlain prevailed upon Czechoslovakia to yield the Sudetenland to Germany after Hitler promised that this demand "is the last territorial claim which I have to make in Europe." Although Chamberlain proclaimed that he had achieved "peace in our time," the German army overran Czechoslovakia in March 1939. Munich thus became a synonym for appeasement or, equally disheartening to world democracies, "surrender on the installment plan."[25]

World democracies, teetering dangerously on the brink of war, anxiously contemplated Hitler's next move. They did not have long to wait. The Nazi dictator demanded that Poland return Danzig and the Polish Corridor to Germany, both of which had been torn away by the Treaty of Versailles. When the Poles stiffened in their resistance by a defensive alliance with Great Britain and France, Hitler surprised world leaders by forming a nonaggression pact with Russia on August 23, 1939. Thus, with the British and French standing firm, and with the Poles refusing to meet German demands, Hitler attacked Poland with powerful aerial and land forces on September 1, 1939. Two decades after the Treaty of Versailles, World War II had begun.[26]

Despite such disquieting world events, a majority of Americans maintained an isolationist stance. And Hearst, whether reflecting or directing their opinions in his newspapers, left no doubt about his foreign policy beliefs. To his way of thinking, American experiences regarding foreign affairs after World War I were costly, often unsuccessful, and at times misguided; they readily proved that the United States must return to Washington's premiere stance of "No Entangling Alliances" and place "America First." During 1938 and 1939 Hearst harped recurringly on this theme in his editorials. To prevent a rash participation in a foreign conflict, he endorsed the so-called Ludlow amendment (in an editorial on February 8, 1938), which proposed a constitutional amendment that would prevent the president and Congress from declaring war without a majority vote by the people. On any number of occasions he displayed articles on the front pages of his newspapers (with the columns heavily lined for effect) titled "KEEP AMERICA FREE" or "LET FREEDOM RING," with the concluding theme condemning "the dreadful consequences of war." Late in October 1938 (less than a month after Munich), Hearst broadcast nationwide on NBC radio a reply to British statesman Winston Churchill, who, upon denouncing Hitler and Mussolini, urged the United States "to join forces with Europe's democracies." Hearst asserted unequivocally that Churchill had misjudged American sentiment and that "America must not be drawn by unwarranted sentiment into the disasters of another foreign war." Nor should Americans, "in the words of Washington, show 'excessive partiality' for any foreign nation," especially the British who had continued to default on World War I loans provided by the United States. "Our firm policy should be," Hearst concluded, "to hope and work for peace and true democracy throughout the world" and "save our strength, our wealth, our arms, to protect and preserve peace and true democracy in . . . the blessed and beloved land in which we live."

Again on April 30, 1939, a month after the Nazis had overrun Czechoslovakia and were pursuing a showdown with Poland, Hearst continued his isolationist theme. In an interview with Damon Runyon he confidently predicted that "there will be no war" because "no nation can afford it economically, politically, or socially." Besides, he asserted, "World War I proved how great a folly it was to depart from our policy of peaceful Americanism. All great American Presidents down to Wilson were right in keeping us free from foreign entanglements."[27]

Nor did Hearst change his rhetoric after Hitler invaded Poland on September 1. In an editorial three days later he reasoned that the "U.S. Must Keep Out of Europe's War," because when that "catastrophe . . . is over," he predicted, "Europe will be prostrated . . . [its] people exhausted and impoverished." The United States would therefore have "a great opportunity, a great mission," that of "reconstruction of the world" after keeping its "resources, its institutions, its democratic principles intact."

And on December 6, after Roosevelt remarked in a fireside chat to the American people that the Hearst newspapers, in maintaining their isolationist theme, were highly critical of his foreign policy, Hearst promptly replied. His editors were never "quite sure" whether to "support or oppose the President's policies," he asserted, "because those policies change[d] so much." But he was "quite sure" that his newspapers did "oppose Russian Communism, German Naziism, and English and French imperialism." In fact, "we support American Liberty and Democracy, American Freedom of the Press and Freedom of Speech, including Freedom of the President to take a few fireside shots occasionally."

In 1940, after German armies overran Denmark and Norway in March, assaulted Holland, Belgium, and Luxembourg in May, and forced France to capitulate late in June, Hearst continued to maintain an isolationist stance, as did a majority of the American people. For instance, in an interview given to Radio's Newsreel on April 25, he was asked, "What do you think of the youth of this country if we should go to war?" Hearst immediately replied that young Americans should be aware of their history, in this case the results affecting the U.S. doughboys who went to France in 1917–1918. Many lost their lives on the battlefields, he noted, while others "came back to find their jobs taken by those who stayed at home, their girls for the most part married to other men, and their opportunities for success and happiness in life considerably handicapped by the devotion they had shown to their country and their fellow citizens." Hearst then quoted Josh Billings, whom he dubbed the "homely philosopher": "Success consists not so much in never making mistakes, but never making the same mistake twice."

Hearst thus concluded, "Let us not make the same mistake twice. Let us keep out of foreign wars."[28]

While continually propounding the "America First" theme, Hearst was ever cognizant of his own financial problems. He focused on improving his economic status, a subject that he might easily have titled the "Hearst First Plan." The results were remarkably good in 1940. Late in March the British, who urgently needed defensive installations against a threatening German invasion, requisitioned St. Donats, thereby turning an expensive Hearst property (costing $342,500 a month) into a welcome profit. Then in October another economic windfall occurred. Because of the increasing necessity for American preparedness as the British fought for survival after the fall of France in June, U.S. Department of Defense officials began negotiating with the Hearst Conservation Committee to buy 154,000 acres of Hearst ranch land in California. On October 24, they closed the deal for $2 million, combining this property with the Los Padres National Forest. As the *New York Times* reported, the army intended to train troops from several nearby camps as soon as possible.[29]

At the same time the Conservation Committee improved the economic status of the Hearst empire substantially. During the March quarter of 1940, Hearst Consolidated Publications reported a net income approximating $1,320,000, equal to 68 cents each on 1,930,000 Class A shares, compared to the previous year of $192,193, or ten cents a share. Even more encouraging, Hearst Magazines, under the able leadership of Richard E. Berlin, netted profits in 1939 totaling $2,364,615, compared to $1,850,936 in 1938. Because of Berlin's demonstrated capabilities, the Committee promoted him to the presidency of the Hearst Corporation.[30]

In one other important financial area—the auctioning of Hearst treasures—the Committee also reached a highly profitable business arrangement. In conjunction with Saks-Fifth Avenue and Gimbel Brothers of New York City, the Committee contracted to place on exhibition and sale approximately 15,000 objects of art, valued at $15 million to $50 million. In turn, these renowned department stores promised to construct galleries as well as rearrange several floors on their premises to accommodate the buying public. As a matter of good business, they provided substantial news coverage, as well as paid advertising, for the Hearst Collection, which was scheduled, by contract, to go on sale on January 20, 1941. And even though the first showing was delayed for two weeks to February 3, the opening was a memorable success. Consequently, by the end of March, Gimbels established Hearst art sales in different areas of the city, providing dinner and entertainment to hundreds of paying guests before offering up the *piece de resistance*, the advertised auctioning of Hearst's most valued treasures.[31]

With the Conservation Committee successfully addressing the economic problems of the Hearst empire and with "the Chief" approaching his seventy-seventh birthday on April 29, 1940, the topic of retirement resurfaced, but not as far as Hearst was concerned. A workaholic imbued with incredible energy, he had been a newspaper man all of his adult life. Journalism was his craft, his trade; he wanted no other. And the Hearst newspapers were "his children," who not only bore his name repeatedly in their columns but, even more, his thinking and personality. After dismissing his guests late in the evening at San Simeon or during the hot summer months at Wyntoon, Hearst routinely retired to his study to examine the forthcoming handiwork of "his children," spreading each edition on the floor before him. Into the wee hours of the morning, he labored assiduously when, as a night person, he was most productive. Through the use of night telegrams and long-distance calls he made his wishes known to anxious night editors awaiting numerous corrections. Although removed from the financial responsibilities of meeting a payroll, he masterfully directed the editorial pages to his viewpoint. With the help of a few trusted subordinates, he decided what subjects to pursue and who should carry out his wishes. But more than that, he critically evaluated the next day's headlines, the placement of local, national, and international news coverage, advertising techniques, even the types of political cartoons and their location effectiveness.

This laborious and time-consuming routine was an important part of the Hearst legacy. Ever seeking to improve his newspapers, ever wishing to make a difference in behalf of his country, Hearst intended to leave an indelible imprint that reflected his personality and point of view. In 1941 he still owned seventeen dailies in the largest cities in the United States, with a circulation of 4,475,264, and thirteen Sunday papers totaling 7,110,890. An estimated one out of four Americans read his newsprint.[32]

Yet Hearst, partly because of the bankruptcies plaguing his media empire, was unwilling to accept as final any negative legacies. He therefore decided to undertake a project of considerable proportions, one in which he hoped to exert a powerful influence on the American public directly—and often. Early in March 1940 to the end of May 1942, he wrote a daily column (always at the top left-hand side of page 1) "In the News," in which he reflected on any subject worthy of his interest. In so doing, he introduced readers to an aging William Randolph Hearst who, instead of being a right-wing, communist-hating fanatic with a fear of the academic community, proved to be a man of wit and charm, well versed in history and literature and modern-day politics, a man who revered the American past and tendered hope for the future. While his sentence structure was at times complicated and lengthy, his stories were interesting and fascinatingly told. For six days a week, this ancient columnist endeared readers to his editorials, which often proved to be empathetic to their ideas and tolerant of their needs.[33]

Although stressing in a number of columns the important theme of American isolation, Hearst intrigued and delighted readers with a lifetime of reminiscences, with the ambitions of a young Californian who had sought—and achieved—the American Dream. He told about his early days in college as editor of the *Harvard Lampoon* and as student campaign manager for presidential candidate Grover Cleveland. He discussed his life as publisher of the *San Francisco Examiner* (1887–1894), the problems arising in its press rooms, and the unusual characters involved in gathering the news. In a number of essays he recalled his association with the Hollywood crowd after 1919, relating interesting anecdotes about such individual stars as Shirley Temple, Greta Garbo, Ann Sheridan, Alice Faye, and Lon Chaney as well as producer and friend Louis B. Mayer of MGM. And in still other essays, he enthralled readers with accounts about the great actress and stage beauty, Lillian Russell, and the "Boston strong boy," heavyweight boxing champion John L. Sullivan.[34]

At times Hearst drifted into the realm of poetry and song. He delighted readers with the lyrics of Charles Kingsley, who recalled the happy, carefree days of youth:

> When all the world is young lad,
> And all the trees are green,
> And every goose a swan, lad,
> And every lass a queen;
> Then hey for boot and horse, lad,
> And 'round the world away.
> Young blood must have its course, lad,
> And every dog his day.[35]

In another column Hearst entertained a growing number of admirers with little Susanna Foster, whose father, Stephen, as well as American pioneers en route to California, immortalized her in verse.

> Oh Susanna, don't you cry
>   for me,
> I'm off to California with
> My banjo on my knee.

In recounting hardships while crossing the Great Plains from Missouri to the Pacific, the settlers also sang:

It rained all night the day I left,
De weather it was dry,
De sun so hot I froze to death,
Susanna, don't you cry.

Hearst fondly remembered another verse that his father sang to "an enfant son" when going to breakfast:

The buckwheat cake was in her mouth,
The tear was in her eye.
Says I, I'm gwine back to de South,
Susanna, don't you cry.

Hearst then explained to readers that Foster, who was a gifted author and composer, died in misery and squalor, hence the sad ending of the song:

I soon will be in New Orleans
To wander all around,
A-looking for Susanna,
My sweetheart must be found.

If I don't find Susanna,
I'll lay me down to die,
But when I'm dead and buried,
Susanna, don't you cry.[36]

Because of the need for daily topics, Hearst led his readers into interesting facets of history. He discussed in detail aspects of the French Revolution and the rise of Napoleon. In a number of columns he noted that England had suffered invasions during at least five eras. Such references led him into reviewing the Roman conquest of Britain, which in turn produced historical accounts regarding Julius Caesar, Cleopatra, and Marc Antony.[37]

Hearst, of course, discussed with his readers the political news of the day. For instance, even though the public speculated about the president's intentions in regard to a reelection campaign bid in 1940, Hearst never seemed to be in doubt. In one of his first "In the News" columns, he noted that Roosevelt had "adopted the Garbo publicity technique." Like the actress who aroused secrecy and mystery by always appearing behind dark glasses, FDR was proving to be "one of the cleverest publicity prestidigitators [tricksters] ever seen"; he was arousing a third term demand among voters by placing in doubt his intentions.[38]

Hearst continued to criticize the New Deal, especially its effects on business and its ultimate goal of drawing the United States into World War II on the side of England. He therefore favored the Republican Party and, ultimately, its presidential nominee. As early as March 19, 1940, more than three months prior to the Republican National Convention in Philadelphia, he devoted a full column to "Mr. Wendell L. Willkie" who had the "common sense" to criticize "extreme New Dealers" for their reactionary policies. "It is time for the American people to wake up," Hearst quoted Willkie, "and call things as they really are." Not surprisingly, the Hearst media empire endorsed Willkie after the Republicans nominated him late in June and the Democrats backed Roosevelt for a third term in July. In an editorial on August 18, titled "Willkie Courageous, True American," Hearst announced that the nominee, who had been a Democrat until 1938, "had found democracy in the Republican Party and not in the New Deal Party." Willkie was "NOW fully and wholly known to the entire nation as a responsible, competent, and loyal AMERICAN, worthy of any and every trust his countrymen may place in him." In fact, Hearst concluded, Wendell Willkie was offering with his candidacy "a change of course and direction, a return to fundamental ways and principles, a restoration of proven AMERICAN ideas and ideals." As a result, he "has made the American way HIS WAY." And the American people, at their peril, should consider the consequences of choosing any other leader as president.[39]

While fully supporting Willkie in his newspapers, Hearst soon lost his enthusiasm for the campaign. Late in August 1940, the Gallup poll began to reflect a drop in popular support for the Republicans. And even though a dynamic and powerful speaker, Willkie was no Roosevelt. Few orators could match the president in charm and substance when delivering a speech. On September 10, Hearst explained the difference in his "In the News" column. "Every time Mr. Willkie speaks he says something—but it is generally something which Mr. Roosevelt has said before and said better." For instance, "Mr. Roosevelt spoke in favor of the draft. So did Mr. Willkie." Hearst then recounted a number of other campaign issues, which the Republican nominee should have differed with or railed against—but did not. As a consequence, Willkie was "like the Indian who used to go to a saloon and get himself some whiskey [which was legally forbidden] and then go out and yell whoopee and raise Cain." The difficulty was that he should "have shouted WHOOPEE loud and wild." The drink "seemed all right," but "the stimulus was not there." Hearst thus cogently asked, "What has happened to Mr. Willkie's stimulus?"

What happened during the remaining two months of the 1940 campaign was that Willkie never found the "stimulus" and suffered a decisive defeat. On November 5, Roosevelt garnered 27 million votes, approximately 5 million more than his opponent, and won a landslide victory in the Electoral College, 449 to 82.[40]

Two days later Hearst summed up this political contest for his readers. Like a skilled surgeon, he deftly cut to the heart of the matter. "President Roosevelt," while not yet "a statesman . . . thank the Lord," Hearst exclaimed, "certainly is the cleverest and wisest politician this country has seen for a century." His opponent, Mr. Willkie, while "a fine man" who "made a heroic campaign," was a washout as a politician. As a result, the president "with characteristic cleverness" sidestepped the domestic mistakes of the New Deal and "boldly made his foreign policy the issue," which Willkie mistakenly endorsed "from top to bottom." And "when he did that," Hearst announced, "he gave Mr. Roosevelt the election on a silver platter." With the president now the major point of contention in the campaign, instead of domestic issues, the American people reacted understandably at this critical time in their history.[41]

Hearst, because of his flamboyant lifestyle as well as an unusual ability to attract myriads of loyal friends or dedicated enemies, became a prototype, an ideal theme for writers to examine, to analyze and portray. From 1928 to 1936 he was the subject of four biographies. Two were overly praiseworthy and two were damning. Then in 1939 Aldous Huxley published *After Many a Summer Dies the Swan,* a best-selling novel depicting the tragic figure of an aging American millionaire, fearful of death. Readers could identify Hearst as Huxley's principal character, who owned a magnificent castle in California and decorated it with expensive objects of art and a beautiful young mistress. On March 13, 1939, when *Time* magazine featured Hearst on its cover, this supposition appeared to be true. *Time* editors, after revealing the financial difficulties of Hearst, evaluated his personal life and career. Unsympathetically, with a sense of writing a final epitaph, they announced that "no other press lord ever wielded his power with less sense of responsibility; no other press ever matched the Hearst press for flamboyance, perversity, and incitement of mass hysteria." For that matter, they harshly concluded, "Hearst never believed in anything much, not even Hearst, and his appeal was not to men's minds but to those infantile emotions which he never conquered in himself: arrogance, hatred, frustration, fear."[42]

Yet an even greater scrutiny and examination of Hearst was in the offing through motion pictures. In 1939, twenty-four-year-old Orson Welles arrived triumphantly in Hollywood. Already hailed as the boy wonder of the New York stage as well as the brilliant architect of the

Mercury Theatre's *War of the Worlds* radio broadcast (on October 30, 1938), which terrified millions of listening Americans by its realistic portrayal of an invasion from Mars, this East Coast prodigy now intended to revolutionize the film industry.[43]

To further his ambitions, Welles fashioned a contract with RKO studio head George J. Schaefer that guaranteed him complete control over developing two feature films. Welles was therefore free to select the subject for his production, develop and amend the script to his liking, hire all cast members, and, as the director, shape the character and performance of the actors. He even had the authority to supervise the construction of scenery for any set. With the signing of this contract on July 11, 1939, the epic film *Citizen Kane* came into being.[44]

For almost a year Welles prepared for his tour de force. He easily persuaded talented screenwriter Herman J. Mankiewicz, who was recovering from a bout with alcoholism and a debilitating automobile accident, to compose a script that Welles would scrupulously edit and revise. As the months wore on, as the first draft lengthened into a seventh one, which was finally designated "the third Revised Final," an intriguing drama emerged. The principle character was Charles Foster Kane, the "greatest newspaper tycoon . . . of any generation," who lived in a gloomy but magnificent castle called Xanadu. In the opening scene Kane, critically ill, uttered to those few at his bedside one final word, "Rosebud." A news editor named Thompson, covering this death scene, decided to resolve the mystery surrounding the word, to discover its importance to Kane. Through a series of flashbacks, the newsman interviewed those who had been closely associated with Kane.

As a result, the career and character of Kane unfolded before the audience. And since Welles decided to assume the starring role and select a number of veterans from the Mercury Theatre of New York as the supporting cast, the biographical study of Kane became even more pronounced. Kane was brilliant but unprincipled in dealing with business competitors, yet a rank amateur in his unsuccessful quest for high political office. In the relationship with his wife, Susan Alexander, who was much younger, he proved to be arrogant and domineering, determined to promote a career for her as an opera singer, despite her lack of talent and her pleadings to the contrary. After her career ended with a disastrous performance, she lived a lonely life with Kane at Xanadu, drinking heavily while working huge jigsaw puzzles to while away the time. Those who had been guests at San Simeon or were part of the Hollywood crowd, upon seeing the movie, immediately identified Kane and Susan as Hearst and Marion.[45]

On July 30, 1940, the shooting of *Citizen Kane* began, and for the next four months Welles relentlessly pushed his RKO crew to final completion. Since the cast was sworn to secrecy, rumors abounded about the *Kane* plot, its subject and content. As early as September, the gossip columnists were already speculating that Hearst was the target, especially since Kane was reported to be "the greatest newspaper tycoon . . . of any generation." And as Welles cleverly continued to avoid such confirmation and as Hollywood insiders surmised that the boy wonder would be foolish to take on an adversary as powerful as Hearst, the rumors persisted.

Louella Parsons, who was Hearst's Hollywood correspondent, had at first befriended Welles, but no longer. In January 1941, after a disquieting yuletide season during which Hearst directed her to get at the truth about *Kane*, she called RKO studio head George Schaefer and demanded a private screening of the film. She arrived at the RKO set accompanied by two Hearst attorneys. Welles greeted her and commenced to present his creation. By the end of the showing, Parsons was, as she later recalled, "horrified. . . . It was a cruel, dishonest caricature." She then stalked out of the projection room "without saying a word to Orson."[46]

Hearst immediately threatened George Schaefer with legal action if RKO did not withdraw *Citizen Kane* from circulation. But when Schaefer refused to knuckle under, Hearst decided to launch a counterattack of devastating proportions. Since a direct frontal assault would stir up even more controversy, thereby creating a massive amount of free publicity for the film, he applied techniques that did not involve him directly but would pressure RKO. Louis B. Mayer, who had never been accused of being a spendthrift, offered Schaefer $800,000—the approximate cost of the *Kane* production—to destroy the negative and all the prints. Other powerful Hollywood executives added their support; hence, in refusing the offer, Schaefer realized daily the political pressure that was directed at him and Welles.

Less subtle and openly venomous, Louella Parsons was allowed to vent her outrage. As Welles biographer Simon Callow put it, she applied "every ugly tactic she could think up," even threatening to publish fictional accounts about the private lives of RKO board executives. And she was surely in agreement with the Hearst editors, who refused to accept any advertisements publicizing *Citizen Kane* or, for that matter, other RKO films.[47]

The most devastating method of attack, however, proved to be an economic boycott. While unable to prevent the release of *Kane* in New York, Chicago, and Los Angeles early in May and in Boston, San Francisco, and Washington later in the month, Hearst executives pressured theater owners into denying its showing. They began a vicious whispering campaign implying that Welles had communistic leanings, that Schaefer was anti-Semitic, and that *Kane* attacked the American way of life. As a result, one independent chain controlling five hundred theaters refused to show it, even though late in 1941 the New York Film Critics and the National Board of Review praised *Citizen Kane* as the best picture of the year. Welles's masterpiece was an economic bust. In 1942, RKO retired it to the company vaults after registering a loss of more than $150,000.[48]

Yet by the end of 1941, this minor Hollywood furor soon receded into the mists of history. On December 7, the Japanese bombed Pearl Harbor.

11 Last Years and Final Edition

Early on Sunday morning, December 7, 1941, the Japanese carried out a surprise attack upon the United States naval base at Pearl Harbor in Hawaii. Against little opposition Japanese fliers bombed and strafed selected targets for several hours, inflicting more than 3,000 casualties on the surprised American military. They also destroyed or immobilized most of the American aircraft while sinking or running aground seven battleships, the backbone of the U.S. Pacific fleet. The next day President Roosevelt, in asking Congress for a declaration of war against Japan, described this attack as "a day which will live in infamy."

Such a devastating aerial strike did not produce the desired results, however. As early as September 1940, the commander in chief of the Japanese Combined Fleet, Admiral Isoroku Yamamoto, had voiced his concern about such an assault, even if successful. "I shall run wild for the first six months or a year," he predicted, "but I have utterly no confidence for the second or third year." He therefore urged the Japanese government to avoid war with the United States at all costs. Or as Hollywood writers dramatically rephrased this quotation in the 1970 movie *Tora! Tora! Tora!* Yamamoto solemnly announced that Japan, instead of demoralizing the United States, "had awakened a sleeping giant and filled him with a terrible resolve." And he was right. The bombs that pulverized Pearl Harbor unified the American people—silencing immediately those advocates of the nation's powerful isolationist movement.

Typical was the reaction of William Randolph Hearst, who had been a leading foreign policy proponent of "no entangling alliances" and the "America First" movement. In a front-page editorial on December 8 in all his newspapers, he announced, "Well, fellow Americans, we are in the war and we have got to win it." And even though "there may have been some difference of opinion among good Americans, there is no difference about how we should come out of it," he asserted. "We must come out victorious and with the largest V in the alphabet."

For that matter, Hearst continued, "the worst thing about the war with Japan is that it will divide our efforts and prevent us from rendering the all out aid to England that we were doing and planning further to do. But we will manage," he confidently stated, "to keep Britain going with our right hand while we poke Japan in the nose with our left."

As for Japan, that nation "has been wanting war for a long time. It has been swaggering around Asia, murdering a lot of unarmed Chinamen." But now, Hearst predicted, "it is going to get a war and a real one." Since Americans "can manufacture ten ships to Japan's one and ten aeroplanes to Japan's one," the United States will soon be on the offensive, putting that "bunch of Oriental marauders back on the right little, tight little, out of sight little island where they belong."

Since this conflict is "going to be a fighting war," Hearst prophesied, "the American people are going to take hold" and dispose of it. And with victory, they will issue the following orders "to the marauding nations" of the world: "Keep the international law, maintain the peace of the world, dismiss your robber bands and pirate hordes, get back in your own confines and stay there."[1]

Within the next few months Hearst proceeded to back up his words with action. Since San Simeon might be a tempting target for shelling by a Japanese submarine, he abandoned his castle on the enchanted hill for the forested wilds at Wyntoon in northern California. And from there he directed his own personal attack on the Japanese. For instance, on January 3, 1942, he began his own crusade in the Hearst newspapers: "LET'S BUY A BOMBER; AVENGE PEARL HARBOR." Hearst urged Americans to contribute their "dollars and dimes" to purchase a heavy bomber (at an estimated cost of $300,000) that would inflict grievous damage on "a ruthless enemy." With the use of daily front-page coverage, this campaign was so successful that within three weeks Secretary of the Treasury Morgenthau singled out the Hearst press for its patriotism, for its "strike for freedom." Again on January 25, Hearst publicized another fund-raiser, in which the Treasury Department asked loyal citizens to invest at least a dollar per month in U.S. saving stamps and bonds. But the Hearst editors captured the imagination of their readers by titling this campaign "LICK A STAMP—LICK A JAP!"[2]

During the first months of war Hearst also helped direct home front energies to benefit American unity. Whereas during the late 1930s Hearst and other isolationist leaders had enrolled hundreds of thousands of American mothers into a political organization to keep the nation out of war, he now helped transform these women into a patriotic association—the Mothers League. Its primary purpose was "to prosecute the war, to aid those fighting . . . and to hurry the war to a successful and speedy conclusion." In turn, Hearst continued to be a prominent promoter and financial contributor to the USO, which focused on providing social activities for American servicemen and women. And in a personal way Hearst reinforced his support of Marion Davies's patriotism as a newly appointed captain in the Medical administrative Corps of the California State Guard. Within weeks after Pearl Harbor, she had made available to the Guard a hospital building from the Marion Davies Foundation.[3]

But possibly Hearst's greatest contribution to the American war effort was his daily editorial, "In the News," to the readers in his newspapers. Besides encompassing a constant diatribe against Oriental barbarism—and an utter disdain for "the Jap" in particular—his columns were a compelling commentary on American patriotism. During the early stages of the war, with American forces on the defensive in the Pacific, he praised the heroism of American marines and sailors who were defending Wake Island and the Midway Islands in the Pacific against overwhelming Japanese onslaughts, guaranteeing that their sacrifices would not be in vain. He singled out General Douglas MacArthur and "his brave men" in the Philippines, "who know how to die, if need be, but . . . do not know the word SURRENDER." And he continually lauded the leadership of Winston Churchill and Franklin Roosevelt in establishing unity of purpose and cooperation against the Axis powers. At the same time, however, Hearst urged them to concentrate on the Pacific theater of war rather than the European front. For instance, he questioned in one editorial, for what purpose was the Allied fight for Libya in comparison to the protection and safety of California and the West Coast against the Japanese. He then concluded, "Let us keep the great Pacific free for the civilizations of our own day."[4]

In 1941 and 1942, Hearst continued to concentrate on putting his financial house in order. Prior to Pearl Harbor the Conservation Committee, together with the assistance of Gimbel's Department Store, had continued to auction Hearst treasures at a brisk—and profitable pace. And on special occasions in 1942, they held sales of priceless Hearst antiques, advertizing bargains to be had at an average of thirty-three cents on the dollar.

During these war years Hearst astounded observers, both friend and foe, by shedding his spendthrift ways and focusing on the superior production of his newspapers, with accounting and costs particularly in mind. As a result, prosperity became a distinguishing feature of the Hearst media empire. He concentrated on making his newspapers informative and readable and entertaining, standards that he had formulated and stressed to his editors upon first publishing the *San Francisco Examiner* in 1887. In this way, he instilled such strengths of purpose, such marks of distinction—especially relating to local and family interests—that had become evident in all Hearst newspapers. Then, with the reporting of stirring world events after December 7, punctuated by dramatic, fist-size headlines (so typically Hearst) that excited readers, circulation increased substantially, which in turn produced a boom in advertising sales. To meet the demands of such growth, Hearst acquired outright half a dozen newsprint paper mills in Canada and Maine.[5]

Other economic moves also reflected this newfound prosperity. Under Richard Berlin's excellent management, the Hearst magazines reported greater profits each year. And Hearst Publications registered a steady growth in quarterly reports. Then in January 1943, with Clarence Shearn's contract as director of the Hearst empire expiring, a revamping of the Conservation Committee occurred, which in turn produced even more efficient management. Besides the reelection to the Committee of Berlin, realty expert Martin Huberth, and family representative William Randolph Hearst Jr., the addition of former Undersecretary of the Treasury and Wall Street banker John W. Hanes provided significant insight and direction. With Hearst loyalists Berlin and Hanes as the strong men in this reorganization, the Committee consolidated ninety-four company organizations, many of which unknowingly owed each other money. But by skimping and saving as well as constantly applying the pruning knife to cumbersome budgets, the new Conservation Committee liquidated millions of dollars in personal debts, while building cash reserves for future projects. Consequently, on October 5, 1944, the Hearst Corporation purchased property in New York City (on Second Avenue between 39th and 40th Streets), in anticipation of postwar newspaper plant expansion. Four days later it announced the sale of the Warwick Hotel (at Sixth Avenue and 54th Street) along with several midtown lots. At the same time the Committee improved the morale of Hearst employees by raising salaries that had suffered during the lean years of bankruptcy proceedings.

After the surrender of Germany in May 1945, and of Japan three months later, the Hearst Corporation emerged smaller and sleeker, although still the most powerful media empire in the world. Despite eight years of severe economic stress, it listed as part of its makeup eighteen daily newspapers, nine American and three English magazines, four radio stations, a wire service, a feature service, and a Sunday supplement. And restored to the leadership of this mighty business organization was eighty-two-year-old William Randolph Hearst. As one biographer put it, "the King was back in the Countinghouse, counting out his money."[6]

Hearst tried to recapture those glorious days prior to Pearl Harbor. In September he eagerly returned to San Simeon, to his monument on Enchanted Hill that vividly proclaimed his raison d'être. Once again he was determined to improve his creation. He immediately hired a large workforce to complete a number of pending projects: rebuild the airport and hangar, rewire all the buildings, extend the North Wing of Casa Grande so that it would appear more symmetrical with the South Wing, and remodel his living quarters on the third floor. He and Marion temporarily took up residence in Casa del Mar (House A).

Once again they resumed their practice of inviting friends to join them for a weekend of luxurious living, reinstituting prewar schedules and routines. For instance, guests from Los Angeles journeyed by special train to San Luis Obispo on a Friday evening and then by limousine to San Simeon early the next morning. After being shown to their quarters, they could partake of a late breakfast and a casual afternoon lunch, followed by dinner at 8:00 P.M. (over which Hearst presided), and ending with a movie, often starring Marion, at the theater in the North Wing.

But life was not quite the same. Hearst was visibly older; he often seemed to proceed in slow motion. Exercise had become a chore; he had lost that spring of step, that agility of movement so prevalent in his younger days. He no longer played tennis and seldom swam or rode horseback. In the evening, however, he tried to maintain a schedule with Marion of walking along the Esplanade, a beautiful pathway lined with trees and shrubs that connected the guest houses (A,B,C) to Casa Grande.[7]

In 1946 Hearst invited his favorite grandson, Bunky, to stay with him at San Simeon and Wyntoon, presumably as a favor to the young man but actually as a precaution to watch over Hearst. But this arrangement did not last for long. By the end of the year his health had deteriorated to an alarming degree. Severe heart palpitations were distressingly frequent, causing a disquieting loss of weight, a noticeable palsy of the hands, and a voice projection scarcely audible above a whisper. Heart specialist Dr. Myron Prinzmetal advised him to leave the seclusion of San Simeon for the Los Angeles area, where medical attention would be more readily available.

Marion moved swiftly to make this idea more plausible to Hearst. She bought a luxurious three-story Spanish-style mansion at 1007 North Beverly Drive in Beverly Hills on an eight-acre plot replete with a swimming pool, spacious gardens, and towering palm trees. She remodeled the second floor of this Mediterranean villa including an elevator to meet specific needs of Hearst. She also hired some two dozen San Simeon employees—drivers, cooks, maids, nurses, and gardeners—whom Hearst had known for years. And to help him feel more at home in this transition, she appropriated some of the statuaries from San Simeon and placed them at prominent spots in the garden.

Early in May 1947, Marion and Hearst left San Simeon. While proceeding down the five-mile drive from Enchanted Hill to the ocean below, Hearst began to cry uncontrollably. Marion gripped his arm and, in an attempt to console him, whispered, "We'll come back, W.R., you'll see." But he knew better. His "look of loss and emptiness," Marion reflected, told a different story.[8]

In the new surroundings at 1007 North Beverly Drive, Hearst accepted medical dictates for a well-structured existence. He maintained a strict diet, exercised (when possible) with short walks during the morning or late evening, and ruled out any situation that might cause unnecessary agitation or excitement. As for visitation by friends or business associates, Dr. Prinzmetal limited visitors to no more than five daily.

Even though "ghastly thin" after a brief bout with pneumonia, weighing no more than 140 pounds, his face distinctive with eyes sunken and hollow-like, Hearst refused to succumb to inactivity. His body was failing, but not his brain. During the late 1940s he continued to write editorials, but not as often. He also maintained a steady flow of instructions to his newspaper editors through night telegrams or phone calls, prompting them to improve their daily editions. And during certain waking hours of quiet and solitude, he at times—through poetry—revealed a certain melancholy about his physical state and eventual death. In "The Song of the River," which he composed prior to leaving Wyntoon in 1945, he queried,

> So why prize life,
> Or why fear death,
> Or dread what is to be?

And then he replied,

> So don't ask why we live or die,
> Or whither, or when, we go,
> Or wonder about the mysteries
> That only God can know.[9]

Hearst did not always accept his physician's strict regimen. As if to taunt death, he enjoyed commemorating his birthday (April 29) with a lavish affair. He and Marion, often with his five sons in attendance, would host a spectacular, albeit exhausting, costume party. He seemed to take a sardonic pleasure in postponing predictions of his impending demise, of holding in abeyance, even for one more day, the prepared obituaries of the press.[10]

Yet Hearst could not postpone the inevitable much longer. He thus intended to protect those closest to him. On November 5, 1950, he instructed his staff to form a trust agreement whereby Marion would receive 30,000 shares of the Hearst Corporation's overall 200,000 shares; she would also have sole voting power in the Hearst Corporation. This proposition, however, never obtained legal authority in the courts.[11]

Hearst in turn left to Millicent and their five sons the bulk of his personal estate (estimated at $59.5 million). In a will encompassing 125 typewritten pages, he established three trusts. In the first one, Millicent received $6 million of Hearst Corporation preferred stock, with an additional $1.5 million in cash to cover the anticipated taxes incurred by this inheritance. The second trust pertained to his five sons. Each would receive enough Hearst Corporation preferred stock to guarantee an annual income of $30,000, which would supplement a comfortable income as a Hearst executive. And the third trust had to do with Phoebe Apperson Hearst. In memory of his beloved mother, he bequeathed substantial sums for "charitable, scientific, educational and public purposes." For instance, the Los Angeles Museum, to which Hearst had already donated at least $3 million from his art collection, received further gifts in her behalf; and the University of California–Berkeley, where Phoebe had served as the first woman trustee, was also a major beneficiary.[12]

On April 29, 1951, Hearst briefly recognized his eighty-eighth birthday. But he had little cause to rejoice. Death was omnipresent. He now needed a wheelchair as transportation, his weight having diminished to 125 pounds, his voice at best a painful whisper. Throughout most of the rooms on the second floor the temperature was an uncomfortable eighty degrees; otherwise he would begin to shiver. Since his emotions were increasingly difficult to control, he asked Marion to invite only five of her closest women friends for a brief celebration. But upon receiving their presents, he began to cry as Marion pressed him to her and said, "It's all right, W.R. It's all right."[13]

Every day now became a death watch, every night a vigil of uncertainty, as Hearst doggedly hung on to life. But during the second week of August 1951, this final drama to outwit death played out its course. Unexpectedly such Hearst Corporation executives as Richard Berlin and Martin Huberth appeared at 1007 North Beverly Drive, supposedly to ask his advice and lay plans for the future. Then four of the Hearst sons, led by Bill Jr., also arrived unannounced, stating that they wanted to visit with Pop and would be nearby for several days. And even though the doctors gave Marion no warning about Hearst's worsening condition, both she and Hearst suspected as much.

In the early morning hours of August 14, Hearst had difficulty breathing, coughing intermittently as mucus in his throat was choking him. Marion sat at his bedside "in the terrible quiet" of the room, recounting stories of their wonderful times together. Eventually Hearst appeared to be sleeping. But Marion continued to reminisce. As she later recalled, "I had this funny feeling that if I stopped, then he would stop—you know, breathing."

Marion would eventually relinquish her post. The stress of the last months, coupled with a growing dependence on alcohol, were telling upon her health and strength. Sometime after daybreak she retired to her room. And that was the last time she saw Hearst.

At approximately 9:50 A.M. on August 14, a day nurse entered Hearst's bedroom and immediately called for help. Hearst did not seem to be breathing. Within an hour a doctor confirmed that Hearst had died.[14]

Hearst corporate executives then took charge. Richard Berlin, upon arriving at the death scene, set in motion a plan that the Conservation Committee and the Hearst family had agreed on as early as 1947. They were determined to stymie any speculative accounts about Hearst and Marion. Consequently Berlin announced to the nurses and servants, "You're all working for me now." He demanded speed and efficiency. Within the hour Pierce Brothers Undertakers in Beverly Hills took the body to their mortuary and prepared it for burial. By 4:00 P.M., the four Hearst sons, together with Berlin and several corporate executives, transported Hearst, ensconced in an ornate bronze casket, onto a chartered plane and flew to San Francisco. En route, they asked the pilot to pass over San Simeon and symbolically "dip his wings." They had also made preparations for a grandiose funeral service, one that Hearst, they believed, would have approved.[15]

For the next two days Hearst's body lay in state at Grace Episcopal Cathedral on Nob Hill, which had also been the location for his mother's last rites in 1919. The tribute to him was indeed spectacular, reminiscent of those Americans who had received their nation's highest honors. In long lines hundreds of well-wishers and curiosity seekers paid their last respects, silently filing by an open casket where Hearst lay clad in a dark blue suit with a monogrammed shirt with cuff links, and a blue tie with the family's coat of arms. Then on the day of his burial 1,500 people crowded into the cathedral to hear the Right Reverend Karl Morgan Block, the Episcopal Bishop of California, give the last rites, while a thousand more waited outside the sanctuary. Designated as honorary pallbearers—numbered at sixty-seven by the *New York Times*—were some of the eminent and great in American life, such as Governor Earl Warren of California, Mayor Elmer Robinson of San Francisco, ex-President Herbert Hoover and former Vice President John Nance Garner, five-star General Douglas MacArthur, New York financial wizard Bernard Baruch, MGM head Louis B. Mayer, and publishers Colonel Robert McCormick of the *Chicago Tribune*, Roy Howard of the Scripps-Howard chain, Arthur Hays Sulzberger of the *New York Times*, and Hugh Baillie of the United Press. Seated in the first two rows of the cathedral, alongside their mother Millicent, were the five Hearst sons and their families. Then sprinkled behind them were Hearst corporate dignitaries, Hollywood notables, and long-standing acquaintances and friends.[16]

But nowhere in this vast assemblage was Marion Davies. She was neither invited nor welcome. During the funeral she grieved alone in her Beverly Hills home. Without Hearst, screenwriter and friend Frances Marion observed, "she is going to be lost" not so much as "a mourning mistress" but as "an orphan." Marion Davies summed up her heartfelt sadness with this bitter comment: "For thirty-two years I had him, and they leave me with his empty room."[17]

Meanwhile, all went smoothly at the funeral in San Francisco. At 11:00 A.M. as the service began, Hearst employees across the nation paused at their workshops in solemn remembrance. In accordance with the church liturgy, the ceremony lasted thirty minutes, during which time Bishop Block never mentioned Hearst by name. At the conclusion of the service a police escort ushered the Hearst family and honored friends through the massive crowd to twenty-two waiting limousines; they efficiently guided them to the Hearst mausoleum at Cypress Lawn Cemetery in Colma ten miles away. Then, after a brief committal service, William Randolph Hearst was laid to rest next to his mother and father.[18]

For someone so controversial, who had earned the reputation as "the most hated man in America" on at least four occasions in his lifetime—accused of abetting the assassination of President William McKinley in 1901, of being pro-German and anti-English during World War I (1914–1918), of favoring Nazi Germany and fascist Italy over England

and France in the 1930s prior to World War II, as well as vigorously opposing FDR and many New Deal programs after 1934—the outpouring of tributes to Hearst was indeed impressive. President Harry S. Truman expressed "his sympathy for the family of Mr. Hearst," and Vice President Alben Barkley praised Hearst's "long and colorful career in the journalistic world. He made a distinct impression in formulating the opinions of the American public." Former President Herbert Hoover, who had ample reasons to despise Hearst, heartily agreed; Hearst "was the most powerful individual journalist of his day. His positive views, his trenchant expression, and his enormous circulation alone warrant that statement. He, however, was more," Hoover concluded, "for he built a great newspaper empire that has endured and will continue to be the most potent force in American life."

Some were more personal and less wordy in their praise. Bernard Baruch called Hearst "a great man," both "brave" and "courageous." Cardinal Spellman of New York mourned "the death of a great American patriot." General Douglas MacArthur described Hearst's voice as "a mighty one in defense of America's freedom." And General of the Army Omar Bradley proclaimed him to be "one of the greatest Americans this country has ever known."

Other public officials, both state and national in scope, were equally effusive in their acclaim. Here were but a few of the many eulogies to Hearst. House Republican leader Joseph W. Martin Jr. proclaimed him to be "one of the most colorful and influential figures of our time." Former National Democratic Party chairman James Farley concurred, stating that "he was in every sense a great American . . . one of the outstanding newspaper publishers of his day and generation." Acting Governor of New York Frank C. Moore noted that Hearst's death marked "the passing of a giant in journalism who exerted vast influence on his profession and on public affairs." And in Massachusetts, both houses of the state legislature adopted a resolution recognizing Hearst as "a commanding figure in the political and business life of the country."[19]

But not all segments of American society grieved the loss of Hearst. The academic community, which Hearst had chastised for promoting communism in the public schools and higher education and which had opposed his "fascist" attempts to demand loyalty oaths of faculty members, showed little remorse. Labor leaders and unionists, whose causes he had promoted prior to World War I but had vigorously opposed with the coming of the New Deal, were also unsympathetic. And the many political opponents whom the Hearst media empire had contested—and often vilified—displayed no feelings of regret.

The British, of whom Hearst had often been critical, gave prominence to his death but in the main were derogatory in their evaluations. While Lord Beaverbrook's *Daily Express* proclaimed Hearst to be "one of the great American figures of the age," the *Manchester Guardian* stated that even in death "it is hard even now to think of him with charity. Perhaps no man did so much to debase the standards of journalism." Washington correspondent Robert Waithman of the *News Chronicle* added to the British assault, denouncing Hearst as "a wicked old reactionary," who used his newspapers to "oppose all that was liberal and progressive." Then he grudgingly conceded that Hearst "invented" journalistic techniques that "were bold and challenging" and "which other people imitated." But the *Daily Telegraph* seemed to sum up best the overall British assessment of his career. Its feature writer observed that Hearst "began by being a sort of revolutionary, denouncing the use of privilege and noisily championing the cause of the common man, and ended by symbolizing, in the eyes of the world at any rate, all that he had denounced."[20]

But Hearst, in any evaluation of his life, would promote controversy, and would have been delighted that he did so. His greatest ambition was to be the leading journalist of his day, and to many observers he was. On March 4, 1887, he became, at age twenty-three, editor and proprietor of the *San Francisco Examiner*, and for half a century he dominated his profession. By 1893 he had revolutionized West Coast journalism, in the main by emulating and improving the techniques of Joseph Pulitzer's *New York World*. Then in 1894 he bought the *New York Morning Journal* and within the next four years challenged Pulitzer for journalistic supremacy in the United States. In this battle royal confrontation, which reached its peak during the Spanish American War, he was triumphant, personally directing his New York newspaper troops to victory. As one observer put it, Hearst's news office, in its determination to scoop the opposition, resembled a Chinese fire drill, which was "PANDEMONIUM WITH PURPOSE."

Hearst developed a formula that produced journalistic success. He concentrated on increasing the circulation of his newspapers and bragged about such growth to readers, which in turn attracted business advertisements. And with this added revenue, he hired the best professionals in their fields: editors, reporters, illustrators, political cartoonists, all at substantial salary increases.

Hearst then concentrated on developing and mastering a new mass media culture in the United States, which attracted readers to his newspapers, especially immigrants and laboring men and women. He believed that his fingers were on the pulse of the American people; in other words, he identified his hopes and trepidations, his likes and dislikes, with theirs. His newspapers were therefore a reflection of his ideas. A master showman, he was an innovator on a grand scale. As one of the creators of yellow journalism, he perfected in his newspapers the use of exciting attention-grabbing, fist-size headlines (underscored in red or black) which succinctly explained provocative front-page stories. He instituted larger type, which made information more legible for readers, thereby reducing the number of columns on a printed page from nine to seven and eventually to five. Editorials accompanied by political cartoons that were often humorous, but at times devastatingly brutal in their portrayal, stimulated readers either to act in protest or praise. And news stories, when possible, encompassed such ingredients as scandal, mystery, human depravity, or natural catastrophes either local or global. Hearst emphasized that such news copy must be interesting and entertaining and above all well written.

In keeping his fingers on the pulse of the American people, Hearst instructed his editors and reporters to identify with the community, not only in promoting projects that would benefit its citizens but in stories that reflected pride in the self-achievement of the local inhabitants. As a result, Hearst newspapers frequently featured stories about regional accomplishments, individual successes, and hometown sports rivalries. Anything having to do with women was also good copy, whether relating to the latest fashions, weddings, beauty contests, or advice to the lovelorn. And Hearst realized that Americans not only loved to read about European royalty but were equally fascinated with American royalty—the superrich, especially the Vanderbilts, Astors, Rockefellers, and Morgans.

The Hearst press, while providing readers with world news, also supplied them with data bordering on the mundane. For instance, page 1 of every edition contained weather forecasts. After October 1896, the first color cartoon, *The Yellow Kid*, appeared in the Sunday edition, and eventually such comic strips as the *Katzenjammer Kids, Mutt and Jeff*, and *Tillie the Toiler* appeared in the dailies.

Another first appeared during the Spanish American War: the *New York Morning Journal* published the first photos relating to that event. By 1904 the *New York American* began listing obituaries (usually on page 4), but also reported births, engagements, and weddings.

In all of his newspapers Hearst entertained readers royally. To increase circulation he instituted games, contests, puzzles, or lotteries for subscribers—with cash prizes or expensive gifts going to the winners. As further entertainment for his readers he published in chapter form the best-sellers of the day such as Erich Maria Remarque's *All Quiet on the Western Front* (1929) and W. R. Burnett's *Little Caesar* (1929).

Understandably, the Hearst newspapers attracted a huge readership. While one of Hearst's first editors stated that the goal of each edition was to elicit an immediate gee-whiz reaction from the reader, *Life* magazine aptly noted that Hearst newspapers were a "one-man fireworks display." They were informative, provocative, entertaining. They contained something for everyone. At the height of their popularity early in the 1930s, approximately one out of four Americans read a Hearst publication.[21]

To a number of journalists, however, Hearst was a source of embarrassment; they believed that he debased their profession. As early as 1896, in an attempt to free Cuba from Spanish rule, he had initiated a crusade formula whose purpose was to persuade readers to the Hearst point of view. In editorials, political cartoons, interviews, and informational stories, Hearst editors and reporters orchestrated the news, presenting only the point of their publisher, especially since his fingers were on the pulse of the American people. When facts did not support their arguments, they manufactured information or photographs as "truthful" evidence, without fear of condemnation or job removal.

By 1916, Hearst rephrased this method of news presentation as "government by newspaper." In an editorial he provided an insight into his thinking and intentions. "The influence of a great newspaper in a great community is," he proclaimed, "almost unlimited, almost illimitable. It enters into the hearts and homes of the people. It informs the mind of the citizen of today and molds the thought of the citizen of tomorrow." As a result, crusading Hearst editors, with instructions to enlist millions of loyal readers to their righteous causes, would be the "mouthpiece of the people" and force both local and national politicians to do their—and Hearst's—bidding.

Hearst's ultimate goal was to become president of the United States. To carry out such a formidable objective, Hearst realized that the control of the news media was imperative. By 1929 he had acquired twenty-eight newspapers in nineteen of the largest cities in the United States, together with thirteen magazines, ten radio stations, a wire service, and a motion picture studio. Even after the presidency was no longer a possibility, he was still a powerful force to be reckoned with in American politics. His continued application of government by newspaper, with complete control over editorial policies, was an awesome weapon, which politicians of the Democratic and Republican parties dared not ignore.

Hearst was an American original. He baffled many contemporaries by his actions. He was, without question, a nonconformist who played by his own rules, often without conscience or concern for the repercussions of his actions. He was the nation's most powerful press lord who confounded observers by the ruthlessness of his attacks on opponents. Yet he could be exceedingly polite to individuals and display unexpected compassion and generosity toward the less fortunate. He was a man of tremendous wealth who believed that money was meant to be spent, while continually seeking additional resources to fulfill his many expensive desires. He became one of the world's foremost collectors of rare artifacts and ancient treasures, housing his acquisitions, when possible, in mansions and castles, yet leaving many priceless possessions unattended in dank warehouses across the nation. And he became known for constructing a magnificent castle on the Enchanted Hill overlooking the Pacific at San Simeon Bay, which he called simply "the ranch."

Hearst hoped to play a significant role in the history of the United States, to make a difference in the lives of his fellow Americans. Of course, he believed that being elected president would be the most effective way of fulfilling this ambition. But that prestigious honor never occurred, although he strove mightily to attain it.

Hearst's changing political outlook was partly responsible for this failure. Early in his career as a journalist (the mid-1890s to 1914) he became an ardent progressive. In foreign policy he, like many progressives, fervently promoted American expansion into the Pacific (Hawaii, Guam, Philippines), as well as espousing a dominant influence in the Caribbean—acquisition of Puerto Rico, construction and controlling of the Panama Canal, securing a base in Cuba at Guantanamo Bay, and providing American financial and military support to the governments in Santo Domingo and Nicaragua.

In domestic policy Hearst also epitomized the progressive thinking of the early 1900s. Like Theodore Roosevelt, he campaigned to bust trusts, to prevent huge corporations such as the railroads, Standard Oil, Armour and Swift meatpacking from taking unfair advantage of Americans in the marketplace. Hearst newspapers also supported unions and their members in a fight to attain better hours, wages, and working conditions. And consistently Hearst editors and reporters campaigned for such economic and political reforms as a graduated income tax (Sixteenth Amendment), monetary and banking regulation (Federal Reserve Act), public utility controls (water and gas socialism), direct election of senators (Seventeenth Amendment), and initiative, referendum, and recall provisions that were enacted in many state constitutions.

After 1918, however, Hearst reversed many of his progressive stances, becoming more conservative with each passing year. Because of American involvement in World War I—and Woodrow Wilson's promotion of the League of Nations at the Treaty of Versailles—Hearst adopted as the logo on his editorial pages George Washington's foreign policy statement of "no entangling alliances." Without reservation he continued to denounce U.S. involvement in the League and was critical of any administration, whether Democratic or Republican, that supported the World Court. For that matter, he warned Hearst readers of a growing Japanese menace, predicting an inevitable conflict between the United States and "the barbarians" from the East. By 1938 Hearst was recognized as one of the leading isolationists, who constantly reminded his fellow countrymen to stay clear of English and French alliances as well as to be ever wary of Japanese aggression. The Hearst newspapers, in a recurring theme, preached "America First."

Concerning the domestic policies of the United States, Hearst also reverted to conservative stances. During the 1920s he became an avowed Jeffersonian Democrat, warning his fellow citizens against the dangers of big government, of unchecked federal power that could infringe on the individual rights of Americans, especially if a charismatic leader was in charge. Although deciding to back the Democrats in 1932 because of President Hoover's inability to solve the problems of the Great Depression, Hearst soon became highly critical of the New Deal. With increasing frequency Hearst newspapers supported big business to the detriment of organized labor. With unabated vigor they condemned higher income tax legislation as a persecution of the "successful." And they repeatedly referred to the New Deal programs as the "Raw Deal," asserting that the leadership was communist led and communist inspired.

Hearst was unable to capitalize on his views in seeking the presidency in part because of his individual makeup. Many aspects of his personality were impressive. He had a brilliant mind, bordering on genius, "so full of ideas," biographer John Winkler put it, "that they tumbled over each other." He was a workaholic, with the rare ability to compartmentalize his many business enterprises, any one of which would have exhausted most men. He was also willing to take an unpopular stand, to endure criticism, no matter how severe, in behalf of what he thought was right. And he was prepared to expend the considerable resources of the Hearst media empire to sustain his beliefs.

Hearst failed to achieve high political office partly because of an inflexible mind-set. He stressed leadership, which meant that he must be the dominant force. In his business enterprises as well as in politics, he had to be the ultimate manager, alone at the top—and in charge. Such an arrangement satisfied him; he wanted no other. Nor did he welcome compromise, unless first proposed by him. And seldom did he seek or acknowledge advice from others, with his mother being one exception and Arthur Brisbane another. Although eventually becoming an effective speaker after overcoming the negatives of a noticeable lisp and a high pitched voice, Hearst was ineffective as a candidate. Besides his inability to take advice, to compromise, to allow others to assume a leadership role in a campaign, he could not suppress his competitive tendencies not just to defeat but savage an opponent in his newspapers.

As a result, Hearst suffered an astonishing number of political defeats during a lifetime of campaigning. While unable to win an elective office, except to Congress (1903–1907), he was consistently unsuccessful in support of presidential candidates of the Democratic and Republican parties for whom he vigorously campaigned—William Jennings Bryan in 1896 and 1900, Champ Clark in 1912, John Nance Garner in 1932, and Alf Landon in 1936. Although endorsing FDR in 1932, Hearst soon became a bitter critic of the Democratic Party; his name was anathema to its members thereafter. Only in New York City, by endorsing John Hylan for mayor, could he claim success—but at the expense of incurring the wrath of Al Smith. To some contemporaries Hearst thus became known in politics as "a connoisseur of catastrophe" who was recognized by the magnificence of his defeats.

Although unable to realize his ultimate ambition, Hearst surely affected generations of Americans who reacted to his ideas, to his multiple crusades to make "America First." And in so doing, he made a difference to his country and his people. *Life* magazine may have assessed the totality of Hearst's life best: "In all aspects he was a fabulous man—such as the U.S. had never produced before and will never produce again."[22]

Notes

Chapter 1

1. Ben Procter, *William Randolph Hearst: The Early Years, 1863–1910* (New York: Oxford University Press, 1998), pp. 180, 193, 216.

2. *Ibid.*, pp. 45, 47–48, 60–65, 89–90, 194–95; Creelman, "The Real Mr. Hearst," *Pearson's Magazine*, November, 1906, p. 267; Lincoln Steffens, "Hearst: The Man of Mystery," *American Magazine*, November, 1906, p. 6; Richard O'Connor, *Ambrose Bierce: A Biography* (Boston: Little, Brown, 1967), pp. 153–58.

3. John K. Winkler, *William Randolph Hearst: A New Appraisal* (New York: Hastings House, 1955), p. 50; George P. West, "Hearst: A Psychological Note," *American Mercury*, November 1930, p. 301; Procter, *Hearst*, p. 50.

4. Mrs. Joseph Marshall Flint, interview by W. A. Swanberg, January 18 and February 20, 1960; Randolph Apperson, interview by W. A. Swanberg, October 23, 1959, Rare Book and Manuscript Library, Columbia University, New York (hereafter cited as in Swanberg Collection); Procter, *Hearst*, p. 194.

5. Procter, *Hearst*, pp. 45–47, 59–60, 81–88, 170–73ff, 177–78; *San Francisco Examiner*, March 11, 1887, p. 1; Oscar Lewis, *Bay Window Bohemia: An Account of the Brilliant Artistic World of Gaslit San Francisco* (Garden City, N.Y.: Doubleday, 1956), p. 137. See masthead of the *New York American*, January 1902.

6. Lewis, *Bay Window Bohemia*, p. 133; Procter, *Hearst*, p. 48.

7. The author determined this assessment by outlining the *San Francisco Examiner* daily from 1887 to August, 1895, as well as the *New York Morning Journal* from November 1895 to 1901. See Procter, *Hearst*, chapters 3–8.

8. For the first "This Day In History" by Thomas B. Gregory, see *New York American*, September 1, 1910, p. 16. The Gregory column is featured daily on the editorial page. For the first Sunday supplement of comics, see *New York Morning Journal*, October 18, 1896, 8 pp. For detailed information, see Procter, *Hearst*, chapters 5–9.

9. In the Sunday *New York Journal*, December 31, 1899, p. 37, Hearst titles this editorial, "The Newspaper of the Twentieth Century." See Procter, *Hearst*, pp. 136–38. For numerous manipulations and distortions of stories during the Spanish American War, see Procter, *Hearst*, chapters 6–7.

10. For "The National Policy" proposals, see editorials beginning in the *New York Morning Journal*, May 10, 1898, p. 10, and then several times a week—and often daily—during 1898, 1899, and 1900. See also Procter, *Hearst*, pp. 102, 137, 146, 152.

11. See the Sunday *New York Morning Journal*, February 5, 1899, p. 24, and thereafter, intermittently, in the editorial section through 1900. An excellent

example of Hearst's commitment to formulating the domestic and foreign policies of the Democratic Party and of the United States is in *ibid.*, November 8, 1900, p. 16. See also Winkler, *Hearst: A New Appraisal*, p. 117; Procter, *Hearst*, pp. 146–48, 152, 174.

12. For an account of Hearst's political activities, see Procter, *Hearst*, pp. 89–94, 152, 156–61, 163–262ff.

13. Mrs. Fremont Older, *William Randolph Hearst: American* (New York: Appleton-Century, 1936), pp. 336–37. For a discussion of the relationship between Phoebe Apperson Hearst and her grandchildren, see Judith Robinson, *The Hearsts: An American Dynasty* (New York: Avon, 1991), pp. 348–55. See also W. R. Hearst to Mrs. P. A. Hearst (telegrams), January 28 and March 14, 1910, MSS, William Randolph Hearst Papers, Bancroft Library, University of California–Berkeley (hereafter cited as WRH Papers). For the birthdates of the three Hearst children, see Procter, *Hearst*, pp. 180, 240–41, 259, 332 n. 58.

14. Concerning Hearst's fascination with cars, see Winkler, *Hearst: A New Appraisal*, pp. 172–73; Procter, *Hearst*, p. 180. For his flight over Los Angeles, see *New York Times*, January 20, 1910, p. 1; and *New York American*, January 20, 1910, p. 1. In regard to the $50,000 prize for the first person to fly coast to coast, see *New York American*, October 9, 1910, p. 1L, October 10, 1910, pp. 1, 2, 20; October 13, 1910, p. 10; October 14, 1910, p. 3; October 15, 1910, p. 5; October 16, 1910, p. 16L; October 19, 1910, p. 3; October 23, 1910, p. 13L; December 25, 1910, p. 9L.

15. *New York American*, April 7, 1910, p. 3. See three interviews of Hearst in Mexico City by the Mexican press, dated March 31, April 1, and April 6, 1910, in *ibid.*, June 28, 1910, p. 18; June 29, 1910, p. 18; June 30, 1910, p. 18. For detailed information concerning the Babicora Ranch, see John Kenneth Turner, *Barbarous Mexico* (Austin: University of Texas Press, 1969), pp. 106, 193, 206–7, 216–17; Procter, *Hearst*, pp. 26, 180, 212, 232. Concerning Diaz, see also Carleton Beals, *Porfirio Diaz: Dictator of Mexico* (Philadelphia: Lippincott, 1932), pp. 395–455ff.

16. Roy Everett Littlefield III, *William Randolph Hearst: His Role in American Progressivism* (Lanham, Md.: University Press of America, 1980), pp. 272, 299–300 (endnotes 59–62); *New York American*, April 15, 1910, p. 3. For Hearst's editorial, see *ibid.*, April 16, 1910, p. 18. For reaction to the Hearst overtures, see *ibid.*, April 15, 1910, p. 3; April 23, 1910, p. 16; April 29, 1910, p. 20. For Hearst's evaluation of Taft after visiting the White House, see *ibid.*, April 21, 1910, pp. 1–2. See also the *New York Times*, April 21, 1910, p. 2. Concerning the political struggle with and victory over Speaker Cannon, see Richard Lowitt, *George W. Norris: The Making of a Progressive* (Syracuse: Syracuse University Press, 1963), pp. 166–84. See also Littlefield, *Hearst: His Role in American Progressivism*, pp. 272–73.

17. Concerning the New York City mayoral contest in the fall of 1919, see Louis Heaton Pink, *GAYNOR: The Tammany Mayor Who Swallowed the Tiger* (New York: International, 1931), pp. 131–38; Mortimer Smith, *William Jay*

Gaynor: Mayor of New York (Chicago: Regnery, 1951), pp. 66–72; Lately Thomas, *The Mayor Who Mastered New York: The Life and Opinions of William J. Gaynor* (New York: Morrow, 1969), pp. 162–92ff; Procter, *Hearst*, pp. 257–62.

18. For the revelation of confidential letters from Murphy to his lieutenants, see the *New York American*, December 15, 1909, p. 1. See also Littlefield, *Hearst: His Role in American Progressivism*, p. 271. Concerning the Cohalan incident, see Pink, *Gaynor*, pp. 156–57; Smith, *Gaynor*, pp. 96–98; Thomas, *Gaynor*, pp. 268–69; *New York Times*, April 16, 1910, p. 10. See many critical references to Gaynor in the *New York American*, January 3, 1910, pp. 1–2, 16; January 6, 1910, p. 11; January 10, 1910, p. 1; January 16, 1910, p. 3; February 4, 7, 1910, p. 1; February 8, 1910, p. 4; February 11, 1910, p. 3; February 14, 1910, p. 1; February 20, 1910, p. 1L; March 30, 31, 1910, p. 1; April 1, 1910, p. 3; April 13, 1910, p. 2; April 15, 1910, p. 1.

19. *New York Times*, April 29, 1910, pp. 1–2; *New York American*, April 29, 1910, p. 11; Thomas, *Gaynor*, pp. 269–73; Smith, *Gaynor*, pp. 98–101; Pink, *Gaynor*, pp. 157–58.

20. *New York Times*, April 29, 1910, p. 1; *New York American*, April 29, 1910, p. 11; Thomas, *Gaynor*, p. 273; Smith, *Gaynor*, pp. 101–2; Pink, *Gaynor*, pp. 158–59. For a firsthand account of the Gaynor–Williams embroglio, see Henry H. Klein, *My Last Fifty Years* (New York: Goldmann, 1935), pp. 29–32.

21. In regard to the immediate orchestration of the news, see the *New York American*, April 29, 1910, p. 11; May 2, 1910, pp. 1, 2, 18; May 3, 1910, pp. 1–3; May 4, 1910, pp. 1–3, 22; May 5, 6, 1910, pp. 1–2; May 8, 1910, pp. 1L-2L-II (concerning Lewis on Gaynor plus Carter cartoon); May 10, 1910, p. 5. For typical testimonials against and criticisms of Gaynor and his administration, which continued almost daily until August 9, 1910, see *ibid.*, May 13 to May 20, 1910.

22. *New York American*, April 30, 1910, pp. 1–2. At the end of the editorial Hearst signed his name in full. See also in *ibid.*, March 23, 30, 1913, p. 1L-IIL, where Henry Watterson, the distinguished editor of the *Louisville Courier-Journal*, apologizes to Hearst "for printing Mayor Gaynor's libellous charges," which were "absolutely untrue." Even after three years, Hearst remembered the Gaynor attack.

23. For the time of sailing to Europe, see *New York Times*, May 11, 1910, p. 6. For the Hearst suit against the *New York Times* and the Associated Press, see *ibid.*, May 1, 1910, pp. 1–2; May 5, 1910, p. 1; May 6, 1910, pp. 1–2; May 8, 1910, p. 9; May 10, 1910, p. 1. See also Will to Mother (telegram), [May, 1910], WRH Papers. For the Hearst editorials of the Edward VII funeral, see the *New York American*, May 21, 1910, pp. 1–2; May 22, 1910, p. 1L; Older, *Hearst*, p. 340. For another vivid account of the funeral of Edward VII, see Barbara W. Tuchman, *The Guns of August* (New York: Macmillan, 1962), pp. 1–4, 12–14.

24. For Hearst's activities in London, see the *New York American*, June 13, 1910, p. 5; Older, *Hearst*, p. 340. See also the Hearst interviews in the *New York American*, June 2, 4, 1910, p. 1; June 8, 1910, p. 4; June 13, 1910, p. 5; June 15, 1910, pp. 1–2; June 27, 1910, p. 4; *New York World*, June 26, 1910, p. 1.

25. Will to Phoebe Hearst (telegram), July 26, 1910, and Geo and William to Phoebe Hearst (telegram), August 12, 1910, WRH Papers. For Hearst's return to Paris, see *New York American*, September 8, 1910, p. 1; September 10, 1910, p. 1L. See also Older, *Hearst*, pp. 340–41, 345.

26. Concerning the American Boy Scout movement, see the *New York American*, May 10, 1910, p. 3; May 12, 1910, p. 4; June 5, 1910, p. 11L; June 7, 10, 1910, p. 10; July 7, 1910, p. 4; July 10, 1910, p. 6L; July 12, 13, 15, and 20, 1910, p. 8; July 26, 1910, p. 5; August 6, 1910, p. 14; August 14, 1910, p. 10L; August 20, 24, 1910, p. 5; September 4, 1910, p. 3-II; September 5, 24, 1910, p. 8; October 9, 1910, p. 11L; October 13, 1910, p. 4. For Hearst's election as national president of the Boy Scouts and his financial contribution, see *ibid.*, July 1, 1910, p. 8; July 18, 1910, p. 5. Note, however, that Hearst resigned his position in December 1910, upon discovering evidence of corruption in fund-raising. See *ibid.*, December 9, 1910, p. 11; December 14, 1910, p. 4; December 21, 1910, p. 7.

27. Concerning the Chicago circulation wars, especially a negative view of Hearst, see Ferdinand Lundberg, *Imperial Hearst: A Social Biography* (New York: Equinox Cooperative, 1936), pp. 149–51. For a more balanced view, see Joseph Gies, *The Colonel of Chicago* (New York: Dutton, 1979), pp. 35–37; W. A. Swanberg, *Citizen Hearst* (New York: Scribner's, 1961), pp. 270–71; Wayne Andrews, *Battle for Chicago* (New York: Harcourt, Brace, 1946), pp. 232–40. For a discussion of the *Boston American* and Hearst's desire to enlarge his news empire, see Moses Koenigsberg, *King News: An Autobiography* (New York: Stokes, 1941), pp. 327–32, 334, 336, 343–44, 348, 352–53.

28. See full-page interview by the *New York World*, June 26, 1910, p. 1, which is also published in the *New York American*, June 27, 1910, p. 4; September 12, 1910, p. 8. See also in *ibid.*, June 28, 1910, p. 5; September 12, 1910, p. 18. See Hearst appeal to Roosevelt in *ibid.*, September 8, 1910, p. 1; and the Roosevelt response in *ibid.*, September 9, 1910, p. 1; and *New York World*, September 9, 1910, pp. 5, 8. For triumphs by Progressives, see *ibid.*, September 14, 15, 1910, p. 1; September 16, 1910, p. 5; Littlefield, *Hearst: His Role in American Progressivism*, pp. 272–74, 300.

29. *New York Times*, October 2, 1910, p. 5; October 7, 1910, p. 2; *New York World*, October 5, 1910, p. 6; October 6, 1910, p. 5; October 9, 1910, p. 12; October 13, 1910, p. 6; October 18, 1910, p. 4; October 22, 1910, p. 10; *New York Times*, October 6, 1910, pp. 1, 3; October 7, 1910, pp. 2, 4; October 8, 1910, p. 6; October 9, 1910, p. 4; October 16, 1910, p. 8; October 18, 1910, p. 5; October 22, 1910, p. 8; October 27, 1910, p. 20. See the *New York American*, October 1, 1910, p. 3; October 3, 1910, p. 10; October 4, 1910, pp. 6, 18; October 5, 1910, p. 8; October 6, 1910, pp. 1–2, 20; October 7, 1910, p. 11; October 8, 1910, pp. 1–2. Then see daily reports of the Independence League campaign in *ibid.*, from October 12, 1910, pp. 6, 10, to November 7, 1910, pp. 1–2. See also Older, *Hearst*, pp. 242–43.

30. For election results noting that Hopper (in greater New York) "received 45,000 votes and Mr. Hearst 60,000," see the *New York American*, November 9, 1910, p. 1; *New York Times*, November 9, 1910, pp. 1–4; November 10, 1910,

p. 3. For numerous telegrams by Democratic victors thanking Hearst, see the *New York American*, November 9, 1910, p. 1; November 10, 1910, pp. 1, 4; November 11, 1910, p. 5; November 12, 1910, p. 1; November 13, 1910, p. 3L-II; December 9, 1910, p. 2. For an evaluation of Hearst's strength with labor in New York City, see Irwin Yellowitz, *Labor and the Progressive Movement in New York State, 1897–1916* (New York: Cornell University Press, 1965), p. 226.

31. *New York American*, November 20, 1910, p. 10L; *New York Times*, November 19, 1910, p. 6.

32. For the Hearst accomplishments concerning criminal trusts, see the *New York American*, December 9, 1910, p. 1; December 10, 1910, p. 11. For Millicent's contribution to the doll bazaar, see *ibid*., December 5, 1910, p. 7; December 7, 1910, pp. 7, 9; December 19, 1910, p. 8. For Hearst's $1,000 donation to the Christmas Fund, see *ibid*., almost daily from November 30 and December 1, 1910, p. 18, to its conclusion on December 26, 1910, pp. 9, 14; December 27, 1910, pp. 4, 5. For Hearst's $1,000 contribution to the widow of the slain policeman, see *ibid*., December 9, 1910, p. 5. And for the story behind Hearst's resignation as head of the Boy Scouts of America, see *ibid*., December 9, 1910, p. 11; December 14, 1910, p. 4; December 21, 1910, p. 7.

33. For the "I am a Democrat" statement and printed signature, see the *New York American*, January 30, 1911, p. 4. For the speech honoring Nathan Straus, see *ibid*., February 1, 1911. For a description of three Hearst dinners, see the *New York Times*, February 21, 1911, p. 11; May 8, 1911, p. 11; May 24, 1911, p. 11. See also Littlefield, *Hearst: His Role in American Progressivism*, pp. 278, 301 n.

34. For articles suggesting Hearst's conservatism, see the *New York American*, February 1, 1911, p. 18; February 14, 1911, p. 1; March 5, 1911, p. 1L-II; June 4, 1911, p. 2L; June 5, 1911, p. 11. Concerning rumors that suggest the acquisition of newspapers, see the *New York Times*, April 16, 1911, p. 1; May 25, 1911, p. 4; June 29, 1911, p. 20.

35. For the New York coverage of the campaign from the Hearst point of view, see the *New York American*, March 1, 1911, pp. 1, 6; April 5, 1911, pp. 1, 2; April 6, 1911, pp. 2, 20. See also the *New York Times*, March 22, 1911, p. 1; April 2, 1911, pt. 6, p. 11. For a different slant on the Chicago campaign, see Carter H. Harrison, *Stormy Years: The Autobiography of Carter H. Harrison, Five Times Mayor of Chicago* (New York: Bobbs-Merrill, 1935), pp. 266–316ff; *New York Times*, April 22, 1911, p. 1. For the political involvement in San Francisco politics, see the *New York American*, March 12, 1911, p. 1L-III; Procter, *Hearst*, pp. 176, 215. And regarding his rapprochement with New York Democrats, see the *New York American*, May 1, 1911, p. 9; May 4, 1911, p. 2; May 16, 1911, p. 5; May 18, 1911, pp. 1–2; May 19, 1911, p. 4; May 24, 1911, p. 7; *New York Times*, May 18, 1911, p. 4.

36. *New York Times*, May 25, 1911, p. 4; Will to Mother [June 1911], Bains de Bormio, Italie; Hearst to Mother [June 1911], from Excelsior Palace Hotel, Venice-Lido; Will to Mother, postcard from [Switzerland], June 22, 1911; Milly and Me to Mother, June 22, 1911, postcard from [Switzerland], WRH Papers. For Hearst's whereabouts on his European tour, see Hearst interviews and editorials

(from Paris) in the *New York American*, August 24, 1911, p. 1; August 25, 1911, p. 16; September 5, 1911, p. 16; and (from London) September 17, 1911, pp. 1L-2L; September 25, 1911, p. 1; September 26, 1911, pp. 1–2. For purchase of Tattershall Castle, see the *New York Times*, September 22, 1911, p. 4.

37. For Hearst's involvement regarding U.S. reciprocity, especially with Canada, see the *New York American*, July 22, 1911, p. 9; July 23, 1911, p. 2L; July 24, 1911, pp. 1, 14; July 30, 1911, p. 2L; August 28, 1911, p. 14; August 31, 1911, pp. 11, 18; September 5, 1911, p. 16; September 17, 1911, pp. 1L–2L; September 19, 20, 1911, pp. 1–2; September 23, 1911, p. 1; September 24, 1911, p. 2L; *New York Times*, September 9, 1911, p. 3. Concerning Hearst's advocacy of world peace, see the *New York American*, August 4, 1911, pp. 3, 16; September 19, 1911, pp. 1–2; September 20, 1911, pp. 1–2.

38. *New York Times*, June 29, 1911, p. 20; August 20, 1911, p. 1; Winkler, *Hearst: A New Appraisal*, p. 173.

39. For the Columbus Day address, see the *New York American*, October 13, 1911, p. 8; October 15, 1911, p. 8L. For Hearst's editorial on Harlan, see *ibid.*, October 16, 1911, p. 18. For the announcements on "$18,000 Rewards," see *ibid.*, October 17, 1911, p. 6, almost daily to November 7, 1911, p. 6. And for Hearst's denunciation of Boss Murphy and Tammany Hall in his "I Am a Democrat" speech, see *ibid.*, October 20, 1911, pp. 1–2; *New York Times*, October 20, 1911, p. 3. See also Littlefield, *Hearst: His Role in American Progressivism*, p. 278.

40. *New York American*, October 22, 1911, p. 2L-IV; October 23, 1911, p. 11; October 25, 1911, p. 22; October 26, 1911, pp. 1, 9. The New York newspaper rivals were even favorable in their coverage. See Littlefield, *Hearst: His Role in American Progressivism*, p. 279. Concerning the Wilson rebuff, see Josephus Daniels, *The Wilson Era: Years of Peace, 1910–1917* (Chapel Hill: University of North Carolina Press, 1944), pp. 79–80.

41. Concerning Hearst's lingering hopes, see editorial entitled "Well Why Not Hearst" in the *New York American*, November 1, 1911, p. 22; *New York Times*, January 28, 1912, p. 1; Littlefield, *Hearst: His Role in American Progressivism*, pp. 278, 284. Concerning the campaign for fusion candidates in New York City, see the *New York American*, October 22, 1911, pp. 4L, 7L, then daily to November 7, 1911, pp. 1–2. See also *ibid.*, November 8, 9, 1911, pp. 1–2; *New York Times*, November 9, 1911, p. 3; Littlefield, *Hearst: His Role in American Progressivism*, pp. 280–81.

42. For Hearst's campaign for the Democratic presidential nomination, see Procter, *Hearst*, chapter 9. For letters and statements of appreciation to Hearst and his newspapers, see the *New York American*, November 9, 1911, pp. 1–2; November 12, 1911, p. 5L-II; November 13, 1911, p. 5; November 20, 1911, p. 18 (editorial); December 14, 1911, p. 1; December 15, 1911, p. 1; *New York Times*, December 11, 1911, p. 9. For story about Hearst's whistle-stop tour in October 1903, see Procter, *Hearst*, pp. 181–82. See also Littlefield, *Hearst: His Role in American Progressivism*, pp. 281–82; Evans C. Johnson, *Oscar W. Underwood: A Political Biography* (Baton Rouge: Louisiana State University Press, 1980), pp. 78–79, 152.

43. Concerning Hearst's advocacy of reciprocal trade agreements and subsequent approval, see the *New York American*, November 17, 1911, pp. 1–2; November 22, 1911, p. 3; November 27, 1911, p. 20; November 28, 1911, pp. 5, 20; December 2, 1911, p. 20; December 3, 1911, p. 8L; December 4, 1911, pp. 9, 20. Concerning appeals to Hearst from the Republic of China, see *ibid.*, November 16, 1911, p. 1; and in regard to Russia, see *ibid.*, December 7, 9, 1911, p. 1; and concerning international recognition of Hearst newspapers, see editorial in *ibid.*, November 20, 1911, p. 20. As for Hearst's progressive agenda regarding the boss system, see *ibid.*, November 10, 1911, pp. 1, 20; November 13, 1911, p. 5; December 10, 1911, p. 4L; *New York Times*, November 9, 1911, p. 3. Concerning a direct primary, see *New York Times*, December 6, 1911, p. 10; *New York American*, December 14, 1911, p. 2. Concerning the curbing of evils within trusts and huge combinations, see Hearst's editorial in the *New York American*, November 17, 1911, p. 18, which was published in the November edition of the *World of Today Magazine*.

44. *New York Times*, December 11, 1911, pp. 1, 9; *New York American*, December 16, 1911, pp. 1–2; December 30, 1911, pp. 1–2. For pleas to Hearst to be a candidate, see the *New York American*, January 3, 1912, p. 4; January 4, 1912, pp. 1–2; Littlefield, *Hearst: His Role in American Progressivism*, pp. 284, 303 n. 125. For the Democratic activities at Washington, see the *New York American*, January 9, 1912, pp. 1–2; January 10, 1912, p. 6; January 16, 1912, p. 2; *New York Times*, January 7, 1912, p. 1; January 9, 1912, p. 2; Arthur S. Link, *Wilson: The Road to the White House* (Princeton, N.J.: Princeton University Press, 1947), pp. 355–56; Louis W. Koenig, *Bryan: A Political Biography of William Jennings Bryan* (New York: Putnam, 1971), p. 478. For Hearst's anticipated acquisition of the *Atlanta Georgian* as well as his final acquisition, see the *New York American*, February 5, 1912, p. 20; February 7, 1912, p. 1; February 8, 1912, p. 3; *New York Times*, January 6, 1912, p. 24; February 6, 1912, p. 4. For a report on his financial wealth, see *ibid.*, February 9, 1912, p. 11.

45. *New York Times*, January 28, 1912, p. 1; Littlefield, *Hearst: His Role in American Progressivism*, pp. 284–85, 303 n. 127–28.

46. For Clark's evaluation of Hearst and his need for Hearst in the 1912 campaign, see Champ Clark, *My Quarter Century of American Politics* (New York: Harper, 1920), 2: 264–67, 401. See also Link, *Wilson: The Road to the White House*, p. 401. For Hearst's acknowledged approval of Clark, see Hearst, interview by William T. Stead, in the *New York American*, September 25, 1911, p. 1; September 26, 1911, pp. 1–2.

47. *New York American*, February 20, 1912, p. 1; February 25, 1912, p. 2L-II. Concerning Chicago politics, see *New York Times*, February 23, 28, 1912, p. 1.

48. Article in *Washington Post*, March 14, 1912, as printed in the *New York American*, March 14, 1912, p. 2.

49. See Link, *Wilson: The Road to the White House*, pp. 382–83; Johnson, *Underwood*, p. 178. For Hearst's brutal assessment of Wilson, which was printed in all the Hearst papers, see the *New York American*, March 14, 1912, p. 2. For anti-Wilson

stories and editorials together with political cartoons, see daily in *ibid.* from March through June 1912. Note, however, that Homer Davenport died on May 2, 1912. See *ibid.*, May 3, 1912, p. 20. For Gaynor's advice to Wilson concerning Hearst, see the *New York Times*, March 13, 1912, p. 3.

50. Alfred Henry Lewis, "The Real Woodrow Wilson," *Hearst's Magazine*, May 1912, pp. 2265–74; Link, *Wilson: The Road to the White House*, pp. 383–87.

51. *New York American*, May 1, 1912, pp. 1, 22; May 2, 1912, pp. 1–2, 4; May 4, 1912, p. 2; May 7, 1912, pp. 1–2; May 8, 1912, p. 2. For Clark victories in California, Iowa, Arizona, and Arkansas, see *ibid.*, May 15, 1912, p. 1; May 17, 1912, pp. 4, 20; May 28, 1912, p. 4; June 6, 1912, p. 1. For the Clark delegate count, see *ibid.*, June 6, 1912, p. 1; June 11, 1912, p. 4. For the story that Clark would receive the New York delegate vote after the first ballot, see *ibid.*, June 14, 1912, p. 7. See also Louis W. Koenig, *Bryan: A Political Biography of William Jennings Bryan* (New York: Putnam, 1971), pp. 474–76.

52. See Link, *Wilson: The Road to the White House*, pp. 384, 402–22ff. For speculation concerning Hearst's role if Clark won the presidency, see the "Editorial Comment" in the *New York American*, April 13, 1912, p. 18; May 12, 1912, p. 14W; Littlefield, *Hearst: His Role in American Progressivism*, p. 286. For the reaction of the Wilson people to Hearst, see also the *New York Times*, April 11, 1912, p. 2; June 26, 1912, p. 1. For one of the most abusive attacks on Hearst, see *Collier's Weekly*, May 25, 1912, p. 8.

53. Concerning Harrison, see the *New York Times*, June 24, 1912, p. 4; Littlefield, *Hearst: His Role in American Progressivism*, p. 285. For preconvention and convention stories and editorials, see the *New York American*, June 20–26, 1912, but see specifically in *ibid.*, June 26–27, 1912, p. 1. In regard to rumors concerning a Hearst deal with Murphy, see the *New York World*, June 25, 1912, p. 3; *New York Times*, June 21, 1912, p. 6; Link, *Wilson: The Road to the White House*, pp. 434–35. For Hearst's organizational techniques at the 1904 national convention, see Procter, *Hearst*, pp. 188–89. For the convention coverage at Baltimore by the Hearst lieutenants, see the *New York American*, June 25–July 1, 1912.

54. For events having to do with the Republicans prior to and during their national convention in Chicago, see Henry F. Pringle, *The Life and Times of William Howard Taft: A Biography* (New York: Farrar & Rinehart, 1939), 2: 796–809; Judith Icke Anderson, *William Howard Taft: An Intimate History* (New York: Norton, 1981), pp. 235–39; Henry F. Pringle, *Theodore Roosevelt: A Biography* (New York: Harcourt, Brace, 1931), pp. 562–65. See also Paolo E. Coletta, *The Presidency of William Howard Taft* (Lawrence: University Press of Kansas, 1973), pp. 235–42.

55. For excellent coverage of the 1912 Democratic Convention, see Link, *Wilson: The Road to the White House*, pp. 435–55; Koenig, *Bryan*, pp. 488–96. See also Paola E. Coletta, *William Jennings Bryan: Progressive Politician and Moral Statesman, 1909–1915* (Lincoln: University of Nebraska Press, 1969), 2: 51–78ff; Clark, *My Quarter Century of American Politics*, 2: 398–442ff; Paul W. Glad, *The Trumpet Soundeth: William Jennings Bryan and His Democracy, 1896–1912* (Lincoln: University of Nebraska Press, 1960), pp. 169–71.

56. Procter, *Hearst*, pp. 191–92, 230; *New York American*, July 1, 1912, p. 20; Older, *Hearst*, p. 350.

57. Link, *Wilson: The Road to the White House*, pp. 458–62; Koenig, *Bryan*, pp. 493–96; Littlefield, *Hearst: His Role in American Progressivism*, pp. 289–90; Glad, *The Trumpet Soundeth*, pp. 171–72; Colleta, *Bryan*, 2: 76–78. See also the *New York American*, June 30, 1912, p. 1L; July 1–2, 1912, p. 1; *New York World*, July 1–2, 1912, p. 3.

58. Daniels, *The Wilson Era*, p. 80; *New York Times*, July 3, 1912, p. 3; Link, *Wilson: The Road to the White House*, p. 508. For a caricature of Hearst attending the Baltimore convention, see the *New York Tribune*, June 30, 1912, p. 1L. See also about Hearst in *ibid.*, July 2, 1912, p. 3; July 3, 1912, pp. 3, 6.

59. Will to Mrs. P. A. Hearst (telegram), May 1, June 12, 1912; Mother to W. R. Hearst (telegram), June 11–12, 1912; affectionate son to mother [1912]; Will to Mother [November 21, 1912], in WRH Papers. See also Robinson, *The Hearsts*, p. 352.

60. Concerning the Hearst business enterprises in London, see affectionate son to mother [1912]; Will to Mother [November 21, 1912], in WRH Papers; Robinson, *The Hearsts*, p. 345. For the Progressive Party convention in Chicago, see Pringle, *Roosevelt*, pp. 566–68. For Roosevelt's intervention in the 1906 New York gubernatorial race, see Procter, *Hearst*, pp. 224–26. See also Hearst's comments about Roosevelt and the 1912 presidential election in editorials and interviews (from London) in the *New York American*, September 1, 1912, p. 3L-II; September 8, 1912, p. 1L-II; September 13, 1912, p. 1. See the announcement supporting Wilson in *ibid.*, September 19, 1912, p. 4 and daily thereafter to Election Day on November 5.

61. For Hearst's role in revealing the Standard Oil letters, see Procter, *Hearst*, pp. 248–54ff; U.S. Congress, Senate, Committee on Privileges and Elections: Campaign Contributions, "Testimony of William R. Hearst, Journalist, New York City, N.Y.," 62d Cong., 3d sess. 1251–95 (hereafter referred to as the Clapp Committee); Everett Walters, *Joseph Benson Foraker: An Uncompromising Republican*, Ohio Governors Series (Columbus: Ohio History Press, 1948), pp. 273–87; Sam Hanna Acheson, *Joe Bailey: The Last Democrat* (New York: Macmillan, 1932), pp. 253–55. For the publication of these letters, see William Randolph Hearst, "The Lesson of the Standard Oil Letters," *Hearst's Magazine*, May 1912, pp. 2204–216. Then see the next in a series in *ibid.*, from June to December 1912. See Roosevelt's reaction to them in Elting E. Morison, ed., *The Letters of Theodore Roosevelt* (Cambridge: Harvard University Press, 1954), 7: 602–9, 611–17. See also the *New York American*, August 16, 20, 22, 1912, p. 1; August 23, 1912, p. 6; August 24, 1912, p. 5; August 26–28, 1912, p. 1; August 29, 1912, pp. 4, 18; September 1, 1912, p. 3L-II; September 2, 1912, p. 2; September 24, 1912, p. 1; September 29, 1912, p. 1L-II; Littlefield, *Hearst: His Role in American Progressivism*, pp. 292–94.

62. Arthur H. Gleason, "Mr. Hearst's Forgeries," *Collier's Weekly*, October 5, 1912, pp. 10–11, 37, 39; see also in *ibid.*, April 20, 1912, pp. 8–9. See also the

New York Times, October 2, 1912, p. 9; *New York American*, October 2, 1912, p. 20; Swanberg, *Citizen Hearst*, p. 279.

63. *New York Times*, November 23, 1912, p. 12; December 18, 1912, p. 6; December 19, 1912, p. 3; December 20, 1912, p. 17; Clapp Committee, 1: 1251–95ff. See the *New York American*, January 11, 1913, pp. 1–2. For a somewhat different evaluation of Hearst's appearance before the Clapp Committee, see Swanberg, *Citizen Hearst*, pp. 280–87.

64. See the following Hearst editorials and interviews in the *New York American*, August 5, 1912, p. 16; September 4, 1912, p. 1; September 8, 1912, p. 1L-II; September 12, 13, 1912, p. 1; September 15, 1912, p. 6L; September 17, 1912, p. 1; October 10, 1912, pp. 1–2.

65. Arthur S. Link, *Wilson: The New Freedom* (Princeton, N.J.: Princeton University Press, 1956), p. 21; Koenig, *Bryan*, pp. 500–502; Coletta, *Bryan*, 2: 89. Hearst's disdain for Bryan in the Wilson administration is portrayed in numerous Frederick Opper political cartoons; for example, see the *New York American*, February 1, 1913, p. 18; February 22, 1913, p. 4; March 4, 1913, p. 20. See also Littlefield, *Hearst: His Role in American Progressivism*, pp. 294–95.

Chapter 2

1. For an excellent evaluation of Wilson and the first two months of his administration, see Arthur S. Link, *Wilson: The New Freedom* (Princeton, N.J.: Princeton University Press, 1956), pp. 55–84ff, 145–56. See also Coletta, *Bryan*, 2: 923–93; Koenig, *Bryan*, 502–3; Josephus Daniels, *The Wilson Era: Years of Peace—1910–1917* (Chapel Hill: University of North Carolina Press, 1944), pp. 104–18ff.

2. Link, *Wilson: The New Freedom*, pp. 152–55, 177–81; Coletta, *Bryan*, 2: 122–23; Johnson, *Underwood*, pp. 197–99.

3. For Wilson's patronage activities in New York in 1913, see Link, *Wilson: The New Freedom*, pp. 164–67.

4. For Hearst's editorial, see the *New York American*, April 14, 1913, p. 16; and continuing praise of the editorial in *ibid.*, April 16–17, 1913, p. 16; April 22, 1913, p. 2. See also his comments concerning the proposed tariff legislation prior to this editorial in *ibid.*, April 4, 1913, p. 18; April 5, 1913, p. 16; April 7, 1913, p. 16. For similar negative reactions to the Wilson address, see Link, *Wilson: The New Freedom*, pp. 152–53.

5. *New York Times*, July 26, 1913, p. 12; Andrew Alpern, *Historic Manhattan Apartment Houses* (New York: Dover, 1996), pp. 30–32; William Randolph Hearst Jr., with Jack Casserly, *The Hearsts: Father and Son* (Niwot, Colo.: Roberts Rinehart, 1991), pp. 24–25; Older, *Hearst*, pp. 345–46; David Nassaw, *The Chief: The Life of William Randolph Hearst* (Boston: Houghton Mifflin, 2000), pp. 231–32.

6. S. N. Behrman, *Duveen* (New York: Random House, 1951), pp. 88, 92–97; Swanberg, *Citizen Hearst*, pp. 288–89. For an example of Hearst's desire to buy only the best-quality merchandise, see the controversy with Charles of

London in the *New York Times*, November 7, 1914, p. 18; *New York American*, November 8, 1914, p. 6L.

7. Hearst Jr. with Casserly, *The Hearsts*, p. 24. For information about their tenth wedding anniversary, see the *New York Times*, April 29, 1913, p. 9; Will to Mrs. P. A. Hearst (telegram), May 1, 1913, MSS, William Randolph Hearst Jr. Papers, Bancroft Library, University of California–Berkeley (hereafter cited as WRHJr. papers); Swanberg, *Citizen Hearst*, pp. 288–89. Concerning the Maine monument fund project, see Procter, *Hearst*, p. 132. For the unveiling of the monument and festivities, see the *New York American*, May 25, 1913, p. 1L-III; May 30, 1913, pp. 1–2; June 1, 1913, p. 1L-II; *New York Times*, May 30, 1913, p. 16; May 31, 1913, p. 3; Older, *Hearst*, p. 362. And concerning the American, Brazilian, and Argentine fete, see *ibid.*, June 24, 1913, p. 11; *New York American*, June 30, 1913, p. 4.

8. Swanberg, *Citizen Hearst*, pp. 290–91; Irene Castle, as told to Bob and Wanda Duncan, *Castles in the Air* (Garden City, N.Y.: Doubleday, 1958), p. 89. Throughout his life, Hearst was seldom denied anything by friends and loved ones. For example, see Behrman, *Duveen*, pp. 94–96; Procter, *Hearst*, pp. 12–14, 44–45.

9. For comments about Hearst for U.S. senator, see *New York Times*, April 10, 1913, p. 1; July 9, 1913, p. 3. Concerning reports about Hearst and Sulzer meeting as well as anti-Murphy comments, see *ibid.*, February 11, 1913, p. 9; May 28, 1913, p. 22; June 15, 1913, p. 7; June 18, 1913, p. 2; June 19, 1913, p. 3. See Murphy's action against Sulzer in *ibid.*, July 2, 1913, p. 4; July 3, 1913, p. 1. Concerning the Sulzer investigation and impeachment, see the *New York American* daily from August 1, 1913, p. 1, to August 20, 1913, p. 1. Concerning Sulzer payoffs, see *ibid.*, September 26–29, 1913, p. 1. And concerning the Sulzer impeachment court, see *ibid.*, October 1–3, 1913, p. 1; October 4, 1913, p. 3; October 7–11, 1913, p. 1; October 17–18, 1913, pp. 1–2. See also Littlefield, *Hearst: His Role in American Progressivism*, pp. 312–13; Swanberg, *Citizen Hearst*, pp. 258, 260; Link, *Wilson: The New Freedom*, p. 167.

10. Concerning the nomination of Mitchel and Hearst's participation and support, see the *New York American*, July 24, 1913, p. 16; August 1, 1913, p. 1; August 2, 1913, pp. 2, 14; August 31, 1913, p. 1L; *New York Times*, August 25, 1913, p. 3; August 26, 1913, pp. 1–2; August 27, 1913, pp. 1–2, 6; August 28, 1913, p. 8; August 31, 1913, p. 2; September 1, 1913, pp. 1–2; September 2, 1913, p. 1; September 5, 7, 1913, p. 2; September 8, 1913, p. 1; September 23, 1913, p. 22; October 10, 1913, p. 1. See specifically Hearst's lengthy telegrams from California in the *New York American*, August 25, 1913, pp. 1–2; August 27, 1913, p. 1. For mass meetings in which Hearst and Mitchel participated, see *ibid.*, October 21, 1913, p. 1; October 22, 1913, pp. 1, 3; October 27, 1913, p. 16. For the Mitchel victory, see *ibid.*, November 5, 1913, pp. 1, 3. For a more detailed discussion of the mayoral campaign of 1913, see also Edwin R. Lewinson, *John Purroy Mitchel: The Boy Mayor of New York* (New York: Astra, 1965), pp. 51–53, 59, 61, 82–87, 89–103ff; Littlefield, *Hearst: His Role in American Progressivism*, pp. 310–15.

11. See the *New York American*, April 13, 1913, p. 7L, for a typical listing of Hearst newspaper campaigns in which Hearst editors bragged about winning

progressive victories. Concerning the Wilson administration's enactment of the Underwood Tariff Act, see Link, *Wilson: The New Freedom*, pp. 177–97. For arguments against the measure, see Richard Lowitt, *George W. Norris: The Persistence of a Progressive, 1913–1933* (Urbana: University of Illinois Press, 1971), pp. 9–11. For arguments in behalf of reciprocity, see the crusade by the *New York American*, July 15, 1913, pp. 2, 16; July 17, 1913, p. 16; July 18, 1913, p. 4; July 20, 1913, p. 4L; July 21, 22, 24, 26, 28, 30, 1913, p. 4; July 27, 1913, p. 4L; see especially the Hearst editorial on December 8, 1913, p. 16; and also July 20, 1916, p. 18. Concerning the Federal Reserve Act, see Link, *Wilson: The New Freedom*, pp. 199–240; *New York American*, September 20, 1913, p. 10. Concerning Hearst's advocacy of trust legislation, see the *New York American*, January 19, 20, 23, 1914, p. 16; January 24, 1914, p. 14.

12. See Hearst editorial in the *New York American*, August 25, 1916, p. 16. Compare it to Roosevelt's thinking as stated in George E. Mowry, *The Era of Theodore Roosevelt and the Birth of Modern American, 1900–1912*, American Nation Series, eds. Henry Steele Commager and Richard B. Morris (New York: Harper & Row, 1958), pp. 143–45, 148.

13. Concerning the Panama Canal tolls controversy, see Link, *Wilson: The New Freedom*, pp. 304–5; Thomas A. Bailey, *A Diplomatic History of the American People* (New York: Appleton-Century-Crofts, 1958), pp. 548–51; Coletta, *Bryan*, 2: 157, 160, 242; Daniels, *The Wilson Era*, pp. 208–10. For a Hearst interview and editorials, see the *New York American*, February 13, 1914, p. 16; February 14, 1914, p. 14; March 29, 1914, p. 1L-II; April 5, 1914, p. 1L. The Hearst crusade on canal tolls was carried in all his newspapers. For a typical example of orchestrating the news through editorials, political cartoons, daily interviews, and mass meetings featuring prominent speakers, see *ibid.*, February 16, 1914, p. 16; February 17, 1914, p. 18; February 19, 20, 1914, p. 16; March 1, 1914, p. 1L; March 6, 1914, pp. 1–2; March 8, 1914, p. 2L; then to the end of March almost daily, then again with equal intensity in *ibid.*, April 1, 1914, pp. 1, 4, 18; April 4, 1914, p. 16; April 5, 1914, p. 4L; April 6–11, 1914, p. 1, and also on the last page (editorials and cartoons); April 13, 1914, pp. 3, 16; April 14, 1914, p. 18; April 19, 1914, p. 1L; then almost daily to May 12, 1914, p. 18. For Hearst's comment about Wilson as the "advance agent of adversity," see *ibid.*, June 14, 1914, p. 1L-II.

14. Link, *Wilson: The New Freedom*, pp. 347–49; Bailey, *A Diplomatic History of the American People*, pp. 554–56; Coletta, *Bryan*, 2: 147–48; Daniels, *The Wilson Era*, pp. 180–205ff.

15. For Hearst editorials, see the *New York American*, November 17, 1913, p. 16; January 27, 1914, p. 16; April 27, 1914, p. 18; January 16, 1915, p. 1L-II. See specifically Hearst editorials in *ibid.*, February 23, 1914, p. 18; April 15, 1914, p. 18; April 16, 1914, p. 18; June 11, 1914, pp. 1–2; May 3, 1916, p. 18. For the history of the U.S.-Mexican relationship, see Link, *Wilson: The New Freedom*, pp. 346–416ff; *Bryan*, 2: 147–81ff; Bailey, *A Diplomatic History of the American People*, pp. 554–59. For a different interpretation of Hearst's motives, see Nasaw, *The Chief*, p. 228.

16. *New York American,* January 4, 1913, p. 18; April 13, 1913, p. 7L; December 1, 1913, p. 16; April 15, 1914, p. 18; June 5, 1914, p. 18; December 7, 1914, p. 16. In reference to the Hearst newspapers as the "yellow peril," see *Selections from the Correspondence of Theodore Roosevelt and Henry Cabot Lodge* (New York: Scribner's, 1925), 2: 275; Bailey, *A Diplomatic History of the American People,* p. 524; Older, *Hearst,* pp. 352–53.

17. Winkler, *Hearst: A New Appraisal,* pp. 173–76; Older, *Hearst,* pp. 346–47; Nasaw, *The Chief,* pp. 233–34; Swanberg, *Citizen Hearst,* pp. 326, 368. For the publication listing of Hearst newspapers and magazines, see the *New York American,* May 10, 1914, p. 1L-II.

18. Nasaw, *The Chief,* pp. 233–35; Older, *Hearst,* p. 359; Gene Fernett, *American Film Studios: An Historical Encyclopedia* (Jefferson, N.C.: McFarland, 1988), pp. 47, 207–13; Donald Crafton, *Before Mickey: The Animated Film, 1898–1928* (Cambridge: MIT Press, 1982), pp. 178–82; Koenigsberg, *King News,* pp. 404–5.

19. See especially Louis Pizzitola, *Hearst Over Hollywood: Power, Passion, and Propaganda in the Movies* (New York: Columbia University Press, 2002), pp. 100–101. See also Raymond William Stedman, *The Serials: Suspense and Drama by Installment* (Norman: University of Oklahoma Press, 1971), pp. 11–18; Crafton, *Before Mickey,* pp. 178–82; Older, *Hearst,* p. 360; Nasaw, *The Chief,* pp. 235–36; Judith Anderson, comp., "Hearst Films by Date," p. 1, MS, San Simeon Library, San Simeon, California. Concerning the advertising of *The Perils of Pauline,* see the *New York American,* March 11, 1914, p. 10; March 15, 1914, p. CE6; March 29, 1915, CE3-5; then every Sunday from May 3 to June 28, September 6 to November 29, 1914, in the CE section. Then concerning advertising of *The Exploits of Elaine,* see *ibid.,* in the Sunday CE section, beginning on December 27, 1914, and then each Sunday from January to June 20, 1915.

20. See specifically W. R. Hearst to Mr. O'Reilly, October 7, 1914, "1903–1914 Editors," Box 1, William Randolph Hearst Correspondence, 1903–1951, Bancroft Library, University of California–Berkeley (hereafter cited as WRH papers). See also Hearst to O'Reilly, September 19, October 2 and 5, 1914, in *ibid.*

21. See specifically Hearst to Mr. Clark, May 9, 1915, "1915 Editors," Box 1, WRH papers. But for other correspondence that demonstrates Hearst's continual demand for excellence from his newspaper editors, see Hearst to Mr. Ranck, January 20, May 16, May 23, 1915; Hearst to Bradford Merrill, January 20, February 6, October 24, 1915; Hearst to Mr. Stanton, October 19, 1915; Hearst to Mr. Van Hamm, October 15, 1915, in *ibid.*; Hearst to Mr. Ranck, January 2, 1916, "1916 Editors," Box 1, *ibid.* For another set of instructions from Hearst "in 1912[?]," see Older, *Hearst,* pp. 356–58. For another assessment of Hearst's relationship with his employees, especially his executives, see Swanberg, *Citizen Hearst,* pp. 252–53, 352–53.

22. For circulation figures, see *New York American,* January 1, 1914, p. 1; then randomly February 25, 1914, p. 7; April 5, 1914, 1L; June 7, 1914, 1L; August 9, 1914, 3L; August 10, 1914, p. 1. Typical advertisement for the Sunday circulation of over 750,000, see *ibid.,* July 2, 5, 11, 21, 23, 26, 1913.

23. The author has outlined daily the *New York Morning Journal* and the *New York American* since Hearst entered the New York market in October 1895. See the editorial section during 1913 and 1914, which is the last page of each issue of the *New York American*, for editorials and accompanying political cartoons. For instance, concerning the advocacy of public utilities and government ownership and operation of communication and transportation, see same pronouncements at top of editorial page from February 1 to March 10, 1915.

24. This information is in the daily reading of the *New York American* during the years from 1910 to 1917. For an example of specifics, see the years 1913–1915 in *ibid*.

25. For Bud Fisher's *Mutt and Jeff*, see the *New York American* daily and thereafter in November 1913, and for McManus's "Bringing Up Father," see *ibid*., July 23, 1913, p. 7 and thereafter. For the World Series trips, see in *ibid*., almost daily from June 1911 to 1914. For an example of the contest announcing five hundred travel trip prizes, see *ibid*., February 14, 1914, p. 6CE. And an example of the promotion of *The Great Republic*, see April 14, 1914, p. 7, and thereafter.

26. See the *New York Sunday American*, March 2, 9, 16, 23, 30, 1913; Procter, *Hearst*, pp. 84–85, 88, 101.

27. For a detailed account of the actions of the major European combatants in World War I, see Tuchman, *Guns of August*, pp. 71–136.

28. See Hearst editorials in the *New York American*, August 22, 1914, p. 12; August 31, 1914, p. 14; September 3 and 4, 1914, p. 16.

29. See specifically the *New York American*, September 5, 1914, p. 5; September 6, 1914, p. L5; September 7, 1914, p. 14; September 10, 1914, p. 16. In *ibid*., also see daily editorials with accompanying political cartoons (on the last page) during September and early in October, 1914.

30. For information concerning parades, see specifically in *ibid*., September 21, 1914, pp. 1–2; September 22, 1914, p. 6; September 23, 1914, p. 4; September 25 and 26, 1914, p. 6; September 27, 1914, p. 4L; September 28, 1914, pp. 1, 4–5; *New York Times*, September 28, 1914, p. 4. See also Older, *Hearst*, pp. 369–70.

31. With rare exceptions from August 1914, to the U.S. entry into the conflict in April 1917, the *New York American* reported the events on the Eastern and Western fronts daily on pages 1 and 2 and often on page 3 of each edition. See also Tuchman, *The Guns of August*, p. 438.

32. Tuchman, *The Guns of August*, p. 333; Older, *Hearst*, p. 372. For an excellent study on American neutrality in 1914, see Ernest R. May, *The World War and American Isolation, 1914–1917* (Cambridge: Harvard University Press, 1959), pp. 3–21ff. For most of the year beginning in May 1915, after the sinking of the *Lusitania*, the daily editorial page heading of the *New York American* read, "Our First Duty Is To Maintain Peace; Our Next Duty Is To Prepare For War." Beginning on January 1, 1916, the daily editorial page heading of the *American* was the following quote by Washington: "To be prepared for war is one of the most effectual means of preserving peace. A free people ought not only to be armed, but disciplined: to which end a uniform and well digested plan is requisite."

33. Concerning Hearst's stance in regard to neutral rights, see Hearst editorials in the *New York American*, February 24, 1915, p. 16; June 6, 1915, p. 2L; July 12, 1915, p. 16. See also Older, *Hearst*, pp. 372–74; Winkler, *Hearst: A New Appraisal*, pp. 192–93. For a discussion of Anglo-American diplomacy during the fall of 1914 and early in 1915, see May, *The World War and American Isolationism*, pp. 25–71ff. For a brief, overall view, see Bailey, *A Diplomatic History of the American People*, pp. 567–71, 577–80.

34. See the Hearst editorial in the *New York American*, August 24, 1915, p. 18. See also May, *The World War and American Isolation*, pp. 145–55; Koenig, *Bryan*, pp. 532–49; Bailey, *A Diplomatic History of the American People*, pp. 564–67, 569–73.

35. See Hearst editorials in the *New York American*, September 20, 1915, pp. 1–2; September 28, 1915, pp. 1–2; October 17, 1915, p. 1L. As a typical example of support for Hearst's stance against war loans to the Allies, see the *New York American*, September 21, 1915, p. 2. See also May, *The World War and American Isolation*, pp. 44–49, 322–23; Bailey, *A Diplomatic History of the American People*, pp. 573–75.

36. For examples of his crusade for a League of Neutral Nations, see the *New York American*, August 9, 1915, p. 16; August 10–15, 1915, p. 3; also in *ibid.*, January 2, 1916, p. 7L; January 3–5, 1916, p. 4; Older, *Hearst*, pp. 374–76. For a typical criticism of Wilson, see the *New York American* editorial, February 26, 1916, p. 18; May 12, 1916, p. 20.

37. Swanberg, *Citizen Hearst*, p. 294. For a discussion of Hearst's actions regarding Germany and England, see also in *ibid.*, pp. 295–96, 298–303ff. See Older, *Hearst*, pp. 378–79, 385–86; Winkler, *Hearst: A New Appraisal*, pp. 192–200ff. For examples of Hearst's Anglophobe editorials, see the *New York American*, July 2, 1916, p. 1L; July 3, 1916, p. 16; July 9, 1916, p. 1L-II; August 28, 1916, p. 16. For typical examples of anti-Wilson editorials and cartoons, see *ibid.*, July 11, 1916, p. 22; July 14, 1916, p. 20; August 10, 1916, p. 16; August 20, 1916, p. 2L; August 28, 1916, p. 16 (reprint of editorial on September 15, 1915).

38. H. D. Wheeler, "At the Front with Willie Hearst," *Harper's Weekly*, October 9, 1915, pp. 340–42. For other negative references concerning Hearst, see *ibid.*, July 24, 1915, p. 73; September 11, 1915, p. 241; October 16, 1915, p. 362. As evidence of obvious pro-Allied comments, see *Harper's Weekly*, July 10, 1915, pp. 25–30; July 17, 1915, p. 49; July 24, 1915, pp. 73–74; July 31, 1915, p. 97; August 7, 1915, p. 121; September 25, 1915, p. 289; October 2, 1915, pp. 313, 323–25. For negative accounts of Hearst—and at times with questionable research—see Oliver Carlson and Ernest Sutherland Bates, *Hearst: Lord of San Simeon* (New York: Viking, 1936), p. 186.

39. Howard Hall, "Hearst: War-Maker," *Harper's Weekly*, October 30, 1915, pp. 436–37; Carlson and Bates, *Hearst: Lord of San Simeon*, pp. 183–85.

40. For the crusades for Bryan in 1896 and Cuba libre in 1897 and 1898, see Procter, *Hearst*, pp. 89–94, 96–97, 102–11, 115–30. For a typical anti-Japanese comment (without proof or foundation), see the article by Albert B. Fall, "600 Miles off West Coast of Mexico in Jap Hands," *New York American*, May 21,

1916, p. 5L-II. See also a criticism of Hearst and other detractors of Japan as "lunatics" by Dr. Stephen H. Wise, rabbi of the Free Synagogue in New York City in the *New York Times*, October 11, 1915, p. 3.

41. Terry Ramsaye, *A Million and One Nights: A History of the Motion Picture* (New York: Simon & Schuster, 1926), pp. 778–80; Michael T. Isenberg, *War on Film: The American Cinema and World War I, 1914–1941* (East Brunswick, N.J.: Associated University Presses, 1981), pp. 26, 151–52, 162, 177; Craig W. Campbell, *Reel America and World War I: A Comprehensive Filmography and History of Motion Pictures in the United States, 1914–1920* (Jefferson, N.C.: McFarland, 1985), pp. 50–52, 60, 63, 164; Fenrett, *American Film Studios*, pp. 263–64. For excellent accounts of the *Patria* story, see also Nasaw, *The Chief*, pp. 261–64; Swanberg, *Citizen Hearst*, pp. 296–97. In the *New York American*, almost daily in January and February 1917, usually on page 5, *Patria* is advertised. But not until May 12, 1917, p. 4 in *ibid.* is *Patria* again mentioned; then in *ibid.*, only on May 20, 1917, p. 8L-II; May 27, 1917, p. 4L-II.

42. For a brief, accurate story of the Huerta fall and the Carranza rise to power, together with the resulting chaos and revolution, see Bailey, *A Diplomatic History of the American People*, pp. 558–62. For reports on the Mexican revolutionaries, see the *New York American* (almost daily on the front pages, January 12, 1916, pp. 1, 16, to January 27, 1916, pp. 1, 4; then March 5, 1916, p. 10L, to June 26–30, 1916, pp. 1–2.

43. *New York American*, January 16, 1916, p. 1L-II; May 3, 1916, p. 18; June 28, 1916, p. 20; July 9, 1916, 5L. For other samples of Hearst's ideas on Mexico, see *ibid.*, May 8, 1916, p. 3; May 20, 1916, p. 1; May 21, 1916, p. 5L-II; June 19, 1916, p. 20; August 10, 1916, p. 16.

44. *New York Times*, December 24, 1915, p. 4; December 25, 1915, p. 3; January 11, 1916, p. 9; January 25, 1916, p. 4; July 11, 1916, p. 6; July 14, 1916, p. 5; July 18, 1916, p. 4; August 25, 1916, p. 10.

45. See Hearst editorials in the *New York American*, June 6, 1916, p. 2; June 7, 8, and 12, 1916, pp. 1–2. For a typical criticism of Wilson, see Winsor McCay's political cartoon in *ibid.*, July 14, 1916, p. 20; but also see Winkler, *Hearst: A New Appraisal*, pp. 195–97. Concerning Millicent's action and Hearst's political stance, see the *New York Times*, September 30, 1916, p. 5. For reports on the presidential election, see the *New York American*, November 8, 1916, pp. 1–2; November 9–10, 1916, p. 1. Concerning Hughes's snub of Governor Hiram Johnson, see Mowry, *The California Progressives*, pp. 243–73; Spencer C. Olin, *California's Prodigal Sons: Hiram Johnson and the Progressives, 1911–1917* (Berkeley: University of California Press, 1968), pp. 132–44; Richard Coke Lower, *A Bloc of One: The Political Career of Hiram W. Johnson* (Stanford: Stanford University Press, 1993), pp. 72–91ff.

46. *New York Times*, November 9, 1916, p. 8; January 27, 1917, p. 2; Swanberg, *Citizen Hearst*, pp. 300–301; Older, *Hearst*, pp. 385–87; Winkler, *Hearst: A New Appraisal*, p. 193; Carlson and Bates, *Hearst: Lord of San Simeon*, pp. 187–88.

47. Winkler, *Hearst: A New Appraisal*, p. 193; Bailey, *A Diplomatic History of the

American People, pp. 586–87; Swanberg, *Citizen Hearst*, p. 301. For a similar Hearst sentiment, see Edmond D. Coblentz, ed., *William Randolph Hearst: A Portrait in His Own Words* (New York: Simon & Schuster, 1952), pp. 83–84. See specifically the U.S. Congress, Senate, Judiciary Committee, Brewing and Liquor Interests and German and Bolshevik Propaganda, Report and Hearings, 66th Cong., 1st sess., 1919, Senate Doc. 62, Serial 7598, pp. 1606–16 (hereafter cited as Senate Judiciary Committee Hearings, 1919).

48. See Senate Judiciary Committee Hearings, 1919, pp. 1606–16; Swanberg, *Citizen Hearst*, pp. 301–3; Koenigsberg, *King News*, pp. 412–14; Carlson and Bates, *Hearst: Lord of San Simeon*, pp. 186–88; Bailey, *A Diplomatic History of the American People*, pp. 582–83. For an example of Hearst's reputation as pro-German, see Lewinson, *Mitchel*, p. 231.

49. For excellent coverage of U.S.-German diplomacy during this time period, see Barbara W. Tuchman, *The Zimmermann Telegram* (New York: Macmillan, 1958); Thomas J. Knock, *To End All Wars: Woodrow Wilson and the Quest for a New World Order* (New York: Oxford University Press, 1992), pp. 73–122ff. See also Bailey, *A Diplomatic History of the American People*, pp. 583–84, 590–94. For examples of increasing tension between Germany and the United States, see the front pages of the *New York American*, January 15 to April 7, 1917. For reference to the sinking of U.S. ships, see *ibid.*, March 19, 20, and 23, 1917, p. 1.

Chapter 3

1. *New York American*, January 3, 1916, p. 13; January 9, 1916, 1W; Procter, *Hearst*, pp. 136–37.

2. For some of the "America First" pronouncements, see the *New York American*, June 18, 1917, p. 16; June 25–26, 1917, p. 18. For the universal military service crusade, see petitions in *ibid.*, April 1–30, 1917. See also Hearst's editorials in *ibid.*, March 19, 1917, p. 18; April 28, 1917, p. 3; May 2, 1917, p. 18. For notices of recruitment booths, which were set up at *American* expense, see *ibid.*, April 1, 1917, p. 1L-II; then daily to April 17, 1917, pp. 1–2, 5, 18; then intermittently thereafter. See also how Marion Davies caused a "rush of recruits" in *ibid.*, November 22, 1917, p. 4. See also Older, *Hearst*, pp. 396–97. Concerning the enactment of the Selective Service Act, see Richard Lowitt, *George W. Norris: The Persistence of a Progressive, 1913–1933* (Urbana: University of Illinois Press, 1971), p. 78; *Congressional Record*, 65th Cong., 1st sess., pp. 1496, 1623.

3. Concerning the Johnson quote, see "dad to my daughter," July 8, 1918, in Robert E. Burke, ed., *The Diary Letters of Hiram Johnson, 1917–1945* (New York: Garland, 1983), 2: 2–3.

4. Concerning the criticism of the Espionage bill, see the Hearst editorials in the *New York American*, May 8, 1917, p. 18; May 28, 1917, p. 1. For petitions "For Free Speech" and articles condemning the Espionage bill, see *ibid.*, May 14, 15, 1917, and thereafter.

5. Hearst Jr. with Casserly, *The Hearsts: Father and Son*, pp. 236–37.

6. Telegrams to Mrs. Phoebe A. Hearst from W. R. Hearst, December 2, 3, and 8, 1915, in WRH Jr. Papers, 1913–1915. In regard to the naming of the second twin, David, biographers Swanberg, *Citizen Hearst*, p. 299; Nasaw, *The Chief*, p. 252; and Robinson, *The Hearsts*, p. 354, differ with the telegram to Mrs. P. A. Hearst from Will, December 8, 1915, in WRH Jr. Papers, 1913–1915, as well as a family picture in the *San Francisco Examiner*, April 14, 1919, p. 3. These biographers state that David was originally named Elbert Willson, not Wil[l]son Whitmire.

7. For evaluations of the Hearst character and mystique, see Procter, *Hearst*, pp. 60–72ff, 112, 125, 151, 165, 179–80, 194–95, 212–13, 230–33; Swanberg, *Citizen Hearst*, pp. 173–82ff; 304–5.

8. Swanberg, *Citizen Hearst*, pp. 304–5; Nasaw, *The Chief*, p. 253; Fred Lawrence Guiles, *Marion Davies: A Biography* (New York: McGraw-Hill, 1972), p. 45; Procter, *Hearst*, p. 194.

9. For an excellent discourse on Broadway life in 1915–1917, see Nasaw, *The Chief*, p. 253; Lewis Erenberg, *Steppin' Out: New York Nightlife and the Transformation of American Culture, 1890–1930* (Chicago: University of Chicago Press, 1981), pp. 215, 219.

10. Guiles, *Marion Davies*, p. 44; Swanberg, *Citizen Hearst*, p. 305; Nasaw, *The Chief*, p. 255. In Marion Davies, *The Times We Had: Life with William Randolph Hearst*, eds. Pamela Peau and Kenneth S. Marx (New York: Ballantine, 1975), p. 131 n, the editors state that Davies was five feet, four inches tall and weighed 120 pounds.

11. Davies, *The Times We Had*, pp. 1–4, 10. In *ibid.*, p. 1, Davies stated that she was born in 1905. At times she also listed 1900 as her birth date.

12. *Ibid.*, pp. 7–8, 9–10, 21–24; Nasaw, *The Chief*, pp. 255–58ff. The first photo of Davies appeared with other chorus girls in the Sunday section of the *New York American*, November 10, 1915, p. 9-M, titled "DRAMA" by Wesley Hamer and Victor Watson. See also photo with accompanying write-up in *ibid.*, February 7, 1916, p. 11. Concerning the *Ziegfeld Follies*, see *ibid.*, May 21, 1916, p. 6-M; June 11, 1916, p. 4-M; June 13, 1916, p. 9; June 18, 1916, p. 4-M; August 27, 1916, p. 4-M. For a notice of Davies in a new play titled *Betty*, see *ibid.*, November 19, 1916, p. 7-M.

13. Hearst Jr., *The Hearsts: Father and Son*, pp. 236–37; Nasaw, *The Chief*, pp. 252–53; Procter, *Hearst*, pp. 194–95.

14. Davies, *The Times We Had*, pp. 11, 13, 17–21; Guiles, *Davies*, pp. 44–49ff, 53–54; Swanberg, *Citizen Hearst*, pp. 305–6; Mrs. Flint interviews, January 18, February 20, 1960, Swanberg Collection. See also Nasaw, *The Chief*, pp. 254–55, especially concerning Hearst attending the *Follies* with friend and fellow publisher Paul Bloch.

15. C. J. "Joe" Hubbell interview, November 1, 1959; Princess Pignatelli interview, November, 1959; Louella Parsons interview, November 2, 1959, Swanberg Collection; Winkler, *Hearst: A New Appraisal*, p. 183.

16. Hubbell interview, November 1, 1959; Princess Pignatelli interview, November, 1959; Parsons interview, November 2, 1959, Swanberg Collection.

17. Hubbell interview, November 1, 1959; William Randolph Hearst Jr. interview, April 27, 1959, Swanberg Collection; Winkler, *Hearst: A New Appraisal*, p. 183. See the *Romance of the Rancho* film in the motion picture archives at the Hearst Castle, San Simeon, California.

18. While the *New York American* described the actions of the candidates jockeying for mayor during the summer of 1917, the *New York Times* often tracked Hearst's efforts. For his rapport with Tammany Hall, see *ibid.*, May 20, 1917, pt. 1, p. 10; June 30, 1917, p. 20; July 31, 1917, p. 24; August 19, 1917, p. 1; August 24, 1917, p. 4. Concerning organizations endorsing Hearst, see *ibid.*, August 4, 1917, p. 4; August 14, 1917, p. 3; August 27, 1917, p. 5; August 29, 1917, p. 20. And for the gathering of petitions for Hearst, see *ibid.*, August 12, 1917, p. 2; August 30, 1917, p. 6. For a typical example of the criticism of the Mitchel administration, see a Hearst editorial in the *New York American*, June 23, 1917, p. 18.

19. Concerning "Big Tom" Foley, see Procter, *Hearst*, pp. 237–39; Henry F. Pringle, *Alfred E. Smith: A Critical Study* (New York: Macy-Masius, 1927), pp. 22–23; *New York Times*, August 25, 1917, p. 16. For more dissention among Tammany leaders, see *ibid.*, August 26, 1917, sec. 1, p. 26. And for a first mention implying that Hearst was unpatriotic and pro-German, see *ibid.*, August 26, 1917, pt. 2, p. 2; August 27, 1917, p. 5.

20. *New York Times*, September 1, 1917, pp. 1, 16. For Hearst's first association with Hylan, see Older, *Hearst*, pp. 389–90.

21. *New York Times*, October 2, 1917, p. 1; *New York Tribune*, October 2, 1917, p. 1; Lewinson, *Mitchel*, pp. 230–32. The most scathing attacks on Hearst and his alleged anti-American activities appeared in a three-part series in the Sunday *New York Tribune*, September 16, 23, and 30, 1917, pt. 1, p. 1.

22. *New York Times*, October 3, 1917, pp. 1, 7; October 4, 1917, pp. 1, 4; *New York Tribune*, October 3, 1917, p. 1; October 4, 1917, pp. 1, 8; October 5–6, 1917, p. 1.

23. *New York American*, October 5, 1917, pp. 1–2, 4; October 6, 1917, pp. 1–2. See also the *New York Times*, October 5, 1917, pp. 1–2; *New York Tribune*, October 5, 1917, p. 1.

24. The *New York Tribune* was especially abusive and negative in its coverage of Hearst from the latter part of September to election day on November 6, 1917. See specifically in *ibid.*, October 7, 14, 21, 1917, p. 1, the editorials by Samuel Hopkins Adams titled "Who's Who Against America." See also in *ibid.*, October 10, 1917, p. 8, where Hearst answered "malicious and slanderous attacks." Hearst was equally vicious in this campaign. For example, see in *New York American*, October 12, 1917, two anti-Mitchel articles on p. 5, an editorial together with a cartoon by McCay on p. 20. Then see daily thereafter to election day in *ibid.*, the full force of the anti-Mitchel crusade, culminating on November 5, 1917, pp. 1, 2, 4, 6, 11, and 20; and November 6, 1917, pp. 1, 4, 6, and 22.

25. Pringle, *Smith*, p. 23; Swanberg, *Citizen Hearst*, p. 308. For Hylan's explanation of refusing interviews to rival presses, see the *New York Times*, October 4, 1917, p. 4.

26. Norman Hapgood and Henry Moskowitz, *Up From the City Streets: Alfred E. Smith* (New York: Harcourt, Brace, 1927), p. 145; Pringle, *Smith*, pp. 35–39. For typical examples of articles, cartoons, and editorials vilifying Hearst, see the *New York Tribune*, November 2, 3, 6, 1917.

27. For examples of Mitchel asking why Hearst was backing Hylan, see the *New York Times*, October 16, 1917, pp. 1, 3; October 28, 1917, pt. 1, p. 4. For the Hearst counterattack during the last week of the campaign, see the *New York American*, October 28, 1917, p. 7L; then Hearst editorials on October 30–31, 1917, p. 4; November 1, 1917, p. 5; November 2, 1917, p. 6; November 4, 1917, pp. 8L, 4L-II. And finally see Nathan Straus's letter to Judge Hylan in *ibid.*, November 6, 1917, p. 6. For the headline of Hylan's victory and his telegram of thanks to Hearst, see *ibid.*, November 7, 1917, p. 1. For a study of the campaign and its issues, see Lewinson, *Mitchel*, pp. 227–47. Hylan eventually won by 150,000 votes—297,000 to 147,000.

28. For purchase of *Puck*, see the *New York Times*, July 14, 1917, p. 14; and the *Boston Advertiser*, see *ibid.*, November 20, 1917, p. 9. For notice of dailies costing two cents, see the *New York American*, January 25, 28, 1918, p. 1. For the first advertisement of the Gravure Section Supreme, see *ibid.*, January 9, 1918, p. 10, then February 24, 1918, p. 6L-III; March 3, 1918, p. 1L. Concerning the defense of Hearst and his newspapers, see *ibid.*, November 22, 1917, p. 6 (full page of testimonials); December 17, 1917, p. 20. For typical examples of the Hearst news media defending the Wilson administration, see *ibid.*, November 17, 1917, p. 20; February 12, 13, 1918, p. 1; April 8, 1918, p. 20; April 23, 1918, p. 24. For the first mention of rebuilding six French cities, see *ibid.*, December 25, 1917, p. 3. Then see the follow-up crusade on December 30, 1917, p. 5L; January 8, 1918, p. 3; January 10, 12, 1918, p. 5; January 13, 1918, p. 3L-II; January 17, 22, 28, 29, 1918, p. 5; January 20, 1918, p. 5L-II; January 21, 1918, p. 6; January 23, 1918, p. 4; January 26, 1918, p. 18; then on February 18, 19, 20, and 22, 1918, p. 4, to March 24, 1918, p. 3L-II.

29. Concerning Hearst's activities for city patronage, see the *New York Times*, December 9, 1917, p. 16; December 21, 1917, p. 20; December 27, 1917, p. 11. For the selection of Mrs. Hearst, see *ibid.*, January 8, 1918, p. 15; *New York American*, January 13, 1918, p. 1L-II.

30. For Mrs. Hearst's appointments and first days in office, see the *New York Times*, January 8, 1918, p. 15; *New York American*, January 12, 1918, pp. 4–5; January 13, 1918, p. 1L-II; January 16, 1918, p. 4. Concerning the New York coal shortage, see *ibid.*, January 15, 1918, p. 4; January 17, 1918, pp. 1–3; January 18, 1918, pp. 1–2; January 19, 1918, pp. 1, 5; January 20, 1918, p. 1L; January 21, 1918, p. 1; January 22, 1918, p. 11; January 27, 1918, p. 8L; January 30, 1918, p. 1; February 2, 1918, p. 4; *New York Times*, January 27, 1918, pt. 1, p. 10. For information concerning membership on Women's National Defense Commission, see *ibid.*, January 30, 1918, p. 9; *New York American*, February 3, 1918, p. 4L-II; February 17, 1918, p. 5L. For information about Camp Upton, see *ibid.*, February 4, 1918, p. 4; February 5, 1918, p. 6; February 9, 1918, p. 18; February 21, 1918,

p. 11; February 23, 1918, pp. 4–5, 22. For items urging men to enlist, see *ibid.*, March 21, 1918, p. 3; *New York Times*, March 21, 1918, p. 15. For information concerning "victory garden," see the *New York American*, April 14, 1918, p. 8L. For Mrs. Hearst's support of Red Cross drives and Liberty Bonds, see *ibid.*, April 24, 1918, p. 7; May 21, 1918, p. 8; *New York Times*, April 19, 1918, p. 15. For first mention of canteens for servicemen, see *New York American*, April 28, 1918.

31. *New York Times*, February 20, 1918, p. 9; February 23, 1918, p. 13; February 24, 1918, pt. 1, p. 6; March 1, 1918, p. 20. For Hearst's speech to the educators at their Florida convention, see the *New York American*, February 26, 1918, p. 20. From February 23 to March 18, 1918, Hearst occupies space in the New York papers almost daily. For instance, see Hearst editorials in the *American*, March 1, 1918, p. 20; March 4–5, 1918, p. 18; March 7–8, 1918, p. 20; March 9, 1918, p. 18. See also the *New York Times*, February 25, 1918, p. 18; February 26, 1918, p. 3; February 28, 1918, p. 13; March 4, 1918, p. 9; March 5, 1918, p. 1; March 6, 1918, p. 8; March 9, 1918, p. 13; March 10, 1918, pt. 1, p. 11. For a prediction that Hearst will run for governor, see *ibid.*, March 17, 1918, pt. 1, p. 1; March 18, 1918, p. 12. Concerning Hearst and Hylan at Palm Beach, see Winkler, *Hearst: A New Appraisal*, pp. 211–12. See also Older, *Hearst*, pp. 389–90.

32. See the five Macgowan articles in the *New York Tribune*, April 28, May 5, 12, 19, 26, 1918, pt. 3, p. 1. Then see five additional essays on June 2, 9, 16, 23, 30, 1918, pt. 3, p. 1. For specific charges and smears against Hearst, see *ibid.*, May 8, 1918, p. 10; June 20, 22, 27, 1918, p. 8; June 29, 1918, p. 10. But see numerous articles daily about Hearst and his newspaper policies from April–July 1918, in *ibid*. Most typical is a full page in *ibid.*, June 19, 1918, p. 16. For the targeting of Hearst, see Richard Kluger, *The Paper: The life and Death of the New York Herald Tribune* (New York: Knopf, 1986), pp. 193–94. See also the *New York Times*, June 1, 1918, p. 20; June 12, 1918, p. 6; June 16, 1918, p. 14; Winkler, *Hearst: A New Appraisal*, pp. 204–5; Older, *Hearst*, pp. 408–9.

33. For the examples duly noted, see the *New York Times*, June 1, 1918, p. 20; June 4, 1918, p. 4; July 3, 1918, p. 6; *New York Tribune*, June 1, 1918, p. 16; June 19, 1918, p. 16; June 24, 1918, p. 14. During June, July, and August, both newspapers list hundreds of incidents in protest of the Hearst publications. In regard to the canteen protest concerning Mrs. Hearst, see the *New York Times*, June 14–15, 1918, p. 11; *New York American*, June 16, 1918, p. 10L; June 19, 1918, p. 22.

34. For date concerning circulation losses, see the *New York American*, September 1, 1918, p. 1; see also in *ibid*. the masthead of the editorial page during the war months in 1917–1918. See the *New York Times*, May 17, 1918, p. 6; June 1, 1918, p. 8. Concerning *The Katzenjammer Kids*, see the *New York Tribune*, June 24, 1918, p. 8. Finally on Sunday, June 13, 1920, the *New York American* replaced *The Shenanigan Kids* with *The Katzenjammer Kids*. For information about Hearst's media empire, see the *New York Tribune*, May 12, 1918, pt. 3, titled "HIS TONGUES." For some similar data on reactions to Hearst, see Winkler, *Hearst: A New Appraisal*, p. 205.

35. Older, *Hearst*, pp. 401–2.

36. *New York Times*, June 28, 1918, p. 7. For the Hearst invitation to the Democratic leadership for the July 4 celebration in New York City and its results, see *ibid.*, June 29, 1918, p. 6; July 1, 1918, p. 6; July 5, 1918, pp. 4, 6; *New York American*, July 5, 1913, p. 13. For Brisbane's statement in the *Washington Times*, see the *New York Times*, July 2, 1918, p. 7. For the report on room reservations at Saratoga, see *ibid.*, July 16, 1918, p. 8. For petitions and testimonies urging Hearst's candidacy, see *ibid.*, July 9, 1918, pp. 1, 9; July 21, 1918, p. 10; *New York American*, June 8, 1918, pp. 4, 18; June 11, 13, 1918, p. 11; July 9, 1918, p. 11; July 10, 1918, p. 18; July 13, 1918, p. 16; July 14, 1918, p. 7L; July 21, 1918, p. 12. For Tammany intrigue, see the *New York Times*, July 15, 1918, p. 18; July 22, 1918, p. 11. And for samples of Hearst's progressive record, see editorials by Hearst or his editors in the *New York American*, June 26, 1918, p. 11; June 27, 1918, p. 22; July 2–3, 1918, p. 11; July 2, 1918, p. 20; August 1, 2, 6, 8, 1918, p. 18; August 10, 1918, p. 16.

37. *New York Times*, April 1, 1918, p. 8; July 6, 1918, p. 18; July 14, 1918, p. 16; July 15, 1918, p. 18; July 17, 1918, p. 6; *New York American*, July 24, 1918, p. 5. For "political typhoid carrier" comment, see the *New York Times*, July 10, 1918, p. 12. For data concerning the Democratic convention, Hearst's withdrawal, and Al Smith's nomination, see *ibid.*, July 23, 1918, p. 6; July 24–25, 1918, p. 1; *New York American*, July 25, 1918, p. 1. For Hearst's endorsement of Smith, see *ibid.*, August 6, 1918, p. 20; *New York Times*, August 6, 1918, p. 24. See also Matthew Josephson and Hannah Josephson, *Al Smith: Hero of the Cities* (Boston: Houghton Mifflin, 1969), pp. 188–91; Pringle, *Smith*, p. 23; Oscar Handlin, *Al Smith and His America* (Boston: Little, Brown, 1958), pp. 70–72.

38. For this two-week assault on Hearst, see the *New York Times*, August 5, 1918, p. 6; August 7, 1918, p. 7; August 10–11, 1918, p. 6; August 12, 1918, pp. 1, 16; August 14, 1918, p. 8; August 15, 1918, p. 7; August 17, 1918, p. 14.

39. *New York American*, August 12, 1918, pp. 1, 10; August 13, 1918, pp. 1–2.

40. For the Hearst attack on Lewis, see the *New York American*, August 8, 1918, p. 6; August 13, 1918, pp. 1–2; August 14, 1918, p. 9; August 15–16, 1918, p. 16; September 5, 1918, p. 18. See Opper, "The Lewis Cabaret" in *ibid.*, August 8, 13, 1918, p. 6; August 19, 1918, p. 7. For McCay, see *ibid.*, August 14, 1918, p. 16; September 5, 1918, p. 18. For opposition news coverage, see the *New York Times*, August 10, 13, 1918, p. 6; August 11, 1918, p. 10; August 12, 1918, pp. 1, 16; August 14, 1918, p. 8; August 15, 1918, p. 7. The *New York Tribune* coverage of Hearst is by far the most vicious.

41. As an example of the lessening of the boycott against the Hearst papers, see the *New York Times*, September 13, 1918, p. 20. Regarding the campaign in behalf of Al Smith, see the *New York American* almost daily from September 16, 1918, p. 4, to November 5, 1918, p. 22. For Heroes Day activities, see *ibid.*, September 1, 1918, p. 1L-II. For promotion of the Fourth Liberty Loan drive, see *ibid.*, September 21, 1918, p. 14; September 27, 28, 1918, p. 18; then almost daily to October 1, 1918, p. 22. Then see specifically in *ibid.*, October 19, 1918, pp. 1, 22, 1918; October 20, 1918, p. 6L.

42. *New York American*, October 8, 1918, p. 6; then daily to November 10, 1918, pp. 6L, 3L-II.

43. *New York American*, September 1, 1918, p. 1L; November 4, 1918, p. 1.

44. For circulation growth of the Sunday *American*, see the *New York American*, November 13, 18–24, 25, 1918, p. 1; December 2, 17, 1918, p. 1. For the subcommittee reports concerning Hearst's correspondence to his editors in February and March 1917, see *ibid.*, December 10, 1918, pp. 1, 3; December 11, 1918, pp. 1, 3, 4; December 12, 1918; *New York Times*, December 7, 1918, pp. 1–2; December 10, 1918, pp. 1, 3; December 11, 1918, pp. 1, 3. For other committee reports as well as editorial comments by Hearst and staff members, see the *New York Times*, December 13, 1918, p. 16; December 14, 1918, pp. 1, 3; *New York American*, December 13, 1918, p. 11; December 14, 1918, p. 3; December 17, 1918, p. 7; December 18, 1918, p. 5; December 19, 1918, p. 4. In regard to the Bolo Pasha inquiry and Senator Reed's inquiry, see the *New York American*, December 20, 1918, pp. 1, 4–5; December 21, 1918, pp. 1, 5; December 22, 1918, pp. 6L-7L; January 10, 1919, p. 4; January 11, 1919, pp. 1, 4, 5; January 12, 1919, pp. 1L, 4L; January 13, 1919, pp. 5, 18.

45. For Hylan's appointment of Hearst as chairman of the New York City welcoming committee for troops, see the *New York World*, December 3, 1918, p. 5; December 5, 1918, p. 11; *New York American*, December 8, 1918, p. 5L. For opposition to Hearst, see the *New York Times*, December 7, 1918, p. 15; December 8, 1918, pt. 1, p. 10; December 11, 1918, p. 3; December 24, 1918, p. 18; January 14, 1919, p. 7; Older, *Hearst*, pp. 410–12; Swanberg, *Citizen Hearst*, pp. 317, 319–20. For continual negatives on Hearst, read articles in the *New York World*, December 8, 1918, p. 5; December 10, 1918, p. 1; December 13, 1918, p. 3; December 22, 1918, p. 7. Peruse the *New York Tribune* from December 4, 1918, p. 8, to December 24, 1919, p. 4, but especially see December 11, 1918, pp. 1–4, which runs an article again titled "COILED IN THE FLAG—HEARSSSST."

46. See the Baker telegram in the *New York American*, December 8, 1918, p. 5L; the open letter by McCay in *ibid.*, December 19, 1918, p. 4; Mayor Hylan's letter in *ibid.*, December 24, 1918, p. 5. For Hearst editorials and letters, see *ibid.*, December 13, 1918, p. 11; December 16, 1918, p. 18; December 22, 1918, p. 1L-II. For other editorials and articles in defense of the Hearst media empire, see *ibid.*, November 19, 1918, p. 18; November 16, 1918, p. 16; December 1, 1918, p. 7L; December 18, 1918, p. 5; December 29, 1918, p. 3L; December 30, 1918, p. 5; January 2, 1919, p. 11; January 6, 1919, p. 5; January 11, 1919, p. 4; January 12, 1919, pp. 1L, 5L. For the approval of the Welcoming Committee by the Board of Aldermen, see *ibid.*, January 22, 1919, p. 1.

47. Older, *Hearst*, pp. 411–12. The comparison between the *New York American* and the *New York Times*, which was Hearst's strongest city competitor, quickly becomes apparent. For example, the *Times* has eight columns per page to five or six in the *American*. The print is therefore much smaller both for headlines and stories. And with few political cartoons and photographs and color cartoons, the *Times* wanes in comparison.

48. After November 11, 1918, through May 1919, New York City is parade conscious. For example, see the *New York American*, November 12, 1918, p. 6. For information on canteens, see *ibid.*, November 9, 1918, p. 9. See entertainment for wounded veterans in *ibid.*, December 13, 1918, p. 11. See in *ibid.*, December 1, 1918, p. 1L, the greeting of soldiers, and December 2, 1918, pp. 1, 4, where state governors send greetings to the arriving troops. See also in *ibid.*, December 26, 1918, p. 7; and for free theater tickets to servicemen, see December 31, 1918, p. 8; January 2, 9, 1919, p. 2.

49. Concerning quote on Hearst, see Winkler, *Hearst: A New Appraisal*, p. 50. For the Hearst editorial on payment of soldiers, together with an accompanying petition, see the *New York American*, December 25, 1918, p. 6. The *American* printed this petition almost daily through April 1919, then intermittently until May 13, 1919, p. 2. See also endorsement of Hearst's six-months payment plan, by Al Smith as well as approval by other politicians in *ibid.*, January 22, 1919, p. 1. In regard to free chevrons, see *ibid.*, December 25, 1918, p. 8. The *American* also ran this chevron notice daily through April 1919. In regard to free ads for positions wanted by servicemen, see *ibid.*, December 26, 1918, p. 7, then almost daily through March 1919.

50. Concerning the first announcement of "The Soldiers' Friend," see the *New York American*, January 13, 1919, p. 6; then see the changing of its name in *ibid.*, January 16, 1919, p. 5. For the rest of 1919, Hearst continues to publicize almost daily his support of the "Soldiers' Service Bureau."

51. For veterans' praise of Hearst, see the *New York American*, January 14, 1919, p. 11; January 17, 1919, p. 3. See also Hearst editorial concerning "a sincere welcome" to veterans in *ibid.*, January 17, 1919, p. 20. See also the growth in advertising for January 1919 in the *San Francisco Examiner*, February 1, 1919, p. 1.

52. For Hearst's purchase of newspapers, see the *New York Times*, November 19, 1919, p. 17. Concerning Ray Long and Hearst magazines, see Winkler, *Hearst: A New Appraisal*, pp. 174–76. As to the formation of Cosmopolitan Productions, see the *New York American*, March 12, 1919, p. 6. For a more detailed discussion, see Pizzitola, *Hearst Over Hollywood*, pp. 174–78; Nasaw, *The Chief*, pp. 279–81.

53. For an excellent account of Phoebe Hearst's last months in New York and California as well as the close relationship with her son, see Robinson, *The Hearsts*, pp. 374–80.

54. Concerning memorials to Phoebe Apperson Hearst and her funeral, as well as her many contributions, see the *San Francisco Examiner*, April 14, 1919, pp. 1–4, 16; April 16, 1919, pp. 1, 6–7, 20; April 17, 1919, pp. 13–15, 17–18; April 20, 1919, p. 2; *New York American*, April 14, 1919, pp. 1, 5, 16; April 15, 1919, p. 5; Robinson, *The Hearsts*, pp. 162–67, 248–50, 268, 286–87, 297–301, 306–15, 318, 364–67.

55. *San Francisco Examiner*, April 18, 1919, pp. 1, 6; *New York American*, April 18, 1919, pp. 1, 4. See also Robinson, *The Hearsts*, pp. 381–83; Swanberg, *Citizen Hearst*, pp. 321–22; Nasaw, *The Chief*, p. 279.

Chapter 4

1. For this assessment of Hearst, see Procter, *Hearst: The Early Years, 1863–1910* as well as the first three chapters of this work. See also Creelman, "The Real Mr. Hearst," pp. 249–67ff; West, "Hearst: A Psychological Note," pp. 298–307ff; and Robert L. Duffus, "The Tragedy of Hearst," *World's Work*, May–October 1922, pp. 623–31.

2. Charles Stetson Wheeler before the U.S. Internal Revenue Bureau, First District of California, "In the Matter of the Estate of Phebe Hearst, Deceased: Re Estate Tax," pp. 1–54, Bancroft Library, University of California–Berkeley; *New York Times*, August 22, 1923, p. 6. Concerning federal estate taxes as well as Wyntoon, see Robinson, *The Hearsts*, pp. 380–83. See also Flint interview, February 20, 1960; Procter, *Hearst*, p. 1; Nasaw, *The Chief*, p. 279; Swanberg, *Citizen Hearst*, pp. 321–22. For an account about Wyntoon, see Sara Holmes Boutelle, *Julia Morgan: Architect* (New York: Abbeville, 1988), pp. 216–32.

3. Older, *Hearst*, pp. 527–28; Nasaw, *The Chief*, p. 287; Swanberg, *Citizen Hearst*, 271–72.

4. Boutelle, *Morgan*, pp. 39, 41–42, 44; Suzanne B. Riess, ed., "The Julia Morgan Architectural History Project," vol. 1, "The Work of Walter Steilberg and Julia Morgan," typed MSS, pp. 51–56, 193, Bancroft Library, University of California–Berkeley (hereafter cited as Riess, ed., "The Julia Morgan Project"); Swanberg, *Citizen Hearst*, pp. 307, 321.

5. Riess, ed., "The Julia Morgan Project," pp. 56–63ff; Boutelle, *Morgan*, pp. 44–46; Older, *Hearst*, p. 531.

6. Riess, ed., "The Julia Morgan Project," pp. 56–64ff; Boutelle, *Morgan*, pp. 176–79; Nasaw, *The Chief*, p. 288.

7. William Randolph Hearst to Julia Morgan, August 8, 11, October 25, [n.d.], December 6, 10, 15, 18, 21, 27, 28, 30, 31, 1919; Morgan to Hearst, October 19, December 5, 1919, MSS, Julia Morgan Collection, Kennedy Archives, California Polytechnic State University, San Luis Obispo, California; Riess, ed., "Julia Morgan Project," pp. 56–57; Boutelle, *Morgan*, pp. 176–77. See also Nasaw, *The Chief*, pp. 288–89.

8. Pizzitola, *Hearst Over Hollywood*, pp. 120–21; 187–94ff; Guiles, *Davies*, pp. 64, 80–85, 89–93. See also Swanberg, *Citizen Hearst*, pp. 323–24; Nasaw, *The Chief*, pp. 281–83, 303–5ff; Older, *Hearst*, p. 360.

9. Concerning the death of Millicent's mother, see *San Francisco Examiner*, September 15, 1919, p. 11. For critical comments by Hearst concerning Smith, especially as to appointments and personal associations, see the *New York Times*, May 10, 1919, p. 16; May 19, 1919, p. 14; *New York American*, May 10, 1919, p. 11; May 12, 1919, p. 3; May 20, 1919, p. 20. For examples of Frederick Opper's cartoons that continued throughout the summer and fall, see the *New York American*, July 16, 1919, p. 11; July 19, 1919, p. 9; July 24, 26, 30, 1919, p. 11; July 29, 1919, p. 13. For further discussion of the Hearst–Smith political controversy, see Pringle, *Smith*, pp. 25–26; Winkler, *Hearst: A New Appraisal*, p. 212; Swanberg, *Citizen Hearst*, pp. 327–28.

10. For daily editorial attacks on the Smith administration, together with caustic cartoons, see the *New York American* and *New York Evening Journal* during October 1919. For the Smith challenge, see the *New York American*, October 27, 1919, p. 6; *New York Times*, October 27, 1919, pp. 1, 3; Winkler, *Hearst: A New Appraisal*, pp. 212–13.

11. For Hearst's reply, see the *New York American*, October 28, 1919, p. 13; *New York Times*, October 28, 1919, pp. 1, 4.

12. See the *New York American*, October 29, 1919, p. 18.

13. Pringle, *Smith*, pp. 25–27; Winkler, *Hearst: A New Appraisal*, pp. 212–13; Swanberg, *Citizen Hearst*, pp. 327–29ff.

14. *New York American*, October 30, 1919, pp. 1, 4; *New York Times*, October 30, 1919, pp. 1, 3; Pringle, *Smith*, pp. 27–32; Winkler, *Hearst: A New Appraisal*, pp. 213–14. See Swanberg, *Citizen Hearst*, p. 331, who suggests that Hearst was on his way to becoming the great American enigma. To this author, Hearst clearly demonstrated his feelings and desires.

15. Winkler, *Hearst: A New Appraisal*, p. 214; *New York Times*, January 3, 1920, p. 4; March 6, 1920, pp. 1, 5; March 10, 1920, p. 17. For evidence of charges and countercharges by Smith and Hearst, see *ibid.*, March 7, 10, 1920, p. 17; *New York American*, January 3, 1920, p. 9; January 5, 1920, pp. 5, 7; January 8, 1920, pp. 2–3; March 8, 1920, p. 3. See typical examples of political cartoons denigrating Smith in the *New York American*, March 8, 1920, p. 18; March 10, 1920, p. 11. See also Pringle, *Smith*, pp. 20, 40.

16. *New York American*, November 5, 1919, p. 1; November 6, 1919, pp. 3, 18; November 7, 1919, p. 3; November 10, 1919, p. 16. See also Hearst editorials in *ibid.*, November 7, 1919, p. 20; December 16, 1919, p. 20; December 22, 1919, p. 16.

17. For the announcement of price increases for dailies and the Sunday newspaper, see *New York American*, July 1, 1919, p. 1, and continually thereafter. See specifically in *ibid.*, February 27, March 25, 1920, p. 1. Concerning high paper costs, see Hearst's letter to close friend Senator James A. Reed of Missouri in the *New York American*, May 2, 1920, 1L; *New York Times*, May 2, 1920, p. 15. For Hearst's purchase of a paper mill and forest lands, see the *New York Times*, May 8, 1920, p. 18. For negotiations of the *San Francisco Call*, see numerous letters and telegrams during May 1919, as well as Charles Francis Neylan to Hearst, May 19, 21, 29, 1919, in the Charles Francis Neylan Correspondence and Papers, Box 63, Series 5, Bancroft Library, University of California–Berkeley (hereafter cited as the Neylan Papers). In regard to Hearst and San Simeon, see Boutelle, *Morgan*, pp. 176–79; for examples of the voluminous correspondence between Hearst and Morgan, see Morgan Papers, December 1919 to March 1920. See specifically in *ibid.*, Hearst to Morgan, February 9, 1920.

18. Nasaw, *The Chief*, pp. 282–85ff; Pizzitola, *Hearst Over Hollywood*, pp. 201–3; Guiles, *Marion Davies*, pp. 99–100, 380–82; Jeanine Basinger, *Silent Stars* (New York: Alfred A. Knopf, 2000), pp. 318–20; Winkler, *Hearst: A New Appraisal*, p. 228. For the Hearst quote at the Hays banquet in New York City, see the *New York American*, March 17, 1922, p. 3. Hearst would not condone

slapstick comedy where Marion Davies was concerned. When a script called for her to be hit in the face with a custard pie, he forced a rewriting of the scene. See King Vidor, *A Tree Is a Tree* (Hollywood: Samuel French Trade, 1953), pp. 166–71.

19. For a succinct history of the Wilson participation in the Treaty of Versailles and the resulting ramifications, see Bailey, *A Diplomatic History of the American People*, pp. 596–613.

20. For arguments against the League of Nations and the Treaty of Versailles, see Hearst editorials in the *New York American*, January 31, 1919, p. 16; May 25, 1919, 1L-II; July 17, 1919, p. 20; August 2, 1919, p. 16; September 30, 1919, p. 22; November 9, 1919, L3; November 24, 1919, p. 24; December 17, 1919, p. 20; January 10, 1920, p. 16; January 15, 1920, p. 20; January 19, 1920, p. 20; January 26, 1920, p. 20; February 8, 1920, 1L-II; March 22, 1920, p. 18. *San Francisco Examiner*, February 19, 1919, p. 18. These editorials appeared in all the Hearst newspapers. For months at a time in 1919 the *New York American* would post the heading "America First" and on the editorial page Washington's statement concerning "No Entangling Alliances." For Hearst's point of view, see Older, *Hearst*, pp. 415–23ff.

21. See note 20 for references to Hearst editorials during 1919 and the first months of 1920. For typical references of praise to Hearst, see the *New York American*, November 21, 1919, pp. 2, 18; November 23, 1919, 3L; December 2, 1919, p. 3; January 16, 1920, p. 2; February 1, 1920, 2L; March 21, 1920, 2L. For the Hiram Johnson quote and his opposition to the League of Nations, see Burke, ed., *Hiram Johnson Diary Letters*, II, "Dad to my dear Jack," January 24, 1919, pp. 2–4; May 22, 1919. See also Older, *Hearst*, pp. 415, 423–26. For a listing of the Hearst newspapers in 1921, see the *New York American*, June 11, 1922 (no page listed); November 8, 1922, p. 9.

22. For a brief attempt at a Hearst boom for president, see the *New York Times*, March 12, 1920, p. 12; March 30, 1920, p. 17; and especially *The New York American*, March 14, 1920, L5-L6; April 18, 1920, 1L-II. For the push for Johnson, see stories and editorials in *ibid.*, April and May 1920, but specifically see June 1–13, 1920, for numerous Johnson stories just prior to and during the Republican Convention in Chicago. For evidence of Hearst's support for Johnson, see also the *New York Times*, April 24, 1920, p. 17; April 30, 1920, p. 2; *New York American*, April 25, 1920, 3L; May 14, 1920, pp. 1, 5; and also Burke, ed., *Diary Letters of Hiram Johnson*, "Dad to my dear Boys," February 12, 1920, p. 1; May 5, 1920, pp. 2–3. In Older, *Hearst*, p. 429, she states that Harding asked Hearst to invite Johnson to be the vice presidential nominee of the Republican Party. Johnson refused.

23. *New York Times*, June 26, 1920, p. 2; July 3, 1920, p. 1.

24. For the third party propaganda in support of the Hearst candidacy, see the *New York American*, July 3, 1920, pp. 1, 3; July 4, 1920, 5L; July 6, 1920, p. 3; July 10, 1920, pp. 1–2; July 11, 1920, 1L; July 12, 1920, p. 2; July 13, 1920, p. 1; July 14, 1920, pp. 1–2. See specifically Hearst interview in *ibid.*, July 8, 1920, p. 4.

See also the *New York Times*, July 1, 1920, p. 5; July 9, 1920, p. 3; July 10, 1920, p. 2; July 12. 1920, pp. 1, 8.

25. Typical of Hearst's criticism of Wilson and the Democratic Party, see the *New York American*, July 8, 1920, p. 4. See also Nicholas Murray Butler, *Across the Busy Years: Recollections and Reflections* (New York: Scribner's, 1940), 2: 327–28.

26. *New York American*, October 27, 1920, p. 1; October 31, 1920, 3L. See in *ibid*. from late in July to the end of October 1920, numerous cartoons by Opper and McCay denigrating Cox as well as editorials denouncing Wilson's League.

27. Concerning anti-Smith editorials and cartoons, see the *New York American* from late in July to October 25, 1920. Then see endorsements of Smith in two Hearst letters (dated October 23 and 25, 1920) in the *New York Times*, October 26, 1920, p. 3; October 28, 1920, p. 3. See further endorsements of Smith in the *New York American*, October 28, 1920, p. 16; October 31, 1920, 3L; November 1, 1920, p. 16.

28. *New York American*, November 4, 1920, p. 1; Winkler, *Hearst: A New Appraisal*, p. 214.

29. Guiles, *Davies*, pp. 58, 62–63, 68–69, 85–88, 92, 94–98ff.

30. Concerning the Hearst–Davies love affair and their plans, see Guiles, *Davies*, pp. 64, 68–69, 94, 102–3. For the increasing public recognition of Millicent, see, for example, the *New York American*, April 16, 1921, p. 8; April 23, 1921, pp. 7, 9; April 24, 1921, 9L; April 26, 28, 1921, p. 6; April 29, 1921, p. 3; June 12, 1921, 3L; June 16, 17, 1921, p. 6. And for mention of Millicent as a Democratic candidate for Congress, see the *New York Times*, July 3, 1921, p. 18. In regard to Millicent knowing about Marion and Hearst prior to his asking for a divorce, see Guiles, *Davies*, p. 103; Elsa Maxwell, *R.S.V.P.: Elsa Maxwell's Own Story* (Boston: Little, Brown, 1954), pp. 128–29; Swanberg, *Citizen Hearst*, p. 341. Pizzitola, *Hearst Over Hollywood*, pp. 126–27, 205–6, states that Millicent definitely knew about Marion in 1921, but suggests that she became aware of the relationship as early as 1918. In the Millicent Hearst interview, May 15, 1959, she stated, "W.R. was a great man. Those who thought otherwise just didn't know him."

31. Concerning the attempt to defeat Manning, see the *New York Times*, January 27, 1921, pp. 1, 3; Swanberg, *Citizen Hearst*, pp. 321, 337. For Hearst's editorial on Wilson and the suit against Houston in regard to foreign loans, see the *New York American*, February 7, 1921, p. 18; February 12, 1921, pp. 1–2; February 13, 1921, 1L-2L; February 14, 16, 22, 1921, p. 1; *New York Times*, February 12, 1921, p. 3; February 16, 1921, p. 2; February 22, 1921, p. 20. And concerning Hearst's ongoing dispute with Gompers, see the *New York Times*, March 21, 1921, p. 15; April 6, 1921, p. 3; June 24, 1921, p. 17. See Hearst editorial titled "Good Wages for Good Work" in the *New York American*, April 5, 1921. He is somewhat critical of unions.

32. Boutelle, *Morgan*, pp. 180, 187–88, 198, 213; Hearst to Morgan, January 2, 11, 1921; February 7, 8, 10, 11, 12, 18, 1921; March 2, 7, 16, 1921; April 2, 3, 7, 8, 10, 12, 19, 26, 1921, Morgan Papers. See specific references to Millicent's

wishes in Hearst to Morgan, December 19, 1920, and April 2, 1921, Morgan Papers; Boutelle, *Morgan*, p. 183.

33. Boutelle, *Morgan*, p. 198. For Hearst's mastery of detail, such as transporting water to San Simeon, see Hearst to Morgan, May 10, 1921, Morgan Papers. Concerning flowers and shrubs, see also Hearst to Morgan, December 4, 5, 9, 1921, Morgan Papers.

34. Boutelle, *Morgan*, pp. 188–90; Older, *Hearst*, pp. 536–37; Nasaw, *The Chief*, pp. 292–93.

35. For a more detailed discussion of Hearst's collecting tendencies and his storage problems, see Nasaw, *The Chief*, pp. 295–302. See also Older, *Hearst*, pp. 537–44ff; Hearst Jr., *The Hearsts*, pp. 74–76. And as evidence of continual purchases, see the *New York Times*, May 1, 1921, p. 20; May 14, 1921, p. 17; Hearst to Morgan, February 18, 1921, Morgan Papers; Boutelle, *Morgan*, p. 184.

36. Boutelle, *Morgan*, p. 184.

37. *New York Times*, May 18, 1921, p. 29; June 15, 1921, p. 26; June 24, 1921, p. 6.

38. For dates regarding the comings and goings of Hearst and Millicent, see Suzanne B. Riess, ed., *The Julia Morgan Architectural History Project* (Berkeley: Regents of the University of California, 1976), 2: 70, Bancroft Library, University of California–Berkeley; Hearst to Morgan, June 28, July 22, 25, August 18–21, 1921, Morgan Papers.

39. Guiles, *Davies*, pp. 104–5; Swanberg, *Citizen Hearst*, pp. 338–39. For the first showing of *Enchantment* in New York City, which would be at the Rivoli Theatre on October 30, see advertisement in the *New York American*, October 27, 1921, p. 8.

40. Hearst surely planned this trip ahead of time. See Hearst to Morgan, October 20, 1921, Morgan Papers. But in regard to the route taken by the Hearst party, accounts differ in regard to certain specifics. I am accepting, at least in part, the reminiscences of Gretl Urban as reported in Nasaw, *The Chief*, pp. 307–8. For instance, Swanberg, *Citizen Hearst*, pp. 338–39, and Guiles, *Davies*, pp. 104–5, state that the participants stopped in Baltimore, instead of New Orleans, for a shopping spree. At the same time, I am accepting Hearst's comments in an editorial of the *New York American*, October 18, 1921, p. 1, in which he details a different route from Texas to Mexico. Then in *ibid.*, November 13, 1921, 1L, 12L, he writes a lengthy editorial describing this trip. Concerning the question of Hearst properties in Mexico, see Gray Brechin, *Imperial San Francisco: Urban Power, Earthly Ruin* (Berkeley: University of California Press, 1999), pp. 217–21; Older, *Hearst*, pp. 434–35. And in regard to Millicent's attempt to curb newspaper publicity about Marion, Hearst would brook no interference in his business affairs. See specifically Hearst to Joseph Moore, October 21, 1921 (telegram); November 7, 1921 (telegram); November 12, 1921 (telegram), in Joseph Arthur Moore Papers, Manuscript Division, Library of Congress, Washington, D.C. See also Pizzitola, *Hearst Over Hollywood*, pp. 205–7.

41. All Hearst newspapers promoted the bonus bill. For evidence, see the *New York American*, almost daily in editorials, during April, May, and June, 1921.

But see specifically in *ibid.*, April 25, 1921, p. 24; April 27, 1921, p. 22; April 28, 1921, p. 1. For the advocacy of a national sales tax to pay for the veterans' bonus, see *ibid.*, June 22, 1921, p. 20; June 29, 1921, p. 18; July 6, 13, 1921, p. 20; July 15, 20, and 27, 1921, p. 18. For the Hearst proposal for Congress to visit Canada "at our cost," and also the trip that occurred, see *ibid.*, October 16, 1921, 3L; October 17, 1921, p. 3; October 19, 1921, p. 3; October 21, 1921, p. 1; October 23, 1921, 6L. For story of visit to Canada, see *ibid.*, November 28, 1921, pp. 1–2; December 3, 1921, pp. 1–2. For circulation numbers of the *Sunday New York American*, see *ibid.*

42. For the Hearst crusade to reelect Hylan, see daily the *New York American*, October 19, 1921, pp. 1–2 (Opper cartoon) to November 9, 1921, p. 1. See specifically the editorial titled "What You Women Ought Not to Forgive or Forget," in *ibid.*, November 5, 1921, p. 18. See also the *New York Times*, November 5, 1921, pp. 1, 3.

43. *New York American*, November 9, 1921, pp. 1–3; November 10, 1921, p. 1; *New York Times*, November 10, 1921, p. 6. Again see negative references to Hylan and Hearst in the *New York Times*, November 5, 1921, pp. 1, 3.

44. Concerning San Simeon, see Hearst to Morgan, October 1, 22, November 12, 26, December 2, 4, 9, 13, 15, 21, 1921, and especially December 24, 1921 (nineteen pages), in Morgan Papers; Older, *Hearst*, pp. 532–38ff; Boutelle, *Morgan*, pp. 184, 187–90. In regard to Cosmopolitan Productions, see Basinger, *Silent Stars*, pp. 317–20; Pizzitola, *Hearst Over Hollywood*, pp. 202–5ff. For a discussion of Hearst newspapers and magazines, see Winkler, *Hearst: A New Appraisal*, pp. 172–77. For the Hearsts' visit to the White House, see the *New York Times*, December 28, 1921, p. 7.

45. See telegram from Hearst to Hylan in the *New York American*, November 12, 1921, p. 1; and a Hearst editorial titled "Mr. Hearst on Winning Issues in Politics," in *ibid.*, December 2, 1921, p. 20.

46. Swanberg, *Citizen Hearst*, pp. 208–9; *New York Times*, January 15, 1922, pp. 14, 16; January 17, 1922, p. 4; January 30, 1922, p. 15; February 5, 1922, p. 5. In defense of his support of Harding, see Hearst editorial in the *New York American*, February 19, 1922, 1L, and two letters by Hearst dated February 19 and 20, 1922, in *ibid.*, February 26, 1922, 2L.

47. Concerning Seabury's activities, see the *New York Times*, January 26, 1922, p. 19; February 2, 1922, p. 6. For Tammany Hall's reactions, see *ibid.*, January 22, 1922, p. 19; January 30, 1922, p. 15; April 4, 1922, p. 21; April 7, 1922, p. 19. In regard to Tom Foley's opposition to Hearst, see *ibid.*, May 18, 1922, p. 1; Procter, *Hearst*, pp. 237–39. For a good summary of Hearst's relationship with Tammany Hall and the continuing hostility of Smith to Hearst, see Pringle, *Smith*, pp. 44–47.

48. For reports of the Hearst campaign's demise, see the *New York Times*, March 12, 1922, p. 26; April 4, 1922, p. 21; April 7, 1921, p. 19. Concerning O'Reilly's death and the effect on the Hearst campaign, see *ibid.*, February 2, 1922, p. 6; April 4, 1922, p. 21. Concerning Conners and his activities, see *ibid.*, April 30, 1922, p. 22; May 3, 1922, p. 4; May 13, 1922, p. 1; May 14, 1922, p. 4;

May 18, 1922, pp. 1, 4. For Hearst's reply to the editor of the *Brooklyn Eagle*, see *ibid.*, May 3, 1922, p. 4. See also Pringle, *Smith*, pp. 44–46.

49. *New York Times*, May 23, 1922, p. 19; Guiles, *Davies*, pp. 105–6; Swanberg, *Citizen Hearst*, p. 342.

50. Guiles, *Davies*, pp. 106–7. See also Nasaw, *The Chief*, pp. 328–29.

51. Guiles, *Davies*, p. 197; Nasaw, *The Chief*, p. 329. For mention of the luncheon with Lloyd George, see the *New York American*, June 2, 1922, p. 4; *New York Times*, June 2, 1922, p. 17. See also interviews of Hearst by London dailies as published in the *New York American*, June 2, 3, 1922, p. 1; June 11, 1922, 1L.

52. Guiles, *Davies*, pp. 108–10; Pizzitola, *Hearst Over Hollywood*, p. 191; Swanberg, *Citizen Hearst*, pp. 342–45; Nasaw, *The Chief*, pp. 329–30. For Hearst's return and plans, see the *New York Times*, June 15, 1922, p. 6; June 22, 1922, p. 19; June 27, 1922, p. 1. As further evidence of the expensive preparations for *When Knighthood Was in Flower*, see the *New York American*, August 13, 1922, 5L; September 3, 1922, 4M; September 14, 1922, p. 1. Concerning Marion and any connection with Hollywood scandals, Hearst specifically tried to protect her. For instance, the Hearst papers protected her in connection with the episode at sister Reine's cottage at Freeport late in June 1922, where Mrs. Oscar A. Hirsh shot and wounded her husband in the neck. Besides excluding Marion's name from early accounts, Hearst newspapers finalized her innocence in the affair in *ibid.*, July 27, 1922, p. 4; July 25, 1922, p. 5.

53. See Conners's statements in the *New York Times*, June 10, 1922, p. 2. See Hylan's comments in *ibid.*, June 8, 1922, p. 1; and in the *New York American*, June 11, 1922, 4L. Concerning women's opposition to Hearst, see the *New York Times*, June 2, 1922, p. 20; June 11, 1922, p. 12; June 21, 1922, p. 19; June 28, 1922, p. 19; July 4, 1922, p. 6; July 10, 1922, p. 15. Concerning Murphy and Tammany Hall, see *ibid.*, June 30, 1922, p. 1; July 16, 1922, sec. 2, p. 1.

54. Pringle, *Smith*, pp. 46–47, 59, 251–52; Hapgood and Moskowitz, *Up from the City Streets*: Alfred E. Smith, p. 210. See also numerous occasions in the *New York Times* and the *New York American* during May, June, July, and early in August, 1922, concerning Smith's silence when asked by different Democratic factions to enter the gubernatorial race against Hearst.

55. Concerning the crescendo of pleas for Smith to run for governor and assume leadership, see almost daily in the *New York Times*, July 20 to August 15, 1922, usually on pages 1 or 19, but sometimes on 3 or 17. See Smith's announcement in *ibid.*, August 16, 1922, p. 1; *New York American*, August 16, 1922, p. 1.

56. See immediate response by Hearst campaign in the *New York Times*, August 17, 1922, pp. 1, 4. Ford wrote an open letter to Hearst in the *New York American*, August 6, 1922, 4L; and Hearst replied in *ibid.*, August 11, 1922, p. 3. See a second Ford letter in *ibid.*, September 3, 1922, 6L, and the *New York Times*, September 3, 1922, sec. 2, pp. 1, 4. See endorsement by Jackson in the *New York American*, September 26, 1922, p. 4; and Hylan's open letter in *ibid.*, September 18, 1922, pp. 1, 4.

57. Concerning the acquisition of upstate newspapers, see the *New York Times*, June 4, 1922, p. 7; September 12, 1922, p. 23; September 13, 1922, p. 31; September 23, 1922, p. 1. Concerning pressuring Murphy and Tammany Hall, see *ibid.*, August 22, 1922, p. 6; September 8, 1922, p. 17; September 24, 1922, p. 18; and especially September 26, 1922, p. 1. See also Hapgood and Moskowitz, *Up From the City Streets: Alfred E. Smith*, p. 144.

58. Pringle, *Smith*, pp. 48–55; Hapgood and Moskowitz, *Up From the City Streets*, pp. 210–12; Winkler, *Hearst: A New Appraisal*, p. 215; Swanberg, *Citizen Hearst*, p. 346.

59. For coverage of New York Democratic Convention at Syracuse, especially with a Hearst slant, see the *New York American*, September 24, 1922, 7L; September 25, 1922, pp. 1, 4; September 26, 1922, p. 4; September 27, 28, 1922, pp. 1–2; September 28, 1922, pp. 1, 4. See Hearst defeat and withdrawal statement in *ibid.*, September 30, 1922, p. 1; *New York Times*, September 30, 1922, p. 1.

60. *New York American*, September 30, 1922, p. 1; October 1, 1922, 1L; *New York Times*, October 1, 2, 1922, p. 1. For a record of full support for Smith, see the *New York American*, October 5 to November 7, 1922, pp. 1 or 2.

61. *New York Times*, October 2, 1922, p. 1; October 3, 1922, p. 1; November 8, 1922, p. 6.

Chapter 5

1. R. L. Duffus, "The Tragedy of Hearst," *World's Work*, October 1922, p. 626; Oswald Garrison Villare, *Prophets, True and False* (New York: Knopf, 1928), p. 302; Procter, *Hearst*, pp. 48–49, 59, 82–83. For a slightly different interpretation from that of the author, see Swanberg, *Citizen Hearst*, pp. 351–55.

2. For Hearst's "Policies of His Organization," see his interview of June 14, 1924, with *Editor and Publisher*, which was reprinted in the *New York American*, June 22, 1924, 2L-II. He will restate these sentiments on numerous occasions.

3. Concerning the revival of the Independence League, see the *New York Times*, January 8, 1923, p. 8. For the purchase of the two Baltimore papers, see *ibid.*, March 29, 1923, p. 1; March 8, 1923, p. 8; April 2, 1923, p. 2; April 6, 1923, p. 3; *San Francisco Examiner*, April 6, 1923, p. 5. For Hearst's favorable reception in Baltimore, see the *New York American*, April 7, 1923, p. 2; April 15, 1923, 8L; *San Francisco Examiner*, April 11, 1923, p. 8; April 15, 1923, 1N. Concerning Dever's mayoral campaign, see the *New York Times*, April 2, 1923, p. 12; *San Francisco Examiner*, April 4, 1923, p. 1.

4. For the court case that Murphy brought against Hertog, see crusade in *New York American*, April 11, 1923, p. 13; April 12, 1923, pp. 11, 12; April 14, 1923, pp. 1, 15; April 17, 1923, p. 1; April 18, 1923, pp. 1, 4; April 19, 1923, pp. 1, 6; April 20, 1923, pp. 1, 7; April 21, 1923, pp. 1, 2, 6; April 22, 1923, 1L, 5L; April 23, 1923, p. 1; April 24, 1923, pp. 1, 7; Nat Ferber, *I Found Out: A Confidential Chronicle of the Twenties* (New York: Dial, 1939), p. 117.

5. Ferber, *I Found Out*, pp. 116–19; Gene Fowler, *The Great Mouthpiece: A Life Story of William J. Fallon* (New York: Grosset & Dunlap, 1931), p. 326. See

"How Bucketeering Works," editorial in the *New York American*, August 11, 1923, p. 6.

6. Ferber, *I Found Out*, pp. 117–31ff; Fowler, *The Great Mouthpiece*, pp. 326–32. For the bucketshop crusade as well as the attacks on Foley and Tammany Hall, see almost daily the *New York American*, May 18, 1923, pp. 1–2, to August 24, 1923, p. 20; and August 25, 1923, p. 18. For especially interesting accounts, editorials, and cartoons, see also in *ibid.*, May 19, 1923, pp. 1, 3; May 20, 1923, pp. 1L, 10L, 14L; May 21–30, 1923, p. 1; June 5, 1923, pp. 1–2; June 8, 1923, p. 24; June 12, 1923, p. 1; June 13, 14, 1923, p. 22; June 15, 1923, p. 24; July 2, 1923, p. 1; July 6, 1923, p. 6; July 7, 1923, p. 20; July 12, 1923, p. 1; July 13, 1923, p. 24; July 17, 1923, p. 20 (anti-Smith); August 7, p. 1; August 11, 1923, p. 16; August 17, 1923, p. 1; August 23, 1923, pp. 6, 20. See also Foley's comments concerning Hearst in the *New York Times*, July 27, 1923, p. 28.

7. *San Francisco Examiner*, January 23, 30, 1923, p. 1; February 4, 1923, 3L; February 5, 1923, p. 1; February 9, 1923, p. 4; April 1, 1923, p. 1; *New York American*, April 16, 1923, p. 20. For Brisbane's comment on salaries, see *ibid*, January 5, 1923, p. 1; *San Francisco Examiner*, January 5, 1923, p. 1. As one example of high pay by Hearst, the *Examiner*, April 9, 1923, p. 3, registered the salary of columnist Cornelius Vanderbilt Jr. at $80,000 a year. See also Oswald Garrison Villard, *Some Newspapers and Newspaper-Men* (New York: Knopf, 1923), pp. 17–20; Swanberg, *Citizen Hearst*, p. 352.

8. For the growing conflict and unhappiness between Cosmopolitan Productions and Famous Players-Lasky, see Pizzitola, *Hearst Over Hollywood*, pp. 192–99ff; Nasaw, *The Chief*, pp. 313–14. For detailed information concerning Goldwyn-Cosmopolitan Distributing Company, see Pizzitola, *Hearst Over Hollywood*, pp. 208–9, 211. Concerning Hearst's speech at Atlantic City in May 1923, see the *San Francisco Examiner*, May 23, 1923, p. 9; Pizzitola, *Hearst Over Hollywood*, p. 213.

9. Jeanine Bassinger, *Silent Stars* (New York: Knopf, 2000), pp. 311–14, 318–21; Pizzitola, *Hearst Over Hollywood*, p. 209. See also Nasaw, *The Chief*, pp. 323–26.

10. Pizzitola, *Hearst Over Hollywood*, p. 208; *San Francisco Examiner*, February 25, 1923, 4E; May 22, 24, 1923, p. 13. Concerning the forty-four big films, see *ibid.*, July 27, 1923, p. 9.

11. *New York American*, July 29, 1923, 10L; August 1, 1923, pp. 8, 9, and 13; August 19, 1923, 10L. For daily promotion, see *ibid.*, during the latter part of July through August 1923. Concerning the costly refurbishing of the Cosmopolitan Theatre, see the *New York Times*, January 6, 1925, p. 5.

12. For one of many promotions, see the *Cosmopolitan* magazine advertisement for Adela Rogers St. John in the *San Francisco Examiner*, April 13, 1923. Louella Parsons began her syndicated column in the *New York American*, December 8, 1923, p. 14; see also Guiles, *Davies*, pp. 114–15. See Hearst's announcement for building three studios in New York in the *New York American*, October 30, 1923, p. 15. For *Variety* comment, see Pizzitola, *Hearst Over Hollywood*, p. 209.

13. Villard, *Prophets, True and False,* pp. 307–11ff; Swanberg, *Citizen Hearst,* pp. 363–67ff. Concerning the Clarendon renovations, see Nasaw, *The Chief,* p. 310. For real estate activities in New York City, see the *New York Times,* February 25, 1923, p. 16; July 15, 1923, sec. 8, p. 2; November 8, 1923, p. 32; February 6, 1924, p. 11; Pizzitola, *Hearst Over Hollywood,* p. 214; Swanberg, *Citizen Hearst,* p. 367.

14. Villard, *Prophets, True and False,* p. 310. Concerning a Palm Beach deal, see the *New York Times,* March 16, 1924, p. 21. For spending in July, see the *New York American,* July 1, 1923, 10L; *New York Times,* July 14, 1923, p. 3; July 15, 1923, p. 2. For the Kansas City purchase, see *New York Times,* April 7, 1923, p. 21.

15. Villard, *Prophets, True and False,* p. 311; Nasaw, *The Chief,* pp. 296–98. For a typical example of the Hearst mania for spending, see the *San Francisco Examiner,* March 22, 1923, p. 5, where one of his representatives bought three art objects at auction for $11,000.

16. Hearst to Morgan, April 28, 1922; Morgan to Hearst, April 6, 1922; May 9, 12, 1922; June 14, 1922; August 3, 1922; February 28, May 13, 1923, Morgan Papers; Boutelle, *Morgan,* pp. 188–93; 193, 213–14; Kastner, *Hearst Castle,* pp. 32, 37–38; 64–75. Victoria Kastner's manuscript is called "San Simeon: The Gardens and the Landscape" and will be published in 2008.

17. For monthly payments and money problems, see Hearst to Morgan, March 23, 1923; Morgan to Hearst, February 28, March 10, 1923, Morgan Papers. For examples of Hearst's involvement with Houses A, B, and C, see Hearst to Morgan, March 2, April 15, 18, 19, August 13, 17, 26, 30, October 1, 5, December 19, 1920; March 7, 16, April 1, 2, 3, 7, 8, 10, 12, May 10, June 7, 9, 12, August 19, 20, October 1, 2, December 4, 21, 24, 31, 1921; March 15, 27, July 22, 24, 30, September 24, 30, October 8, 9, 1922; Morgan to Hearst, May 7, 1920; April 2, 8, 1921, April 19, October 5, 1922, April 3, 1923, *ibid.* See also Kastner, *Hearst Castle,* pp. 34, 39, 43–44, 64, 67; Boutelle, *Morgan,* pp. 177, 179, 183–84; Nasaw, *The Chief,* pp. 290, 293, 294; Older, *Hearst,* pp. 532–34. For a description of San Simeon in August 1923, see Arthur Brisbane's column in the *San Francisco Examiner* and the *New York American,* August 15, 1923, p. 1.

18. *San Francisco Examiner,* August 1, 1923, p. 6; August 3, 1923, p. 14.

19. For the naming of the New York City ferryboat in honor of Hearst, see the *New York Times,* March 17, 1923, p. 26; March 18, 1923, L21. For the Hearsts' visit to the White House, see *ibid.,* December 2, 1923, pp. 1, 3. For Hearst's public support of Millicent's milk fund, see the *New York American,* February 21, 1923, p. 9; March 18, 1923, L7; April 13, 1923, p. 12; April 16, 1923, p. 13; April 17, 1923, p. 9; April 18, 1923, p. 7; April 19, 1923, p. 11; April 21, 1923, p. 13; April 22, 1923, p. 22; May 13, 1923, 8L. And for the *American* Christmas fund, see specifically in *ibid.,* December 19, 1923, p. 7; December 22, 1923, p. 6; December 25, 1923, pp. 10, 11, 15. Regarding the marriage of son George as well as a costume ball in New York, see *ibid.,* April 17, 1923, p. 11; April 27, 1923, p. 11; *San Francisco Examiner,* April 8, 1923, 8S; April 19, 1923, p. 14;

May 5, 1923, p. 11; May 24, 1924, p. 12. For mention of the Hearst's twentieth wedding anniversary, see the *New York Times,* April 29, 1923, sec. 1, pt. 2, p. 8. Concerning Millicent's trip to Europe and good press, see the *New York American,* September 16, 1923, 2L; November 5, 1923, p. 15; November 24, 1923, p. 7; November 27, 1923, p. 5; *New York Times,* September 12, 1923, p. 19. For other recognition concerning Millicent's civic affairs, see the *New York American,* February 21, 1923, p. 9; February 23, 1923, p. 1; June 16, 1923, pp. 1, 7. For a personal reminiscence, see Hearst Jr., *The Hearsts,* p. 240.

20. Guiles, *Davies,* pp. 64, 122; Hearst Jr., *The Hearsts,* p. 240.

21. Guiles, *Davies,* pp. 71, 106, 121–23, 128. Concerning Davies's filming in the winter and spring of 1923, see the *San Francisco Examiner,* January 10, 1923, p. 13; January 14, 1923, 4E; February 1, 1923, p. 14, to February 22, 1923, p. 17; May 23, 1923, p. 13; August 6, 1923, p. 10. For ads concerning the second run of *Little Old New York* at the Capitol theater, see the *New York American,* November 4, 1923, 2L, to November 28, 1923, p. 5. See also *ibid.,* December 26, 1923, p. 7. For the announcement of Millicent's trip to Europe, see *ibid.,* September 16, 1923, 2L; *New York Times,* September 12, 1923, p. 19.

22. *New York Times,* August 22, 1923, p. 6; October 26, 1923, p. 19.

23. For Murphy's attempt to placate, see the *New York Times,* August 26, 1923, p. 17; August 27, 1923, p. 10; October 2, 1923, p. 1. For Hearst's reply, see the *New York American,* October 8, 1923, p. 20. For the crusade against Tammany, see daily in *ibid.,* October 9 to November 6, 1923. But also see the coverage in this campaign by the *New York Times,* October 7, 10, 1923, p. 23; October 11, 1923, p. 1; October 17, 1923, p. 21; November 2, 1923, p. 19; November 4, 1923, sec. 2, p. 1.

24. "Dad to my dear boys," May 19, 1922, p. 5, in Burke, ed., *Hiram Johnson Diary.* Concerning the anonymous pamphlet, see the *New York Times,* November 3, 1923, p. 13. For Smith's speeches, see *ibid.,* November 4, 1923, p. 3, and sec. 2, p. 1; November 5, 1923, p. 3. Regarding Smith's disdain for Hearst, see chapter 4, endnotes 13–15.

25. For results of the election, see the *New York American,* November 7, 1923, p. 1; *New York Times,* November 7, 1923, p. 1. For Tammany's postelection reaction, see *ibid.,* November 7, 1923, p. 2; November 8, 1923, pp. 1, 4; November 16, 1923, p. 19; November 21, 1923, p. 23.

26. Concerning newspaper purchases, see the *New York Times,* April 4, 1924, p. 3; May 24, 1924, p. 5; Hearst to John Francis Neylan, July 15, 1924, MSS, William Randolph Hearst General Correspondence, 1924–1927, Folder 5, Bancroft Library, University of California–Berkeley (hereafter cited as WRH Gen. Corresp.). For Hearst's attempt to seek the Democratic nomination, see the *New York Times,* January 16, 1924, p. 2. For the Democratic National Convention and Hylan's reactions, see the *New York American,* January 16, 1924, pp. 1–2; January 17, 1924, pp. 1–4; January 19, 1924, pp. 2, 7. For action by the New York Independence League, see *ibid.,* February 1, 1924.

27. See "Dad to my dear boys," February 28, 1924, in Burke, ed., *Hiram Johnson Diary.* For Hearst's withdrawal as a candidate, see Hearst to Neylan, February 14,

1924, WRH Gen. Corresp. For his approval of McAdoo, see Hearst to McAdoo, May 1, 1924, *ibid.*; "Hearst in Capital Gives an Interview on Political Questions," *New York American*, March 27, 1924, pp. 1–2. See Hearst's support of Reed in *New York American*, February 6, 1924, p. 9; *New York Times*, February 18, 1924, p. 17. See also Pringle, *Smith*, pp. 326–27. For a brief description of McAdoo and Smith, see Arthur M. Schlesinger Jr., *The Age of Roosevelt*, vol. 1, *The Crisis of the Old Order, 1919–1933* (Boston: Houghton Mifflin, 1957), pp. 94–96.

28. Concerning Murphy's death, see the *New York American*, April 26, 1924, pp. 1, 6–8; April 27, 1924, pp. 1, 9. For the fight over Murphy's replacement, see *ibid.*, April 30, 1924, pp. 1–2; May 4, 1924, 1L; May 15, 1924, p. 1; *New York Times*, May 1, 1924, p. 2; May 5, 1924, pp. 1–2; May 6, 1924, p. 1; May 7, 1924, pp. 1, 5; May 15, 1924, p. 1. See also Pringle, *Smith*, pp. 304–5.

29. For evidence of the Hearst-Hylan and Smith rapprochement, see the *New York Times*, June 19, 1923, p. 1; June 20, 1924, pp. 3, 18. For a rejection of Hylan as a state delegate at large, see *ibid.*, May 1, 1924, p. 2. See also *ibid.*, May 11, 1924, p. 1. For Hearst editorials just prior to and during the Democratic National Convention, see *ibid.*, June 21, 1924, p. 7; *New York American*, June 21, 1924, p. 1; June 22, 1924, 1L, 2L-II; June 29, 1924, 1L; June 30, 1924, p. 30; July 1, 1924, p. 1; and July 8, 1924, p. 4.

30. *New York American*, June 20, 1924, p. 8; June 25, 1924, p. 10; *New York Times*, June 21, 1924, p. 3. Concerning the Hearst extravaganza at the Ritz-Carlton and an accompanying guest list, see *ibid.*, p. 9.

31. For a brief summary of the 1924 Democratic National Convention as well as an evaluation of Davis, see Schlesinger Jr., *The Crisis of the Old Order*, pp. 98–100. See also the *New York American*, July 10, 1924, pp. 1, 8. For coverage of the convention, see *ibid.* daily from June 26 to July 10, 1924. For a rumor that Hearst made an overture of support to Davis, see Swanberg, *Citizen Hearst*, p. 371.

32. For Hearst's trip to San Simeon, see the *New York Times*, July 12–13, 1924, p. 1; *New York American*, July 20, 1924, 14L; July 31, 1924, p. 2. Concerning the Fallon case, see Ferber, *I Found Out*, pp. 149–54, 214–31ff; Fowler, *The Great Mouthpiece*, pp. 372–87; *New York Times*, July 23, 1924, p. 17; July 29, 1924, p. 1; August 7–8, 1924, p. 1; August 9, 1924, p. 1. See also Swanberg, *Citizen Hearst*, pp. 368–72ff; Nasaw, *The Chief*, pp. 337–39; Carlson and Bates, *Lord of San Simeon*, pp. 211–12; Guiles, *Davies*, pp. 132–34, 136–37.

33. For the Fallon trial and verdict, see the *New York Times*, July 23, 1924, p. 17; July 29, 1924, p. 1; August 7–9, 1924, p. 1; Fowler, *The Great Mouthpiece*, pp. 384–87. Concerning Millicent and her three-month European tour, see the *New York American*, September 11, 1924, p. 8; November 17, 1924, p. 15; December 9, 1924, p. 13; December 16, 1924, p. 5; *New York Times*, December 16, 1924, p. 16. Concerning Victor Watson's exile, see Ferber, *I Found Out*, p. 229.

34. Ferber, *I Found Out*, pp. 229–31; Swanberg, *Citizen Hearst*, pp. 373–75; Guiles, *Davies*, pp. 135–37.

35. Guiles, *Davies*, p. 134; Nasaw, *The Chief*, p. 340.

36. Guiles, *Davies*, pp. 134–37.

37. Guiles, *Davies*, pp. 135–36; *New York American*, August 4, 1924, p. 6; August 6, 1924, p. 17; August 10, 1924, 8M; August 18, 1924, p. 4; September 4, 1924, p. 4. In *ibid.*, during September, Marion Davies and Cosmopolitan Productions received a tremendous amount of publicity. See also Nasaw, *The Chief*, pp. 340–41.

38. Pizzitola, *Hearst Over Hollywood*, pp. 216–17; Charles Higham, *Merchant of Dreams: Louis B. Mayer, MGM, and the Secret Hollywood* (New York: Fine, 1993), pp. 66–69.

39. Pizzitola, *Hearst Over Hollywood*, pp. 216–19ff; Higham, *Mayer*, p. 79; Nasaw, *The Chief*, pp. 341–42, 348–49. For the premiere of *Zander*, see the *Los Angeles Examiner*, April 16, 1925, sec. 2, p. 1; April 19, 1925, sec. 1, pp. 1, 9, 10; *New York American*, May 2, 1925, p. 2; May 3, 1925, 9M; May 4, 1925, p. 11.

40. For Hearst's real estate developments in New York, see the *New York American*, March 30, 1924, 18L; *New York Times*, April 12, 1924, p. 25; September 25, 1924, p. 36; November 9, 1924, sec. 11, p. 2. For purchase of newspapers, see *ibid.*, April 4, 1924, p. 3; May 24, 1924, p. 5. Concerning the buffalo sale for San Simeon, see *ibid.*, December 20, 1924, p. 27.

41. *New York Times*, April 25, 1924, p. 31; April 26, 1924, p. 26; April 30, 1924, p. 2; May 3, 1924, p. 24; May 6, 1924, p. 30; May 7, 1924, p. 31.

42. Hearst to all Hearst newspapers, July 10, 1924, WRH Gen. Corresp., Folder 6; *New York Times*, October 3, 1924, pp. 1–2; *New York American*, November 4, 1924, p. 24 (no political endorsements). For Hearst's editorials and reactions after the National Democratic Convention, see the *New York American*, July 20, 1924, 1L; July 26, 1924, p. 1; July 27, 1924, 1L; August 3, 1924, 1L. For typical editorials and political cartoons critical of Davis, see *ibid.*, September 24, 1924, p. 26; September 26, 1924, p. 24; September 30, 1924, p. 26; October 11, 1924, p. 22; October 13, 1924, p. 20; October 15, 1924, p. 26; November 3, 1924, p. 26. For anti-Smith editorials and cartoons, see *ibid.*, August 6, 1924, p. 26; August 9, 1924, p. 22; August 16, 1924, p. 18; August 20, 21, 1924, p. 22; August 25, 1924, p. 20; August 26, 1924, p. 22; August 28, 1924, p. 24; September 4, 1924, p. 24; October 6, 1924, p. 22; October 30, 1924, p. 28; November 1, 1924, p. 22. For Hearst editorial concerning the 1924 election, see *ibid.*, November 9, 1924, 1L.

43. For those in agreement concerning the Ince death, see Pizzitola, *Hearst Over Hollywood*, pp. 220–24; Nasaw, *The Chief*, pp. 344–45; Carlson and Bates, *Lord of San Simeon*, pp. 198–201.

44. Kastner, *Hearst Castle*, pp. 68–69, 72, 82–83, 101–3, 169–71; Boutelle, *Morgan*, pp. 200–202, 206.

45. Pizzitola, *Hearst Over Hollywood*, pp. 226–29ff; Higham, *Mayer*, p. 91; Bosley Crowther, *Hollywood Rajah: The Life and Times of Louis B. Mayer* (New York: Holt, 1960), pp. 122–25; "unless he was permitted," *Variety*, March 4, 1925.

46. For property acquisitions, see the *New York Times*, January 6, 1925, p. 5; January 7, 1925, p. 25; June 13, 1925, p. 25. For the sale of *Town and Country*, see

ibid., June 28, 1925, p. 20; and for the *Syracuse Journal*, see *ibid.*, November 4, 1925, p. 10; November 5, 1925, p. 15. For other acquisitions, see *ibid.*, November 7, 1925, p. 27; November 28, 1925, p. 25; December 4, 1925, p. 12. For the sale of the Fort Worth newspaper, see *ibid.*, October 26, 1925, p. 14.

47. Alice Head, *It Could Never Have Happened* (London: Heinemann, 1939), pp. 81, 85–86; Clive Aslet, *The Last Country Houses* (New Haven: Yale University Press, 1982) p. 199; *New York Times*, August 16, 1925, p. 1; September 16, 1925, p. 16.

48. *New York Times*, April 19, 24, 1925, p. 1. See Hearst editorial in the *New York American*, May 24, 1925, 1L. For Smith's and Tammany's reactions to the "Hearst threat," see the *New York Times*, April 25, 1925, p. 1; April 30, 1925, pp. 1, 4. Concerning this controversy, see editorial in *ibid.*, May 10, 1925, sec. 9, p. 1.

49. Pro-Hylan stories in the *New York American* appeared daily. For typical crusade headlines with accompanying stories or editorials, see *ibid.*, June 20, 1925, p. 2; June 30, 1925, p. 1; July 6, 1925, p. 18; July 20, 1925, p. 5; July 26, 1925, 1L; July 29, 1925, p. 20; August 1, 1925, p. 6; August 3, 1925, p. 16; August 5, 1925, p. 1.

50. Williams displayed his work on the editorial page, while Opper was usually on pages 2, 3, or 4. For an example of Opper's *Ten-Cent Troubadours*, see the *New York American*, August 17, 1925, p. 3.

51. *New York Times*, August 6, 1925, pp. 1–2; August 11, 1925, p. 1; Gene Fowler, *Beau James: The Life and Times of Jimmy Walker* (New York: Viking, 1949), pp. 136–46ff. For reports of the Democratic campaign, see the *New York Times*, August 14, 1925, p. 12; August 16, 1925, sec. 8, p. 5; August 19, p. 2; August 20, 1925, p. 2; August 26, 1925, p. 1; August 27, 1925, p. 18; August 28–29, 1925, pp. 1–2.

52. For comments by political pundits, see the *New York Times*, August 16, 1925, sec. 8, p. 5; August 20, 25, 1925, p. 2; August 26, 1925, p. 1; August 30, 1925, p. 3. Concerning Smith's criticism of Hearst, see September 3, 1925, p. 4; September 4, 1925, p. 1.

53. *New York American*, September 4, 1925, p. 1; *New York Times*, September 4, 1925, p. 18.

54. While the *New York American*, September 5–16, painted an optimistic picture of Hylan's strength on its front-page and editorial section, the *New York Times* presented an accurate account. See *ibid.*, September 5, 1925, p. 5; September 6, 1925, p. 1; September 8, 1925, p. 3; September 13, 1925, p. 3; September 15, 1925, p. 2; September 16, 1925, p. 24. For the Democratic primary election results, see *ibid.*, September 17, 1925, p. 1.

55. Concerning Hylan's retirement statement, see the *New York Times*, September 17, 1925, p. 1. See Hearst's editorial offering to support Hylan in the *New York American*, September 18, 1925, p. 1. Concerning the Progressive Party's offer to nominate Hylan, see *ibid.*, September 19, 1925, p. 1; September 20, 1925, 1L. For Hearst's renewed offer of support, see the *New York Times*, September 26, 1925, p. 3. For the endorsement of Walker by Hearst and Hylan, see *ibid.*, October 30, 1925, p. 1; October 31, 1925, p. 16. For scant coverage of

the mayor's race after the Democratic primary on September 16, observe the *New York American* to the end of October 1925.

56. See "Mr. Hearst Answers 7 Political Queries," which was published in the *New York Evening Post* and reprinted in the *New York American*, November 3, 1925, p. 2.

Chapter 6

1. Kevin Brownlow, *The Parade's Gone By* (New York: Knopf, 1969), pp. 30–35, 38–40; Kevin Starr, *Material Dreams: Southern California Through the 1920's* (New York: Oxford University Press, 1990), pp. 65, 67–68, 90–96ff. For the headline in the *Los Angeles Examiner*, see heading of editorial page in January 1925.

2. Brownlow, *The Parade's Gone By*, pp. 39, 170; Pizzitola, *Hearst Over Hollywood*, pp. 233–34; Davies, *The Times We Had*, pp. 46, 48.

3. Guiles, *Davies*, pp. 175–76; Davies, *The Times We Had*, pp. 139–42; Charles Chaplin, *My Autobiography* (New York: Simon and Schuster, 1964), pp. 309–10; Nasaw, *The Chief*, pp. 362–64; Jesse Lasky Jr., *Whatever Happened to Hollywood* (New York: McGraw-Hill, 1972), pp. 175–76.

4. Pizzitola, *Hearst Over Hollywood*, pp. 231–35; Charles Higham, *Merchant of Dreams: Louis B. Mayer, M.G.M., and the Secret Hollywood* (New York: Fine, 1993), pp. 72, 91, 122. For advertisement of movie star spoons in regard to Marion Davies, see the *New York American*, October 4, 1925, 8L, CE5; October 5, 1925, p. 6; October 8, 1925, p. 5; October 9, 1925, p. 15; October 10, 1925, p. 7.

5. Pizzitola, *Hearst Over Hollywood*, pp. 231–32; Davies, *The Times We Had*, p. 61; Chaplin, *My Autobiography*, p. 312; Donald L. Barlett and James B. Steele, *Empire: The Life, Legend, and Madness of Howard Hughes* (New York: Norton, 1979), p. 70; interviews of Colleen Moore, "The Jazz Age's Movie Flapper at San Simeon," by Gerald Reynolds, 1972, and Metta Hake and Tom Scott, January 25, 1977, p. 4, Oral History Project, Hearst San Simeon State Historical Monument, San Simeon, California (hereafter cited as San Simeon Oral History Project); interview of Colleen Moore by Gerald Reynolds, June 8, 1972, pp. 22–23, *ibid.*; interview of Joel McCrea by Metta Hake, December 5, 1982, p. 4, *ibid.*

6. Davies, *The Times We Had*, pp. 61–67ff; Kastner, *Hearst Castle*, pp. 68–71, 72, 74–76, 110–11, 119, 121, 127, 144–47; Moore interview, pp. 6, 8; interview of Alice Marble by Marie Nay, June 4, 1977, pp. 3–5, 17, San Simeon Oral History Project; interview of King Vidor by Rosie Wittig, 1975, *ibid.*; interview of Adela Rogers St. John by Jerry Reynolds, 1971, *ibid.*; interview of Patricia and Arthur Lake by Metta Hake, April 4, 1984, pp. 5, 11, 16, *ibid.*; interview of Charles Gates by Thelma Anderson, October 4, 1978, pp. 4, 7–9, 12, *ibid.* Chaplin, *My Autobiography*, pp. 312–13.

7. For the site plan of San Simeon, see Kastner, *The Hearst Castle*, pp. 134–35. Concerning the theater, see *ibid.*, pp. 126–28. For discussion of the Neptune and Roman pools, see *ibid.*, pp. 169–71, 172–79, 207. See also Marble interview, pp. 5–11, 17; interview of Edna and Gertrude Calkins by Tom

Scott, pp. 13, 15, 17, *ibid.*; McCrea interview, pp. 9, 67; Vidor interview; St. John interview; Patricia and Arthur Lake interview, pp. 10, 28, 31, 32; Gates interview, pp. 21–22, 25.

8. Moore interview, pp. 5, 24; Gates interview, p. 25; Edna and Getrude Calkins interview, pp. 1–2; Marble interview, pp. 3–4; McCrea interview, p. 4; interview of Norman Rotanzi by Tom Scott, *ibid.*

9. Interview of Vince DeBarry by Dave Hibbs, July 30, 1984, p. 3, *ibid.*; Moore interview, p. 12.

10. For a listing of the twenty-six Hearst newspapers, five of which were in California, see the *New York American*, July 7, 1926, p. 4. For the crusade for progressive causes in southern California, see the editorial page of the *Los Angeles Examiner* during April and May 1926, and specifically April 6, 1926, sec. 2, p. 20. During May 1926, in *ibid.* the demand for Boulder Dam appeared daily. In turn, during April and May, the *Examiner* published its increased circulation figures almost daily. For an example of Hearst's growing popularity in California, see article that "gives thanks to Brisbane" and lauds policies of Hearst in the *New York American*, February 17, 1926, p. 7.

11. For typical editorials and political cartoons favoring Mellon, see the *New York American*, February 1, 1926, p. 26; February 2, 19, 26, 1926, p. 28; *Los Angeles Examiner*, April 6, 1926, sec. 2, p. 20. Concerning Mellon, see Schlesinger Jr., *The Crisis of the Old Order*, pp. 61–63. For a Hearst editorial concerning the Volstead Act, see the *New York American*, February 7, 1926, 1L. See also referendum poll on Prohibition in *ibid.*, March 7, 1926, 1L, and almost daily thereafter during March 1926. See the *New York Times*, April 2, 1926, p. 2.

12. For a typical denunciation of the League of Nations and the World Court in all Hearst newspapers, see the editorials and political cartoons in the *New York American*, January 7, 1926, p. 28; January 9, 1926, pp. 4, 24; January 11, 1926, p. 26; January 12, 1926, p. 34; January 14, 1926, p. 30; January 17, 1926, 1L; January 18, 1926, p. 22; January 20, 23, 1926, p. 24.

13. For senatorial candidates who suffered defeat in political primaries in 1926, see the *New York American*, April 15, 1926, p. 1; June 9, 1926, p. 1; July 26, 1926, p. 26; *Los Angeles Examiner*, April 15, 1926, p. 1. For Hearst's support of Hiram Johnson, see the *New York Times*, August 23, 1926, sec. 2, p. 3; September 12, 1926, sec. 2, p. 3.

14. Pringle, *Smith*, pp. 263–65; *New York American*, October 5, 1926, p. 26; October 6, 1926, p. 28; *New York Times*, October 5, 1926, p. 3; October 6, 1926, p. 2.

15. *New York American*, October 5, 1926, p. 26. For the attack on Smith concerning the milk scandal, see *ibid.*, October 8–9, 1926, pp. 1–2; October 10, 1926, 1L; October 11, 1926, p. 1; October 12, 1926, p. 6; October 13, 1926, pp. 1, 30; then daily to November 1, 1926, p. 1. See also the editorial pages for these same dates in *ibid.* And for the 1919 milk controversy between Smith and Hearst, see chapter 4, pages 12–17. See also the *New York Times*, October 5, 1926, p. 3; October 15, 16, 1926, p. 1. See especially in *ibid.*, October 20, 1926, p. 1.

16. *New York Times*, October 15, 1926, pp. 1, 4, 22; October 20, 24, 1926, p. 1.

17. *New York Times*, October 15, 1926, pp. 1, 4; October 16, 1924, pp. 1, 3, 6; October 20, 1926, p. 1; October 24, 1926, p. 1; October 25, 1926, pp. 1–2; *New York American*, October 15, 1926, pp. 1–2.

18. *New York Times*, October 27, 1926, p. 1; October 28, 1926, p. 2; *New York American*, November 3, 1926, p. 1.

19. Kastner, *Hearst Castle*, pp. 100–10ff; *New York Times*, December 14, 1926, pp. 1, 3. For evidence of Hearst's interest in the San Simeon zoo, see the *New York Times*, July 21, 1927, p. 8.

20. *New York Times*, August 2, 1927, p. 23; Villard, *Some Newspapers and Newspaper-men*, pp. 15–21; Villard, *Prophets, True and False*, pp. 304–11ff. In regard to *Cosmopolitan*, see the advertisement in the *New York American*, August 11, 1927, p. 9; September 14, 1927, p. 9. Concerning Hearst magazines, see also Villard, *Some Newspapers and Newspaper-men*, p. 19. For radio license application, see the *New York Times*, April 26, 1926, sec. 9, p. 17.

21. *New York Times*, February 2, 1927, p. 43; May 25, 1927, p. 40; August 18, 1927, p. 37. For previous purchases of property, see chapter 5, endnotes 13–14.

22. For the Hearst quote to Neylan, see Swanberg, *Citizen Hearst*, p. 383. See also Hearst Jr., *Hearsts: Father and Son*, pp. 238–41; Pizzitola, *Hearst Over Hollywood*, p. 233. Concerning Millicent's activities in 1926, see the *New York American*, February 9, 1926, p. 21; February 13, 1926, p. 12; March 11, 1926, p. 11; April 13, 1926, p. 14; June 28, 1926, p. 7; *New York Times*, March 17, 1926, p. 19; July 15, 1926, p. 23; August 12, 1926, p. 19. For reports of Millicent's activities in 1927, see the *New York American*, January 23, 1927, 13L; February 16, 1927, p. 9; March 8, 11, 1927, p. 9; March 13, 20, 1927, 2M; May 2, 1927, p. 15; October 3, 1927, p. 15; *New York Times*, May 7, 1927, p. 14; October 18, 1927, p. 12. Concerning report of the Hearsts' costume ball celebrating their wedding anniversary, see the *New York American*, April 29, 1927, p. 9.

23. *New York Times*, October 7, 1927, p. 48; October 30, 1927, sec. 12, p. 13; *New York American*, October 7, 1927, p. 4.

24. Guiles, *Davies*, pp. 190–93, 388–91; Crowther, *Hollywood Rajah*, pp. 123–26ff; Swanberg, *Citizen Hearst*, pp. 387–88. For the sale of Hearst's Cosmopolitan studio in New York, see the *New York Times*, November 30, 1926, p. 31. For typical examples of the promotion of Davies, see the *Los Angeles Examiner*, April 1, 1926, sec. 2, p. 5; April 3, 1926, sec. 2, p. 2; April 4, 1926, sec. 1, p. 12; April 5–10, 12–17, 1926, sec. 2, p. 2; April 18, 1926, sec. 2, p. 7; April 20, 1926, sec. 1, pp. 6, 12. Although Davies is noted less often in Hearst's New York newspapers, she still receives some mention in the *New York American*; see December 2, 1926, p. 25; December 8, 10, 1926, p. 11; December 12, 19, 1926, 6M; February 6, 1927, 5M; February 7, 1927, p. 5; February 9, 1927, p. 8.

25. See the Hearst editorial in the *New York American*, January 2, 1927, 1L–2L. Concerning a follow-up crusade in the Hearst newspapers, see *ibid.*, almost daily, from January 4, 1927, pp. 1–2, 32, to January 28, 1927, p. 2. For criticism of Hearst's proposal, see *ibid.*, January 7, 1927, p. 2; January 24, 1927, p. 4; *New York Times*, January 4, 5, 1927, p. 4; January 9, 1927, pp. 2, 18. For progressive

ideas concerning American foreign policy prior to World War I, see chap. 2, pp. 10–11, and endnote 12.

26. For the full text of the Hearst baccalaureate address, see the *New York American*, May 29, 1927, 1E. See also an editorial in *ibid.*, May 30, 1927, p. 22.

27. A. Scott Berg, *Lindbergh* (New York: Putnam, 1998), pp. 5, 26, 128–31; *New York American*, May 22, 1927, 1L, 3L-4L. For quote concerning Lindbergh, see Schlesinger Jr., *The Crisis of the Old Order*, pp. 75–76.

28. Berg, *Lindbergh*, pp. 143–59ff.

29. *New York Times*, June 16, 1927, p. 2; Berg, *Lindbergh*, pp. 160, 162–63, 165–67; Swanberg, *Citizen Hearst*, pp. 391–92. For Lindbergh's "We," see the *Los Angeles Examiner*, January 8, 1928, sec. 6, pp. 1, 7; January 9, 12, 17, 18, 22, 25, 26, 27, 1928, sec. 2, p. 2. See also the *New York American* from early in January to February 10, 1928, p. 12, which concluded with Lindbergh's chapter 30 of "We."

30. After Lindbergh's flight to Paris on May 21, 1927, the Hearst newspapers promoted stories about aviators for the rest of the year, usually in headlines on the front page. For the offer to Chamberlin and Levine, see the *Los Angeles Examiner*, June 9, 1927, p. 1; *New York Times*, June 9, 1927, p. 2. For mention of the Dole and the Old Glory disasters, see Hearst messages in the *New York American*, September 8, 1927, p. 1. See every day thereafter in *ibid.*, September 9–13, 1927, p. 1. See also the *New York Times*, August 1, 1927, p. 7.

31. The lead journalist for the Mexican documents exposé was John Page of the *Washington Herald*. For his articles, which ran in all the Hearst papers, see daily in the *New York American*, November 14, 1927, pp. 1–3, to December 9, 1927, pp. 1–2. See also the *New York Times*, November 14, 1927, p. 2; November 15, 1927, p. 3; November 16, 1927, p. 5; December 10, 1927, p. 3; Swanberg, *Citizen Hearst*, pp. 394–96; Lundberg, *Imperial Hearst*, pp. 284–85; John A. Britton, *Carleton Beals: A Radical Journalist in Latin America* (Albuquerque: University of New Mexico Press, 1987), pp. 58–59; Hunt, *One American and His Attempt at Education*, pp. 293–94.

32. *New York Times*, December 11, 1927, p. 11; December 12–13, 1927, p. 2; December 14, 1927, p. 21; December 15, 1927, p. 11. See also the *New York American*, December 10, 12, 13, 1927, p. 1; December 14, 1927, pp. 1, 26; December 15, 1927, p. 1.

33. *New York Times*, December 15, 1927, p. 11; December 16, 1927, pp. 1, 16. See also Swanberg, *Citizen Hearst*, pp. 396–99ff.

34. *New York Times*, December 16, 1927, pp. 1, 16; Swanberg, *Citizen Hearst*, pp. 397–98.

35. *Congressional Record*, 70th Cong., 1st sess., December 19, 1927, pp. 806–8; Richard Lowitt, *George W. Norris: The Persistence of a Progressive, 1913–1933* (Urbana: University of Illinois Press, 1971), pp. 369–72ff. For the Senate committee's final investigation, see the *New York Times*, January 3, 1928, p. 30; January 4, 1928, p. 7; January 5, 1928, pp. 1, 20; January 7, 1928, p. 3; January 8, 1928, p. 5; January 12, 1928, p. 9. See also Villard, *Prophets, True and*

False, pp. 302–3; Swanberg, *Citizen Hearst*, pp. 397–403; Lundberg, *Imperial Hearst*, pp. 284–90. The *New York Times*, August 31, 1928, p. 33, stated that Hearst paid $15,000 for the Mexican documents.

For an interesting observation about Hearst and the Mexican documents—and also about the bitterness toward Hearst by competitor newspapers—see "Dad to my dear Arch," December 10, 1927, January 7, 1928; "Dad to my dear Jack," December 10, 1927, in *Hiram Johnson Diary Letters*, vol. 4.

36. Concerning Koenigsberg's comment, see Koenigsberg, *King News*, p. 428. For lunch at the White House, see the *New York Times*, November 23, 1927, p. 8. In regard to Mellon, see Harvey O'Connor, *Mellon's Millions: The Life and Times of Andrew W. Mellon* (New York: Blue Ribbon Books, 1933), pp. 140–41; Lundberg, *Imperial Hearst*, pp. 264–70ff; Swanberg, *Citizen Hearst*, pp. 404–5. Concerning the Boulder Dam bill, see Lowitt, *Norris: The Persistence of a Progressive, 1913–1933*, pp. 350–54ff. For the Hearst crusade against the Power Trust, see policies that Hearst advocated daily during 1927–1928 in the *Los Angeles Examiner*. For example, see *ibid.*, June 1, 1927, sec. 2, p. 16. The first policy is Boulder Canyon, High Dam. See also for 1927–1928, numerous editorials in the *New York American*.

37. Concerning the Ritz Tower acquisition, see the *New York Times*, January 17, 1928, p. 51; February 7, 1928, p. 48; Swanberg, *Citizen Hearst*, p. 406. For other property purchases, see the *New York Times*, February 18, 1928, p. 30; August 14, 1928, pp. 4, 42; October 26, 1928, p. 45; November 3, 1928, p. 35.

38. Morgan to Neylan's office, January 18, 29, 1928; Hearst to Morgan, January 18, 1928, Box 6, Julia Morgan Papers. Concerning expansion at Casa Grande, see Kastner, *Hearst Castle*, pp. 101–2, 133–48ff, but see especially the site plan on pp. 134–35. In regard to the zoo, see Kastner, *Hearst Castle*, pp. 16–17, 102–3, 106, 123, 124, 207; Nasaw, *The Chief*, pp. 370–71.

39. *New York Times*, June 28, 1927, p. 3; Taylor Coffman, *Building for Hearst and Morgan: Voices from the George Loorz Papers* (Berkeley: Berkeley Hills, 2003), pp. 23–24, 25.

40. Hearst to Morgan, February 19, 1927, Box 6, Julia Morgan Papers; Kastner, *Hearst Castle*, pp. 108, 110.

41. For the engagement and marriage of Alma Walker and Bill Jr., see the *New York Times*, February 11, 1928, p. 21; March 25, 1928, sec. 2, p. 8. For the review of Winkler's biography, see *ibid.*, May 27, 1928, sec. 2, p. 1; sec. 4, p. 1; see also West, "Hearst: A Psychological Note," *American Mercury*, November, 1930, p. 308; Swanberg, *Citizen Hearst*, p. 406.

42. John D. Hicks, *Republican Ascendancy, 1921–1933* (New York: Harper & Row, 1963), pp. 201–5ff; O'Connor, *Mellon's Millions*, pp. 301–5. For Mayer's backing of Hoover, see Crowther, *Mayer*, pp. 136–37. See Hearst editorial predicting Smith's defeat in the *New York American*, September 2, 1928, 1L–2L. See also *ibid.*, September 19, 1928, p. 30; September 23, 1928, 1L, 4L; September 30, 1928, 1L, 4L; November 4, 1928, 10E; *New York Times*, September 1, 1928, pp. 1, 3; September 2, 1928, p. 4; September 20, 1928, p. 6; October 6, 1928,

p. 2. For a Hearst editorial assessing his views on GOP candidates, see the *New York American*, December 11, 1927, 1L-2L. In regard to Hearst's purchase of the *Omaha Bee*, see the *New York Times*, July 1, 1928, p. 23; July 4, 1928, p. 22.

43. *New York Times*, July 21, 1928, p. 29; Guiles, *Davies*, pp. 211–13; Nasaw, *The Chief*, pp. 399–401; Head, *It Could Never Have Happened*, pp. 103–6, 112–13.

44. Head, *It Could Never Have Happened*, pp. 113–18; Guiles, *Davies*, pp. 214–16. See also reports about Marion in the *New York American*, August 20, 1928, p. 14; September 2, 1928, 4M; September 12, 1928, p. 15; October 18, 1928, p. 16.

45. Head, *It Could Never Have Happened*, 113–14; Guiles, *Davies*, pp. 213–14.

46. Head, *It Could Never Have Happened*, pp. 118–24; Older, *Hearst*, pp. 456–61ff; Swanberg, *Citizen Hearst*, pp. 407–8; Nasaw, *The Chief*, pp. 402–4; *New York Times*, October 6, 1928, p. 2.

47. *New York Times*, October 6, 1928, p. 2. As evidence of Hearst's support for the Republicans, see *ibid.*, November 25, 1928, sec. 2, p. 6. For the 1928 straw vote poll by the Hearst newspapers, see daily in the *New York American*, August 12, 1928, 8L, to November 3, 1928, 2L. See also *ibid.*, November 8, 1928.

48. In Villard, *Some Newspapers and Newspaper-Men*, p. 319, statistics show that the *Times* had a greater circulation than the *American* as early as 1923 by almost 20,000 readers daily. For Hearst's arrangement with NBC, see the *New York American*, December 16, 1928, 1L; December 17, 1928, p. 6; December 24, 1928, pp. 1–2.

49. *Los Angeles Examiner*, January 3, 1929, pp. 1–2; *New York American*, January 3, 1929, p. 3; January 4, 1929, p. 2; January 20, 1929, 6L; *New York Times*, January 3, 1929, p. 6; January 20, 1929, p. 2. The temperance contest was a daily crusade in the *American* from January 22, 1929, p. 2, through April 1929. In *ibid.*, May 5, 1929, 1L, readers had submitted 70,002 temperance plans. See announcement of winners in *ibid.*, June 2, 1929, 2L, 8L; *New York Times*, June 2, 1929, p. 11.

50. See editorial concerning an income tax slash in the *New York American*, March 2, 1929, p. 24, then daily with petition in *ibid.*, from March 4, 1929, pp. 1, 4, to May 29, 1929, p. 8.

51. For flag contest rules, see the *New York American*, February 17, 1929, 10L. For information concerning the contest as well as the questions, usually four at a time, see *ibid.*, February 4, 6, 9, 1929, p. 4, through February 28, 1929, p. 12. See also *ibid.*, March 3, 1929, 8L; March 10, 1929, 28L; March 16, 21, 1929, p. 9; and especially June 15, 1929, p. 1.

52. Concerning Coolidge, see the *New York American*, March 31, 1929, 1L; September 8, 1929, 1L–2L, through September 15, 1929, 1L, 18L; September 22, 29, 1929, 1L–2L. Concerning *All Quiet on the Western Front*, see daily in *ibid.*, July 14, 1929, 1L, to August 17, 1929, p. 6. For *Little Caesar*, see daily in *ibid.*, August 19, 1929, p. 6, to September 21, 1929, p. 12. And for *The Life of Jimmy Walker*, see advertisement in *ibid.*, September 24, 1929, p. 8; and story from September 29, 1929, 14L-15L, to October 16, 1929, p. 10.

53. See *New York American*, August 1, 1929, p. 1, to August 30, 1929, pp. 1, 5, 8, 9, 11–13. See also advertisement of RKO Cameo in *ibid.*, November 2, 1929, p. 6. See specifically Pizzitola, *Hearst Over Hollywood*, pp. 239–41.

54. For Hearst's deal with MGM, see the *New York American*, June 23, 1929, 16L; Pizzitola, *Hearst Over Hollywood*, pp. 234, 474. In regard to Hearst's further acquisition of property in New York City, see the *New York Times*, June 10, 1929, p. 47; July 10, 1929, p. 49; July 24, 1929, p. 45. Concerning the purchase of the *San Francisco Bulletin*, see *ibid.*, August 29, 1929, p. 20; September 2, 1929, p. 14.

55. For some of Millicent's activities at Palm Beach in 1929, see the *New York American*, February 12, 1929, 6S; February 20, 1929, p. 14; February 21, 1929, p. 16; February 23, 1929, p. 14; February 24, 1929, 2M; February 28, 1929, p. 14; March 1, 1929, p. 14; March 5, 1929, p. 18; March 10, 1929, 2M; March 12, 1929, 5S; March 14, 16, 1929, 6S; March 18, 1929, p. 5. See also mention of her charity work in *ibid.*, April 10, 1929, p. 4; April 11, 1929, p. 16; April 12, 1929, p. 5; June 26, 1929, p. 4; October 7, 1929, p. 13; October 24, 1929, p. 7. Concerning the Hearsts' luncheon at the White House, see the *New York Times*, May 23, 1929, p. 4. And for hosting a party for Churchill, see *ibid.*, October 19, 1929, p. 18; and the *New York American*, October 19, 1929, p. 18.

56. Guiles, *Davies*, pp. 202–4, 205–6, 235–39ff; Pizzitola, *Hearst Over Hollywood*, pp. 257–59; Crowther, *Hollywood Rajah*, pp. 125–27. Concerning Churchill in California, see Chaplin, *My Autobiography*, pp. 339–40; *New York American*, September 23, 1929, p. 16; September 27, 1929, p. 28. For Millicent's party for Churchill in New York City, see the *New York American*, October 19, 1929, p. 18; *New York Times*, October 19, 1929, p. 12.

57. Schlesinger Jr., *Crisis of the Old Order*, pp. 157–59; John Kenneth Galbraith, *The Great Crash, 1929* (Boston: Houghton Mifflin, 1955), pp. 93–132ff; Harris Gaylord Warren, *Herbert Hoover and the Great Depression* (New York: Oxford University Press, 1959), pp. 104–6; Hicks, *Republican Ascendancy, 1921–1933*, pp. 223–24.

Chapter 7

1. Schlesinger Jr., *The Crisis of the Old Order*, pp. 161–69, 170–71; Hicks, *Republican Ascendancy, 1921–1933*, pp. 223–40ff; Galbraith, *The Great Crash, 1929*, pp. 113, 140–48ff.

2. For the Hearst open letter, see the *New York American*, November 15, 1929, p. 1; *New York Times*, November 15, 1929, p. 3.

3. In regard to actions by the Federal Reserve and tax cuts, see Galbraith, *The Great Crash, 1929*, pp. 125, 142; *New York American*, November 14, 15, 20, 1929, p. 1. For a daily report on the activities of the Hoover administration, see the *New York American*, November 16 to December 10, 1929, p. 1. See specifically in *ibid.*, November 22, 23, 29, 1929, p. 1; December 1, 1929, 1L.

4. For the return of prosperity statement, see Galbraith, *The Great Crash, 1929*, p. 146. For Hoover's statements about the U.S. economy, see the *New York American*, March 17, 19, 1930, p. 1. Concerning typical support of the Hoover

administration by Hearst newspapers, see *ibid.*, March 16, 1930, 1L. For the front-page item titled "GOOD NEWS," see *ibid.*, March 25–June 2, 1930, p. 1 (daily).

5. See the *New York Times*, December 13, 1929, p. 1; March 21, 1930, p. 50; April 3, 1930, p. 54. Concerning St. Donat's, see *ibid.*, March 24, 1930, p. 9.

6. *New York Times*, April 29, 1930, p. 28; May 19, 1930, p. 20. For architectural improvements at the Davies compound and the Rogers–Hearst land deal, see Swanberg, *Citizen Hearst*, pp. 409–10.

7. Boutelle, *Julia Morgan, Architect*, pp. 196–97; Kastner, *Hearst Castle*, pp. 134 (site plan), 166, 169. For discussion of Hearst and the building of San Simeon, see chapter 5, pp. 14–16.

8. Pizzitola, *Hearst Over Hollywood*, pp. 256–58; Guiles, *Davies*, pp. 245–46, 394–96. For the comedian's comment concerning the Hearst media coverage of Marion, see Sol Chaneles and Albert Wolsky, *The Movie Makers* (Secaucus, N.J.: Derbibooks, 1974), p. 123; Norman Zierold, *The Moguls* (New York: Coward-McCann, 1969), pp. 282–86, 287. See also Lawrence Grobel, *The Hustons* (New York: Scribner's, 1989), pp. 159–60. Louella Parsons chronicled Marion's activities in her newspaper column. For instance, see the *New York American*, January 27, 1929, 4M; February 7, 9, 1929, 6S; February 26, 1929, p. 14; March 21, 1929, 6S; April 10, 1929, p. 17; April 11, 1929, p. 16; April 28, 1929, 3D; June 6, 1929, p. 18; July 3, 1929, p. 16; July 4, 1929, p. 13; July 14, 1929, 4M; July 25, 1929, p. 16; July 30, 1929, p. 15; August 2, 5, 12, 1929, p. 14; August 8, 1929, p. 17; August 31, 1929, p. 23; September 1, 1929, 4M; October 18, 1929, p. 13; January 3, 1930, p. 16; January 30, 1930, p. 18; February 5, 1930, p. 7; February 8, 1930, p. 20; February 28, 1930, p. 16; April 5, 1930, p. 18; April 16, 1930, p. 16; May 9, 1930, p. 16; May 18, 1930, 6M; May 25, 1930, 19L, 2M. For the close relationship between Hearst and Mayer, see Crowther, *Hollywood Rajah*, pp. 123–26. To see the growth of motion picture coverage in the Hearst newspapers, compare the *New York American* daily and Sunday in the early 1920s to that of 1929–1930.

9. Irvin S. Cobb, *Exit Laughing* (New York: Bobbs-Merrill, 1941), pp. 122–23; Swanberg, *Citizen Hearst*, p. 389.

10. See Hearst editorials in the *New York American*, February 16, 1930, 1L; April 1, 1930, p. 1. See also Hicks, *Republican Ascendancy, 1921–1933*, pp. 241–42.

11. For a brief discussion of the London Naval Conference, see Hicks, *Republican Ascendancy, 1921–1933*, pp. 241–44; Bailey, *A Diplomatic History of the American People*, pp. 650–52. For the brunt of the crusade against the London Conference, see the *New York American*, March 23, 1930, 1L, to April 2, 1930, p. 1. See in *ibid.*, other editorials and political cartoons intermittently from February to July 1930, but especially April 27, 1930, 1L.

12. Concerning the tariff, see Schlesinger Jr., *The Crisis of the Old Order, 1919–1933*, pp. 163–66; Hicks, *Republican Ascendancy, 1921–1933*, pp. 221–23; *New York American*, April 1, 5, 1930, p. 30; May 3, 1930, p. 32; May 19, 1930, p. 28.

Typical of Hearst's support of war veterans is an editorial in *ibid.*, June 25, 1930, p. 1. Editorials and political cartoons critical of Hoover appear daily in *ibid.*, May 1930. For the summation of Hearst's disillusionment, see *ibid.*, June 2, 1930, p. 30.

13. *New York American*, May 13, 1930, p. 18. While in Rome, Millicent interviewed Benito Mussolini; see *ibid.*, May 8, 1930, 8L. For Brazilian president dinner see the *New York Times*, June 20, 1930, p. 23.

14. Older, *Hearst*, pp. 462–65, 505; Head, *It Could Never Have Happened*, pp. 139–42; Swanberg, *Citizen Hearst*, p. 418.

15. Head, *It Could Never Have Happened*, pp. 141–44.

16. *Ibid.*, p. 144; Swanberg, *Citizen Hearst*, p. 419.

17. In regard to the exposé concerning the secret Franco–British naval document, see the *New York American*, September 25, 1928, pp. 1, 6; September 26, 1928, p. 24. See also related articles in the *New York Times*, October 10–12, 14, 1928; Guiles, *Davies*, pp. 219–20. For a reproduction of the Hearst interview in the *Frankfurter Zeitung*, see the *New York American*, August 29, 1930, p. 1. See also the *New York Times*, September 3, 1930, p. 1.

18. *New York American*, September 3, 1930, p. 1; September 10, 1930, p. 2; *New York Times*, September 3, 1930, p. 1.

19. See the *New York American*, September 4, 1930, p. 2; September 13, 1930, p. 1. For acquisition of the great chamber at Gilling Castle, see *ibid.*, September 6, 1930, p. 18; *New York Times*, September 6, 1930, p. 18.

20. *New York American*, September 19, 1930, p. 2.

21. *New York American*, September 13, 1930, p. 1; September 14, 1930, 3L; September 15, 1930, p. 3; September 16, 1930, pp. 1–2; *New York Times*, September 15, 1930, p. 25; September 16, 1930, p. 24. See also Coblentz, ed., *William Randolph Hearst: A Portrait in His Own Words* (New York: 1952), pp. 98–99.

22. *New York American*, September 23, 1930, p. 1; September 24, 1930, p. 2; September 25, 1930, p. 3; October 10, 1930, pp. 1–2. Regarding Hearst's radio address, see *ibid.*, September 29, 1930, pp. 1–2, September 30, 1930, p. 2; *New York Times*, September 29, 1930, p. 23. For the protest by Polish Americans in Chicago, see *ibid.*, October 6, 1930, p. 32.

23. *New York American*, October 4, 1930, p. 4; October 16, 1930, p. 16.

24. *Ibid.*, October 17, 1930, p. 2; *San Francisco Examiner*, October 17, 1930, pp. 1, 10–13; October 18, 1930, p. 1; *New York Times*, October 17, 1930, p. 9. Concerning Hearst for president buttons, see the *New York Times*, October 23, 1930, p. 11.

25. Concerning James W. Gerard's list of fifty-nine rulers of America, see the *New York Times*, August 21, 1930, pp. 1, 3. For disclaimer in regard to political office, see *ibid.*, December 1, 1930, p. 6; *New York American*, December 1, 1930, p. 3.

26. For the Hearst announcement concerning political office, see *New York American*, December 1, 1930, p. 3; *New York Times*, December 1, 1930, p. 6. For

depression effects in 1931, see Schlesinger Jr., *Crisis of the Old Order*, pp. 167–68, 171–72, 174–75; Hicks, *Republican Ascendancy, 1921–1933*, pp. 229–33.

27. See Hearst editorial in the *New York American*, October 9, 1930, pp. 1–2. As typical of Hearst's nationwide editorials in his twenty-eight newspapers, see the *San Francisco Examiner*, February 6, 1931, p. 2. See also the *San Francisco Examiner*, February 7, 1931, p. 1.

28. *New York Times*, June 3, 1931, p. 15. For the full text of Hearst's radio address, see the *New York American*, June 7, 1931, 1E.

29. For evidence of the Hearst prosperity crusade, see the *New York American*, June 5, 1931, p. 2; June 6, 1931, p. 16; June 7, 1931, 1E; June 8, 1931, p. 12; June 9, 1931, p. 16; June 11, 1931, p. 18; June 12, 1931, p. 16; June 14, 1931, 14L, E2. Then for the rest of 1931, editorials and cartoons will appear intermittently in *ibid*.

30. For Hearst's whereabouts on this vacation, see the *New York American*, June 24, 1931, p. 18; June 27, 1931, p. 16; *New York Times*, August 16, 1931, p. 12. See also Swanberg, *Citizen Hearst*, pp. 430–31; Pizzitola, *Hearst Over Hollywood*, pp. 262–64; Head, *It Could Never Have Happened*, p. 157. For Hearst's arrival in New York City, see the *New York American*, September 11, 1931, p. 2; *New York Times*, September 11, 1931, p. 23.

31. *New York American*, September 13, 1931, 1L-2L.

32. See Hearst editorials, which were published in all Hearst papers, in the *New York American*, September 13, 1931, p. 14; September 24, 1931, pp. 1–2; October 4, 1931, 1L; October 18, 1931, 1L. Concerning the Hoover moratorium policy with France, see Hicks, *Republican Ascendancy, 1921–1933*, pp. 245–47. See Hearst's reaction to the moratorium in the *New York American*, October 27, 1931, p. 1; December 16, 1931, p. 1; and a follow-up on December 17, 1931, pp. 1–2. See also Hearst editorial in *ibid*., December 21, 1931, p. 1.

33. For Hearst's support of Coolidge for president, see the *New York Times*, June 23, 1931, p. 15. See Hearst editorial in the *New York American*, December 24, 1931, p. 1.

34. *New York Times*, January 3, 1932, p. 3; *New York American*, January 3, 1932, 1L. See also Norman D. Brown, "Garnering Votes for 'Cactus Jack': John Nance Garner, Franklin D. Roosevelt, and the 1932 Democratic Nomination for President," *Southwestern Historical Quarterly*, October, 2000, 165–66; Frank Freidel, *Franklin D. Roosevelt: The Triumph* (Boston: Little, Brown, 1956), 3:245.

35. Coblentz, ed., *Hearst: A Portrait in His Own Words*, pp. 126–29; Brown, "Garnering Votes for 'Cactus Jack,'" p. 166.

36. See Hearst editorial in the *New York American*, January 3, 1932, 1L. See also Hearst editorials in *ibid*., January 8, 1932, p. 1; January 10, 17, 31, 1932, 1L. For radio talk on newsreel, see *ibid*., January 11, 1932, p. 11.

37. Brown, "Garnering Votes for 'Cactus Jack,'" p. 165; Schlesinger Jr., *The Crisis of the Old Order, 1919–1933*, p. 227.

38. Brown, "Garnering Votes for Cactus Jack," p. 167; Bascom N. Timmons, *Garner of Texas: A Personal History* (New York: Harper, 1948), p. 158; Thomas L.

Stokes, *Chip Off My Shoulder* (Princeton, N.J.: Princeton University Press, 1940), p. 326.

39. Coblentz, ed., *Hearst: A Portrait in His Own Words*, pp. 129–30. For one publication of the Garner biography, see the *New York American*, February 21 to February 28, 1932, 1L. For a promotion of the *Cosmopolitan* article, see *ibid.*, March 15, 1932, p. 9. For the reprint of the article in *Good Housekeeping*, see *ibid.*, May 1, 1932, 2E. See also Schlesinger Jr., *The Crisis of the Old Order, 1919–1933*, pp. 228–29; Eldon Stephen Branda, ed., *The Handbook of Texas: A Supplement* (Austin: Texas State Historical Association, 1976), 3: 326–27.

40. Brown, "Garnering Votes for 'Cactus Jack,'" pp. 168–76ff. For further evidence of FDR's growing delegation support, see Freidel, *Franklin D. Roosevelt: The Triumph*, 3: 275–90; Lowitt, *Norris: The Persistence of a Progressive, 1913–1933*, pp. 551–52.

41. For Hearst's letter requesting FDR's stance on the League of Nations and the governor's reply, see the *New York Times*, February 2, 1932, p. 4; February 18, 1932, p. 2. See also Freidel, *Franklin D. Roosevelt: The Triumph*, 3: 250–54; Brown, "Garnering Votes for 'Cactus Jack,'" pp. 176–77; Thomas M. Storke, *California Editor* (Los Angeles: Westernlore, 1958), pp. 299, 301.

42. Brown, "Garnering Votes for 'Cactus Jack,'" pp. 176–78; Storke, *California Editor*, pp. 299, 301; Coblentz, ed., *Hearst: In His Own Words*, pp. 129–30.

43. For the staff of twelve writers covering the Republican and Democratic conventions in June, see the *New York American*, June 12, 1932, 2L. See also Swanberg, *Citizen Hearst*, p. 436. Concerning the Republican Convention, see Harris Gaylord Warren, *Herbert Hoover and the Great Depression* (New York: Oxford University Press, 1959), pp. 251–53.

44. Schlesinger Jr., *The Crisis of the Old Order, 1919–1933*, pp. 305–7; Freidel, *Franklin D. Roosevelt: The Triumph*, 3: 304–7; Brown, "Garnering Votes for 'Cactus Jack,'" pp. 185–86.

45. Freidel, *Franklin D. Roosevelt: The Triumph*, 3:172–74, 307–8; Brown, "Garnering Votes for 'Cactus Jack,'" pp. 186–87.

46. Coblentz, ed., *Hearst: A Portrait in His Own Words*, pp. 132–34; Freidel, *Franklin D. Roosevelt: The Triumph*, 3: 308–9.

47. Brown, "Garnering Votes for 'Cactus Jack,'" pp. 186–88; Storke, *California Editor*, pp. 327–30; Freidel, *Franklin D. Roosevelt: The Triumph*, 3: 308–11. For a somewhat different interpretation of Hearst's importance in the Roosevelt selection, see Coblentz, ed., *Hearst: A Portrait in His Own Words*, p. 134; Swanberg, *Citizen Hearst*, pp. 437–38.

48. For Hearst's interpretation of the Roosevelt and Garner nominations, see Coblentz, ed., *Hearst: A Portrait in His Own Words*, p. 134; Swanberg, *Citizen Hearst*, pp. 437–38; Nasaw, *The Chief*, pp. 455–56. But for Hearst's own assessment of his role at the Democratic convention, see Hearst editorial in the *New York American*, January 15, 1933, 1L-2L.

49. For criticism of Hoover in Hearst editorials, which were published in all his newspapers, see typically in the *New York American*, September 19, 1932, p. 1;

November 2, 1932, pp. 1–2. For praise of Roosevelt, see typical editorials in *ibid.*, October 24, 1932, pp. 1–2; November 6, 1932, 1L-2L. Concerning the catch phrase about "Vote for Hoover," see specifically *ibid.*, October 30, 1932, 1L-2L. Hearst also contributed $25,000 to the Roosevelt campaign. See Nasaw, *The Chief*, p. 458.

50. *New York Times*, October 3, 1932, p. 19; October 4, 1932, p. 23; October 5, 1932, p. 23; October 23, 1932, p. 2; October 24, 1932, p. 14. Dr. Crile stated that the operation was "for oesophageal diverticulum."

51. *New York Times*, October 12, 1932, p. 4.

52. See Hearst editorials in the *New York American*, October 24, 1932, p. 1; October 30, 1932, 1L-2L. See also *ibid.*, November 7, 1932, p. 2. For an excellent recitation of the 1932 presidential campaign from the Democratic side, see Freidel, *Franklin D. Roosevelt: The Triumph*, 3: 312–71. For a daily account of the presidential campaign, see the *New York American* from late in August to November 9, 1932. And for Hearst's support of FDR in California, see Pizzitola, *Hearst Over Hollywood*, pp. 289–92.

Chapter 8

1. For a discussion of progressive ideology, see Otis L. Graham, Jr., *An Encore for Reform: The Old Progressives and the New Deal* (New York: Oxford University Press, 1967), pp. 46, 181–85ff. For Hearst's reminiscence, see Coblentz, ed., *Hearst: A Portrait in His Own Words*, p. 48. For Hearst correspondence pertaining to some of Roosevelt's thinking and activities from November 1932 to March 1933, see *ibid.*, pp. 141–54. For certain Hearst activities after the November election involving Roosevelt, see Nasaw, *The Chief*, pp. 458–62.

2. John Tebbel, *The Life and Good Times of William Randolph Hearst* (New York: Dutton, 1952), pp. 308–15; Nasaw, *The Chief*, pp. 462–63; Swanberg, *Citizen Hearst*, p. 439. In going public with Hearst Consolidated, see the *New York Times*, May 11, 1930, sec. 2, p. 5; July 7, 1930, p. 31; *New York American*, July 8, 1930, p. 21.

3. Swanberg, *Citizen Hearst*, pp. 414–16ff, 432, 455. For evidence of Hearst's workaholic tendencies, see Edmond David Coblentz Correspondence and Papers, Box 3, Bancroft Library, University of California–Berkeley. See also *Time*, May 1, 1933, p. 19.

4. *Time*, May 1, 1933, pp. 19–20, 22; *Los Angeles Examiner*, April 30, 1933, p. 3; *New York American*, April 28, 1933, p. 7; *New York Times*, April 29, 1933, p. 15; April 30, 1933, p. 31. See also Guiles, *Davies*, pp. 266–67.

5. W. R. Hearst to Governor Roosevelt, February 7, 1933, in F.D.R.: President's Personal File, File 62 (W. R. Hearst) in Franklin D. Roosevelt Library, Hyde Park, New York (hereafter cited as FDR Papers); Hearst to the President, March 6, 1933, *ibid.*; Roosevelt to Hearst, March 9, 1933, *ibid.*; Coblentz, ed., *Hearst: A Portrait in His Own Words*, pp. 141–58ff; Frank Freidel, *Franklin D. Roosevelt: Launching the New Deal* (Boston: Little, Brown, 1973), 4: 58, 63, 142, 152; Nasaw, *The Chief*, p. 469. For mention of George Hearst, see the *New York Times*, February 8, 1933, p. 2.

6. Schlesinger Jr., *The Crisis of the Old Order*, pp. 453, 458; Coblentz, ed., *Hearst: A Portrait in His Own Words*, pp. 142–54ff. For Hearst editorials and interviews, see the *New York American*, January 3, 1933, pp. 1–2; January 7, 1933, p. 1; January 15, 1933, 1L-2L; January 18, 1933, pp. 1–2; February 6, 1933, p. 1; February 15, 1933, pp. 1–2; February 19, 1933, 1L-2L; February 22, 1933, pp. 1–2; February 26, 1926, 1L-2L. Concerning the Buy America crusade, see daily in *ibid.*, December 26, 1932, through February 1933. For a notice of Hearst Metrotone News regarding the public showing of Roosevelt's inauguration, see *ibid.*, March 6, 1933, p. 19.

7. For an excellent account of *Gabriel Over the White House*, see Pizzitola, *Hearst Over Hollywood*, pp. 293–300, 301, 325, 330; Nasaw, *The Chief*, pp. 463–66. See also Roosevelt to Hearst, April 1, 1933, in F.D.R.: President's Personal File, File 62 (W. R. Hearst), FDR Papers.

8. See Arthur M. Schlesinger Jr., *The Coming of the New Deal* (Boston: Houghton Mifflin, 1958), pp. 1–23ff; Freidel, *Franklin D. Roosevelt: Launching the New Deal*, 4: 96–101, 220, 226–29, 257–59, 350–54, 436–53.

9. Concerning Hearst's ideas to remedy the depression, see his views to the U.S. Senate in the *New York American*, February 22, 1933, pp. 1–2; February 26, 1933, 1L; *New York Times*, February 22, 1933, pp. 31, 33. For Hearst editorials critical of Congress, see the *New York American*, April 24, 1933, p. 1; April 28, 1933, p. 1; April 29, 1933, pp. 1–2; May 11, 1933, pp. 1–2; May 30, 1933, pp. 1–2; *Los Angeles Examiner*, April 28, 1933, p. 1.

10. See Schlesinger Jr., *The Coming of the New Deal*, pp. 522–32ff; Coblentz, ed., *Hearst: A Portrait in His Own Words*, p. 154; Freidel, *Franklin D. Roosevelt: Launching the New Deal*, 3: 60–65, 71–74, 81.

11. For an excellent history of the creation of the NRA, see Freidel, *Franklin D. Roosevelt: Launching the New Deal*, 4: 408–35ff, 447–50; Schlesinger Jr., *The Coming of the New Deal*, pp. 97–102.

12. Coblentz, ed., *Hearst: A Portrait in His Own Words*, p. 161. See Hearst editorial in the *New York American*, July 19, 1933, pp. 1–2.

13. Coblentz, ed., *Hearst: A Portrait in His Own Words*, pp. 158–60.

14. *New York American*, August 13, 1933, 1L-2L.

15. See Hearst editorials concerning the NRA in the *New York American*, September 4, 1933, p. 1; September 10, 1933, 1L-2L. For examples of the Buy Now crusades, see daily in *ibid.*, usually on page 1, during September and October 1933. For his NBC radio address and the reaction to it, see *ibid.*, September 17, 1933, p. 1; *New York Times*, September 17, 1933, p. 29; October 9, 1933, p. 16. Concerning Hearst's disenchantment with the NRA, see the *New York American*, October 31, 1933, pp. 1–2; Coblentz, ed., *Hearst: A Portrait in His Own Words*, pp. 160–63. In regard to Hearst's growing fear of federal power, see editorials in the *New York American*, November 17 and 22, 1933, p. 1. See also a Hearst editorial in *ibid.*, December 10, 1933, 1L-2L.

16. Kastner, *Hearst Castle*, pp. 164, 166–69.

17. Boutelle, *Julia Morgan, Architect*, pp. 217–32ff; Kastner, *Hearst Castle*, pp. 87–88, 164.

18. Guiles, *Marion Davies*, pp. 260–61, 265–73; Davies, *The Times We Had*, pp. 185–98ff; Swanberg, *Citizen Hearst*, pp. 352, 359–61; Pizzitola, *Hearst Over Hollywood*, pp. 230–32, 288. For a description and reviews of Marion's four motion pictures during 1932–1934, see Guiles, *Marion Davies*, pp. 398–401.

19. Guiles, *Marion Davies*, pp. 270–73ff; Swanberg, *Citizen Hearst*, p. 242; Davies, *The Times We Had*, pp. 303–6; Pizzitola, *Hearst Over Hollywood*, p. 304; *New York Times*, May 27, 1934, p. 3; *New York American*, May 27, 1934, 2L. For a reference to Harry Crocker, see Nancy Dowd and David Shepard, *King Vidor* (Metuchen, N.J.: Directors Guild of America Scarecrow, 1988), p. 91.

20. See Franklin D. Roosevelt to Hearst, May 18, 1934; Hearst to the President, May 18, 1934, in FDR: President's Personal File, File 62 (W. R. Hearst), FDR Papers; *New York American*, May 25, 1934, p. 18; May 26, 1934, p. 1; *New York Times*, May 27, 1934, p. 3; Swanberg, *Citizen Hearst*, p. 442.

21. Concerning the NRA criticisms, see editorials and NBC broadcast in the *New York American*, January 11, 1934, p. 16; February 4, 1934, 1L-2L; March 4, 1934, 1L-2L; March 10, 1934, p. 10; March 11, 1934, 1L-2L; March 15, 1934, pp. 1–2. See also the *New York Times*, February 9, 1934, p. 15; March 11, 1934, p. 5. Hearst also employed Richard Washburn Child, who wrote an editorial daily during the first months of 1934 in the *New York American*, usually on page 1. Most of his editorials were anti–New Deal. For a typical example, see *ibid.*, January 8, 1934, pp. 1–2. For a sample of Hearst's opposition to a higher income tax, see the *New York Times*, April 13, 1934, p. 4. And for the FDR influence on Hearst, see the *New York American*, May 27, 1934, 2L; *New York Times*, May 27, 1934, p. 3. See conclusions of Hearst interview in London in the *New York American*, June 24, 1934, 1L-2L.

22. *New York Times*, June 11, 1934, p. 13; June 22, 1934, p. 9. For Hearst's unforgiving disdain of the French, see Coblentz, ed., *Hearst: A Portrait in His Own Words*, pp. 99–102. See also Guiles, *Marion Davies*, pp. 273–74. For an excellent description of Hearst on this trip, see Harry Crocker, "That's Hollywood," chap. 3, pp. 3–8, MSS, Margaret Herrick Library, Academy of Motion Picture Arts and Sciences, Los Angeles, California (hereafter cited as Herrick Lib.). See also Pizzitola, *Hearst Over Hollywood*, pp. 304–8ff; Nasaw, *The Chief*, pp. 490–91, 492; Swanberg, *Citizen Hearst*, pp. 442–43.

23. Crocker, "That's Hollywood," chap. 11, pp. 6–7, Herrick Lib.

24. Coblentz, ed., *Hearst: A Portrait in His Own Words*, pp. 212–14.

25. *New York Times*, May 27, 1934, p. 3; August 19, 1934, p. 25. For the Hearst–Hitler meeting, see Crocker, "That's Hollywood," chap. 11, pp. 8–12, Herrick Lib.; Coblentz, ed., *Hearst: A Portrait in His Own Words*, pp. 103–4. For one reason that Hearst was refusing to avoid Nazi politics and propaganda, see the *New York Times*, August 23, 1934, p. 10.

26. Crocker, "That's Hollywood," chap. 11, pp. 10–12, Herrick Lib.; Coblentz, ed., *Hearst: A Portrait in His Own Words*, pp. 103–4; Crowther, *Mayer*, p. 196. See Pizzitola, *Hearst Over Hollywood*, pp. 308–13, 483–84, who discusses the Hearst–Hitler meeting thoroughly.

27. For one of Hearst's incentives for the interview with Hitler, see the *New York Times*, September 17, 1934, p. 8. For other specifics, see Crocker, "That's Hollywood," chap. 11, pp. 12–17, Herrick Lib.; Winkler, *Hearst: A New Appraisal*, pp. 270–71; Coblentz, ed., *Hearst: A Portrait in His Own Words*, pp. 104–7. See also Pizzitola, *Hearst Over Hollywood*, pp. 311–17; Nasaw, *The Chief*, pp. 510–11.

28. Coblentz, ed., *Hearst: A Portrait in His Own Words*, p. 106. For Hearst editorials concerning Hitler, see the *New York American*, September 28, 1934, pp. 1–2; September 30, 1934, 2L; *Los Angeles Examiner*, September 28, 1934, p. 5; September 30, 1934, p. 2.

29. Crocker, "That's Hollywood," chap. 11, p. 11, Herrick Lib.; Winkler, *Hearst: A New Appraisal*, p. 270.

30. Swanberg, *Citizen Hearst*, p. 444; Nasaw, *The Chief*, pp. 509–10; *New York American*, September 28, 1934, p. 5; *New York Times*, September 28, 1934, p. 25.

31. See "W. R. Hearst Discusses Sinclair Nomination," editorial, *Los Angeles Examiner*, September 3, 1934, p. 1; *New York American*, September 3, 1934, pp. 1–2. Concerning Sinclair and his race for governor, see Leon Harris, *Upton Sinclair: American Rebel* (New York: Crowell, 1975), pp. 294–315ff; Upton Sinclair, *The Autobiography of Upton Sinclair* (New York: Harcourt, Brace & World, 1962), pp. 268–76; Arthur M. Schlesinger Jr., *The Politics of Upheaval, 1935–1936* (Boston: Houghton Mifflin, 1966), pp. 111–21; Pizzitola, *Hearst Over Hollywood*, pp. 332–35; Crowther, *Hollywood Rajah*, pp. 197–200; John D. Weaver, *Los Angeles: The Enormous Village, 1781–1981* (Santa Barbara: Capra, 1980), pp. 120–21. See letter titled "Mr. Hearst Gives Reasons for Supporting Merriam," *Los Angeles Examiner*, October 25, 1934, p. 1. It is reprinted or referred to daily in *ibid.* until the day prior to the election on November 5, 1934, p. 2.

32. Pizzitola, *Hearst Over Hollywood*, pp. 203, 330–32; Crowther, *Hollywood Rajah*, pp. 185–86, 198–201.

33. Pizzitola, *Hearst Over Hollywood*, pp. 330–31; Crowther, *Hollywood Rajah*, pp. 196–97, 200–201. For Hearst's visit to the White House and his comments thereafter, see the *Los Angeles Examiner*, October 10, 1934, p. 1. See also Roy D. Keehn to Roosevelt, September 24, 1934; the President to Keehn, September 27, 1934, in FDR: President's Personal File, File 62 (Hearst), FDR Papers.

34. Pizzitola, *Hearst Over Hollywood*, pp. 330–32, 486–87; Crowther, *Hollywood Rajah*, pp. 200–201.

35. For Hearst's visit to the White House, see the *Los Angeles Examiner*, October 10, 1934, p. 1; Elliott Roosevelt, ed., *F.D.R.—His Personal Letters* (New York: Duell, Sloan & Pearce, 1950), 1:424. See also Hearst interview in the *New York American*, October 8, 1934, as well as the 1934 election results in Schlesinger Jr., *The Coming of the New Deal*, pp. 505–7, and the Hearst telegram to Roosevelt in Coblentz, ed., *Hearst: A Portrait in His Own Words*, p. 166.

36. See editorial in the *New York American*, November 8, 1934, p. 1, "W. R. Hearst Gives His Views on the Election."

37. Concerning the Brain Trust, see the *New York American*, January 7, 1935, p. 14; March 16, 1935, p. 1; March 23, 1935, p. 12; Coblentz, ed., *Hearst: A Portrait*

in His Own Words, p. 176; William E. Leuchtenburg, *Franklin D. Roosevelt and the New Deal, 1932–1940* (New York: Harper & Row, 1963), pp. 32–35.

38. Concerning Hearst's advocacy of veterans' bonuses, see the *New York American*, March 24, 1935, 1L-2L; May 22, 1935, p. 2; May 23, 1935, pp. 1–2; Leuchtenburg, *Franklin D. Roosevelt and The New Deal*, pp. 12, 45, 171; Schlesinger Jr., *The Politics of Upheaval, 1935–1936*, pp. 10–11, 504; Freidel, *Roosevelt: Launching the New Deal*, 4:238–40, 243–45.

39. See Hearst editorials in the *New York American*, January 14, 1935, p. 1; February 17, 1935, 1L; March 14, 1935, pp. 1–2; March 16, 1935, p. 1. See also *ibid.*, January 7, 1935, p. 14. See also Swanberg, *Citizen Hearst*, p. 449.

40. Coblentz, ed., *Hearst: A Portrait in His Own Words*, pp. 167–80ff. See specifically Hearst editorials in the *New York American*, January 15, 1935, p. 8; January 20, 1935, 1L; February 13, 1935, p. 1; February 21, 1935, pp. 1–2; April 8, 1935, p. 2. See also articles concerning the World Court in *ibid.*, January 22, 1935, p. 1; January 24, 1935, p. 2; January 28, 1935, p. 1; January 29, 1935, p. 2; January 30, 1935, p. 1; January 31, 1935, p. 1; *New York Times*, January 30, 1935, pp. 1–2.

41. For a history of the administration's tax program and Roosevelt's thinking, see Schlesinger Jr., *The Politics of Upheaval, 1935–1936*, pp. 325–34; Leuchtenburg, *Franklin D. Roosevelt and The New Deal*, pp. 152–56. For Hearst's actions and thinking see Coblentz, ed., *Hearst: A Portrait in His Own Words*, pp. 172, 173, 177–80ff.

42. For examples of Hearst's thinking, see the *New York American*, June 2, 1935, 1L-2L; July 2, 1935, p. 6; August 30, 1935, pp. 1–2; Coblentz, ed., *Hearst: A Portrait in His Own Words*, pp. 169–72. See also the *New York Times*, August 29, 1935, pp. 1, 8; August 30, 1935, pp. 5, 16.

43. See the *New York American*, April 21, 1935, 1L; May 22, 1935, p. 2; June 2, 1935, 1L-2L; July 3, 1935, p. 2; August 30, 1935, p. 1; September 19, 1935, p. 4.

Chapter 9

1. *New York American*, November 26, 1934, p. 1; Coblentz, ed., *Hearst: A Portrait in His Own Words*, pp. 106, 114. See also Schlesinger Jr., *The Politics of Upheaval, 1935–1936*, pp. 82–85.

2. Schlesinger Jr., *The Politics of Upheaval, 1935–1936*, pp. 84–86; Leuchtenburg, *Franklin D. Roosevelt and the New Deal, 1932–1940*, pp. 111–14; Harvey Klehr, *The Heyday of American Communism: The Depression Decade* (New York: Basic, 1984), pp. 124–29. For reports on the San Francisco strike, see also the *New York American*, July 16, 17, 19, 20, 1934, p. 1.

3. See the *New York Times*, December 24, 1934, p. 2. See also Carlson and Bates, *Hearst: Lord of San Simeon*, pp. 253–54; Ferdinand Lundberg, *Imperial Hearst: A Social Biography*, pp. 347–48.

4. See specifically the *New York Times*, December 24, 1934, p. 2. See also Lundberg, *Imperial Hearst*, pp. 348–51; Carlson and Bates, *Hearst: Lord of San Simeon*, pp. 254–62. Concerning Hearst's orders to seek out communists at major

universities, see J. Willicomb to T. V. Ranck, February 6, 1936, Hearst Papers, 1874–1951. For a typical example of Hearst editorials against academia, see the *New York American* editorial titled "Throw Them All Out!" on November 22, 1934, p. 16. See editorials concerning loyalty oath and communist professors in *ibid.*, January 8, 1935, p. 18; February 13, 1935, p. 18; February 18, 1935, p. 1; March 7, 1935, p. 16; March 23, 1935, p. 12 (cartoon); May 3, 1935, p. 2.

5. *New York Times*, December 24, 1934, p. 2; January 1, 1935, p. 25; January 15, 1935, p. 17; February 25, 1935, p. 18. See also Carlson and Bates, *Lord of San Simeon*, pp. 256–57.

6. *New York Times*, February 4, 1935, p. 9; February 26, 1935, p. 8. See report of Hearst's nationwide radio address in *ibid.*, January 6, 1935, p. 29. See Beard's assessment of Hearst in Richard Hofstadter, *The Progressive Historians* (New York: Knopf, 1968), pp. 291–92. See also "A Preface and a Farewell to William Randolph Hearst," in Lundberg, *Imperial Hearst*, p. vii. And for a concise account of Hearst's troubles, see Schlesinger Jr., *The Politics of Upheaval, 1935–1936*, p. 88.

7. *New York American*, March 11, 1935, p. 12; April 19, 1935, p. 20; October 9, 1935, p. 14; October 17, 1935, p. 14.

8. In 1935 the *New York American* is rife with articles, editorials, and cartoons concerning communist activities. For example, see Hearst editorial in *ibid.*, December 11, 1935, p. 1. For continuing charges of communist infiltration into U.S. organizations, see *ibid.*, January 10, 1936, p. 12; January 20, 1936, p. 11; February 9, 1936, 1L; February 17, 1936, p. 16; February 18, 1936, pp. 5, 15. See also John Tebbel, *The Life and Good Times of William Randolph Hearst* (New York: Dutton, 1952), pp. 256–457; Schlesinger Jr., *The Politics of Upheaval, 1935–1936*, pp. 86–88.

9. See the *New York American*, April 21, 1935, 1L, which is reprinted (full-page) in *ibid.*, July 2, 1935, p. 6. See also Schlesinger Jr., *The Politics of Upheaval, 1935–1936*, pp. 88, 667 (endnote 8).

10. Concerning Yale and Harvard, see the *New York American*, June 19, 1935, p. 14; October 5, 1935, p. 5; October 9, 1935, p. 14. See also Schlesinger Jr., *The Politics of Upheaval, 1935–1936*, p. 88.

11. The editorials and political cartoons in the *New York American* daily remind readers of Hearst's opposition to the Roosevelt administration. For typical examples, see *ibid.*, May 11, 1935, p. 1; May 28, 1935, p. 1; May 30, 1935, p. 1; June 2, 1935, 1L-2L; July 3, 1935, p. 2; August 23, 1935, p. 16; August 30, 1935, p. 1; September 8, 1935, 2L; September 18, 20, 1935, p. 4; October 6, 1935, 1L-2L. See also Coblentz, ed., *Hearst: A Portrait in His Own Words*, pp. 170–80.

12. *New York Times*, August 29, 1935, pp. 1, 8; August 30, 1935, pp. 5, 16; *New York American*, August 30, 1935, pp. 1–2; September 20, 1935, p. 4. See also Schlesinger Jr., *The Politics of Upheaval, 1935–1936*, pp. 515–19; and George Wolfskill, *The Revolt of the Conservatives: A History of the American Liberty League, 1934–1940* (Boston: Houghton Mifflin, 1962), pp. 17–55ff.

13. Donald R. McCoy, *Landon of Kansas* (Lincoln: University of Nebraska Press, 1966), pp. 230–31; Coblentz, ed., *Hearst: A Portrait in His Own Words*, pp. 181–84. See also the *New York Times*, October 11, 1935, p. 24, concerning

Runyon. For an example of the investigation of Landon, see the *New York American*, October 1, 1935, p. 1, Arthur Brisbane's Today Column.

14. *New York Times*, September 30, 1935, p. 2; McCoy, *Landon of Kansas*, p. 231. See also Hearst's editorial in the *New York American*, October 6, 1935, 1L-2L.

15. McCoy, *Landon of Kansas*, p. 231; Winkler, *Hearst: A New Appraisal*, pp. 265–66. See also Schlesinger Jr., *The Politics of Upheaval, 1935–1936*, pp. 536–39.

16. *New York American*, December 11, 1935, p. 3; *New York Times*, December 11, 1935, p. 6; McCoy, *Landon of Kansas*, p. 232. Concerning Landon's differences with Hearst over campaign issues, see McCoy, *Landon of Kansas*, pp. 232–33.

17. McCoy, *Landon of Kansas*, pp. 234–39.

18. Schlesinger Jr., *The Politics of Upheaval, 1935–1936*, pp. 538–39; McCoy, *Landon of Kansas*, p. 236. See Hearst's assessment of Landon and Roosevelt in Coblentz, ed., *Hearst: A Portrait in His Own Words*, pp. 182–85ff.

19. See the *New York American*, January 11, 13, 1936, p. 6; January 16, 1936, p. 3. Concerning the American Liberty League dinner in New York City and Al Smith's speech denouncing FDR, see *ibid.*, January 26, 1936, 1L; January 27, 1936, p. 1. On further publicity for Landon, see *ibid.*, January 29, 1936, p. 6; January 30, 1936, pp. 1–2; January 31, 1936, p. 21. See also Coblentz, ed., *Hearst: A Portrait in His Own Words*, p. 186.

20. Although articles appear almost daily in the *New York American*, see specifically March 17, 19, 1936, p. 1; March 20, 1936, p. 9; March 21, 1936, p. 7. For a Landon crusade, see *ibid.*, daily during April, May, and June, 1936. For a history of the Landon preconvention campaign, see McCoy, *Landon of Kansas*, pp. 234–52. For Hearst's evaluation of Landon, see Coblentz, ed., *Hearst: A Portrait in His Own Words*, pp. 183–85.

21. McCoy, *Landon of Kansas*, pp. 256–61. For Ickes's remark and Hearst's reaction, see Coblentz, ed., *Hearst: A Portrait in His Own Words*, pp. 182–83; *New York Times*, June 8, 1936, p. 4.

22. See the *New York American* from January to June 1936, for numerous anticommunist articles and editorials. Concerning Thomas's remark, see the *New York Times*, January 7, 1935, p. 31; Swanberg, *Citizen Hearst*, pp. 368–71. In regard to the Hearst boycott, see the *New York Times*, January 29, 1936, p. 14; February 27, 1936, p. 21. For the Farmer-Laborite meeting, see *ibid.*, March 29, 1936, pp. 1, 26; and concerning the League Against War and Fascism, see *ibid.*, April 14, 1936, p. 13.

23. In regard to the Older Hearst biography, see Older, *William Randolph Hearst: American*, p. x; Swanberg, *Citizen Hearst*, p. 471. Materials that Hearst sent to Older are housed in the Bancroft Library at the University of California–Berkeley. For the two critical biographies of Hearst, see Lundberg, *Imperial Hearst: A Social Biography*, and Carlson and Bates, *Hearst: Lord of San Simeon*. See the book reviews of these two works in the *New York Times*, April 26, 1936, sec. 6, p. 5.

24. For evidence of his arguments against higher taxation by the New Deal, see Hearst editorials in the *New York American*, March 16, 1935, p. 1; March 19,

1935, pp. 1–2; March 24, 1935, 1L-2L. Concerning Hearst's fight against the California income tax, see the *New York American*, April 3, 1935, pp. 1–2; November 8, 1935, p. 3; November 10, 1935, 1L-2L; *New York Times*, April 20, 1935, p. 17; October 23, 1935, pp. 1, 17. For invitations to settle in other states, see *ibid.*, October 24, 1935, p. 17; October 25, 1935, p. 44; October 27, 1935, sec. 4, p. 10; *New York American*, October 26, 1935, p. 1.

25. *Fortune Magazine*, October, 1935, pp. 43–54ff; Tebbel, *Hearst*, pp. 308–15; Cobb, *Exit Laughing*, p. 125; Swanberg, *Citizen Hearst*, pp. 465–68. Concerning Neylan and Hearst, see John F. Neylan, Carton 8, Folders 42–46, Hearst Papers, 1874–1951.

26. Concerning the London auction, see the *New York Times*, May 31, 1935, p. 15. At this time the British pound in currency was "about $4.93 and 1/2." For purchase of the architecture magazine, see *ibid.*, April 29, 1936, pp. 17, 39. And for acquisition of the radio stations, see *ibid.*, May 6, 1936, p. 9; *New York American*, May 10, 1936, 7L. In regard to reports of corporate earnings of Hearst Magazines, Hearst Publications, and Hearst Consolidated Publications, see the *New York Times*, June 13, 1935, p. 38; June 20, 1935, p. 34.

27. *New York Times*, August 9, 1936, p. 25. See mention of Marion's plans in the *New York American*, August 4, 1936, p. 8; August 7, 1936, p. 10. For comment on art dealers, see Crocker, "That's Hollywood," chap. 10, pp. 1–2. Concerning the European trip, see Davies, *The Times We Had*, pp. 211–13; Guiles, *Davies*, pp. 289–90; Swanberg, *Citizen Hearst*, pp. 477–78.

28. *New York Times*, October 5, 1936, p. 6; October 11, 1936, sec 4, p. 2; October 24, 1936, p. 9; Swanberg, *Citizen Hearst*, p. 479.

29. *New York American*, October 15, 1936, p. 12; *New York Times*, October 27, 1936, p. 2; November 1, 1936, p. 38; *New York American*, November 1, 1936, 1L.

30. Coblentz, ed., *Hearst: A Portrait in His Own Words*, p. 186.

31. See the *New York American* during July and August 1936. For typical days, see *ibid.*, July 17, 1936, pp. 1, 5, 6, 11, 16, and August 25, 1936, pp. 1, 2, 5, 6, 12, for anti-Roosevelt and\or pro-Landon articles.

32. McCoy, *Landon of Kansas*, pp. 262–77ff; Schlesinger Jr., *The Politics of Upheaval, 1935–1936*, pp. 601–15ff.

33. See Hearst editorial concerning Farley in the *New York American*, July 16, 1936, pp. 1–2. See also Coblentz, ed., *Hearst: A Portrait in His Own Words*, pp. 192–93.

34. In regard to Morgenthau, see the Morgenthau Diary, September 11, 1936, book 2, pp. 67–68, MSS, in FDR Papers; John Morton Blum, *From The Morgenthau Diaries: Years of Crisis, 1928–1938* (Boston: Houghton Mifflin, 1959), p. 335; John Morton Blum, *Roosevelt and Morgenthau* (Boston: Houghton Mifflin, 1970), p. 170; Coblentz, ed., *Hearst: A Portrait in His Own Words*, p. 173; Schlesinger Jr., *The Politics of Upheaval, 1935–1936*, pp. 325–29.

35. See Harold L. Ickes, *The Secret Diary of Harold L. Ickes: The First Thousand Days, 1933–1936* (New York: Simon & Schuster, 1953), pp. 153, 155, 493, 614–15, 639, 644, 647–48, 657, 659–60, 668–71, 683–85. See also Ickes's

speeches and activities in the *New York Times*, August 27, 1936, p. 20; August 28, 1936, pp. 1, 6, 8; August 29, 1936, pp. 1, 4, 5, 12; August 30, 1936, p. 1; August 31, 1936, p. 4; September 5, 1936, p. 14; *New York American*, August 26, 1936, p. 1; August 30, 1936, 17L.

36. For the Hearst editorial, see the *New York American*, September 6, 1936, and then daily references linking the New Deal to communist support.

37. See the *New York American*, September 20, 1936, p. 1; *New York Times*, September 20, 1936, p. 1.

38. See the *New York American*, September 21, 1936, pp. 1–2; Coblentz, ed., *Hearst: A Portrait in His Own Words*, pp. 186–87, 189–90; *New York Times*, September 21, 1936, pp. 1–2.

39. *New York Times*, September 22, 1936, p. 4. See also denunciations of Hearst in *ibid.*, September 22, 1936, pp. 9, 11; September 24, 1936, pp. 7, 9, 13; September 27, 1936, sec. 4, p. 12; October 1, 1936, p. 24; October 4, 1936, p. 42; October 5, 1936, p. 17; October 18, 1936, sec. 4, p. 5; October 22, 1936, p. 16; October 23, 1936, p. 15; October 28, 1936, p. 21. See also Schlesinger Jr., *The Politics of Upheaval, 1935–1936*, pp. 618–22.

40. See signed Hearst editorials in the *New York American*, November 1, 1936, 1L; November 2, 1936, pp. 1, 5; *New York Times*, November 3, 1936, p. 27. See also Coblentz's comment on Hearst in Coblentz, ed., *Hearst: A Portrait in His Own Words*, p. 189. See also Swanberg, *Citizen Hearst*, p. 479. Concerning the fall campaign, see McCoy, *Landon of Kansas*, pp. 313–42; Schlesinger Jr., *The Politics of Upheaval, 1935–1936*, pp. 622–44ff; Leuchtenburg, *Franklin D. Roosevelt and the New Deal*, pp. 195–96. For mention of Hearst's radio broadcast message in behalf of Landon, see the *New York Times*, November 1, 1936, p. 38.

41. Ickes, *Secret Diary*, 1: 704; Swanberg, *Citizen Hearst*, p. 479. For the Hearst editorial, see the *New York American*, November 5. 1936, p. 1; *New York Times*, November 6, 1936, p. 6. Concerning the appointment of Boettiger, see the *New York American*, November 27, 1936, p. 1; November 27, 1936, p. 1.

42. See Procter, *Hearst: The Early Years, 1863–1910*, pp. 45–55. See Hearst editorial in the *New York American*, February 4, 1937, p. 12. The author outlined the *American* from the election on November 3, 1936, to its demise on June 24, 1937. See also the announcement of consolidation in *ibid.*, June 23, 1937, p. 8.

43. See "A TRIBUTE" in the *New York American*, December 26, 1936, p. 1. See also *ibid.*, December 27, 1936, 1L; *New York Times*, December 26, 1936, p. 7; Swanberg, *Citizen Hearst*, p. 483.

44. John Francis Neylan to Hearst, August 10, 1937, Hearst Papers, 1874–1951.

Chapter 10

1. John Francis Neylan to W.R., August 10, 1937, in Hearst Papers, 1903–1951, Box II. For a different assessment of Neylan see Davies, *The Times We Had*, pp. 266–67; Guiles, *Davies*, pp. 292–93.

2. Concerning earlier magazine corporation debentures amounting to $13 million, see the *New York Times*, March 11, 1937, p. 33; and see the SEC's permission to withdraw debentures in *ibid.*, September 2, 1937, p. 33. See also *ibid.*, March 21, 1938, p. 6; Winkler, *Hearst: A New Appraisal*, p. 278.

3. *New York Times*, January 7, 1937, p. 28; *New York American*, January 7, 1937, p. 5. For information on tax dodgers, see the *New York Times*, June 18, 1937, p. 6; June 19, 1937, pp. 1, 5; July 14, 1937, p. 1.

4. Forrest Davis, "Mr. Hearst Steps Down," *Saturday Evening Post*, August 27, 1938, pp. 5, 65; *New York Times*, March 21, 1938, pp. 1, 6; Winkler, *Hearst: A New Appraisal*, p. 278; Nasaw, *The Chief*, pp. 538–39; Swanberg, *Citizen Hearst*, pp. 484–85.

5. See Winkler, *Hearst: A New Appraisal*, pp. 278–79; Swanberg, *Citizen Hearst*, p. 484; Nasaw, *The Chief*, p. 538.

6. See the announcement about the demise of the *New York Journal-American* in the *New York American*, June 23, 1937, p. 1; June 24, 1937, p. 8. Concerning the Chicago papers, see the *New York Journal-American*, July 4, 1937, 1L. For sale of certain Hearst newspapers, see the *New York Times*, March 21, 1938, p. 6.

7. Nasaw, *The Chief*, pp. 537–39ff; Swanberg, *Citizen Hearst*, pp. 484–87ff. For notices of Hearst sales in London, see the *New York Times*, September 8, 1938, p. 1; October 26, 1938, p. 24; December 15, 1938, p. 27; May 19, 1939, p. 24; June 23, 1939, p. 17.

8. Swanberg, *Citizen Hearst*, pp. 484–85; Nasaw, *The Chief*, pp. 538–39.

9. Swanberg, *Citizen Hearst*, pp. 485, 487. For a brief history of the Clarendon property, see the *New York Times*, January 21, 1940, p. 1.

10. Martin Huberth Interview, *New York Times*, April 1, 1938, pp. 1, 24; April 2, 1938, p. 32; Davis, "Mr. Hearst Steps Down," p. 65; Swanberg, *Citizen Hearst*, pp. 485, 487.

11. *New York Times*, October 11, 1937, p. 19; November 18, 1937, p. 25.

12. For an excellent account concerning Shearn and the Conservation Committee, see Nasaw, *The Chief*, pp. 538–42. See also Swanberg, *Citizen Hearst*, pp. 485–88; Davis, "Mr. Hearst Steps Down," p. 67.

13. See the *New York Times*, March 21, 1938, pp. 1, 6. For advertisements about the Hearst collection, see *ibid.*, April 10, 1938, p. 2. For the Rockefeller purchase, see *ibid.*, April 21, 1938, p. 37. For reference to van Dyck's portrait of Queen Henrietta Maria, see in this work Chapter 2, endnote 6; Swanberg, *Citizen Hearst*, pp. 289, 486. For a good account of the Hearst auctions and bankruptcy proceedings, see Nasaw, *The Chief*, pp. 539–42. See also Davis, "Mr. Hearst Steps Down," pp. 5–6, 64–65. Concerning other Hearst auctions and sales, see the *New York Times*, September 8, 1938, p. 1; September 20, 1938, p. 24; September 29, 1938, p. 28; October 12, 1938, p. 25; October 20, 1938, p. 25; October 26, 1938, p. 24; November 13, 1938, sec. 7, p. 14; November 15, 1938, p. 20; November 17, 1938, p. 22; November 19, 1938, p. 21; November 20, 1938, sec. 2, p. 4; December 1, 1938, p. 26; December 2, 1938, p. 13; December 15, 1938, p. 27; January 6, 1939, p. 19; January 7, 1939, p. 7; January 8, 1939, p. 45; January

12, 1939, p. 20; August 20, 1939, sec. 2, p. 2; October 29, 1939, p. 40; November 19, 1939, p. 40; November 22, 1939, p. 18; November 23, 1939, p. 32; November 28, 1939, p. 24; December 19, 1939, p. 30; December 24, 1939, sec. 2, p. 9. See also Tebbel, *The Life and Good Times of William Randolph Hearst*, pp. 267–70, 276–77.

14. Davies, *The Times We Had*, pp. 266–71; Guiles, *Davies*, pp. 292–94.

15. Concerning Davies's three years at Warners, see Guiles, *Davies*, pp. 279–85ff. See also the reviews of her four pictures in *ibid.*, pp. 401–5. See also Pizzitola, *Hearst Over Hollywood*, pp. 348–49.

16. Pizzitola, *Hearst Over Hollywood*, p. 350; Nasaw, *The Chief*, pp. 534–35; Swanberg, *Citizen Hearst*, p. 486.

17. *Time*, March 13, 1939, pp. 49–56. In regard to Hearst Consolidated, see Nasaw, *The Chief*, pp. 430–32, 544–45. See also in *ibid.*, pp. 531–32.

18. For quote concerning Hearst, see Schlesinger Jr., *The Coming of the New Deal*, p. 565.

19. For background material on the Supreme Court's rulings that declared the NIRA and the AAA as well as several other New Deal acts unconstitutional, see Schlesinger Jr., *The Politics of Upheaval, 1935–1936*, pp. 6, 214, 254, 275–76, 470–71, 472–74, 488, 490, 504. See also Leuchtenburg, *Franklin D. Roosevelt and the New Deal, 1932–1940*, pp. 144–45; 170–71; and also concerning the Court-packing bill, pp. 231–38. For Hearst editorials that were critical of the New Deal while expressing his philosophy, see the *Los Angeles Examiner*, January 2, 1938, pp. 1–2; January 28, 1938, p. 1; January 30, 1938, pp. 1–2; April 1, 1938, pp. 1–2; April 7, 1938, pp. 1–2; April 10, 1938, p. 1; May 1, 1938, p. 1; May 29, 1938, p. 1; September 17, 1938, p. 6; September 18, 1938, p. 5. See specifically the Sunday editorial in *ibid.*, April 28, 1938, p. 1.

20. Concerning Hearst's views on foreign affairs, see Ian Mugridge, *The View from Xanadu: William Randolph Hearst and United States Foreign Policy* (Montreal: McGill-Queen's University Press, 1995), pp. 3–6.

21. The information for this paragraph is from the day-to-day research by the author in the *New York American* from 1900 to 1937. But see the Hearst editorial in the *New York American*, March 9, 1918, p. 18. In Mugridge, *The View from Xanadu*, see the chapter titled "Hearst and the Yellow Peril," pp. 46–59, and the chapter titled "Hearst and United States Foreign Policy," pp. 144–52. See also Winkler, *Hearst: A New Appraisal*, p. 283.

22. For an excellent study of American foreign policy under Roosevelt, see Robert Dallek, *Franklin D. Roosevelt and American Foreign Policy, 1932–1945* (New York: Oxford University Press, 1979); Cole, *Roosevelt and the Isolationists, 1932–1945*; Bailey, *A Diplomatic History of the American People*, pp. 692–710; Mugridge, *The View from Xanadu*, pp. 30–59ff, 90–152ff; Leuchtenburg, *Franklin D. Roosevelt and the New Deal, 1932–1940*, pp. 212–13.

23. Bailey, *A Diplomatic History of the American People*, pp. 692–701. Concerning the passage of Neutrality acts, see Dallek, *Franklin D. Roosevelt and American Foreign Policy, 1932–1945*, pp. 117–292ff; Leuchtenburg, *Franklin D. Roosevelt and the New Deal*, pp. 219–22ff, 224–25.

24. Dallek, *Franklin D. Roosevelt and American Foreign Policy, 1932–1945*, pp. 126–80ff; Bailey, *A Diplomatic History of the American People*, pp. 701–2; Leuchtenburg, *Franklin D. Roosevelt and the New Deal*, pp. 222–24, 284.

25. Dallek, *Franklin D. Roosevelt and American Foreign Policy, 1932–1945*, pp. 148–68; Bailey, *A Diplomatic History of the American People*, pp. 707–8.

26. Dallek, *Franklin D. Roosevelt and American Foreign Policy, 1932–1945*, pp. 171–98; Bailey, *A Diplomatic History of the American People*, pp. 708–10.

27. Mugridge, *The View from Xanadu*, pp. 108–25ff. For editorial advocating a constitutional amendment, see the *Los Angeles Examiner*, February 8, 1938, pp. 1–2; Cole, *Roosevelt and the Isolationists, 1932–1945*, pp. 253–62 (the Ludlow amendment). See Hearst editorials in the *San Francisco Examiner*, June 6, 1938, p. 10; June 12, 1938, p. 1; June 13, 1938, p. 8. For Churchill's speech and Hearst's reply, see the *San Francisco Examiner*, October 17, 1938, p. 1; October 23, 1938, pp. 1–2. See Runyon interview in the *New York Journal and American*, April 30, 1939, pp. 1, 16. See also Hearst editorials in *ibid.*, January 29, 1939, 1L-2L; February 2, 1939, p. 1; April 11, 1939, p. 14; July 16, 1939, 1L-2L. Concerning the American public's isolationist attitude, see Leuchtenburg, *Franklin D. Roosevelt and the New Deal*, pp. 292–301ff.

28. See the *New York Journal and American*, September 4, 1939, p. 1; December 6, 1939, p. 1. Concerning the interview given to Radio's Newsreel, see "In The News," *Los Angeles Examiner*, April 25, 1940, 1A. For the isolationist struggle in the United States, see Mugridge, *The View from Xanadu*, pp. 124–25; Berg, *Lindbergh*, chaps. 13–14; Leuchtenburg, *Franklin D. Roosevelt and the New Deal*, pp. 292–305ff, 326–27; Cole, *Roosevelt and the Isolationists, 1932–1945*, pp. 409–12.

29. Although the British requisitioned St. Donat's soon after the German invasion of Poland on September 1, 1939, they did not announce the arrangements with Hearst until reports in the *New York Times*, March 26, 1940, p. 28; March 28, 1940, p. 28. See also information concerning St. Donat's in footnote 7 of this chapter. See sale of Hearst's California property in *New York Times*, September 12, 1940, p. 3; October 25, 1940, p. 8.

30. See the *New York Times*, April 9, 1940, p. 41; May 3, 1940, p. 35; July 5, 1940, p. 22.

31. For contract negotiations with Saks-Fifth Avenue and Gimbel Brothers, see the *New York Times*, December 29, 1940, pp. 1, 26; December 30, 1940, p. 16. Concerning the Hearst collection and forthcoming sales, see *ibid.*, January 4, 1941, p. 15; January 18, 1941, p. 13; January 28, 1941, p. 22; January 29, 1941, p. 13; February 2, 1941, sec. 1, p. 40, sec. 9, p. 9; February 4, 1941, p. 18; February 21, 1941, p. 21. For Hearst art sales, see *ibid.*, March 5, 1941, p. 23; March 16, 1941, p. 48; March 22, 1941, p. 17; March 23, 1941, p. 43; March 26, 1941, p. 21. See also Tebbel, *The Life and Good Times of William Randolph Hearst*, pp. 267, 277–79.

32. Mugridge, *The View from Xanadu*, pp. 19–23.

33. Winkler, *Hearst: A New Appraisal*, pp. 279, 282; Swanberg, *Citizen Hearst*, p. 494.

34. As typical of Hearst's isolationist theme, see "In The News," *Los Angeles Examiner*, March 8, 1940, pp. 1–2; March 18, 1940, pp. 1–2; March 25, 1940, pp. 1–2; April 17, 1940, pp. 1–2. Concerning Hearst's Harvard days, see *ibid.*, March 9, 1940, pp. 1–2; June 13, 1940, pp. 1–2. In regard to stories about the *San Francisco Examiner*, see *ibid.*, June 4, 1940, pp. 1–2; June 6, 1940, pp. 1–2. Concerning the Hollywood scene, see *ibid.*, March 11, 1940, pp. 1–2; May 17, 1940, pp. 1–2; May 22, 1940, pp. 1–2; May 27, 1940, pp. 1–2. For the story of John L. Sullivan, see *ibid.*, June 19, 1940, pp. 1–2; June 29, 1940, pp. 1–2. See also in *ibid.*, July 5, 1940, pp. 1–2.

35. See Swanberg, *Citizen Hearst*, pp. 494–96.

36. "In The News," *Los Angeles Examiner*, March 27, 1940, pp. 1–2; June 15, 1940, p. 1.

37. Concerning stories about the French Revolution, see "In The News," *San Francisco Examiner*, July 18, 1940, pp. 1–2; July 19, 1940, pp. 1–2; July 22, 1940, pp. 1–2. For columns regarding Caesar, Cleopatra, and Roman life, see *ibid.*, July 8, 1940, pp. 1–2; July 29, 1940, pp. 1–2; August 1, 1940, pp. 1–2; August 2, 1940, pp. 1–2; August 6, 1940, pp. 1–2; August 9, 1940, pp. 1–2; August 28, 1940, pp. 1–2; August 29, 1940, pp. 1–2; August 30, 1940, pp. 1–2. For discussions of the invasions of England, see the *Los Angeles Examiner*, September 15, 1940, pp. 1–2; September 17, 1940, pp. 1–2; September 18, 1940, pp. 1–2; September 19, 1940, pp. 1–2; September 20, 1940, p. 1.

38. "In The News," *Los Angeles Examiner*, March 7, 1940, p. 1. See also in *ibid.*, March 15, 1940, pp. 1–2; April 8, 1940, p. 1; Leuchtenburg, *Franklin D. Roosevelt and the New Deal*, pp. 314–16; Winkler, *Hearst: A New Appraisal*, pp. 282–83; James MacGregor Burns, *Roosevelt: The Lion and the Fox* (New York: Harcourt, Brace, 1956), pp. 422–30.

39. "In The News," *Los Angeles Examiner*, March 19, 1940, pp. 1–2; August 18, 1940, pp. 1–2. See also Ellsworth Barnard, *Wendell Willkie: Fighter for Freedom* (Marquette: Northern Michigan University Press, 1966), pp. 142–208ff.

40. See Barnard, *Wendell Willkie: Fighter for Freedom*, pp. 209–29; "In The News," *Los Angeles Examiner*, September 10, 1940, pp. 1–2. For evidence of Hearst's full support of Willkie, see daily on page 1 from August to November 4, 1940, Hearst's political campaign coverage in the *Los Angeles Examiner* and the *San Francisco Examiner*. See also the continued negative slant concerning Roosevelt and the New Deal by Hearst "In The News." For the presidential election returns, see Leuchtenburg, *Franklin D. Roosevelt and the New Deal*, pp. 321–22; Burns, *Roosevelt: The Lion and the Fox*, pp. 453–55.

41. "In The News," *Los Angeles Examiner*, November 7, 1940, pp. 1–2. For similar evaluations, see Leuchtenburg, *Franklin D. Roosevelt and the New Deal*, pp. 317–22; Burns, *Roosevelt: The Lion and the Fox*, pp. 454–55.

42. For a discussion of other works describing a Hearst character, see Pizzitola, *Hearst Over Hollywood*, p. 391. Concerning the four biographies of Hearst written by John K. Winkler (1928), Mrs. Fremont Older (1936), Ferdinand Lundberg (1936), and Oliver Carlson and Ernest Sutherland Bates (1936), see

Chapter 9, footnote 23 of this text. See also Aldous Huxley, *After Many a Summer Dies the Swan* (New York: Harper, 1939); and Robert L. Carringer, *The Making of Citizen Kane* (Berkeley: University of California Press, 1985), p. 17, for reference to Huxley. And see specifically *Time* magazine, March 13, 1939, pp. 49–56.

43. Orson Welles and Peter Bogdanovich, *This Is Orson Welles* (New York: Da Capo, 1998), chap. 9, p. 346; Carringer, *The Making of Citizen Kane*, pp. 2, 82, 100; Guiles, *Davies*, p. 305. See also Peter Noble, *The Fabulous Orson Welles* (London: Hutchinson, 1956), pp. 62–72, 107–19.

44. Carringer, *The Making of Citizen Kane*, pp. 1–15ff; Guiles, *Davies*, p. 305.

45. Besides reviewing the film *Citizen Kane* several times, the author has used Noble, *The Fabulous Orson Welles*, pp. 127, 131–32; Pizzitola, *Hearst Over Hollywood*, pp. 15, 29, 392–95ff, 495; Nasaw, *The Chief*, pp. 564–74ff.

46. Louella O. Parsons, *Tell It to Louella* (New York: Putnam, 1961), pp. 116–32ff; Noble, *The Fabulous Orson Welles*, pp. 126–28; Pizzitola, *Hearst Over Hollywood*, pp. 396, 495; Nasaw, *The Chief*, pp. 565–67; Carringer, *The Making of Citizen Kane*, p. 111; Guiles, *Davies*, pp. 313–17. See also Simon Callow, *Orson Welles: The Road to Xanadu* (New York: Viking, 1995), pp. 507–39ff.

47. Crowther, *Hollywood Rajah*, pp. 257–60; Noble, *The Fabulous Orson Welles*, pp. 130–35ff; Pizzitola, *Hearst Over Hollywood*, pp. 396–400ff; Callow, *Welles*, p. 632; Nasaw, *The Chief*, pp. 568–69.

48. Carringer, *The Making of Citizen Kane*, pp. 115–17; Noble, *The Fabulous Orson Welles*, pp. 134–38; Pizzitola, *Hearst Over Hollywood*, pp. 396–99.

Chapter 11

1. See "In The News," *Los Angeles Examiner*, December 8, 1941, pp. 1–2. For background material concerning Pearl Harbor, see Dallek, *Franklin D. Roosevelt and American Foreign Policy, 1932–1945*, pp. 299, 311–13, 317–18. See also the Yamamoto quote to the Japanese government in September 1940 in David M. Kennedy, *Freedom From Fear: The American People in Depression and War* (New York: Oxford University Press, 1999), p. 526.

2. Concerning the move to Wyntoon, see Swanberg, *Citizen Hearst*, p. 500. By December 22, 1941, Hearst was at Wyntoon; see "In The News," *Los Angeles Examiner*, December 23, 1941, pp. 1–2. For the Buy a Bomber campaign, see *ibid.*, January 3, 1942, p. 1 (daily) for the months thereafter on p. 1. See also Morgenthau's praise of Hearst in *ibid.*, January 25, February 1, 1942, p. 1. In regard to the U.S. Saving Stamps and Bonds campaign ("LICK A STAMP, LICK A JAP!") see *ibid.*, January 25, 1942, p. 1 and daily thereafter.

3. For a discussion of the Mothers Leagues, see "In The News," *Los Angeles Examiner*, December 21, 1941, pp. 1–2. For information about USO groups, see *ibid.*, January 17, 1942, pp. 1–2. And concerning the Marion Davies appointment to the California Guard, see *ibid.*, January 13, 1942, p. 3.

4. For a discussion of the early battles in the Pacific, see "In The News," *Los Angeles Examiner*, December 24, 25, 26, 30, 31, 1941, pp. 1–2; January 13, 1942,

pp. 1–2. For the leadership of Churchill and FDR, see *ibid.*, January 2, 8, 20, 24, 30, 1942, pp. 1–2. Concerning Hearst's emphasis on the Pacific theater of war, see *ibid.*, January 2, 6, 10, 13, 19, 29, 1942, pp. 1–2. In the editorial on Libya, see *ibid.*, February 3, 1942, pp. 1–2. For the diplomatic history of Allied military concentration, see Dallek, *Franklin D. Roosevelt and American Foreign Policy, 1932–1945*, pp. 317–61.

5. Concerning the activities by Gimbel's, see the *New York Times*, April 29, 1941, p. 15; June 28, 1942, pp. 35–36; June 30, 1942, p. 19; September 22, 1942, p. 24; November 15, 1942, p. 53; Swanberg, *Citizen Hearst*, pp. 499–500. In regard to Hearst's direction of his newspapers, see Winkler, *Hearst: A New Appraisal*, p. 285. The *Los Angeles Examiner*, which replaced the *New York American* in July 1937, as the flagship of the Hearst newspapers, typified Hearst rules on publishing. See the *Examiner*, daily, from 1939 through 1944 for further verification.

6. For the notice of a new board of Hearst trustees, see the *New York Times*, January 12, 1943, p. 25. For the fight to remove Shearn, see *ibid.*, July 31, 1943, p. 15. See also Winkler, *Hearst: A New Appraisal*, p. 285; Swanberg, *Citizen Hearst*, p. 500; Nasaw, *The Chief*, pp. 579–81. For the acquisition or sale of properties in New York City, see the *New York Times*, October 5, 1944, p. 31; October 9, 1944, p. 31. For a listing of Hearst newspapers and American magazines, see the *New York Times*, August 15, 1951, p. 20.

7. Kastner, *Hearst Castle*, pp. 199–202; Winkler, *Hearst: A New Appraisal*, p. 291; Swanberg, *Citizen Hearst*, pp. 511–12; Nasaw, *The Chief*, pp. 580–81.

8. Guiles, *Davies*, pp. 11, 328–30; Winkler, *Hearst: A New Appraisal*, p. 291; Tebbel, *The Life and Good Times of William Randolph Hearst*, pp. 10–11, 13; Swanberg, *Citizen Hearst*, pp. 514–16.

9. For descriptions of Hearst's last years at the Beverly Hills mansion, see Guiles, *Davies*, pp. 330–32; Nasaw, *The Chief*, pp. 588–90; Swanberg, *Citizen Hearst*, pp. 515–18. Concerning *The Song of the River*, see Tebbel, *The Life and Good Times of William Randolph Hearst*, pp. 353–54. The presiding minister read this poem at Hearst's funeral.

10. For pictures of birthday celebrations with Hearst's five sons in attendance, see Ken Murray, *The Golden Days of San Simeon* (Garden City, N.Y.; Doubleday, 1971), p. 97; Hearst Jr. with Jack Casserly, *The Hearsts: Father and Son*, pp. 112–13.

11. Winkler, *William Randolph Hearst: A New Appraisal*, pp. 296–97; Nasaw, *The Chief*, pp. 595–96; Tebbel, *The Life and Good Times of William Randolph Hearst*, pp. 360–61; Swanberg, *Citizen Hearst*, pp. 522–23.

12. *New York Times*, August 16, 1951, pp. 1, 20, 25; Winkler, *William Randolph Hearst: A New Appraisal*, pp. 296–97; Nasaw, *The Chief*, pp. 600–601; Tebbel, *The Life and Good Times of William Randolph Hearst*, pp. 360–62.

13. Guiles, *Marion Davies*, pp. 232–33; Swanberg, *Citizen Hearst*, pp. 518–19.

14. *Life*, August 27, 1951, p. 23; *New York Times*, August 15, 1951, p. 1; Guiles, *Davies*, pp. 4–11; Swanberg, *Citizen Hearst*, pp. 518–20; Hearst Jr. with Jack Casserly, *The Hearsts: Father and Son*, pp. 248–49.

15. Hearst Jr. with Jack Casserly, *The Hearsts: Father and Son,* pp. 249–51; Tebbel, *The Life and Good Times of William Randolph Hearst,* pp. 355–56.

16. *New York Times,* August 16, 1951, p. 25; August 17, 1951, p. 17; Hearst Jr. with Jack Casserly, *The Hearsts: Father and Son,* pp. 249–52; Swanberg, *Citizen Hearst,* pp. 520–21.

17. Guiles, *Davies,* p. 334; Tebbel, *The Life and Good Times of William Randolph Hearst,* p. 357. For another viewpoint about Marion, see Hearst Jr. with Jack Casserly, *The Hearsts: Father and Son,* pp. 248–51.

18. *New York Times,* August 18, 1951, p. 18; *Life,* August 27, 1951, pp. 23–34; Tebbel, *The Life and Good Times of William Randolph Hearst,* pp. 358–59; Hearst Jr. with Jack Casserly, *The Hearsts: Father and Son,* pp. 251–52.

19. *New York Times,* August 15, 1951, p. 19.

20. *New York Times,* August 15, 1951, p. 20.

21. See *Life,* August 17, 1951, p. 22.

22. *Life,* August 27, 1951, p. 22.

Index